STATE CENSUS
OF
NORTH CAROLINA
1784-1787

Second Edition
Revised

Transcribed and Indexed
by

MRS. ALVARETTA KENAN REGISTER

Originally Published
Second Edition, Revised
Norfolk, 1971

Reprinted in an Improved Format
Genealogical Publishing Co., Inc.
Baltimore, 1973, 1974, 1978, 1983, 1987, 1993, 2001

Library of Congress Catalogue Card Number 73-3664
International Standard Book Number 0-8063-0556-8

TABLE OF CONTENTS

Page

MICROFILMED BY
NORTH CAROLINA DEPARTMENT OF ARCHIVES AND HISTORY
DIVISION OF ARCHIVES AND MANUSCRIPTS
RALEIGH, NORTH CAROLINA

December 7, 1965

GOVERNOR'S OFFICE
STATE CENSUS
IN ACCORDANCE WITH
LAWS OF 1784, Chapter 1

1785 - 1787

S. 51. 56   Red. Ratio 16 to 1

LAWS OF NORTH CAROLINA
1784

At a General Assembly begun and held at New Bern on the Twenty Second of October, in the Year of our Lord One Thousand Seven Hundred and Eighty-Four, and in the Ninth Year of the Independence of the said State: Being the First Session of this Assembly, Alexander Martin, Esq. Governor.

Chapter 1

An Act to ascertain the number of White and Black Inhabitants, and the Citizens of every age and condition in the State.

I.   Whereas it is recommended by the United States in Congress assembled, that the number of white and black inhabitants, and free citizens of every age, sex and condition, including those bound to servitude for a term of years, and three-fifths of all other persons not comprehended in the foregoing description shall be taken in each State; and in order to comply with the above recommendation.

II.   Be it Enacted by the General Assembly of the State of North Carolina, and it is hereby Enacted by the authority of the same, That the several county courts in this State, shall within six months after the passing this Act, appoint a proper person in each captain's district to take a list of the number of white and black inhabitants and the free citizens of every age, sex and condition in each district which list shall distinguish the number of blacks from whites and other free inhabitants in the following manner:

White males from twenty one years old to sixty	White males under twenty one years old and above sixty	White females of every age	Blacks of each sex from twelve to fifty	Blacks upwards fifty and under twelve years old

And the list by them so taken, shall be returned to the court which shall sit next after their appointment, which list shall by the clerk of the court be immediately transmitted to the Governor, under the penalty of fifty pounds, recovered from any jurisdiction, having cognizance thereof, and applied to the use of the county, and by him sent to our delegates at Congress; and in failure of the appointment aforesaid, by the several county courts within the time limited by this Act, the sheriffs of the several counties, are hereby required to summon three of the justices in the respective counties, who are hereby authorized to make the appointments aforesaid.

III.   And be it further Enacted by the authority aforesaid, That if any person who shall be appointed to receive the lists, shall fail or neglect to do the duty by this Act appointed, he shall forfeit and pay the sum of one hundred pounds, to be recovered in any court of record having cognizance thereof, in the name of the Governor, for the use of the State; and if any master or mistress of a family, his or her agent, director, manager, or attorney, after due notice given by advertisement of the same at the most public place of the district, shall fail to give in a list of his or her family, as by this Act required, he or she so failing or neglecting, shall forfeit and pay the sum of fifty pounds, to be recovered and applied as in the case last mentioned.

4

NORTH CAROLINA CENSUS OF 1784 – 1787

County	Formation	Census	Summary	Names	None
Anson	1750				x
Beaufort	1712				x
Bertie	1787	1787		x	
Bladen	1734				x
Brunswick	1764				x
Burke	1777	1787	x[1]	x	
Camden	1777	1787	x[1]		
Carteret	1722	1786	x[1]		
Caswell	1777	1787	x		x
Chatham	1771	1787	x[1]		
Chowan	1670	1787	x		x
Craven	1712				x
Cumberland	1754		x[1]		x
Currituck	1670	1787			
Duplin	1750	1786		x	
Edgecombe	1741		x[2]		
Franklin	1779		x[2]		
Gates	1779	1786			x
Granville	1746	1786			x
Guilford	1771				x
Halifax	1758	1786		x	
Hertford	1759				x
Hyde	1712	1786			x
Johnston	1746	1787			x
Jones	1778	1786			x

County	Formation	Census	Summary	Names	None
Lincoln	1779				x
Martin	1774	1787		x	
Mecklenburg	1762			x	
Montgomery	1779	1787		x	
Moore	1784				x
Nash	1777	1786	x[2]	x	
New Hanover	1729	1786		x	
Northampton	1741	1786		x	
Onslow	1734	1786		x	
Orange	1752				x
Pasquotank	1670			x	
Perquimans	1670	1786		x	
Pitt	1760	1786		x	
Randolph	1779				x
Richmond	1779	1785		x	
Rockingham	1785				x
Rowan	1753				x
Rutherford	1779				x
Sampson	1784		x[2]	x	
Surry	1771	1786		x	
Tyrrell	1729	1786		x	
Wake	1771				x
Warren	1779	1786		x	
Wayne	1779				x
Wilkes	1777	1787		x	

1. Original summaries; no names unless found subsequent to microfilming.

2. Printed summaries, Walter Clark (ed.) "The State Records of North Carolina" (16 volumes, 1895–1914) XVIII, 433.

State of North Carolina
Department of Archives and History, Raleigh, N. C.

CERTIFICATE OF AUTHENTICITY

This is to certify that the micro-photographs appearing on this reel are true and accurate reproductions of the records listed on the target (title) sheet preceding each volume or series of records microfilmed hereon; that the records were microfilmed on the date and at the reduction ratio indicated; and that on the date of microfilming, the records were in the custody of the official or other individual listed on the target sheet(s).

It is further certified that the records listed on the aforesaid target sheet(s) were microfilmed in conformity with the provisions of Sections 8-45. 1 - 8-45. 4, General Statutes of North Carolina; and that in order to insure archival quality and authentic reproduction of records filmed, they were microfilmed in the manner prescribed, and with equipment and film approved, by the State Department of Archives and History.

(Signed)   Denald E. Horton
            Camera Operator

Date. 12-7-65

* * * * *

The transcriber of the microfilm certifies that the records have been typed as near exactly as they were written by the census-taker as possible. Some census takers had miserable handwriting, and others could not spell properly. Names have been typed as spelled by the census taker.

(Mrs.) Alvaretta Kenan Register

CENSUS OF 1784 – 1787

STATE-WIDE ABSTRACT AND RETURNS NOT IDENTIFIED BY COUNTY

The following Abstract contains the agrigate (sic) amount of each description of persons in North Carolina agreeable to the Returns made to the Marshall of that district by his Assistants.

Districts	Counties	No. of Heads of Families including (illegible)	Free white males 16 yrs. & upwards including Heads of Families	Free white males under 16 yrs. of age	Free white females including Heads of Families	All other Free Persons	Slaves	Amount of free persons of every description	Total of Every Description
Edenton	Chowan	556	641	559	1,182	41	2,588	2,423	5,011
	Perquiman	709	885	1,156	1,717	37	1,878	3,795	5,673
	Pasquotank	800	951	1,034	1,810	79	1,623	3,874	5,497
	Camden	583	727	758	1,480	30	1,038	2,995	4,033
	Currituck	795	1,017	1,024	1,960	115	1,103	4,116	5,219
	Gates	631	790	775	1,515	93	2,219	3,173	5,392
	Herford	655	814	823	1,533	216	2,442	3,386	5,828
	Bertie	1,440	1,762	1,840	3,514	349	5,141	7,465	12,606
	Tyrrell	709	807	959	1,777	35	1,166	3,578	4,744
									53,770 (sic)
Newbern	Craven	1,438	1,709	1,538	3,227	337	3,658	6,811	10,469
	Jones	581	736	794	1,541	70	1,681	3,141	4,822
	Johnston	775	1,039	1,119	2,083	64	1,329	4,305	5,634
	Dobbs	914	1,162	1,293	2,478	45	1,915	4,978	6,893
	Wayne	805	1,064	1,219	2,256	37	1,557	4,576	6,133
	Pitt	1,088	616	2,354	2,915	23	2,367	5,908	8,275

A Return of the Number of Persons in Captain Carson's Militia Company as Described in the Act of Assembly 1784.

Number of White Males 21 yrs. old to 60 yrs.	Number of White Males above 60 and under 21 yrs.	Number of Females of all ages	Number of Negroes from 12 to 50 yrs. of age	Number of Negroes under 12 and over 50 yrs. age
61	96	148	24	27

Taken by

Jo[s]. U. Donell

* * * * *

Return of the Number of Persons in Capt. Carson Camp.

| 8 | 30 | 8 | 30 | 10 |

* * * * *

House of half lot in middle street No. 68

1 free white Canage
2 Negroes as Poles and himself

(Signed) Jacob Johnston

* * * * *

The number of Souls in Capt. Vancez District:

| 86 | 148 | 229 | 29 | 30 |

The above is a true list of the number of souls
as returned to me in the District to which I was
appointed. Certified.

David Vance
16th April '87

Delinquents:

McCoy   John Cosby - white males 1
Wallace   females 1

[On reverse side of page]

Return of Souls in Vancez District - Total 522

Head of Household	WM 21-60 yrs.	WM under 20 & above 60	WF all ages	Blacks 12-50	Blacks under 12 & above 50

BERTIE COUNTY

"North Carolina Bertie County a list of
the inhabatanc of Capt. Francis Pughs
Company taken in 1787"

Pg. 1

Head of Household	WM 21-60 yrs.	WM under 20 & above 60	WF all ages	Blacks 12-50	Blacks under 12 & above 50
Stevens Gray	1	.	.	4	5
Willian Johnson	1	2	4	.	.
James Latham	1	2	3	.	.
John Dowers	1	2	1	.	.
Stephen Outerdbridge	1	1	1	.	2
Ceasar Chavis	1	.	.	.	2
Samuel Laughton	1	1	.	.	.
Henry Dunelo	1	.	1	.	.
John Leming	1	.	.	.	.
George West	1	1	2	10	8
Joseph Collins	1	5	.	3	3
John Warfenden	2	.	2	6	7
James Warren	1	1	1	.	.
James Turner	1	2	6	2	1
Josiah Thomas	1	3	3	2	2
Jacob Bass	1	1	4	.	1
Susanah Holder	.	4	5	.	.
Agness Moore	2	1	1	.	1
Joseph Stiles	1	.	.	.	.
Francis Sowell	2	4	2	.	.
James Doers	3	.	2	.	.
James Miller	.	1	2	.	.
Thomas Barry	3	.	.	1	1
Dennis Dwyer	1	.	5	.	2
James Penney	1	3	5	.	.
John Cowen	1	.	7	.	.
James Rice	1	1	1	1	1
David Taloe	1	3	2	4	1
Benjamin Turlington	1	1	3	.	.
Benjamin Roads	1	.	.	.	.
James Burn	1	1	2	7	4
James Taloe	1	1	5	1	1
Henry Hill	4	.	1	17	10
Gilbert Liegh	1	5	2	8	1
Anthoney Darlet	1	1	2	3	3
Rebecka Ganes	.	.	2	1	.
Alexander Urquhart	1	2	4	.	.
Joshua Morriss	1	.	5	.	.
Moses Sheen	1	3	3	.	.
John Moore	1	1	3	3	3
John Hagan	1	.	.	.	.
David Province	2	.	.	.	.
David Hughs Pg. 2	1	3	2	.	.
John Pearche	1	.	2	1	.

Head of Household	WM 21-60 yrs.	WM under 20 & above 60	WF all ages	Blacks 12-50	Blacks under 12 & above 50
Isaac Williams	1	6	2	1	3
Jacob Sumerlen	1	1	2	.	.
Samuel Melborn	1	5	3	1	3
Benjamin Bryer	2	.	6	3	4
Frances Pugh	1	2	2	12	14
Peter Clifton	1	3	4	6	5
Thomas Mullen	1	.	2	.	.
John Slade	1	.	1	4	2
Richard Dawson	3	1	7	6	7
John Hix	1	.	2	.	.
Thomas Newbern	1	1	2	.	.
William Cowan	1	.	2	.	.
Josiah Collins	2	4	4	.	.
James Wilford	1	1	2	.	.
Joel Britt	1	2	3	.	.
Cader Bass	1	1	.	2	.
William Gray, J. P.	1	2	6	15	10
Amos Turner	2	2	.	6	2

List taken by Willian Gray, J. P.

Feby. Term 1787. List taken by Hum
(blurred) Hardy, Esq. in Capt[n].
Moore's district.

Stevens Gray

(One page only)

Head of Household	WM 21-60 yrs.	WM under 20 & above 60	WF all ages	Blacks 12-50	Blacks under 12 & above 50
Hugh Himon	1	2	2	7	1
Ann James	.	.	4	.	.
Jer. James	1	3	3	.	.
Arthur Williams	1	.	.	.	.
Joab Williams	1	4	3	6	3
Charles Sowell	1	3	5	1	1
John Barrette	1	1	1	.	.
Sol[o]. Weston	1	2	6	.	.
Joseph Simons	1	2	4	2	.
Thomas Callaway	1	4	4	2	1
Charles Boswell	1	.	.	.	.
Obediah Lawrence	1	.	2	.	.
Nicholas Cobb	1	2	3	.	.
Henry Cobb	1	2	3	1	.
Ben Bourn	1	5	3	.	.
James Baker	1	3	1	.	.
(Blurred) Davis	1	1	1	.	.
(Wi?)lliam Castelow	1	1	2	.	.
Ransom Billups	1	2	6	1	3
Thomas Bozwell	1	5	4	1	.
Rob[t]. Lawrence	1	1	2	.	.
Aarchibald Wilford	4	1	1	.	.
John Castelow	1	1	1	.	.
Martha Castelow	.	1	3	.	.

9

Head of Household	WM 21-60 yrs.	WM under 20 & above 60	WF all ages	Blacks 12-50	Blacks under 12 & above 50
Stephen Buck	1	4	5	.	.
John Bozman	1	3	2	2	5
Thomas Harden	1	5	1	1	.
Jas. Curry	1	4	2	.	.
Ephrain Weston	1	2	5	.	3
Thos. Shehan	1	1	2	4	3
George Outlaw	1	3	2	4	3
Andrew South	1	2	4	.	.
Amos Weston	1	2	3	.	.
John Lawrence, Jr.	1	.	4	.	.
Abner Lawrence	1	1	4	.	.
John Lawrence	1	1	2	1	3
John Corbet	1	2	3	.	.
John Moss ?	1	1	3	4	.
William Briant	1	3	3	.	2
Eliz. Dirkins	6	1	4	.	.
Jams Moore	1	3	1	1	1
William Weston	1	4	2	1	1
William Yeates	1	2	4	.	1
Peter Yeates	.	1	3	1	1
Edw. Griffin	2	1	1	3	5
Thomas Yeates	1	4	3	1	1
Bobt. Butler	1	2	1	.	.
John Hopkins	1	3	1	3	3
Lute Hawkins	1	.	.	.	.
Thomas Hawkins	.	2	1	.	.
Thomas Hawkins Jr.	1	.	.	.	.
John Hawkins	1	.	.	.	.
Elisabeth Hardy	.	1	3	.	.
Joseph Mitchell	1	2	3	.	.
Thomas Sutton	1	.	.	.	4
Hum. Hardy	1	5	2	12	20
Luke Collins	1	1	.	13	3
Whitml. Pugh	1	1	6	12	25
Cader Cooper	1	3	5	1	.
William Hodder	1	.	2	.	1
Abigal Charlton	.	.	1	7	8
Capt. Speller's Dist. Pg. 2					
Thomas Rasco	1	1	2	3	2
Sameul Rasco	1	1	1	.	.
James Rasco	1	2	2	3	.
William Smith	1	1	2	.	.
Ann Ryan	.	2	4	7	8
John Hall	4	.	1	.	.
Benjamin Williams	1	7	6	13	16
John Miller, Jun.	1	.	.	.	.
Moses Craft	1	6	2	.	.
Minnit Rodgers	1	3	3	.	.
Mary Seals ?	.	2	3	.	.
Mary Booth	.	.	2	.	.
Mary Rhodes	.	1	2	.	.
William Holley	1	.	1	.	.
John Kittrell	3	1	3	9	15
William Armistead	3	3	4	14	4
James Jordan	.	2	4	9	9
Lidea Whitehouse	.	1	1	.	.
Joseph Carley	3	1	1	2	.
Andw. Oliver	1	5	3	9	11
John Cherry	1	1	2	.	.

Taken by Andw. Oliver

A list of the inhabitants in Capt. Spellers District. Taken by Andw. Oliver. The number of whole is 959

Pg. 1					
Samuel Garrot	1	?	1	1	.
Luke Mannin	1	?	.	1	.
Anthony Armistead	2	?	1	11	1
Soloman Pender	1	3	3	4	4
John Bently	2	3	3	.	.
Bird Hubberd	1	.	6	1	1
Benjamin Cory	2	1	1	1	2
William Warburton	1	.	3	5	6
Melven Demsey	1	2	4	1	.
James Jones	1	.	3	.	.
Nottingham Monk	1	1	2	.	.
Arthur Rasco	1	1	4	1	1
John Himan	2	2	4	4	7
William Jordan	2	.	5	34	24
John Smithwick, Sr.	1	2	1	.	.
Elizabeth Barber	.	1	5	.	.
Nottingham Monk Jr.	2	2	3	5	6
Ritter Swain	.	1	5	1	.
John Leggett	1	2	4	4	2
William Hardy	3	1	6	.	.
Thomas Vass	1	8	3	1	.
Absalom Tadlock	1	2	3	1	2
Mary Jordan	.	.	1	5	4
Samuel Ray	1	1	5	3	1
Peter Burnet	2	1	1	.	.
Thomas West	2	1	4	7	2
Peter West	1	.	3	3	1
Ann Durgan	2	.	2	7	3
Demsey Kittrell	1	4	2	3	1
John Smithwick Jr.	1	1	.	2	2
James Baker	2	4	2	.	.
Joseph Champin	2	4	2	1	.

Head of Household	WM 21-60 yrs.	WM under 20 & above 60	WF all ages	Blacks 12-50	Blacks under 12 & above 50
John Johnston	1	1	5	.	.
William Bently	1	2	1	.	.
Joseph North	1	2	2	2	3
John Garrot	2	1	2	.	.
Joseph Avis	1	.	.	1	.
Stephen Garrot	1	.	1	.	1
John Thomas	1	2	3	.	.
William Burlingham	1	.	1	2	.
John Mardre	1	1	2	.	.
George Creetch	1	2	4	1	.
Abraham Avis	1	1	2	8	1
Luther Everitt	1	1	.	.	.
Ephafroditus Moore	1	2	1	1	.
Sawyer Avis	.	.	?	?	7
Edmond Dunston	3	3	4	4	2
Jesse Bently	1	1	5	.	.
John Sutton	1	2	3	8	5
Job Swain	1	1	2	5	8
William Pender	1	1	1	2	1
Mary Ward	.	1	2	5	6
Sylus Belote	1	1	1	1	1
James Ward	1	.	1	.	.
Isaac Jordan	2	2	6	12	12
Tabitha Swain	2	5	4	3	2
Mary Butler	.	.	4	.	.
George Clements	1	1	1	.	1
John Miller	1	8	3	.	.
Charles Barber	1	4	4	1	.
Benjamin Whitfield	1	1	5	7	7
Elizabeth Whitfield	.	.	1	1	2
John Rhodes	1	.	3	4	.
Christian Reed	1	5	3	7	9
Thomas Collins	1	1	2	5	4
Luke Warberton	1	2	.	2	3
Thomas Leggett	1	.	1	3	5
James Leggett	1	1	5	2	1
Jeremiah Leggett	2	1	5	4	3
Henry Speller	1	2	3	4	3
William West	1	3	2	6	4

A List of the Inhabitants of All Sex and Condition within Captn. Solomon Freeman's District in Bertie County. Taken by Jas Campbell.

Pg. 1

Head of Household	WM 21-60 yrs.	WM under 20 & above 60	WF all ages	Blacks 12-50	Blacks under 12 & above 50	Total
1. Thomas Sowell	1	3	2	1	.	7
2. Luke White, Sen.	.	4	8	.	1	13
3. Samuel Burrass	1	2	1	.	.	4
4. Peter White	2	3	1	.	.	6
5. James Campbell	1	5	5	13	11	35
6. John Campbells Estate	.	.	.	12	15	27
7. James Wilson	1	4	5	.	1	11
8. Luke White, Jr.	1	5	1	2	.	9
9. Moses Freeman	1	2	5	4	1	13
10. Dempsy Kail	1	1	5	.	.	7
11. David Meredith	2	1	3	23	21	50
12. Thomas Cochran	1	2	5	3	2	13
13. Solomon Baker Jr.	1	2	4	.	.	7
14. Solomon Baker Sr.	.	1	2	.	.	3
15. Dempsy Baker	1	1	3	.	.	5
16. Isaac Harrell	1	4	4	.	.	9
17. John Peircey	1	1	3	.	.	5
18. William Harrell	1	3	5	.	.	9
19. Joshua Evans	1	4	4	.	.	9
20. James Asbell	1	3	3	.	.	7
21. Joseph Harrell	1	1	2	.	.	4
22. Thomas Harrell	.	1	2	.	.	3
23. Widow Mary Lassiter	1	3	4	.	.	8
24. Michael Capeheart	1	.	.	.	1	2
25. John Kail	2	1	4	.	1	8
26. Godfrey Askew	.	3	1	.	.	4
27. Cader Kail	1	.	2	.	.	3
28. Widow Rebecca Kail	.	1	5	.	.	6
29. George McClelan	1	2	1	.	.	4
30. Widow Ann Sowell(?)	1	.	2	1	2	6
	27	63	92	60	55	297

Pg. 2

Head of Household	WM 21-60 yrs.	WM under 20 & above 60	WF all ages	Blacks 12-50	Blacks under 12 & above 50	Total
31. Joseph Laurence	1	1	2	.	.	4
32. Edward Sparkman	1	5	3	.	.	9
33. Samuel Haste	1	2	3	.	.	6
34. Adem Harrell	1	1	7	.	.	9
35. Herbert Pritchard	1	3	3	.	.	7
36. Benjamin Stone	.	3	3	1	.	7
37. William Stone	1	2	2	.	.	5
38. Amos Davison	1	3	3	1	2	10
39. Christian Hallam (widow)	.	.	2	.	.	2
40. Judith Hallam (widow)	.	3	4	.	.	7
41. James Robinson	1	1	3	.	.	5
42. William Peircey	1	2	1	.	.	4
43. Elizabeth Rayner (widow)	1	1	3	.	.	5
44. Ann Hallam (Husband ran away)	1	1	.	.	.	2
45. Thomas Ward, Jr.	1	3	5	.	.	9
46. Cader Hunter	1	1	2	2	3	9

Head of Household	WM 21-60 yrs.	WM under 21 & above 60	WF all ages	Blacks 12-50	Blacks under 12 & above 50	
47. Josiah Harrell	1	.	2	.	.	9
48. John Meizell	.	1	4	.	.	5
49. Samuel Ward, Gave in at Pasquotank						
50. Lewis Belch	1	5	1	.	.	7
51. Robert Henry	1	5	2	1	.	9
52. Elias Baker	1	.	1	.	.	2
53. James Madre	1	3	1	.	1	6
54. Joshua White, Gave in Chowan Co.						
55. David Curry	1	6	6	.	.	13
56. Solomon Stone	1	6	2	1	.	10
57. John Capeheart	1	2	7	.	1	11
58. William White	1	2	2	.	1	6
59. Moses Todd	1	6	1	.	.	8
60. James Askew	1	1	3	.	2	7
61. John Robinson	1	3	3	.	.	7
62. Robert Barton (single)	1	.	.	.	.	1
63. John Harrell Jr.	1	2	4	.	.	7
	53	137	178	66	65	499
Pg. 3						
64. Hardy Hunter	1	2	4	8	6	21
65. Job Hunter	1	5	3	1	.	10
66. John Askew Sr.	1	1	5	1	.	8
67. Lewis Sowell	1	1	1	.	.	3
68. William Evan Jr.	1	4	4	1	.	10
69. John Berry, Sr.	.	2	1	.	.	3
70. Wright Berry	1	1	2	.	.	4
71. John Berry, Jr.	1	2	5	.	.	8
72. William Laurence	1	1	2	.	.	4
73. Abraham Perry	1	1	2	.	.	4
74. Aaron Freeman	1	2	4	1	1	9
75. Peter Vanpelt	1	2	1	1	1	5
76. Samuel Williams	1	1	4	.	.	6
77. George Williams	2	3	2	.	.	7
78. Sarah Tyner	.	.	1	.	.	1
79. John Jordan	1	2	7	.	.	10
80. Obediah Sowell	2	2	6	.	.	10
81. James Lane	1	3	4	.	.	8
82. Jacob Outlaw	1	.	4	1	1	7
83. John Howell Sr.	1	.	4	.	.	5
84. William Miezell	1	3	3	.	.	7
85. James Jordan	1	3	2	.	.	6
86. John Oxley	2	4	6	4	.	16
87. John Davison	1	3	3	2	.	9
88. William Robinson	1	1	5	.	.	7
89. Thomas Gaskins	1	1	2	.	.	4
90. Moses Williams	4	1	2	.	.	7
	84	188	267	86	73	698

91. John Todd[no figures given]

List taken by Jas. Campbell, Esq.
Inhabitants in Capt. Freeman's
District. Feby. Term 1787.
Stevens Gray, C. C.

State of North Carolina: Bertie Co.
Capt. John Folks District 1787.

Head of Household	WM 21-60 yrs.	WM under 21 & above 60	WF all ages	Blacks 12-50	Blacks under 12 & above 50
Pg. 1					
Arnold, Richard	1	1	3	4	2
Bunch, Embroy	1	1	3	1	3
Bunch, Fredderick	1	2	2	.	.
Bunch, Jeremiah	.	3	2	1	.
Bunch, Jeremiah Sr.	1	1	1	3	1
Bunch, Meiach (?)	1	.	.	.	.
Bunch, Nehemiah	1	4	3	.	.
Bunch, William	1	1	2	.	.
Barrns, Henery	1	3	6	1	.
Barrns, Solomon	1	.	2	.	.
Baker, Susanah	.	1	6	5	5
Baker, John	1	.	.	1	1
Bazmore, John Sen.	1	1	.	2	4
Bazmore, James	1	4	2	.	.
Bazmore, John	2	2	8	.	.
Bazmore, Jesse	2	9	4	7	4
Bazmore, Malicha	1	1	3	.	.
Bond, Thomas	1	3	1	1	.
Boyce, John	1	3	2	.	5
Baker, Richard	1	.	.	.	.
Barrett, Jennet	.	1	3	.	.
Cherry, Aaron	3	.	4	.	.
Cherry, John	1	.	.	.	.
Cherry, Solomon	1	2	5	3	7
Cob, Lewis	1	4	2	.	.
Clark, Thomas	1	3	3	3	.
Carter, William	1	2	3	1	.
Cherry, William	1	3	6	1	2
Dement, Charles	1	3	2	.	1
Dwyer, Elizabeth	.	.	2	6	12
Dunning, Shadrick	1	1	4	.	.
Davis, Sarah	1	.	1	.	.
Duglass, John	1	2	2	.	.
	33	60	87	40	47
Pg. 2					
Eason, Joseph	1	2	1	2	4
Edwards, Nathan	1	.	3	.	.
Eason, Abner Jr.	1	1	3	2	2
Edwards, John	1	2	2	.	.
Edward, Benjamin	1	.	4	1	1

STATE CENSUS OF NORTH CAROLINA 1784-1787

Head of Household	WM 21-60 yrs.	WM under 21 & above 60	WF all ages	Blacks 12-50	Blacks under 12 & above 50
Fryer, Willis	1	2	2	.	.
Folk, John	2	4	3	1	2
Freeman, King	1	2	1	3	3
Farmer, James	1	.	2	.	.
Griffin, Thomas	1	.	2	.	.
Gardiner, John Sr.	1	5	6	3	6
Gardiner, John	1	2	3	1	.
Gardiner, James	1	2	5	3	5
Gardiner, Sarah	2	1	2	2	10
Gardiner, John Jr.	1	1	1	.	3
Goff, Andrew	1	.	.	.	.
Hail, Jesse	1	3	3	.	.
Howard, Benjamin	1	.	2	1	.
Holder, Elisha	1	2	1	.	.
Howard, Elijah	1	5	3	.	.
Holder, Elizabeth	.	.	3	.	.
Holland, Joel	1	1	1	2	2
Henderson, Isaac	1	1	1	.	.
Holland, Joseph	.	1	2	2	3
Harris, John	1	1	5	.	.
Hermon, Nicholas	1	7	4	.	.
Hogard, William	1	3	1	.	.
	27	51	66	23	41

Pg. 3

Head of Household	WM 21-60 yrs.	WM under 21 & above 60	WF all ages	Blacks 12-50	Blacks under 12 & above 50
Jenkins, Cadar	1	3	3	.	.
Jinkins, Lewis	1	1	5	1	4
King, Charles Sr.	.	5	4	8	1
King, Charles	1	2	2	2	.
King, Henery	1	.	.	1	2
King, William	1	3	2	4	6
Martin, Michal	1	.	3	.	.
Outlaw, Edward	1	1	3	1	1
Poythress, William	1	.	.	.	.
Pritchard, Christian	.	2	5	.	.
Pritchard, Darcus	1	6	2	.	.
Perry, Thomas	1	.	1	3	4
Perry, George	1	1	2	1	1
Parker, Joseph	1	4	3	8	5
Parker, Richard	1	3	3	2	2
Priddim, David	1	.	.	.	2
Rhoades, John Sr.	1	1	2	3	.
Rhoades, John	1	2	5	.	.
Rhoades, Henery Sr.	1	.	2	4	4
Rhoades, Henery	1	1	2	2	.
Rhoades, James	1	3	4	1	.
Rhoades, Isaac	1	1	2	.	.
Ruffin, William	1	6	3	6	6

Rice, James (erased in original; no figures)

Head of Household	WM 21-60 yrs.	WM under 21 & above 60	WF all ages	Blacks 12-50	Blacks under 12 & above 50
Sholar, John	2	1	3	.	.
Sholar, James	1	.	.	.	.
Standley, Edmond	2	2	6	4	6
Sholar, Benjamin	1	3	3	.	.
Sumerlin, Jonas	1	1	2	.	.
Smith, William	1	.	1	.	.
Sholar, Thomas	1	2	2	.	.
	29	55	75	51	46

Pg. 4

Head of Household	WM 21-60 yrs.	WM under 21 & above 60	WF all ages	Blacks 12-50	Blacks under 12 & above 50
Stone, Zedekiah	1	1	2	14	13
Thompson, John	1	.	3	.	.
Thomas, Ezekiel	1	.	2	.	1
Thomas, James	1	.	3	.	.
Thompson, William	1	2	1	.	1
Thompson, Charles	1	.	.	.	.
Thompson, James	1	.	.	.	.
Vail, Thomas	1	4	5	4	1
Willson, Edward	2	.	4	.	.
William, James	1	1	5	1	1
Willson, Edward Jr.	2	2	1	.	.
Willson, Josiah	1	1	2	.	.
Williams, Elizabeth	.	1	1	.	.
Warren, Josiah	1	4	4	.	.
Wood, Jonas	1	.	1	5	2
Abner, Eason	1	1	1	8	9

Above list taken by Abner Eason.

13

BURKE COUNTY

	WM 21–60 yrs.	WM under 21 & above 60	WF all ages	Blacks 12–50	Blacks under 12 & above 50

The Number of Souls in Capt. Brittain's District.

109	white males from 21 yrs. old to 60
241	white males under 21 & above 60
319	white females of every age
21	Blacks of both sexes from 12 to 50
9	Blacks under 12 & above 50 yrs.

The above is a true list of the number of souls as returned to me in the district in which I was appointed.
Certified.
State North Carolina)
Burke County   ) James Brittain
                    19th April 1787

The Number of Souls in John Bradburn's Esq. District in Burke County, taken 6th April 1787.

70	white males above 21 yrs. & under 60
139	white males under 21 & over 60
211	white females of all ages
9	Blacks above 12 & under 50
10	Blacks under 12 & above 50
439	Total

On back of paper –
"A List of the Number of Souls in Capt. Conolys Comply."

A list of white and Black inhabitants, and free citizens of every age, sex and condition in Captain Henry Reed's District, State of North Carolina, Burke County.

Pg. 1

48	white males from 21 to 60 yrs.
108	white males under 21 & above 60
135	white females of every age
4	Blacks of every sex from 12 to 50
0	Blacks above 50 and under 12 yrs.

Pg. 2

53	white males from 21 to 60 yrs.
126	white males under 21 & above 60
158	white females of every age
7	Blacks of each sex from 12 to 50
0	Blacks above 50 & under 12

Pg. 3

35	white males from 21 to 60 yrs.
67	white males under 21 & above 60
190	white females of every age
3	Blacks from 12 to 50 yrs.
3	Blacks above 50 & under 12

Totals of above pages

136	white males from 21 to 60
295	white males under 21 & above 60
513	white females of every age
14	Blacks from 12 to 50 yrs.
3	Blacks above 50 & under 12 yrs.

On back of page:
A Return of Inhabitants of Capt. Henry Reeds Comy."
By Pat Sloan

A list of the Number of Souls in Capt. William Null's Old Company, in Burke County. Taken April 5th, 1787.

There is a blurred streak down the left side of the microfilm, which of course, is on the original returns. This streak obliterates the first several letters of many names in the two pages of this return.
(Compiler).

Pg. 1

	WM 21–60 yrs.	WM under 21 & above 60	WF all ages	Blacks 12–50	Blacks under 12 & above 50
[ ] Wofford	2	4	5	3	4
[ ] Ainswork	1	2	4	3	.
John Sisco, Sr.	1	3	4	.	.
John Sisco, Jr.	1	.	3	.	.
[ ]ob Sisco	1	.	2	.	.

14

Head of Household	WM 21-60 yrs.	WM under 21 & above 60	WF all ages	Blacks 12-50	Blacks under 12 & above 50
John Van	1	1	1	.	.
[Mart?]ha Oakley	1	.	2	.	.
[ ] [--]owell	1	2	4	.	.
[ ] Wison	1	.	1	.	.
[ ] Wilson	1	2	6	.	.
[ ] [De?]loch	1	1	2	.	.
[ ] Wilson	1	3	3	1	1
[Name illegible]	1	4	5	.	.
[?]omas Young	1	3	1	.	.
William Phillips	1	4	3	.	.
[De]lilah McNalls	.	3	1	.	.
Catherine Pepper	1	5	4	.	.
Frederick Miller	2	1	1	.	.
James Lee	1	3	2	.	.
William Moodie	1	4	1	.	.
James Bennett	.	2	2	.	.
[ ] Hensley	1	3	2	.	.
[ ] Hensley	1	3	4	.	.
[ ] [Hen?]sley	1	2	4	.	.
[ ] [---]erstaff	2	.	2	.	.
[ ] Billins	3	2	4	.	.
[ ] [Whi?]taker	1	2	4	.	.
[---]mas (?) Bright	.	5	4	.	.
[ ] Hensley	2	3	4	.	.
[---]liam Bright	1	2	1	.	.
[ ] Pickeral	1	3	4	.	.
[ ] Ruddock	1	4	7	.	.
[Al?]bert Turner	1	2	4	.	.
[---]uel Gray	1	2	3	.	.
	37	80	104	7	5
Pg. 2					
Jonas Griffith	1	2	4	.	.
George Holebrok	2	.	6	.	.
David McCraken	1	3	5	.	.
Thomas Baker	1	.	1	.	.
John Armstrong	.	5	4	.	.
Henry Gillispie	.	3	2	.	.
Richard Jacks	1	2	5	.	.
Thomas Barnard (?)	1	.	1	.	.
[ ] [Mon?]tgomery	2	2	2	1	2
[ ] [Bra?]dshaw	1	2	3	.	.
[ ] [---]ling	.	2	3	.	.
[ ] [---]way	1	1	1	.	.
[ ] [W?]right (?)	1	1	1	.	.
	49	103	142	8	7

Grand Total 30(9?)

15

CAMDEN COUNTY

State of No. Carolina. A List of the Number of white and black Inhabitants &c of the county of Camden, distinguish'd agreeable to Act of Assembly of October 1784 as returned to June court &c 1787 by the several Justices appointed for that purpose agreeable to the Governor's Proc. of the 13th Jany. in the same year.

Names of the Persons who, by order of Court have taken these lists in the 8 Militia districts of the County	White males 21-60 yrs. age	White males under 21 over 60 yrs.	White females of every age	Blacks 12-50 years of age	Blacks under 12 over 50 years age	Total
Willis Brite, Esquire	86	167	221	27	30	531
Elisha McBride, Esq.	80	135	197	63	55	530
Caleb Grandy, Esq.	79	155	230	61	64	589
Enoch Sawyer, Esq.	70	96	178	137	129	610
Isaac Gregory, Esq.	61	110	156	34	37	398
William Nevell, Esq.	64	95	163	33	20	375
Stephen Sawyer, Esq.	73	154	216	67	80	590
Isaac Guilford, Esq.	67	119	188	44	52	470
Total	580	1,031	1,549	466	467	4,093

Camden Co. This may certify that the above is an exact account of the number of white and black inhabitants, & the free citizens of every age, sex & condition in the County of Camden, State of No. Carolina, as far as they have been returned by the several persons appointed for that purpose agreeable to his Excellency the Governors Proclamation of 13th Jany. last, which returns were made to June Term. In faith and Testimony whereof I have hereunto set my hand and seal this xxviiith day of June, A. D. 1787, and xlth of Independence.

D. Burgess, C. C. C. (Seal)

[On back of page:]

Camden; No. of Inhabitants, A. D. 1787 - 4,093

To His Excellency the Governor or Secretary's Office.

By the Honble. Genl. Gregory, one of the members of the General Assembly for the County of Camden.

CARTERET COUNTY

Beaufort, June 20th, 1786, Carteret County.

The Subscriber being appointed Commissioner for the District of Beaufort agreeable to an Act of Assembly to take the lists of the inhabitants of Carteret County, have taken the same as follows:

James Parrett

	White males 21-60 years age	White males under 21; over 60 years	White females of every age	Blacks 12-50 years age	Blacks under 12; over 50 years age
	122	175	297	153	112
White Oak District. Abraham Dudley, Commissioner	68	149	232	88	90
Bogus Sound District Absolam Shepard, Commissioner	77	143	196	64	78
Hunting Quarters District Taken by Joseph Gaskill Commissioner	60	133	172	7	10
Straits District. Taken by John Fulford, Commissioner	92	217	264	67	64
Ocacock District Adam Gaskill, Commissioner	39	79	107	42	0
[Totals by Compiler]	458	896	1,268	421	354

Total as given in census

3,375　　　　　　　　　　　Robt. Read, Clk.

[On back of page]

Number of Souls in Carterett County

CASWELL COUNTY

A true list of the number of the inhabitants in Caswell County agreeable to the different returns from the several Districts taken and returned to January and April counts 1786.

	White males 21-60 years age	White males under 21; over 60 years	White females of every age	Blacks 12-50 years age	Blacks under 12; over 50 years age
St Luke's District Taken by Peter Farrar	134	290	336	99	115
Richmond D⁰. Taken by John J. Farley	215	448	629	222	224
Caswell D⁰. Taken Robert Burton	194	424	566	118	104
Gloucester D⁰. Taken by William Gooch, Jun.	122	261	339	45	41
Added to Glouster	61	152	164	34	32
Nash D⁰. Taken by Yancey Bailey	132	233	360	168	197
St. James D⁰. Taken by Robert Payne	105	225	281	101	81
St. Lawrence D⁰. Taken by John Cumbers	168	365	509	151	153
St. David D⁰. Taken by Waddy Tate	142	350	427	172	150
Total Amount	1,273	2,748	3,611	1,110	1,097

A true copy.

Test. Ae^d. (Archibald) Murphy, C. C.

List of the No. of the inhabetents of Caswell County - 9,839.

* * * *

Note by Compiler: Subsequent to microfilming the above summary, two of the Districts have been located in the Archives, and were sent to the compiler on xerox. These two returns - Caswell and Gloucester Districts and St. David's District total 4,004 inhabitants. This still leaves 5,835 not yet found.   a. k. r.

STATE CENSUS OF NORTH CAROLINA 1784-1787

Head of Household	WM 21-60 yrs.	WM under 20 & above 60	WF all ages	Blacks 12-50	Blacks under 12 & above 50
Caswell District					
Pg. 1					
Dudley Gatewood	1	5	3	6	5
Robert Paul	1	2	1	3	.
Peter Smith	2	10	4	3	6
Berry Turner	1	1	3	5	12
Spill Coleman	1	2	2	9	7
Thos. Bartin	1	3	7	.	.
Jno. Waters	1	2	2	.	1
Jno. Ware	1	1	2	.	.
Jno. Ingram	1	4	4	.	.
Willm. Quine	1	2	3	.	.
Jno. Walker	1	2	4	1	1
Saml Paul	2	.	2	4	1
Paul McClarny	.	2	2	.	.
Obediah Holloway	1	1	5	.	.
Thos. Gaddis	1	2	4	.	.
Jane Musick	.	2	5	.	.
Wm. Leak	1	1	2	.	.
Chs. Hanie	1	3	2	.	.
James Ingram	1	3	3	.	.
Thos. Baxter	.	5	5	.	.
Mary Quine	.	1	2	.	.
Reuben Hanie	.	2	1	.	.
Shadd. Jackson	1	5	1	.	.
IgnaTinnison	1	3	6	.	.
James Miller	1	3	3	.	.
Saml. Bullock	1	2	3	.	.
Isaac Middlebrook	1	1	4	.	.
Abram. Perkins	.	2	2	2	1
Benje. Hubbert	1	3	4	.	.
Robt. Lyon	1	2	3	2	3
Jas. Perkins	1	6	4	1	1
Jesse Perkins	1	.	1	.	.
	28	83	99	36	38
Pg. 2					
Jno. Perkins	.	2	1	1	1
Joel Connon	1	2	2	.	.
Jno. Summers	1	1	3	.	.
Wm. Cannon	1	2	4	3	4
Henry Dixon	.	2	2	7	6
Ann Middlebrook	.	4	2	.	.
Jno. Middlebk.	1	2	1	.	.
Richd. Boggess	1	7	4	.	.
Christ. Dudley	1	1	4	.	.
Wm. Ware, Sen.	1	2	3	.	.
Wm. Ware, Junr.	1	.	3	.	.
Geo. A. Davis	1	4	2	.	.
Geo. Whitton	2	3	5	.	.

Head of Household	WM 21-60 yrs.	WM under 21 & above 60	WF all ages	Blacks 12-50	Blacks under 12 & above 50
Danl. Gossage	1	5	1	.	.
Benje. Rose	1	1	3	.	.
Edwd. Oneal	1	6	4	.	.
Danl. Adams	1	2	2	.	.
Jno. Sammon	2	3	6	1	1
Wm. Parr, Senr.	.	2	2	.	.
Wm. Parr, Junr.	1	.	.	1	.
Henry Baldwin	1	3	5	.	.
Obediah Tucker	1	1	2	.	.
Mary Hatfield	1	2	2	.	.
Jno. Baldwin	1	.	2	.	.
Gideon Hogg	.	1	5	.	.
Nathl. Dickerson	1	6	3	3	1
Wm. Otwell	1	3	3	.	.
Olive Terry	1	.	2	.	.
Rebk. Terry	.	.	2	2	.
Martha Dixon	.	3	3	5	8
Thos. Tiffin	1	3	2	1	.
Elexs. Thompson	1	.	1	.	.
Wm. Leake	1	3	3	.	.
Wm. Hanie	1	3	2	.	.
Jas. Grant	.	4	3	3	.
Hez. Fanning	1	3	5	.	.
	30	86	99	27	21
Pg. 3					
Peter Smith	1	2	2	1	4
Benje. Quine	1	2	2	.	.
Abram Miles	1	3	2	2	3
Thos. Miles	1	.	1	.	.
Jno. Miles	1	1	4	.	.
James Richardson	1	1	9	.	.
Thos. Richdson	1	1	2	.	.
Wm. Standfield	.	1	1	2	1
Peter Hill (Hitt?)	1	2	3	.	1
Jones Broach	1	2	2	.	.
Jno. Foster	1	1	1	.	1
Bridgar Hanie	1	2	2	1	.
Lal. Richardson	1	.	1	.	.
Jno. Roberts	.	3	4	.	.
Limage Stringer	1	.	2	.	.
Jno. Cannon	1	3	4	1	2
James Walker	1	3	5	.	.
Milly Brown	.	2	4	.	.
Jno. Beaver	1	2	3	.	.
Wm. Beaver	1	4	3	.	.
Jerm. Beaver	1	2	1	.	.
Jno. Talbot	1	.	1	.	.
Alexr. Porter	1	2	5	.	.
Elijah Nunn	1	3	3	.	.

19

Head of Household	WM 21-60 yrs.	WM under 20 & above 60	WF all ages	Blacks 12-50	Blacks under 12 & above 50
Robt. Farguson	1	3	2	.	.
Jno. Grant	1	2	2	.	.
Thos. Poor	1	3	3	.	.
Thos. Forster	1	6	2	.	.
Jno. Graves	.	.	.	3	.
Jas. Alverson	1	2	1	.	.
Christ. Huston	.	1	1	.	.
Jeff. Rice	1	1	1	1	1
Robt. Embry	1	5	6	.	.
Wm. Embry	1	.	1	.	.
Wm. Page	1	5	6	.	.
	30	66	92	11	13
Pg. 4					
Wm. Atkins	1	.	3	.	.
Wm. Atkins	1	.	4	.	.
Nathl. Page	1	1	2	.	.
Jno. Pendergrass	1	1	5	.	.
Thos. Wht. head (Whitehead)	1	.	3	.	.
Jno. Alverson	.	2	3	.	.
Davd. Pendergrass	1	.	5	.	.
Henry Cobb	2	6	3	4	2
Jno. Cobb	1	1	2	.	.
Thos. Thaxton	1	1	2	.	.
Wm. Morgan	1	2	5	.	.
Saml. Morgan	1	3	1	.	.
Saml. Brakin	1	3	6	.	.
Thos. Waters	1	2	7	.	.
Wm. Wht. head (Whitehead)	1	3	3	.	.
Widow Tribble	.	2	1	.	.
Henry Strader	1	.	1	.	.
Robt. White	1	3	4	.	.
Geo. Elmore	.	1	4	.	.
James Landmon	1	1	3	.	.
Wm. Graham	.	6	6	2	4
Wm. Graham	1	3	5	.	.
Edwd. Graham	1	.	.	.	.
Jno. Graham	1	2	1	.	.
Peter Graham	1	.	3	.	.
Chs. Elmore	1	3	3	.	.
Peter Elmore	1	5	5	.	.
Archer Alverson	1	3	2	.	.
Robt. King	1	6	2	.	.
Widow Ransom	.	1	4	.	.
Geo. Summers	1	1	3	.	.
Jno. Summers	1	2	1	2	1
Henry Curtis	1	.	3	.	.
Thos. Murphy	1	4	3	.	.

Head of Household	WM 21-60 yrs.	WM under 20 & above 60	WF all ages	Blacks 12-50	Blacks under 12 & above 50
Jno. Powell	1	3	3	.	.
Wm. Smith	1	3	2	.	.
Wm. Lyon	1	.	1	.	.
	33	74	114	8	7
Pg. 5					
Wyatt Stubblefd (Stubblefield)	1	2	4	5	5
Majr. Brocmn. (Brockman)	1	4	2	.	.
Abram Womack	1	3	3	3	3
Jno. McCollum	2	6	3	.	.
Alexr. Jnoson (Johnson)	1	2	2	1	.
Thos. McLane	1	2	1	.	.
Thos. Weatherfd (Weatherford)	1	.	2	.	.
Thos. Weathrford	2	.	1	.	.
Wm. Chapman	1	5	6	.	.
Jas. Chapman	1	1	1	.	.
Conrad Strader	1	4	3	.	.
Wm. Moss	1	3	2	3	1
Richd? Beasley	1	1	4	3	1
Jas. Powell	1	3	4	2	1
Pat Adams	.	.	1	.	.
Widow Smith	.	.	1	.	.
Simeon Ford	1	4	4	.	.
Joel Gibson	1	5	4	.	.
Ezel. Walters	1	.	2	.	.
James Snow	1	.	5	.	.
Mary Durham	.	2	4	.	.
Isaac Durhm. (Durham)	1	3	8	.	.
James Arnett	1	3	2	.	.
Andw. Arnett	1	7	4	.	.
Patk. McGongl. (McGonegal?)	1	3	3	.	.
Wm. Watts	4	2	4	.	.
Timy. Ragon	1	3	3	.	.
Edwd. Baldwin	1	.	1	.	.
Fred. Spoolman	1	1	2	.	.
Geo. Humphs (Humphreys)	1	5	5	.	.
Thos. Swann	2	2	4	.	.
Jas. Brown	1	4	2	1	.
Jane Burton	.	2	4	8	7
Josh. Jones	1	2	3	.	.
Jno. Southerld (Southerland)	1	1	4	.	.
Totals	37	85	108	26	15

20

Head of Household	WM 21-60 yrs.	WM under 20 & above 60	WF all ages	Blacks 12-50	Blacks under 12 & above 50
Pg. 6					
Robt. Burton	1	2	6	10	10
Jonath^n. Greenhaw	1	3	3	.	.
Jas. Underwood	1	2	2	.	.
Thos. Skinner	1	1	3	.	.
Jas. Gibson	1	3	5	.	.
Jno. Gibson	1	1	2	.	.
Thos. Whalebone	1	2	5	.	.
Abr. Gillon (Gilton?)	1	1	2	.	.
Henry Clemens	1	.	5	.	.
Jno. Gelton?					
(Gilton or Gillon)	3	3	3	.	.
Nancy McCubbins	.	1	3	.	.
Timy. Rooks	2	3	2	.	.
Ez^l. Rooks	1	2	3	.	.
Jona. Cummins	1	5	7	.	.
Dav^d. Benton (?)	1	1	3	.	.
Henry McClarney	1	.	.	.	.
Wm. McClarney	1	.	.	.	.
Raw^l. Horton	1	.	.	.	.
James Boggess	1	.	.	.	.
Thos. Middlebr^k.					
(Middlebrook)	1	.	.	.	.
Isaac Avery	1	.	.	.	.
Thos. Ware	1	.	.	.	.
Wynne Dixon	1	.	.	.	.
Tilmon Dixon	1	.	.	.	.
Ch^r or Ch^s Dixon	1	.	.	.	.
James Burton	1	.	.	.	.
Bryan(t) Leak	1	.	.	.	.
James Hayes	1	.	.	.	.
James Grant	1	.	.	.	.
Vincent Robts					
(Roberts)	1	.	.	.	.
Benj. Ransom	1	.	.	.	.
Jas. Hopkins	1	.	.	.	.
Wm. Dix	1	.	.	.	.
F. Roland	1	.	.	.	.
Totals	36	30	54	10	10

Mulattoes:
Jno. Wright	1
Arthur Toney	1
Wm. Hood	1
free Winney	3
	3 3

A list of the number of souls in
Caswell District.
Robert Burton   Jany 16, 1786
Total 1, 412

Head of Household	WM 21-60 yrs.	WM under 20 & above 60	WF all ages	Blacks 12-50	Blacks under 12 & above 50
Accumulated Total					
Caswell District	194	424	566	118	104

Gloucester District: Caswell Co.

Head of Household	WM 21-60 yrs.	WM under 20 & above 60	WF all ages	Blacks 12-50	Blacks under 12 & above 50
Pg. 1					
Robert Parks	1	7	5	.	.
James Barker	1	2	3	1	.
Shadrach Gibbs	1	.	1	.	.
John Shanks	1	4	2	.	.
Wm. Gooch, Junr.	1	6	2	1	.
James Gooch	1	.	1	.	.
Wm. Gooch, Senr.	1	4	4	4	4
Edward Anderson	1	.	.	.	.
Henry Fuller	1	4	6	.	.
Robert Kimbro	1	2	4	2	1
James Turner	1	2	2	.	.
Wm. Kimbro	1	3	6	1	1
John Kimbro	1	5	6	3	8
Thomas Graves	1	4	4	2	4
Thomas Kimbro	1	2	1	1	2
Robert Bruice	2	3	4	1	.
Joseph Bush	1	1	7	1	3
John McIntosh	1	4	3	.	.
Elenor Kimbro	1	.	1	3	3
Anthorite Martin	.	1	4	.	.
Robert Martin	1	1	2	.	.
Poll Saunders	.	.	3	.	.
George Spilmon	1	.	1	.	.
Wm. Jones	2	4	4	2	5
Thomas Jones	2	1	5	1	1
Jonathan Anthony	1	1	2	.	.
Henry Davis, Senr.	.	1	3	.	.
Jonathan Davis	1	2	1	.	.
Nicholas Davis	1	.	1	.	.
Edward Roberson	1	2	3	.	.
	30	66	91	23	32
Pg. 2					
Wm. Cantrell	1	.	5	1	.
Wm. Austin	1	5	3	.	.
Thomas Roberson	1	2	1	.	.
Thomas Rice	1	4	4	.	.
Edward McClusky	1	3	3	.	.
Hutson Berry	1	1	3	1	.
Tabitha Lannum	.	4	3	.	.
John Shy	.	5	5	.	.
Clifton Allen	1	2	4	1	1
John Polson	1	3	2	.	.

Head of Household	WM 21-60 yrs.	WM under 20 & above 60	WF all ages	Blacks 12-50	Blacks under 12 & above 50
John Anthony	1	4	2	2	2
James Anthony	1	1	1	.	.
James Rice	2	5	4	.	.
John Rice	1	4	5	.	.
James Jones	1	4	3	3	2
David Jones	1	3	1	2	3
Ann Jones	.	.	1	.	.
Moses Pierce	1	3	4	.	.
Joel Corder	1	1	1	.	.
Christopher Porter	1	3	3	.	.
Obed Florence	1	2	6	.	.
Benjamin Enucks	2	4	2	1	.
Edmund Browning	1	2	4	.	.
Joseph McReynolds	1	2	1	.	.
Alexdr. McIntosh	.	2	2	.	.
Jesse Shy	1	.	1	.	.
John White	1	.	.	.	.
Luke Pendergrass	1	4	4	.	.
James Colman	1	2	1	.	.
Orasha Coope	1	1	1	.	.
Joseph Jones	1	1	2	.	.
James Hopper	1	6	3	.	.
Gabriel Murphy	1	3	8	.	.
	31	86	93	11	8
Pg. 3					
Richard Arwin	1	.	.	.	.
Richard Arnal	1	1	1	.	2
John Pleasant	1	.	1	.	.
James Benton	1	5	7	1	.
Wm. Barnwell	2	6	3	.	.
John Murphy	1	1	1	.	.
Nicholas Browning	.	1	3	.	.
Henry Warson	1	.	2	1	.
John Pyron(t)	1	3	7	.	.
Elijah Mason	1	5	5	.	.
John Tardy	1	2	2	.	.
Pierce Aswell	1	4	1	.	.
Samuel Browning	1	2	3	.	.
George Browning	1	.	3	.	.
Jonathan Poe	1	5	2	.	.
Eliz. Browning	.	3	4	.	.
Roland McReynolds	1	4	4	.	.
Bleuford Pleasant	2	3	9	.	.
James Barton	1	.	.	.	.
John McMeneny	2	.	2	.	.
Timothy Burges	1	4	1	.	.
Edward King	1	2	2	.	.
Samuel Mothrel	1	4	.	.	.
Samuel Warren	1	.	4	.	.

Head of Household	WM 21-60 yrs.	WM under 20 & above 60	WF all ages	Blacks 12-50	Blacks under 12 & above 50
Elijah Fuller	1	1	2	.	.
Ann Grear	1	2	4	1	.
Richard Johnston	1	4	3	.	.
Samuel Grear	1	1	5	.	.
James Wray	1	2	5	1	.
Acquilla Compton	2	6	4	.	.
David Dickie	1	1	2	.	.
Martha Wisdom	.	4	5	1	.
Wm. Bridgewaters	1	.	2	.	.
	34	76	99	5	2
Pg. 4					
Wm. Culbertson	1	2	3	.	.
Nathaniel King	.	1	2	.	.
John Curry, son of Jas.	1	2	2	.	1
John Dickie	2	1	3	.	.
Elias Wallis	1	1	4	.	.
John Wallis	1	4	2	.	.
James Culbertson	.	1	2	.	.
Isaac Boren	1	1	2	.	.
Charles McIntosh	1	.	.	.	.
John Hopper	.	3	2	.	.
David Harrington	1	3	6	.	1
Wm. McIntosh	1	1	2	.	.
Susannah Hopper	.	1	1	.	.
Ralph Shaw	1	2	6	.	.
John Graves Jr.	1	5	4	5	3
Benjamin French	1	1	1	.	.
Thomas Wiley	1	2	5	.	.
Samuel French	1	1	1	.	.
Thomas Evins	.	2	2	.	.
Joseph Carney	1	3	2	1	.
Alexander Wiley	2	3	3	.	.
John Bates	1	2	2	1	2
Meshach Morton	1	5	3	.	.
Zacheriah Evins	1	.	2	.	.
Daniel Evins	1	2	1	.	.
Thomas Langly	1	4	3	.	.
James Richmond	1	3	2	.	.
Thomas Serjant	1	6	2	.	.
Henry Turney	1	4	5	3	1
James Noel	1	1	4	.	.
Joshua Carney	1	.	.	.	.
John Richmond Sr.	1	3	2	1	.
James Serjant	1	5	4	.	.
Jeremiah Gilmore	1	4	2	.	.
William Lea	1	2	2	1	.
Neal McCoy	.	1	1	1	.
	32	82	90	13	8

STATE CENSUS OF NORTH CAROLINA 1784–1787

Head of Household	WM 21-60 yrs.	WM under 21 & above 60	WF all ages	Blacks 12-50	Blacks under 12 & above 50
Pg. 5					
Barzilla Graves	1	2	1	.	.
John Kerr	1	3	3	1	.
Samuel Bullison	.	5	3	.	.
Thomas Jones	1	2	2	.	.
John Cochran Sr.	.	3	3	2	4
John Cochran Jr.	1	.	.	.	.
Wm. Cochran	1	.	.	.	.
Reuben Cochran	1	.	.	.	.
Edward Nowel	1	3	6	.	1
John Richmond	1	2	4	1	1
Larkin Wisdom	.	1	2	.	.
Thomas Phelps	1	.	3	.	1
Thomas Rhone	1	.	2	.	.
John Christmass	1	1	2	.	.
Richard Martin	1	1	2	.	.
John Payne	.	2	2	1	.
Jane Love	1	1	6	1	.
Solomon Parks	1	.	1	1	.
Samuel Kelley	1	.	1	1	1
Wm. Donoho	1	3	3	2	2
Mathew Richmond	1	4	2	.	.
James Martin	1	1	1	.	.
Ann Yancey	1	3	7	6	5
Alexander Bruice	1	6	3	.	.
Wm. Carrel	1	1	3	.	.
Wm. Richmond	1	5	3	1	2
Thomas Tuning	1	1	2	.	.
Wm. Kelley	.	1	1	.	.
Wm. Saunders	1	5	2	4	6
James Kitchen	1	.	1	.	.
John Siddall	1	2	5	.	.
Hannah Carrell	.	2	4	.	.
John Roberson	2	1	6	.	.
	28	61	86	21	23
Pg. 6					
John Corder	2	5	6	.	.
Lewis Corder	1	.	1	.	.
Charles Taylor	2	2	4	.	2
James Johnston	1	5	4	.	.
John Ashbourne	1	.	1	.	.
Benjamin Wallis	1	1	2	.	.
Thomas Evins	2	2	2	.	.
Anderson Ashbourn	1	3	3	.	.
Thomas Kilgore Jr.	1	.	1	.	.
Lydda Kilgore	.	2	1	.	1
James Lea	1	3	4	1	.
Wm. Hughs	1	.	1	.	.
George Hughston	1	2	3	.	1
Archd. Carmical	1	3	3	.	.

Head of Household	WM 21-60 yrs.	WM under 20 & above 60	WF all ages	Blacks 12-50	Blacks under 12 & above 50
John Hix	1	.	1	.	.
Jeremiah Carmical	1	1	2	.	.
Mary Curry	.	1	5	2	3
Henry McMullin	.	1	2	1	1
John McMullin	1	.	.	1	.
Richd. Currier	1	2	3	.	.
James Currier	1	3	1	.	.
John Curry Sr.	2	2	6	.	.
Thomas Cole	1	1	1	.	.
Harman Hopper	1	.	2	.	.
John Jackson	1	.	.	.	.
Daniel Melton	1	2	4	.	.
Henry Cooper	1	1	1	1	.
	28	42	64	6	8

Per William Gooch, Junr. Jany. 14, 1786

Accumulated Totals
Gloucester Dist. 183 413 503 79 73

Grand Total
Gloucester Dist. 1, 251

Saint David's District
Pg. 1

Head of Household	WM 21-60 yrs.	WM under 20 & above 60	WF all ages	Blacks 12-50	Blacks under 12 & above 50
Anderson, John	1	1	6	.	.
Addams, James	1	1	1	.	.
Adcock, Edmond	.	3	7	.	.
Angling, Wm.	1	2	3	.	.
Adcock, Joshua	1	4	2	.	.
Berton, Liewes	1	6	8	.	.
Burton, Sam¹	1	1	1	.	.
Blackwill, Robt.	1	4	5	4	1
Berry, John	1	.	.	.	.
Barton, Susannah	.	1	2	.	.
Burton, David	1	1	3	.	1
Barker, Israil	1	4	1	1	.
Brown, Wm.	1	4	5	.	.
Brothers, John	1	1	5	.	.
Brown, Leonard	1	5	4	.	.
Burton, Cutbud	1	.	.	.	.
Butler, Anderson	1	3	3	.	.
Browning, Wm.	1	2	7	.	.
Barker, George	4	1	1	7	5
Barton, James	1	1	4	.	.
Brown, John	1	8	4	10	13
Brown, Wm. (C)	3	2	4	.	.
Barker, Geo. Jr.	1	.	2	1	.

23

Head of Household	WM 21-60 yrs.	WM under 21 & above 60	WF all ages	Blacks 12-50	Blacks under 12 & above 50
Cobb, Noah	1	7	3	.	.
Cantral, Joseph	.	3	3	4	7
Davis, Henry	1	3	2	1	.
Dennis, John	1	2	4	.	.
	29	70	90	28	27
Pg. 2					
Dill, John	1	6	2	.	.
Dorress, Wm.	1	1	1	.	.
Davis, Cornelius	1	2	1	.	.
Dill, Annels	1	.	3	.	.
Dill, John Sr.	.	2	2	.	.
Dabney, Cornelius	1	1	3	2	3
Dickens, James	1	2	2	.	.
Dill, John Jr.	1	2	5	.	.
Estes, Richard	1	3	6	.	1
Fitchgarrell, Wm.	1	.	1	.	.
Fitchgarrell, Charles	1	1	3	.	.
Foote, George Jr.	1	2	1	1	.
Foote, George Sr.	1	5	3	6	6
Foote, Newton	1	.	.	.	.
Gwyn, Daniel	1	4	3	1	.
Graves, John Sr.	.	2	1	12	9
Haggard, Edmond	2	5	3	.	.
Hughes, Roland	2	.	5	2	3
Haggard, Wm.	1	3	2	.	.
Hinslee, John	1	3	4	1	.
Herbin, John (Cl)	1	3	6	.	.
Henslee, David	1	1	.	.	.
Henson, Richd	1	2	4	.	.
Henslee, Macksfield	.	1	3	1	.
Herbin, John (C. C. C.)	1	3	5	.	.
	54	126	163	54	49
Pg. 3					
Hughes, James	1	1	4	.	.
Harress, Tyree Jr.	1	1	1	.	.
Henslee, Wm.	1	.	.	.	.
Hughes, Charles	.	1	2	.	.
Hayes, John	1	.	2	.	.
Hughes, John	.	2	1	.	.
Herbin, Wm.	1	2	2	.	.
Harress, Tyree Sr.	1	3	2	12	15
Hart, David	1	6	3	8	6
Harden, Presly	2	3	3	.	.
Jackson, George	1	.	1	.	.
Jones, John	1	.	1	.	.
Johnston, Lancelot	2	5	4	4	.
Johnston, James	1	2	2	.	.
Keer ?Kerr), Alexr	1	.	4	7	4
Lay, John	1	4	3	.	.

Head of Household	WM 21-60 yrs.	WM under 20 & above 60	WF all ages	Blacks 12-50	Blacks under 12 & above 50
Lachkey, John	1	4	3	.	.
Martin, George	1	4	2	.	.
Mallery, John	1	2	5	2	.
McCulley, John	1	.	2	.	.
Mitchell, Geo.	1	2	3	.	.
Martin, Joseph	1	1	1	.	.
Mitchell, Wm.	1	3	6	.	.
Murrey, Jonathan	1	3	1	.	.
Murrey, James	1	1	6	.	.
Mallery, John	1	2	2	.	.
	80	178	229	87	74
Pg. 4					
Mayhan, Wm.	1	1	2	.	.
Murphy, John	1	2	1	.	.
Loveings, Arthur	1	2	6	.	1
Nance, Shearwood	1	1	3	.	.
Oldham, Geo.	1	2	5	.	.
Oldham, John	1	2	1	4	2
Orre, James	1	2	5	.	.
Oldham, James	1	7	2	.	.
Oldham, Moses	1	5	4	1	.
Oldham, Jesse	1	4	5	2	2
Oldham, Richd Jr	1	.	.	.	.
Ponder, Thomas	1	.	1	.	.
Pike, Liewis	1	5	3	.	.
Ponder, Morgan	1	6	2	.	.
Pinnex, John	1	.	4	.	.
Poston, Jeramiah	1	2	3	1	.
Payne, Josiah	1	2	3	.	.
Payne, Greenwood	1	4	3	2	.
Redmond, Barbery	.	1	1	.	.
Rice, H. Wm.	1	2	2	1	.
Reid, John	1	.	1	.	1
Rice, Wm.	1	3	4	2	3
Rice, Hezakiah	1	4	2	2	.
Rice, Thomas (CB)	1	1	1	3	1
Reid, Nathl	1	2	4	.	.
Rice, Nathan	1	3	3	.	.
	105	241	300	105	84
Pg. 5					
Rice, Thomas Esq.	.	4	1	4	1
Rice, Nathl.	1	1	2	.	.
Rice, Japtha	1	3	1	1	1
Rice, Asa	1	.	3	.	.
Rice, John	.	3	5	2	1
Swift, Antho.	1	.	1	2	.
Swift, Thomas	1	1	2	4	.
Simpson, Richd Jr.	.	1	.	7	6
Sawyears, Stephen	1	.	.	.	.
Smith, Francis	1	1	3	.	.
Spencer, John	1	1	3	.	.

Head of Household	WM 21-60 yrs.	WM under 21 & above 60	WF all ages	Blacks 12-50	Blacks under 12 & above 50
Sawyears, John	1	5	3	.	.
Scoot (?Scott) John	.	2	2	.	.
Slade, Thomas	1	2	1	2	3
Sanders, Smith	1	1	1	.	.
Smith, Richard	1	2	5	.	.
Scott, James	1	2	2	.	.
Sims, Geo.	1	4	7	1	5
Sawyears, Wm.	1	4	5	.	.
Spencer, Eliz.	1	1	4	.	.
Spencer, Benjamin	1	4	4	1	.
Simpson, Mary	.	.	2	.	.
Swift, Wm.	.	4	2	7	5
Slade, Wm.	1	.	.	.	.
Triplett, Nimrod	1	.	1	.	.
Thompson, John	1	3	2	.	.
	125	290	362	136	106
Pg. 6					
Thompson, Antho.	.	1	.	.	.
Tate, Waddy	1	4	4	3	1
Triplett, John	1	2	3	.	.
Thompson, Wm.	.	1	1	.	.
Taylor, Mary	.	2	4	.	.
Thornton, Joel	1	3	4	.	.
Vaugh, Giddian	1	1	1	.	.
Williamson, Nathan	1	4	5	2	5
Whitlock, Robt.	.	7	4	.	.
Walker, James	.	4	2	.	.
Windsor, John	1	3	3	2	.
White, Timothy	.	2	1	.	.
Williamson, Hawley	1	4	3	.	.
Willis, Henry	1	2	1	.	.
Williamson, Jera.	1	2	4	1	.
Williams, Elizabeth	.	3	5	7	10
Washington, Wm.	1	1	1	.	.
Walker, Samuel	.	2	3	.	.
Williams, Daniel	.	1	1	2	1
Wright, William	1	1	3	.	.
Walker, James Jr.	1	2	1	.	.
Williams, John	1	1	3	6	12
Williamson, Stephen	2	2	4	10	15
Wisdom, Joseph	1	3	3	.	.
Moore, Saml	1	2	1	3	.
Accum. Tot.	142	350	427	172	150

Tot. St. David's Dist.   1, 241

Chatham County

Amount of the white and Black inhabitants in Chatham County as Returned
by the several persons appointed by
the Court to receive the same.

900	white males 21-60
1, 037	white males under 21 and over 60 yrs.
2, 550	white females of every age
493	Blacks 12-50 yrs. of age
472	Blacks under 12 & above 50
5, 452	Total by Compiler

Test.

John Ramsey, C. C.

Received   1 August 1787

CHOWAN COUNTY

A list of the Inhabitants in Capt. Stallins District:

Pg. 1

Head of Household	WM 21-60 yrs.	WM under 21 & above 60	WF all ages	Blacks 12-50	Blacks under 12 & above 50
John Parkes	1	2	2	.	.
John Evens	1	1	6	.	.
Amos Perey	1	1	3	.	.
Silas White	1	3	4	1	.
Charles White	1	.	2	.	.
James Lain	1	4	1	.	.
Elias Stalings	1	2	3	.	.
Thomas Ward	1	2	3	.	.
Moses Ward	1	2	5	.	.
Lowdrick Ward	1	3	2	.	.
Ephriam Ward	1	.	.	.	.
William Ward	1	.	.	.	1
James Byrum	1	4	2	.	.
Abner Halawell	1	4	2	1	3
Willis Griffin	1	3	2	.	.
James Ward	.	5	6	.	.
Nathen Jordan	1	.	.	.	.
Samuel Lain	1	2	.	.	.
Calob Jordan	1	.	1	1	1
Samuel Parker	1	1	4	.	.
Sarah Bufkin	.	1	2	.	.
Thomas Ward	1	3	4	.	.
Joseph Jordan	1	4	3	.	.
James Woodward	1	.	1	.	.
Charles Powell	1	.	1	1	4
Fedrick Gurley	1	2	3	.	.
Lewis Ward	2	1	5	.	.
Thomas Ward	1	4	2	2	.
Joseph Jordan	1	2	4	.	.
Nicholas Stalings	1	3	7	.	.
	29	59	80	6	9

Pg. 2

Head of Household	WM 21-60 yrs.	WM under 21 & above 60	WF all ages	Blacks 12-50	Blacks under 12 & above 50
Jacob Jordan	2	.	2	6	7
Josiah Copeland	3	.	3	16	12
Marten Hurdle	1	2	4	.	.
William Felton	1	1	1	1	3
John Felton	2	1	1	2	1
Shadrick Felton	1	1	1	2	2
John Lee	1	3	2	.	.
Willis Moore	1	.	2	.	.
Micajah Chapel	2	1	1	.	.
Marget Moore	1	1	2	.	.
Henery Jacobs	1	1	3	.	.
Ezeblun Mansfield	1	4	5	.	.
Jacob Cullens	1	.	1	2	1

Head of Household	WM 21-60 yrs.	WM under 21 & above 60	WF all ages	Blacks 12-50	Blacks under 12 & above 50
Benjamin Gregory	1	1	1	.	.
Benjamin Hurdle	1	1	2	2	1
Benjamin Jordan	1	2	3	.	.
Thomas Jones	1	2	2	.	.
Edward Welch	2	5	2	.	.
Joseph Copeland	1	2	3	.	.
Josiah Copeland Jr.	1	.	2	.	.
Thomas Hobbs	1	.	2	.	.
Mary Copeland	.	.	2	.	.
Micajah Blanshard	1	2	1	3	2
Jonathan Jordan	1	.	4	3	2
Isaac Byrum	2	2	3	.	.
Joel Byrum	1	1	3	.	.
Sarah Smith	2	1	4	.	.
Mary Ross	.	1	3	.	.
Joshua Copeland	1	4	4	.	.
Michel Bond	.	.	4	3	1
Bond Jameson	1	.	2	.	.
William Webb	1	1	4	.	.
Job Winslow	1	.	1	2	1
	38	40	80	42	33

Pg. 3

Head of Household	WM 21-60 yrs.	WM under 21 & above 60	WF all ages	Blacks 12-50	Blacks under 12 & above 50
Ruth Fulaw	.	1	2	.	.
Judah Wood	.	1	2	.	.
John Coffield Jr.	1	.	1	8	8
Hardy Hurdle Jr.	1	2	4	5	1
Samuel Pery	2	4	2	.	.
Hardy Hurdle	.	2	2	6	3
Henery Hurdle	1	.	2	.	2
John Robarts	1	2	4	1	1
Josiah Jordan	1	1	3	.	.
Edward Parish	1	3	4	.	.
Job Parker	1	3	6	1	.
Nathen Parker	1	.	3	3	.
Joseph Scott	1	1	4	1	.
Champin Spivey	1	1	4	.	.
John Ward	.	3	2	.	.
David Welch	1	6	6	1	.
Thomas Goodwin	1	1	5	1	.
Exhem Goodwin	1	.	.	.	.
Joseph Goodwin	1	.	1	.	.
Jacob Tomas	1	2	4	.	.
Joshua White	1	1	2	.	.
Jarvis Forhand	1	2	4	.	.
Totals (sic)	19	36	66	27	15

579

Josiah Copeland

26

Head of Household	WM 21-60 yrs.	WM under 21 & above 60	WF all ages	Blacks 12-50	Blacks under 12 & above 50

"A List of the White and Black inhabitants of the Town of Edenton, 1786. Chowan County.   1,112

Pg. 1

Head of Household	WM 21-60	WM u21	WF	Bl 12-50	Bl u12
Lott Brewster	1	.	5	3	1
William Borritz	1	.	2	7	3
Samuel Dickinson	2	1	3	34	12
Michael Payne	1	.	4	21	6
John Mare	3	1	2	9	10
William McDonnald	1	2	1	7	3
Stephen Cararrus	1	.	2	30	30
Ann Sinclair	4	4	5	2	2
James Dunscombe	1	.	1	2	1
Benjamin Hardy	1	.	2	2	2
Francis Porree	1	.	2	1	1
Joseph Whedbee	1	2	1	2	2
Mary Littledale	.	.	3	3	1
Frances Black	1	.	1	8	2
Mary Darling	.	.	2	.	.
Sacker Savage	1	1	3	1	.
Zachariah Webb	1	2	2	.	.
Ann Anderson	.	.	2	7	4
James Yeomans	1	.	2	1	1
Elizabeth Stewart	.	.	1	1	.
	22	13	46	141	81

Pg. 2

Head of Household	WM 21-60	WM u21	WF	Bl 12-50	Bl u12
Sarah Sweaney	.	.	3	.	1
James Webb	.	.	1	1	.
John Williams	1	2	1	.	.
Josiah Collins	4	.	1	19	.
Alexander Black	2	1	.	3	.
Thomas Britain	1	1	4	.	1
Sarah O'Neal	.	2	2	4	2
Thomas Bents	1	1	1	3	1
William Parker	8	.	4	4	1
Charles Loughrea	2	2	1	1	1
John Small	1	3	3	1	1
William Dolbey	1	.	4	.	.
Penelope Kirby	3	.	5	2	1
Mary Roddy	2	1	4	1	2
Elizabeth Hays	.	.	2	.	.
Elizabeth Eagan	1	.	2	8	6
Elizabeth Mand/Maud	.	2	3	.	.
Mary Lafong	.	2	3	.	.
Matthews O'Malley	2	1	.	3	1
Maliche Collins	1	.	2	.	.
Isaiah Burdick	1	.	1	1	.
Margaret Watson	.	1	2	.	.
Accum. Totals	56	32	95	193	99

Pg. 3

Head of Household	WM 21-60	WM u21	WF	Bl 12-50	Bl u12
Mary Wallace	.	.	3	2	.
Elizabeth Saterfield	1	1	2	2	.
Henry Neal	2	1	.	.	1
Penelope Wynans	.	.	2	.	2
Joseph Faribault	1	1	.	.	.
John Mallary	1	.	2	.	2
John Frazel	2	2	2	2	.
Mary Redick	.	2	2	3	1
George Dear	1	.	2	1	3
William Gardner	5	5	4	8	3
Elizabeth Minerva	.	1	1	1	.
Mary Wilkinson	1	.	3	2	.
Frederick Rameke	1	1	4	13	8
Henderson Luten	1	.	2	2	1
Elizabeth Russell or Fussell(?)	.	.	1	3	1
James Iredell	2	1	5	8	6
Thos. Clarkson	1	1	1	.	.
Elizabeth Askins	.	1	2	1	.
Ivey Purdie	1	1	2	2	3
Francis Beasley	1	.	2	2	.
James Farrow	1	1	1	2	.
	78	51	138	247	130

Pg. 4

Head of Household	WM 21-60	WM u21	WF	Bl 12-50	Bl u12
Ann Williams	.	1	2	1	2
William Lester	2	2	3	1	.
Robert Millar	1	.	3	.	1
John Fife	1	.	1	.	.
Abraham Brown	1	.	2	.	.
Thomas King	2	4	3	7	3
Peter Groshon	1	4	2	1	1
James Jennet	1	1	3	3	.
James Hays	1	4	2	4	5
Absolom Luten	3	.	1	1	.
William S. Daws	1	.	1	1	.
John Bigar	1	.	1	1	.
Henry Bond	3	2	3	4	2
Mary Blackbourn	.	1	2	3	3
Thomas Chambers	3	.	2	.	.
William Littlejohn	1	2	6	27	13
Samuel Cooley	1	1	1	5	1
William Bennet	3	2	4	23	11
Stephen Miles	1	.	5	3	2
Samuel Butler	1	1	1	9	2
John Ready	4	.	3	1	.
William Rumbough	1	3	2	2	1
John Wallace	1	.	2	1	2
Accum. Totals	112	79	193	345	180

27

Head of Household	WM 21-60 yrs.	WM under 21 & above 60	WF all ages	Blacks 12-50	Blacks under 12 & above 50
Pg. 5					
George Morgan	1	3	3	2	3
Thomas Barker	.	1	1	6	13
Walsey Hathaway	1	3	3	2	1
John Ecleston	1	.	1	1	1
Hannah Ker	.	.	3	.	.
Fanny Anderson	.	.	2	.	.
Nathaniel Allen	1	2	4	16	1
Alexander Hamilton	1	.	2	.	1
Dominique Murear	2	.	4	2	.
Thomas Waff	1	2	3	2	.
James Martin	1	.	1	.	.
Emillia Lawrence	2	2	4	4	2
Henry Watson	4	4	2	3	1
John Powers	3	.	2	2	.
Mary Bateman	3	.	2	1	.
Joseph Blount	1	3	2	17	8
Richard Reeves	1	.	3	1	.
John Wright	.	.	2	.	.
Henry Cheshire	1	4	2	1	1
Sarah Montgomery	4	1	1	4	5
Thomas Cox	1	1	4	5	1
Accum. Totals	141	105	234	414	218

Grand Total 1, 112

March 29, 1786   Saml Cooley

Currituck County

A return of the number of inhabitants in each Captain's district in Currituck County, Anno Dom. 1787

Companies: [All names preceded by Capt.]

	WM 21-60 yrs.	WM under 21 & above 60	WF all ages	Blacks 12-50	Blacks under 12 & above 50
Saml. Ferebees	97	169	294	114	96
William Northern's	104	128	205	61	62
John William's	84	155	255	69	60
John William's (HiFile?)	73	119	205	61	36
Andrew Dukes	98	138	216	44	35
Thomas Poyners	83	141	222	56	47
Nathan Halls	55	122	169	58	38
Thomas Farrows	100	166	255	25	19
Stephen Westcots	118	206	277	52	42
Total	812	1344	2098	540	435

Grand Total (Compiler) 5, 229

Currituck County; June Term 1787.

I do hereby certify the above return to be a Just Account of the number of inhabitants in this county agreeable to the returns made to my office (I am not furnished with a list of names).

Test.

William Ferebee, C. C. C.

28

Head of Household	WM 21-60 yrs.	WM under 21 & above 60	WF all ages	Blacks 12-50	Blacks under 12 & above 50

DUPLIN COUNTY

List of Capt. Stallin's District taken by
Dan[l] Teachy & returned April 1786.
Pg. 1

Head of Household	WM 21-60 yrs.	WM under 21 & above 60	WF all ages	Blacks 12-50	Blacks under 12 & above 50
1. Daniel Teachy	1	2	1	6	10
2. Wimbert Boney	2	5	2	3	3
3. Anthony Francis	1	3	1	.	.
4. Lott Green	1	.	4	.	.
5. John Teachy	1	2	6	.	.
6. Joseph Morgan	1	3	4	.	.
7. Jas. Morgain	1	.	1	.	.
8. John Morgan	2	.	3	.	.
9. Adam Platt	2	1	4	.	.
10. Jacob Wells	1	.	1	.	.
11. Nicholas Bryan	1	2	1	.	.
12. Peter Young	1	2	4	.	.
13. Hardy Parker	1	.	1	.	.
14. Lavin Allen	1	.	1	.	.
15. John Williams	1	2	1	.	.
16. John Young	1	.	1	.	.
17. John Holden	1	.	.	.	.
18. Zach[n] Carter	1	2	1	.	.
19. Henry Allen	1	.	2	.	.
20. Andrew Thally	1	4	3	1	.
21. Henry Allen Sr.	.	2	1	.	.
22. Emanuel Bowzer	.	2	2	.	.
23. Thos. Green	.	1	3	.	.
24. John Cooke	1	3	3	.	.
25. Thos. Evans	1	2	3	.	.
26. Henry Jones	1	2	2	.	.
27. Thos. Cumings	1	4	3	.	.
28. William Allen	1	6	1	.	.
29. William Hall	1	2	6	.	.
30. William Savage	2	1	2	.	.
31. Jas. Knowles	1	4	3	.	.
32. Robt. Wallace	1	.	6	.	.
33. Jas. Rollins	1	6	2	.	.
34. Simon Rivenbark	1	6	4	.	.
35. John Evens	1	2	5	.	.
36. Jos. Williams Jr.	1	1	4	1	1
37. John Williams	3	3	5	.	.
	40	73	97	11	14
Pg. 2					
38. David Davis	1	.	3	.	.
39. John Wilson	1	1	1	.	.
40. John Green	1	3	3	.	.
41. James Wright	1	.	1	1	.
42. Jonathan Davis	1	1	1	1	1
43. Britton Powell	1	1	4	.	.
44. Geo. Willis	1	1	3	.	.
45. John Alderman	1	1	5	.	.
46. Simon Wood	1	2	4	.	.
47. William James	2	3	2	1	.
48. David Williams	1	.	1	.	.
49. Mesheck Stallins	1	2	4	1	.
50. Eliz[h] Fussell	.	2	4	.	.
51. Wm. Duff	3	2	4	.	.
52. John Cook (J. C.)	1	2	3	2	.
53. Mary Cook	.	1	2	1	4
54. Martin Hanchy	1	1	4	.	.
55. Luke Bowzer	1	1	3	.	.
56. Sarah Murray	.	2	2	1	.
57. Walter Bryan	1	.	.	.	.
58. Silvester Cavanah	1	2	1	.	.
59. Sarah Bailey	.	1	5	.	.
60. Jesse Norris	1	3	2	.	.
61. Jacob Teachy	1	1	1	1	.
62. Jesse George	1	3	1	.	.
63. Daniel Boney	1	1	2	.	.
64. Adam Murray	2	.	4	.	.
65. James Padget	1	.	.	.	.
66. Aaron Hodgeson	1	4	3	.	.
67. Andrew Rouse	1	5	1	.	.
68. Sarah Shuffield	.	2	3	.	.
69. Joseph Wilson	.	2	2	1	3
70. Daniel Bowen	1	5	4	.	.
71. David Tucker	1	4	2	.	.
72. Lewis Brock	2	1	4	3	1
73. David Sloan	.	2	3	3	1
74. Benj. Lanier	1	2	4	.	.
	35	64	97	17	9
Pg. 3					
75. David Carleton	1	.	1	.	.
76. Joseph Wms.	3	1	3	4	5
77. Alexr. Porter	1	1	2	.	.
78. Wm. Merrit	1	4	5	.	.
79. Abrm. Newton	1	1	3	.	.
80. Chas. Merrit	1	1	2	.	.
81. Rice Matthews	1	3	3	.	1

29

Head of Household	WM 21-60 yrs.	WM under 21 & above 60	WF all ages	Blacks 12-50	Blacks under 12 & above 50
82. Wm. Goff	1	1	1	.	1
83. Robt. Rollins	1	4	5	.	.
84. John Vann	1	1	2	.	.
85. TholCrumpton	1	2	2	1	.
86. Joshua Blake	1	1	2	.	.
87. David Hall	1	.	2	.	.
88. David Alderman	1	2	7	.	.
89. Richd. Welch	1	1	4	.	.
90. John Mathis	1	1	3	1	.
91. John Goff Jr.	1	1	3	1	1
92. Wm. Beven	1	2	2	.	.
93. Jacob Mathis	2	3	4	.	.
94. Arthur Mathis	1	1	1	.	.
95. Wm. Knight	1	2	1	.	.
96. Joseph Beven	1	1	1	.	.
97. Robt. Knowles	1	.	2	.	.
98. Jacob Beverit	1	1	4	.	.
99. Wm. Tilmon	1	3	4	.	.
100. Fredk. Williams	1	5	1	.	.
101. Wm. Cooke	.	1	1	.	.
102. John Newton	1	2	6	.	.
103. Daniel Aldeman	1	2	4	.	.
104. Joseph Beven	1	3	3	1	.
105. Auston Beesley	1	1	2	.	.
106. David Hennesy	1	.	1	.	.
107. Hardy Powell	1	1	2	.	.
108. Shadrick Stallins	1	2	4	3	3
109. Peter Newell	1	2	4	.	.
	37	57	97	11	11
Pg. 4					
110. John Baker	1	.	1	.	.
111. Michael Ezel	4	2	3	.	1
112. Nathl. Edwards	.	1	2	.	.
113. Timothy Murphy	.	3	1	5	5
114. Edward Dickson	1	1	4	9	3
115. Wm. Murphy	1	1	4	1	1
116. Joshua Edwards	1	2	2	.	.
117. John Goff Sr	.	1	1	4	2
118. Fredk. Wells	1	2	5	1	.
119. John Carleton	1	5	2	.	.
120. Jacob Wells Sr	1	2	5	5	3
121. Jacob Wells Jr	1	.	2	.	2
122. John Blanton	1	7	4	.	.
123. James Blanton	1	1	1	.	.
124. Elias James	1	1	.	.	.
125. John Parker	1	3	4	.	.
126. Charles James	1	.	4	.	.
127. Jacob Powell	1	1	1	.	.
128. Mary Hill	.	.	6	.	.

Head of Household	WM 21-60 yrs.	WM under 21 & above 60	WF all ages	Blacks 12-50	Blacks under 12 & above 50
129. Jeremiah Pearsall	1	3	1	1	2
130. George Powell	1	.	.	.	.
131. John Whitman	1	4	5	.	.
132. John Bryan	1	1	2	.	.
133. John Merchant	1	1	6	.	.
134. John Evers Sr	1	1	3	.	.
135. John Evers Jr	1	.	1	.	.
136. Willoby Tillis	1	2	1	.	.
137. Wm. Harvill	1	6	3	.	.
138. Mathew Beck	1	4	1	.	.
139. Wm. Bland	1	2	3	.	.
140. Thomas James	2	3	5	9	8
141. Thomas Carleton	1	2	5	.	.
142. Hardy Gilstrap	1	.	1	.	.
143. Mary Bland	.	4	4	.	.
	33	66	93	35	27

List of Capt. Hubbard's Company taken by Samuel Houston & returned April 1786.

	WM 21-60 yrs.	WM under 21 & above 60	WF all ages	Blacks 12-50	Blacks under 12 & above 50
Pg. 1					
1. Ann Worley	.	1	2	3	.
2. Loftis Worley	1	1	4	.	.
3. Lewis Barfield	1	3	6	1	1
4. Absalom Mercer	1	.	2	.	.
5. Rachel Mercer	.	1	2	.	.
6. Fredk. Smith	1	5	2	1	.
7. Jas. Williams	2	3	6	.	.
8. Jas. Holland	1	2	3	.	.
9. Lewis Smith	2	3	3	.	.
10. Geo. Smith Sr.	1	4	5	.	.
11. Saml. Jones Jr.	1	2	5	.	.
12. John Johnston(B. C)	1	1	2	.	.
13. John Jones	1	2	3	.	.
14. Stephen Brady	1	1	1	.	.
15. John Williams	1	4	7	13	11
16. Joseph Bray Sr	1	1	2	.	.
17. Joseph Bray Jr	1	2	3	.	.
18. Joseph Canaday	1	2	3	.	.
19. Mills Mumford	1	2	6	.	.
20. Andrew Erickson	1	1	2	.	.
21. Jones Boyet	1	1	3	.	.
22. Wm. Nethercut	1	.	1	.	.
23. Wm. Nethercut Sr.	1	4	3	.	.
24. Wm. Barlow	1	.	1	.	.
25. Steph. Martindel	1	1	6	.	.
	25	47	79	18	12

Head of Household	WM 21-60 yrs.	WM under 21 & above 60	WF all ages	Blacks 12-50	Blacks under 12 & above 50
26. Saml Martindel	1	2	4	.	.
27. Joseph Morgan	1	1	2	.	.
28. Thos. Shelton	1	.	3	.	.
29. John Morrow	1	1	2	.	.
30. Jos. Canaday Sr.	1	4	3	.	.
31. Jas. Frazar	1	1	4	.	.
32. John Southerland	2	1	2	.	.
33. Absolom Boyed	1	3	5	.	.
34. Geo. Smith Jr.	2	4	1	.	.
35. Richd Prescut	1	4	2	.	.
36. Elizh Boyet	.	.	3	.	.
37. John Richards	1	.	1	.	.
38. Anthony Miller	1	3	4	3	1
39. Chas. Miller	1	.	2	.	1
40. Wm. Hubbard	1	.	3	1	.
41. Jas. Dobson	.	1	3	.	.
42. Lewis Barnes	1	3	3	7	6
43. Wm. Hall	1	4	1	6	4
44. Jas. Conner	1	3	5	.	.
45. Anthony Lewis	.	2	3	.	.
46. Edward Houston	1	2	2	1	2
47. Joseph T. Rhodes	1	.	.	3	1
48. Saml Whaley	1	2	2	.	.
49. Benj. Rhodes	1	2	5	2	4
50. Joseph Twilley	1	1	1	.	.
	24	44	66	23	19
Pg. 3					
51. Robt. Twilley	1	.	3	1	.
52. Thos. Quin	1	1	5	.	.
53. Francis Whaley	1	.	2	.	.
54. John King	1	2	4	.	.
55. Robt. King	1	2	6	.	.
56. David Greear	1	2	.	2	.
57. Zadock Mumford	1	.	2	.	.
58. Caleb Quin	1	.	.	.	.
59. Jas. Whaley	1	2	5	1	.
60. Wm. Whaley	1	3	5	.	.
61. Griffith Houston	4	1	5	1	.
62. Wm. Houston	.	2	1	2	9
63. Chas. Sowell	1	1	2	.	.
64. Shadk Sowell	1	1	3	.	.
65. Wm. Mercer	1	3	2	.	.
66. Henry Houston	1	2	8	2	1
67. Saml Houston	1	3	7	6	4
68. Eliza Maxwell	.	.	2	.	.
	19	25	62	15	14

Head of Household	WM 21-60 yrs.	WM under 21 & above 60	WF all ages	Blacks 12-50	Blacks under 12 & above 50
List of Capt. Whitehead's District, taken by Frederick Barfield and returned April 1786.					
Pg. 1					
1. Fredk Bearfield	1	5	3	4	1
2. John Durrell	1	2	2	.	.
3. Saml Tanner	1	1	5	.	.
4. James Taylor	1	1	5	.	.
5. Diana Taylor	.	.	1	.	.
6. Buckingham Killigrew	1	.	2	1	.
7. Wm. Whitfield	.	1	1	1	3
8. Daniel Parker	1	2	3	.	.
9. Jonathan Parker	1	3	2	.	.
10. Anthony Jones	1	4	3	.	.
11. Solomon Dobson	1	3	3	.	.
12. Michael Sulliven	1	1	2	.	.
13. John Sulliven	1	4	3	.	.
14. Sabrit Sollis	1	2	2	.	.
15. Eliza Parker	.	1	4	.	.
16. Ann Jones	.	2	1	.	.
17. Demsey Taylor	1	.	.	.	.
18. James Outlaw	1	5	5	3	3
19. Auston Swinson	1	.	.	.	.
20. Demsey Westbrook	1	1	2	.	.
21. Lewis Hines Jr	2	.	2	.	.
22. Lewis Pipkin	1	.	3	1	.
23. Wm. Alberson	1	.	.	.	.
24. Daniel Hines	1	.	1	.	.
25. Besent Brock	1	.	3	.	.
26. Benj. Brock	1	1	6	.	.
27. Wm. Stroud	1	1	3	.	1
28. John Dever	.	6	2	.	.
29. James Wilkins	.	2	3	.	.
30. Thos. Tanner	1	3	5	.	.
31. Wm. Wilkins	1	1	3	.	.
32. John Wilkins	.	2	1	.	.
33. Jesse Jones	1	.	2	.	.
34. Samuel Goff	1	.	1	.	.
	28	54	84	10	10
35. Richd Roberts	.	3	3	.	.
36. Solomon Carter	1	3	2	1	2
37. Wm. Bullard	1	2	4	.	.
38. Richd Roberts Jr	1	1	1	.	.
39. Ollive Johnston	.	2	3	.	.
40. David Carter	1	1	1	.	.
41. Hezikiah Blizzard	1	.	3	.	.

31

Head of Household	WM 21-60 yrs.	WM under 21 & above 60	WF all ages	Blacks 12-50	Blacks under 12 & above 50
42. Lott Gray	1	1	2	.	.
43. Michael Glisson	1	2	2	1	1
44. Ann Pomfrey	.	2	2	1	2
45. Jonathan Kitley	1	1	5	.	.
46. Silas Carter	1	4	1	.	.
47. James Roberts	1	.	.	.	.
48. Kesia Blizzard	.	1	1	.	.
49. Saml Alberson	1	2	5	3	1
50. Benj. Adams	2	2	2	.	.
51. Josiah Stafford	1	.	4	.	.
52. Richd. Mouns	1	3	5	.	.
53. Wm. Roberts	1	1	1	.	.
54. Elisha Fairles	1	4	3	.	.
55. John Smith	.	2	3	.	.
56. Margaret Carter	.	3	3	.	.
57. Benj. Snipes	1	1	5	.	.
58. Wm. Mainer	1	2	3	.	.
59. Alexr Graddy	1	4	3	2	3
60. Isaac Dawson	1	3	4	1	1
61. Jacob Summerlin	1	8	3	.	.
62. Jacob Glisson	1	2	2	.	.
63. Bethia Massey	1	2	5	.	.
64. Edee Smith	.	1	1	.	.
65. John Alberson	1	.	.	.	.
66. John Glisson	1	3	2	.	.
67. Fredk Graddy	1	4	3	1	1
68. John Graddy	1	1	3	2	.
	28	71	90	12	12

Pg. 3

Head of Household	WM 21-60 yrs.	WM under 21 & above 60	WF all ages	Blacks 12-50	Blacks under 12 & above 50
69. Andrew Guilford	1	1	4	2	.
70. Stephen Guilford	1	.	.	.	.
71. Wm. Kornegay	1	5	4	2	.
72. Eliza Thomson	.	3	3	.	.
73. Benj. Thomson	1	2	2	.	.
74. Isaac Herring	1	1	3	.	.
75. Samuel Sowell	1	2	3	.	.
76. Sulliven	.	3	3	.	.
77. John Barnet	1	1	5	.	.
78. William Sulliven	1	2	1	.	.
79. Lewis Sowell	.	2	4	.	.
80. Stephen Herring	1	1	4	1	.
81. Whitfield Herring	1	1	1	.	.
82. Owen O. Daniel	1	.	2	.	.
83. Sampson Grimes	1	.	5	1	1
84. Elizabeth Grimes	.	.	1	1	1
85. Stephen Barfield	1	.	.	3	1
86. Lewis Graddy	1	4	3	1	.
87. John Tetterton	1	1	3	.	.

Head of Household	WM 21-60 yrs.	WM under 21 & above 60	WF all ages	Blacks 12-50	Blacks under 12 & above 50
88. William Powers	1	.	2	.	.
89. Aliff Taylor	.	.	2	.	.
90. Samuel Rogers	1	1	3	1	.
91. Rubin Weston	1	5	2	.	.
92. Benj. Herring	1	3	2	.	.
93. John Houseman	1	5	1	2	.
94. James Mathews	1	3	3	.	.
95. Elijah Bowen	1	2	1	.	.
96. William Graddy	1	4	4	2	2
97. Jethro Mainer	1	2	3	.	.
98. Mary Sulliven	.	.	4	1	1
99. Cason Harris	1	3	1	.	.
100. John Sulliven	1	5	4	.	.
101. John Mainer	1	3	2	.	.
	28	67	87	17	6

Pg. 4

Head of Household	WM 21-60 yrs.	WM under 21 & above 60	WF all ages	Blacks 12-50	Blacks under 12 & above 50
102. Mourning Williams	.	1	1	.	.
103. Lewis Hines Sr.	1	5	5	.	.
104. Jacob Taylor	1	3	4	.	.
105. Lutson Stroud	1	2	3	.	.
106. Beckford Garris	1	1	1	.	.
107. Thomas Taylor	.	2	2	.	.
108. Lewis Jones	.	1	1	.	.
109. Lewis Herring	.	1	1	.	.
110. John Whitehead	1	3	2	.	.
	5	19	20	.	.

List of Capt. Bowden's Company taken by Francis Olliver & returned April 1786.

	WM 21-60 yrs.	WM under 21 & above 60	WF all ages	Blacks 12-50	Blacks under 12 & above 50
1. Nicholas Bowden	1	4	2	.	.
2. Baker Bowden	1	1	1	.	.
3. Geo. Homes	1	3	5	.	.
4. Shadk Daniel	1	1	4	.	.
5. Hardy Reeves	1	3	5	.	.
6. Chloe Simpler	.	1	2	.	.
7. John Shuffield	2	5	5	.	.
8. Wm. Dunkin	1	3	3	1	3
9. Elisha Harrell	1	.	2	.	1
10. Wm. Taylor	1	.	1	.	.
11. John Daniel Sr.	1	1	4	.	.
12. John Wade	1	2	1	.	.
13. Simon Flowers	1	.	1	.	.
14. Wm. Harris	1	5	5	.	.
15. Jacob Millard	1	3	1	.	.
16. Joseph Wade	.	1	6	.	.

Head of Household	WM 21-60 yrs.	WM under 21 & above 60	WF all ages	Blacks 12-50	Blacks under 12 & above 50
17. Rubin Johnston	1	5	6	.	.
18. Jacob Kornegay	1	1	2	6	11
19. Jesse Swinson	1	1	2	.	.
20. Theo. Williams	1	1	3	1	2
21. Elisha Carrol	1	3	3	.	.
22. John Swinson	1	2	1	1	.
23. Teresa Warrin	.	.	1	.	1
24. Joshua Chambles	1	2	4	.	.
25. John Daniel	1	1	3	.	.
26. John Bradley	1	4	3	.	.
27. Jesse Brock	1	3	2	.	.
	25	56	78	9	18

Pg. 2

Head of Household	WM 21-60 yrs.	WM under 21 & above 60	WF all ages	Blacks 12-50	Blacks under 12 & above 50
28. Caleb Beck	1	2	4	.	1
29. John Haines	1	3	5	.	.
30. Nathanl Kinnard	1	1	1	.	1
31. Tho. Wiggins	1	.	4	4	5
32. Michl Kinnard	1	5	4	1	4
33. James Oates	1	1	1	2	3
34. John Kornegay	1	1	1	.	1
35. Adam Reeves	1	.	2	.	.
36. Wm. Hines	1	3	2	.	.
37. Jesse Cook	1	2	1	.	.
38. Robl Brock	1	2	1	.	.
39. David Walker	1	2	1	.	.
40. Mary Jones	2	1	7	.	.
41. Jerusha Parker	.	.	2	.	.
42. John Winders	4	.	5	4	3
43. Edmund Dunkin	2	1	5	.	.
44. John Rogers	1	6	3	.	.
45. Geo. Kornegay	1	5	2	6	4
46. Geo. Kornegay Jr.	1	1	2	.	1
47. Elisha Jernigan	1	1	1	.	.
48. John Gibbs	1	3	5	1	.
49. Tho. Bennet	2	5	3	.	.
50. Jacob Taylor	1	2	2	.	.
51. Lavin Watkin	1	5	2	2	3
52. Isaac Dunkin	1	.	1	.	.
53. Tho. Bradley	1	2	1	.	.
54. Wm. Gulley	2	2	7	1	.
	33	54	75	21	26

Pg. 3

Head of Household	WM 21-60 yrs.	WM under 21 & above 60	WF all ages	Blacks 12-50	Blacks under 12 & above 50
55. Saml Bowden	1	3	3	.	.
56. Mark Rogers	1	.	1	.	.
57. Tho. Flowers	1	2	3	.	.
58. Jesse Flowers	1	2	1	.	.
59. Richd Bradley	1	1	1	.	.
60. Jas. Grimes	1	5	1	.	.
61. Jas. Hurst	1	.	.	.	.
62. Wm. Beemam	1	7	3	1	2

Head of Household	WM 21-60 yrs.	WM under 21 & above 60	WF all ages	Blacks 12-50	Blacks under 12 & above 50
63. Alexr. Sanders	1	1	3	.	.
64. Jas. Bizzel	1	1	2	.	.
65. Robt. Henderson	1	.	2	.	.
66. Francis Cogdell	1	1	8	.	.
67. Stephen Snell	2	.	3	1	.
68. Chrisr Burch	1	2	2	.	.
69. Jesse Branch	1	2	3	.	.
70. Charity Herring	.	1	2	1	1
71. Mary Denmark	.	2	4	.	.
72. Wm. Taylor	2	1	5	10	3
73. Francis Olliver	1	2	5	1	2
74. Wm. Bizzel	1	2	4	.	2
75. Willis Cherry	1	2	4	1	.
78. John Rogers Jr	1	2	3	.	.
79. Thos. Gray	1	5	4	15	7
	23	44	67	30	17

[76 & 77 omitted from original]

List of Capt. Kenan's District taken by Daniel Hicks and returned April Term 1786.

Pg. 1

	WM 21-60 yrs.	WM under 21 & above 60	WF all ages	Blacks 12-50	Blacks under 12 & above 50
1. James Kenan	1	2	5	11	12
2. Wm. Dickson	1	4	5	13	9
3. Samuel Ward	1	2	1	2	1
4. Daniel Glisson	2	1	1	1	.
5. James Morris	2	.	1	9	8
6. Wm. Sharples	1	1	2	.	.
7. David Cannon	3	1	5	2	1
8. Wm. Stevens	1	6	6	5	2
9. Loammy Stevens	1	6	6	5	2
10. Shadk Byrd	1	.	4	.	.
11. Stephen Herring	1	3	3	5	7
12. Warrin Blount	1	4	2	.	2
13. Joseph Wms.	.	1	2	.	1
14. Elijah Croom	1	4	3	.	.
15. Tho. Hooks Sr.	1	4	4	6	7
16. Wm. Hooks	1	3	5	1	.
17. Alexr Wilson	1	.	.	.	.
18. John Stuckey	1	4	5	3	3
19. Robert Byrd	1	3	2	2	5
20. John Wright	3	1	3	4	4
21. Solomon Hines	2	1	5	.	.
22. John Clarke	4	1	5	2	3
23. Patrick McCann	1	.	3	.	.
24. Wm. Ward	1	3	6	.	.
25. Jas. Winders	1	.	3	.	.
26. James Ward	2	3	1	.	4

Head of Household	WM 21-60 yrs.	WM under 21 & above 60	WF all ages	Blacks 12-50	Blacks under 12 & above 50
27. William Beck	2	4	5	5	3
	38	56	88	41	72
Pg. 2					
28. John Beck	2	4	3	5	3
29. Stephen Beck	1	.	2	.	1
30. George Frazar	2	3	4	4	4
31. Thomas Kea	1	1	2	.	.
32. Noel Pennington	1	3	4	.	.
33. Thos. Hooks Jr	1	1	1	.	.
34. John Southerland	1	1	2	.	.
35. Benjamin Johnston	1	.	1	1	.
36. Benja. Blount	1	1	2	.	.
37. Philip Ward	1	3	7	.	.
38. William Ward	1	1	4	.	.
39. Daniel Ward	1	1	2	.	.
40. Luke Ward	2	1	3	.	.
41. Wm. Sullivan	1	4	2	2	3
42. James Bud Lee	1	.	1	.	.
43. Wm. McCurdy	1	3	1	.	.
44. Hillary Hooks	1	4	2	.	1
45. John C. Slocumb	1	1	3	.	.
46. John Ward	1	.	3	1	.
47. Joseph Hutson	2	1	3	.	.
48. Cullen Connerly	1	2	6	.	.
49. Hardy Carrol	2	.	1	.	.
50. Aaron Bowen	.	2	1	.	.
51. Hancock Hatcher	1	.	8	.	.
52. Thomas Tarrans *	1	5	4	5	3
53. Fredk Rivenbark	2	1	7	.	.
54. Lamuel Guy	2	3	4	.	.
	33	46	83	18	15
55. James Guy	1	1	2	.	.
56. Stephen Smith	1	2	3	.	.
57. Jane Love	.	4	2	9	15
58. Wm. Newton	1	.	4	.	.
59. Rubin Cook	1	.	2	.	.
60. John Cook	.	2	2	.	.
61. James Baker	.	2	.	.	.
62. William Guy	1	4	3	1	.
63. Patrick Newton	2	2	4	3	.
64. Nathan Cook	1	2	3	.	.
65. Martha Henry	.	2	2	.	.
66. Thomas Phipps	2	1	5	.	.
67. M. J. Kenan	1	4	3	7	12
68. Daniel Hicks	1	6	2	7	6
69. Abra. Molten	.	4	2	5	7
70. Felix Frederick	2	2	3	.	.
71. Thomas Hill	1	1	3	7	10

Head of Household	WM 21-60 yrs.	WM under 21 & above 60	WF all ages	Blacks 12-50	Blacks under 12 & above 50
72. Henry Faison	2	2	4	10	7
73. Richd Singleton	1	.	.	.	.
74. Richd Meares	1	1	2	.	.
75. Wm. Ward	1	1	2	.	.
76. Robt. Wilkinson	1	3	1	1	2
77. James Wright	1	2	1	1	.
78. Jeremh Whitman	2	3	4	.	.
79. Clemt Armstrong	.	2	2	.	.
	24	53	62	51	59

List of Capt. Southerland's Dist. taken by Danl Southerland and returned April 1786.

Head of Household	WM 21-60 yrs.	WM under 21 & above 60	WF all ages	Blacks 12-50	Blacks under 12 & above 50
Pg. 1					
1. Wm. McCann	1	2	2	1	.
2. Robt. Cottle	2	3	2	.	.
3. Wm. Southerland	1	5	1	1	1
4. Jesse Brown	1	.	1	.	1
5. Wm. McCann Sr.	2	2	3	1	2
6. Abrm Andrews	1	2	3	.	.
7. Joseph Brooks	1	1	8	.	.
8. Burwell Mobley	1	1	3	.	.
9. Henry Fountain	1	2	2	.	.
10. Nathan Fountain	1	1	2	.	.
11. Henry Fountain Sr.	1	.	2	.	.
12. Francis Land	.	1	3	.	.
13. Rebeckah Meradith	.	.	3	.	.
14. Thos. Lanier	2	2	2	.	.
15. Elisabeth Halso	1	2	3	.	.
16. John Halso	1	1	3	.	.
17. John Brown	1	1	2	.	.
18. Jesse Lanier	1	1	2	.	.
19. John Lanier	1	6	4	.	.
20. John Parker	1	5	4	.	.
21. Chrisr Mashburn	1	.	5	.	.
22. Abe Jones	1	1	4	.	2
23. Solomon Rhodes	1	2	6	.	.
24. Joab Fountain	1	2	4	.	.
25. Benja. Lanier	1	1	.	.	.
26. James Murrow Sr	.	2	5	3	.
27. Eliza Hollingsworth	.	2	4	2	3
28. Wm. Wallace	1	1	5	.	.
29. Benja. Brinson	1	2	2	.	.

* Shown on other records as Thomas Torrans

Head of Household	WM 21-60 yrs.	WM under 21 & above 60	WF all ages	Blacks 12-50	Blacks under 12 & above 50
30. Henry ? Picket	1	1	3	.	.
31. James Evens	1	4	4	.	.
32. James Picket	1	4	4	.	.
33. Liddia Casteen	.	2	4	.	.
34. Sarah Rogers	.	.	4	.	.
	31	62	109	8	9
Pg. 2					
35. Bird Lanier	1	.	3	.	.
36. Wm. Hollingsworth	1	.	1	.	.
37. Chrisr. Butler	1	2	.	.	.
38. Elisabeth Batchelor	.	1	3	.	.
39. John Cook	1	.	2	1	.
40. Elisha Woodward	1	1	1	.	.
41. Robert Cole	1	2	1	1	.
42. Solomon Picket	1	2	3	.	.
43. Moses Shoaler	3	1	3	.	.
44. Martha Shoaler	1	2	1	.	.
45. Peter Wood	1	3	7	.	.
46. Elisab. Lockhart	.	2	2	2	3
47. Charles Goff	1	1	3	.	1
48. Daniel Ranier?	1	1	2	.	.
49. Solomon Cox	1	.	3	.	.
50. Henry Edwards	1	1	2	.	.
51. Sihon Picket	2	1	5	.	.
52. Stepn Thisselwood	1	2	1	.	.
53. Wm. Picket Sr	1	.	1	1	1
54. Wm. Picket Jr	1	.	.	.	.
55. William Harpe	.	2	3	.	.
56. Isaiah Harpe	1	.	2	.	.
57. James Ellis	1	2	1	.	.
58. John Baily	1	.	1	.	.
59. Richd. Chaison	1	4	2	.	.
60. Richd Williams	3	1	4	2	4
61. John Williams	1	2	5	.	.
62. Sarah Batts	.	3	3	1	.
63. Hanah Batts	.	1	3	.	.
64. Jacob Brown	1	4	5	2	3
65. Saml Sanderlin	2	3	2	.	.
66. Abram Newkirk	1	2	6	2	4
67. Chas. Bostick	1	5	6	.	.
68. Henry Newkirk	1	2	4	.	.
	35	53	91	12	16
Pg. 3					
69. Simon Davis	1	2	2	.	.
70. Nichos Sanderlin	1	2	2	.	.
71. Temple Tullos	1	1	1	.	.
72. Elisabeth Tullos	.	.	2	.	.
73. Daniel Southerland	1	4	2	2	1

Head of Household	WM 21-60 yrs.	WM under 21 & above 60	WF all ages	Blacks 12-50	Blacks under 12 & above 50
74. Job Thegpen	1	3	3	.	.
75. John Waller Sr	1	3	3	.	.
76. John Waller Jr	2	2	4	.	.
77. James Lanier	1	3	4	.	.
78. Mary Bratcher	.	3	3	.	.
79. Margaret Picket	.	3	1	.	.
80. Jonathan Parker	1	.	3	.	.
81. Renatus Land	2	1	3	.	.
82. Wm. Shoaler	1	.	1	.	.
83. James Floyd	1	2	4	.	.
84. Drury Hall	1	1	2	.	.
85. Mary Smith	.	.	2	.	.
86. James Brooks	1	2	1	.	.
87. Prissillia Coleman	.	2	1	.	.
88. Steph Williams	1	.	1	.	.
89. Amos Parker	1	3	4	.	.
90. John Woodward	2	.	5	1	1
91. Susana Edwards	.	.	4	.	.
92. Edmond Britton	1	.	2	1	.
93. John Britton	1	.	3	.	.
94. Rachel Carter	.	.	1	.	.
95. Abigal Brice	.	.	1	.	.
96. Wm. Farrier	1	.	5	.	.
97. James Hall	1	.	.	.	.
98. John Brice	1	.	.	.	.
99. Sarah Hall	.	1	2	.	.
100. Saban Williams	1	4	5	.	.
101. Auston Bryan	1	1	1	4	2
102. Jas. Wallace Sr	.	2	3	.	.
	27	45	81	8	4
103. Sherrad Picket	1	.	2	.	.
104. Jas. Wallace Jr	1	2	3	.	.
105. Wm. Thomas	2	5	2	2	1
106. Isaac Thomas	1	1	1	1	3
107. Robt. Bishop	1	3	4	.	.
108. John Humphry	.	3	3	.	1
109. Matthew Edwards	1	.	5	5	3
110. Hicks Mills	1	.	2	1	.
111. Thomas Canaday	1	1	1	.	.
112. Robt. Southerland	2	2	3	.	.
113. John Farrior	1	3	2	3	.
114. Wm. Batchelor	1	.	.	.	.
115. Margaret Sumner	.	2	3	.	.
116. Hugh McCann	2	2	5	.	.
117. George Evens	1	1	2	.	.

Head of Household	WM 21-60 yrs.	WM under 21 & above 60	WF all ages	Blacks 12-50	Blacks under 12 & above 50
118. Saml Ratcliffe	1	3	1	.	.
119. Joseph Johnston	1	3	4	.	.
	18	31	43	12	8

List of Capt. Gillespie's Company, taken by Thomas Routledge & returned April 1786.

Head of Household	WM 21-60 yrs.	WM under 21 & above 60	WF all ages	Blacks 12-50	Blacks under 12 & above 50
Pg. 1					
1. Thos. Routledge	1	3	3	4	7
2. James James	1	2	5	8	3
3. Kedar Bryan	1	2	1	10	12
4. Joseph Dickson	1	4	2	4	5
5. James Wilson	1	5	4	.	.
6. Andrew Edwards	1	2	3	.	.
7. John Venters	1	.	.	.	.
8. James Midleton	1	2	2	.	.
9. John Phillips	1	3	4	1	3
10. John Molten	1	1	5	5	3
11. Jas. Midleton Jr.	2	1	3	4	3
12. Wm. Magee	1	3	8	.	.
13. Jas. Midleton	1	1	8	1	.
14. James Mills	1	4	5	5	7
15. John Tilman	.	1	2	.	.
16. Wm. Cole	1	4	2	.	.
17. Isaac Hunter	1	2	4	3	4
18. Nicholas Hunter	1	2	3	2	2
19. John Armstrong	1	7	4	.	.
20. John Cranford	1	1	3	.	.
21. Robt. Miller	1	1	4	.	.
22. John McCulloh Jr.	1	.	2	.	.
23. John McCulloh Sr.	1	1	3	.	.
24. Wm. Flowers	1	4	5	.	.
25. John Mallard	1	3	3	.	.
26. Alexr Dickson	1	.	.	4	1
27. Robt. Dickson	1	5	6	9	11
	27	64	94	60	61
Pg. 2					
28. Denis Cannon	1	5	5	.	.
29. Benja. Tanner	1	1	1	.	.
30. Nathl Wells	1	3	3	.	.
31. Wm. Rigbee	1	4	4	2	.
32. John Rigbee	1	.	1	.	.
34. Wm. Stokes	2	5	2	.	.
35. Arthur Stokes	1	5	5	.	.
36. Benja. Dulany	1	2	2	.	.
37. Thos. Heath	1	3	2	.	.
38. Eliza Gibbons	.	3	4	.	.
39. Geo. Mallard	1	1	2	.	.
40. Daniel Mallard	1	.	.	.	.
41. Phil. Southerland	1	.	2	.	1
42. James Evens	1	3	4	.	.
43. Joseph Mallard	1	.	3	.	.
44. William Carr	3	1	3	.	.
45. James Carr	1	.	.	2	.
46. Wm. Best	1	3	2	3	.
47. Isaac Midleton	1	.	1	.	.
48. Moses Hanchy	1	.	3	.	.
49. James Maxwell	1	6	1	1	.
50. Absalom Stricklin	1	2	2	.	.
51. Solomon Beesley	1	4	6	.	2
52. James Heath	1	3	5	.	.
53. James Murrow	1	3	2	.	1
54. Ebenr Garrison	1	.	4	1	2
55. Adonijah Garrison	1	1	1	.	.
	29	58	70	9	6
Pg. 3					
56. John Collins	1	.	1	.	.
57. James Rogers	1	4	2	.	.
58. Stephen Rogers	1	.	1	.	.
59. Wm. Frederick	1	2	5	.	.
60. Ephm Garrison	2	2	3	.	.
61. Mary Pearse	2	2	5	.	.
62. Martha Pickins	.	3	3	.	.
63. Watson Burton	1	1	2	1	.
64. Tho. Johnston	4	4	2	.	.
65. Griffith Jones	1	2	1	.	.
66. Theophs Swinson	1	2	3	.	.
67. Wm. Bush	1	1	4	.	.
68. Kedar Harrell	1	3	2	.	.
69. James McIntire	1	1	1	4	5
70. Geo. Rouse	1	5	1	.	.
71. Rebecka Bryan	.	2	2	.	.
72. James Cooke	1	.	2	.	.
73. Andrew Wallace	1	2	2	.	.
74. Frans. Gallemore	.	2	1	.	.
75. Peter Simpson	1	4	1	.	.
76. Adam Runcie	1	1	1	.	.
77. John Cox	1	1	2	.	.
78. Joseph Cox	1	.	1	.	.
79. Joseph Cox Jr.	1	1	2	.	.
80. Wm. M. Gowen	1	7	1	8	5
81. Jas. Gillespie	2	3	5	11	10
82. Peter Morris	1	3	3	.	.
	30	58	59	24	20

STATE CENSUS OF NORTH CAROLINA 1784-1787

List of Capt. Ward's District taken by Charles Ward and returned April 1786.

Pg. 1

Head of Household	WM 21-60 yrs.	WM under 21 & above 60	WF all ages	Blacks 12-50	Blacks under 12 & above 50
1. Charles Ward	2	1	2	8	5
2. John Gore	1	4	5	.	.
3. Jas. Chambers	1	5	2	3	.
4. John Johnston	1	.	2	3	3
5. John Matchet	1	1	4	2	3
6. Joab Padget	1	5	2	.	.
7. John Hill	2	1	3	12	10
8. David Cannon	1	4	5	.	.
9. William Boyet	1	.	5	.	.
10. William Hunter	1	4	2	.	.
11. Geo. Cooper Jr.	1	2	3	1	3
12. Arthur Boyet	1	.	3	.	.
13. Lamuel Boyet	1	2	1	.	.
14. John Best Sr.	2	6	2	.	.
15. Ephraim Boyet	1	2	2	.	.
16. John Best Jr.	1	1	2	.	.
17. Uriah Gurganus	1	5	2	.	1
18. John Auston	1	.	3	.	.
19. John Neale	2	.	1	.	.
20. Andrew Reed	1	2	4	.	.
21. Archibald Carr	1	1	5	1	2
22. John Chambers	1	4	3	3	1
23. Edward Sloan	1	2	5	.	.
24. Robt. Williams	1	1	6	1	.
25. Chris^r Martin	1	2	5	.	.
	29	55	79	34	28

Pg. 2

Head of Household	WM 21-60 yrs.	WM under 21 & above 60	WF all ages	Blacks 12-50	Blacks under 12 & above 50
26. Geo. Williams	3	2	4	2	1
27. Joseph Smith	2	1	1	.	.
28. Ivey Smith	1	2	1	1	.
29. Joseph Welts	1	.	1	2	3
30. Joseph Johnston	3	2	4	1	.
31. David Murdock	1	2	3	5	4
32. Sarah Matchet	.	1	1	.	.
33. Widow Quin	2	2	2	.	.
34. Widow Huggins	.	3	1	.	.
35. Geo. Cooper Sr.	2	3	1	2	4
36. Richard Cooper	1	2	1	.	.
37. Arthur Herring	1	.	1	.	.
38. Wright Williams	1	.	1	.	.
39. Joseph Grimes	4	3	3	4	1
40. Edward Pearsall	1	.	.	2	1
41. Clem^t Godfrey	1	.	1	.	.

Head of Household	WM 21-60 yrs.	WM under 21 & above 60	WF all ages	Blacks 12-50	Blacks under 12 & above 50
42. Geo. Miller	3	.	1	7	7
43. William Kenan	2	1	2	37	27
44. Felix Frederick	2	2	3	.	.
45. Lamuel Dunn	2	2	2	.	.
46. Mourning Harrell	.	2	2	.	.
47. Lewis Thomas	1	.	3	8	6
	34	30	39	71	54

Pg. 3

Duplin County:

The within lists contains the full number of all the inhabitants of Duplin County as appears by the several returns made by persons appointed by the County Court to take the lists in the said several Districts in the said County agreeable to an Act of Assembly passed at Newbern in the Ninth Year of the American Independence, Anno Dom 1784.

Of which Lists the within is a true copey.

Test.

W. Dickson, C. C.

[On reverse]   1786

A list of the white and Black inhabitants of Duplin County.

No. 6   Total   5,240

37

GATES COUNTY

"List of the Number of White & Black Inhabitants in the County of Gates in the Year 1786." Persons names who returned list of Familys.

Pg. 1

Head of Household	WM 21-60 yrs.	WM under 21 & above 60	WF all ages	Blacks 12-50	Blacks under 12 & above 50
Solomon King	2	3	5	7	12
Joseph Speight	1	1	3	11	10
Henry Speight	1	.	1	5	3
Isaac Pipkin	1	2	4	12	16
James Goodin	1	.	6	.	.
William Boyce	1	.	2	.	.
James Jones	1	2	2	.	.
William Wallis	1	.	2	.	.
Francis Parker	1	1	8	1	1
Demsey Sumner	1	4	3	.	.
John Varnell	1	3	2	.	.
Joil Goodman	2	5	3	1	8
Ann Bethey	.	.	1	2	5
Miles Benton	1	.	1	11	9
James Skinner	1	.	.	.	.
John Weatherley	2	3	2	5	4
John Vann	1	.	.	.	.
Thomas Vann	1	4	3	1	6
William Warren	1	4	.	.	3
Joseph Brady	1	1	1	.	.
Edward Vann	1	.	.	.	.
Francies Speight	1	1	1	9	8
Mary Hare	.	.	1	3	3
James Bethey	1	1	2	.	.
John Bethey	1	.	4	5	1
Charles Dilday	1	2	1	.	.
Henry Dilday	1	2	2	.	.
Thomas Rooks	1	2	1	7	.
	29	41	61	81	89

Pg. 2

Head of Household	WM 21-60 yrs.	WM under 21 & above 60	WF all ages	Blacks 12-50	Blacks under 12 & above 50
David Lewis	4	2	5	8	3
George Gatling	1	.	.	1	3
David Watson	1	2	2	2	1
Uriah Parker	1	.	2	.	.
John Gatling	3	3	4	5	7
Benjamin Barnes	1	2	1	3	2
Phillip Winborne	1	2	6	.	.
William Odom	1	1	1	2	3
Milley Rogers	1	3	1	.	.
Joseph Rooks Jr.	1	.	.	.	.
Demsey Rooks	2	.	2	1	3
Abel Cross	1	1	5	6	.
Charity Saunders	1	2	2	3	4
Ann Walters	.	1	1	.	.
Sarah Saunders	1	1	1	3	2
Joseph Saunders	1	.	.	.	.

Head of Household	WM 21-60 yrs.	WM under 21 & above 60	WF all ages	Blacks 12-50	Blacks under 12 & above 50
Sarah Boon	.	.	1	.	.
Jesse Jones	1	2	1	.	.
John Odom	1	.	.	7	10
Jesse Vann	1	3	5	4	1
Elisha Brinkley	.	2	3	1	.
Demsey Barnes	2	5	3	5	4
Cyprian Cross	1	6	3	2	4
Edward Warren	1	2	3	3	2
Joseph Rooks Sr	.	1	1	3	.
Thomas Barnes	1	.	.	3	2
Thomas Highatt	1	.	2	.	.
Watson Howell	1	1	2	.	.
Jacob Walters	1	4	5	.	.
Jesse Highatt	1	1	1	.	.
Phillip Lewis	1	.	1	8	2
Josiah Parker Jr	1	1	4	.	.
Wm. Gatling Jr	1	1	3	7	5
James Wells	1	1	4	.	.
Josiah Parker Sr	1	1	1	.	.
	67	92	137	157	147

Pg. 3

Head of Household	WM 21-60 yrs.	WM under 21 & above 60	WF all ages	Blacks 12-50	Blacks under 12 & above 50
Henry Lee	1	6	4	3	5
James Brady Jr.	1	2	4	1	1
Demsey Williams	1	5	2	.	.
Ebon Sears	1	.	3	1	.
David Cross	1	.	.	2	.
Uriah Odom	1	.	.	.	.
James Crafford	2	1	2	1	.
William Goodman	1	.	3	6	5
Henry Goodman	1	3	2	7	7
Hardy Cross	2	2	8	2	5
Phillip Dunford	1	3	3	.	.
Jesse Saunders	1	5	4	7	4
James Lang	1	2	3	1	.
John Warren	1	.	.	.	.
James Parker	1	2	1	1	1
Priscilla Rogers	.	3	4	7	6
Francis Osmont	1	1	1	.	.
Amos Dilday	1	.	.	.	.
Aaron Ellis	1	1	2	.	.
Charity Ellis	.	.	3	.	.
James Curle	1	1	2	.	.
Anthony Matthews Sr	1	5	1	1	3
Anthony Matthews Jr	1	2	2	.	.
Aaron Harrell	.	1	2	.	.
Benjamin Harrell	1	4	2	.	.

Head of Household	WM 21-60 yrs.	WM under 21 & above 60	WF all ages	Blacks 12-50	Blacks under 12 & above 50
Christopher Riddick	1	2	5	4	7
Charles Smith	1	.	.	.	.
Demsey Parker	1	1	4	.	1
Edward Piland(of Geo)	1	.	3	.	.
Edward Piland(of Ewd)	1	.	.	.	.
Elizabeth Riddick	.	3	3	3	4
Sarah Riddick	.	1	1	4	6
Easter Marthews	.	.	2	.	.
George Piland	.	2	3	1	.
Geo. Williams Sr.	.	2	5	.	.
George Allen	1	3	2	.	1
Geo. Williams Jr.	1	1	3	.	.
	98	156	226	209	203
Pg. 4					
George Williams	1	6	6	2	.
Henry Smith	1	1	4	.	1
Henry Forrest	1	3	4	4	7
Hardy Browne	1	2	3	.	.
Humphry Hudgins	1	4	3	2	4
Joseph Tigg	2	1	4	2	1
Jesse Browne	1	3	4	1	.
Isaac Parker	1	2	3	.	.
Jacob Hayes	1	3	5	.	1
James Tugwell	1	.	.	.	.
Isaac Miller	1	3	3	.	2
John Hall	1	.	4	.	.
John Felton	1	4	1	1	.
John Shephard	1	5	3	3	.
Joseph Norfleet	1	.	1	.	.
John Raby	.	1	.	.	.
Jeremiah Speight	1	4	11	11	7
John Baker	2	1	5	9	12
Jonathan Smith	1	.	.	.	.
John Duke, Sr.	.	2	4	.	.
John Duke, Jr.	1	2	6	2	.
James Piland Sr	2	1	4	.	.
John Slavin	.	2	5	.	.
Israel Beeman	1	3	5	2	5
James Carter	1	1	2	.	.
John Swann	1	.	.	.	.
James Rooks	1	1	1	.	.
Kedar Odom	1	2	2	2	3
Lawrence Baker	2	2	4	20	15
Lewis Walters	1	1	2	.	.
Matthias Green	1	1	4	.	.
Moses Spivey	2	.	4	.	.
Michael Lawrence	1	.	3	.	.
Moor Carter	1	2	4	1	1

Head of Household	WM 21-60 yrs.	WM under 21 & above 60	WF all ages	Blacks 12-50	Blacks under 12 & above 50
Moses Williams	1	.	.	.	.
Mary Parker	.	1	2	.	.
Mary Allen	.	.	2	.	.
Peter Piland	1	.	2	.	.
	39	63	124	62	59
Pg. 5					
Robert Parker Sr	2	5	4	1	2
Richard Felton	1	.	.	.	.
Richard Green	1	2	4	1	.
Samuel Williams	1	5	2	.	.
Seth Riddick	1	1	4	5	6
Samuel Smith	1	3	3	1	1
Sarah Felton	3	2	3	2	3
Sarah Odom	1	.	4	3	3
Samuel Eure	1	2	6	1	.
Sarah Polson	.	2	2	.	.
Stephen Harrell	1	1	3	.	.
Sarah Smith	.	2	1	.	.
Thomas Fryer or Frycer	1	4	5	.	.
Thomas Smith	1	4	.	.	.
Thomas Robertson	1	.	.	.	.
Willis Browne	1	.	.	3	1
William Baker	1	2	5	11	15
William Powell	.	1	2	5	5
William Boyce	1	3	2	.	.
William Harriss	1	1	2	13	15
Wright Hayes	1	6	5	1	3
William Williams	1	.	4	.	.
William Cleaves	1	3	2	3	1
Willis Parker	1	.	3	.	1
William Green	2	3	2	.	.
William Brooks	2	.	2	1	1
Stephen Parker	1	.	1	.	.
Isaac Walters	1	1	9	1	2
Micajah Riddick	2	4	4	3	3
William Draper	1	1	2	.	.
Samuel Williams	.	5	3	.	.
Samuel Parker	2	1	5	.	.
Demsey Odom	1	2	4	4	4
Henry King	2	4	4	2	2
Elisha Parker	3	3	6	5	5
Joseph Dilday	1	3	2	.	.
Peter Parker	1	1	4	2	2
Mary Parker	.	1	1	1	1
	82	141	235	131	127
Pg. 6					
Ann Parker	.	1	1	1	1
Joseph Griffin	.	3	2	1	1
Samuel Baker	1	4	3	4	5

STATE CENSUS OF NORTH CAROLINA 1784-1787

Head of Household	WM 21-60 yrs.	WM under 21 & above 60	WF all ages	Blacks 12-50	Blacks under 12 & above 50
Jonathan Williams	1	4	5	2	2
Jesse Benton	1	.	1	1	1
Elizabeth Benton	.	2	1	2	1
Mary Benton	1	2	2	3	1
William Barr	1	1	2	1	1
Moses Haynes	1	1	3	.	.
Edward Daughtiee ?	2	1	3	2	2
William Daughtiee ?	1	2	4	2	3
Rachel Willey	1	1	3	1	.
William Walters	1	.	2	4	3
William Dunford	1	6	3	.	.
Miles Parker	1	1	3	2	2
James Bristow	1	1	3	2	2
Enos Rogers	1	2	2	1	.
Zilpha Rogers	.	1	1	4	2
Phillip Rogers	1	3	2	.	1
James Brady	1	2	2	6	10
Solomon Ross	1	.	1	.	.
Robert Parker	1	3	2	2	.
Henry Griffin	1	2	5	.	1
Moses Boyce	1	2	2	.	.
Francis Daughtiee ?	1	.	1	.	.
Mills Odom	1	.	3	.	1
Demsey Williams	1	3	1	4	4
Elisha Cross	1	4	3	2	1
Josiah Benton	1	1	4	4	2
John Cuffe	1	5	2	.	.
John Arline	1	1	1	3	2
George Russell	1	.	1	.	.
William Matthews	1	6	3	.	1
William Vann	2	4	3	1	1
James Phelps	2	3	4	.	.
	153	229	311	263	256
Pg. 7					
Thomas Parmer	1	.	3	.	.
Kedar Benton	1	2	4	.	.
John Polson	1	1	4	.	.
Calob Polson	2	.	4	.	1
Kedar Parker	1	.	1	.	.
Josiah Brinkley	1	4	1	.	.
James Pruden	1	5	5	.	.
Abraham Morgan	1	5	2	2	2
Matthias Morgan	1	3	2	.	1
John Arnold	1	1	2	2	1
John Saunders	1	1	2	.	.
James Parker	1	2	2	1	3
Joseph Peel	2	1	2	.	.
Hardy Wells	1	.	2	.	.
Moses Kittrell	1	3	6	5	5

Head of Household	WM 21-60 yrs.	WM under 21 & above 60	WF all ages	Blacks 12-50	Blacks under 12 & above 50
Jesse Eason	.	3	2	1	3
Moses Speight	.	3	3	1	2
David Rice	1	1	2	6	7
James Daves	1	1	4	1	.
John Riddick	1	.	5	3	4
Isaac Harrell	1	1	4	6	8
Josiah Granbery	1	4	4	10	10
Daniel Gwinn	1	1	1	.	1
Joshua Small	2	.	1	4	4
John Rice	1	3	3	3	2
Noah Harrell	1	.	.	.	.
David Jones	.	1	3	5	3
William Ellis	1	2	6	1	3
James Jones	1	2	3	3	5
Moses Davis	1	2	3	.	.
Richard Brigg	1	1	2	.	.
William Hinton	1	1	4	23	21
Isaac Reed	1	.	2	.	.
John Small	1	.	.	.	.
David Small	1	3	4	1	.
John Miller	1	3	1	.	.
Edward Kelley	1	4	2	.	.
Isaac Benton	1	2	6	.	.
Moses Benton	1	6	4	.	.
Thomas Parker	1	2	6	2	.
Kedar Ballard	1	2	1	8	6
	194	303	419	351	450
Pg. 8					
Jacob Powell	1	6	2	1	2
Lewis Jones	1	6	5	2	2
Elisha Benton	1	.	.	.	.
Moses Hare, Sr.	.	2	1	2	1
Isaac Lamb	1	4	4	.	.
Moses Hare, Jr.	2	1	.	.	1
Edward Arnold	1	1	2	1	3
Elizabeth Norfleet	.	1	4	2	3
John Duke	1	.	.	.	.
James Knight	2	3	7	3	2
John Davis	.	3	3	.	.
John R. Wilkinson	1	1	4	3	5
Ann Speight	.	2	4	.	.
Feriba Phelpes	.	.	2	.	.
Mary Haslet	.	2	1	5	6
James Jones	1	.	1	1	.
Elisha Norfleet	1	.	.	3	2
John Powell	1	3	6	8	16
Charles Jones	1	.	.	.	.
Solomon Briggs	1	3	2	.	.
Hannah Cortney	.	3	4	1	2

STATE CENSUS OF NORTH CAROLINA 1784-1787

Head of Household	WM 21-60 yrs.	WM under 21 & above 60	WF all ages	Blacks 12-50	Blacks under 12 & above 50
James Small	1	.	.	.	.
James Norfleet	1	.	4	7	12
Ann Gibson	.	1	1	4	3
Bridget Wiggins	.	.	4	.	.
Hezekiah Alphin	1	.	.	.	.
Hezekiah Jones	1	1	4	.	.
Jethro Ballard	1	2	4	3	13
Rachel Brinkley	.	2	3	2	5
John Ellis	1	1	1	.	.
James Sumner	2	2	4	22	24
John Briggs	1	2	3	.	.
Jethro Benton	1	1	1	1	3
Easther Copeland	.	1	1	.	.
Benjamin Gordon	1	.	3	6	7
Alexander Eason	1	2	1	2	4
John Darden	1	.	2	5	3
Joseph Hare	1	1	2	.	1
	225	359	512	451	578
Pg. 9					
Jethro Sumner	1	1	2	8	9
Martha Sumner	1	1	2	6	.
William Arnold	1	.	2	1	.
Willis Wiggins	1	6	2	.	1
David Jones	1	.	.	.	.
Joseph John Sumner	1	.	3	4	4
William Parker	2	5	3	2	4
Amos Parker	1	4	3	3	2
William Mattias	1	3	1	2	1
John Jones	2	1	3	.	1
Simon Stallings	1	2	2	5	7
James Walten	1	.	.	2	.
William Robertson	1	.	.	.	.
Amos Sivels	1	.	1	.	.
Aaron Hobbs	1	3	5	1	2
Thomas White	1	3	3	.	.
John White	1	1	3	.	.
William Berriman	1	2	5	.	.
Lamuel Taylor	1	2	4	.	.
Nathaniel Taylor	1	.	1	.	.
Thomas Hoffler	1	1	2	3	4
Moses Hill	1	2	6	1	.
Amerias Blanshard	1	.	1	1	.
Amos Trotman	1	3	1	8	6
Jacob Hobbs	1	3	2	.	.
Seth Stallings	1	5	.	.	.
Thomas Trotman	1	3	3	8	10
Jacob Outlaw	1	.	2	1	2
Jethro Lassiter	1	1	3	6	5
Zadock Hinton	1	1	2	1	.
Levi Eason	1	2	4	.	2
Jacob Eason	1	.	.	3	5
George Eason	1	.	.	.	.
Gabril Martin	1	2	3	.	.
Jacob Spivey	1	2	3	1	.
Ann Walton	.	1	6	1	.
William King	1	5	4	.	.
William Hinton	1	4	5	5	8
Robert Taylor	.	3	1	.	.
Ephraem Morriss	1	1	1	.	.
Richard Freeman	1	1	3	1	1
Jesse Ward	1	1	3	.	.
Richard Ward	1	.	1	.	.
	268	434	613	525	666
Pg. 10					
Charrity Morris	.	3	1	.	.
Jonas Hinton	1	.	.	.	.
Robert Ward	1	3	2	.	.
Jesse Spivey	1	2	3	2	.
Lamuel Colley	1	2	6	.	.
Amos Hobbs	1	2	3	.	.
Elijah Spivey	1	.	4	.	.
William Freeman	1	1	4	6	6
Demsey Bond	2	3	3	5	4
Mordica Perry	1	1	3	3	3
Kedar Hill	1	5	2	5	11
Nathaniel Spivey	1	1	3	.	.
James Taylor	1	1	2	.	.
Reuben Hobbs	1	2	2	.	.
Edmond Hobbs	1	.	.	.	.
Henry Hobbs	1	2	3	.	.
Moses Hobbs	1	2	5	.	.
William Ward	1	1	2	.	.
Guy Hill	1	1	2	.	.
George White	1	.	2	.	.
Stephen Thomas	1	.	.	.	.
Seth Rountree	.	.	2	2	3
Joseph Brinkley	2	1	1	6	7
William Hurdle	1	5	1	2	1
Benjamin Berryman	.	2	2	.	.
James Freeman	1	3	1	6	7
Edward Briscow	1	2	3	1	.
Casbrook Hinton	1	.	.	.	.
James Outlaw	1	.	1	2	6
George Outlaw	1	2	5	8	9
Levis Outlaw	1	1	1	1	1
Charles Rountree	1	3	4	8	7
Jonathan Roberts	2	2	4	8	7
Jethro Meltear	1	3	3	2	1
Henry Hill	2	.	4	1	.
David Hill	1	.	1	1	.

STATE CENSUS OF NORTH CAROLINA 1784-1787

Head of Household	WM 21-60 yrs.	WM under 21 & above 60	WF all ages	Blacks 12-50	Blacks under 12 & above 50
Clemant Hill	1	2	3	.	.
	305	492	702	594	739
Pg. 11					
Richard Bond	1	.	1	3	3
Thomas Hunter	3	3	5	10	12
William Kelley	2	3	4	.	.
Joseph Riddick	1	4	6	6	7
Patrick Hegerty	1	.	.	.	.
Osten Nixon	1	6	6	.	.
Penelope Onley	.	3	2	.	.
Samuel Green	1	3	3	.	.
Ephraim Griffin	1	.	.	.	.
James Gregory	1	1	3	10	9
John Gordon	.	2	2	5	7
Ezekiel Trotman	1	5	3	4	4
William Hunter	1	1	3	1	1
Abraham Green	1	3	4	.	.
Abraham Hurdle	1	.	1	.	1
Thomas Hurdle	1	4	5	3	1
Seth Eason	1	3	2	6	5
Moses Eason	1	.	.	.	.
John B. Walton	1	.	1	3	6
Moses Blanshard	1	.	1	2	9
Edward Berryman	1	2	2	1	1
Isaac Pierce	1	.	4	.	.
Abraham Harrell	1	4	3	2	.
Josiah Lassiter	1	4	4	1	.
Richard Pierce	1	.	.	.	.
Judith Fullington	.	.	1	.	.
Martha Harrell	.	.	1	.	.
Thomas Walton	1	4	6	2	1
Jacob Pierce	1	3	4	1	.
Mary Pierce	.	.	2	.	.
Christopher Pierce	.	1	2	.	.
Abraham Pierce	1	.	1	.	.
Abner Pierce	1	.	.	.	.
Joseph Hurdle	1	1	4	4	6
James Costen	1	.	4	7	6
Aaron Lassiter	1	2	6	.	.
Jonathan Nichols	1	1	2	.	.
John Wells	1	.	2	.	.
Maximillion Minshew	1	1	4	1	1
	341	553	815	670	818
Pg. 12					
Bond Minshew	1	.	.	1	.
John Hare	1	1	2	.	.
Christian Costen	.	.	5	4	6
William Pierce	1	2	2	.	.
Demsey Jones	1	4	2	.	.
Demsey Jones, Jr.	1	.	1	1	.

Head of Household	WM 21-60 yrs.	WM under 21 & above 60	WF all ages	Blacks 12-50	Blacks under 12 & above 50
Joseph Brown	1	1	.	.	.
George Lassiter	1	2	4	2	2
George Lassiter Jr	1	.	.	.	.
Jacob Gordon	1	4	5	4	2
Thomas Traviss	1	1	1	.	.
James Lassiter	1	.	2	.	.
Elisha Harriss	1	1	3	.	.
Reuben Lassiter	1	.	2	.	.
William Bond	1	1	2	.	.
Amos Lassiter	1	4	3	.	.
Amos Smith	1	4	3	.	.
Kedar Hinton	1	3	3	2	1
Joseph Parker	.	5	3	.	.
Aaron Lassiter	1	1	1	.	.
Abisha Lassiter	1	5	4	.	.
Jonathan Laaister	1	4	5	.	2
Demsey Blanshard	1	1	4	1	.
Aaron Blanshard	1	3	2	1	1
Michael Lassiter	.	2	2	1	.
Isaac Hunter	1	.	1	9	3
Elisha Hunter	.	2	2	7	6
James Scott	1	4	2	.	.
Abraham Sumner	1	.	.	6	4
John Sedgley	1	.	.	.	.
Abner Blanshard	1	.	.	2	5
Samuel Browne	1	.	3	.	.
Abraham Spivey	1	.	2	1	.
Elizabeth Blanshard	.	2	3	.	.
Robert McCallock	1	.	1	2	2
Timothy Lassiter	1	.	2	11	11
Richard Rolling	1	1	1	1	.
Job Riddick	1	3	6	12	14
George Eason	1	1	2	6	5
	375	628	897	797	882
Pg. 13					
Isaac Eason	1	.	.	.	.
Abraham Eason	1	.	2	4	3
Moses Briggs	1	.	1	1	1
Solomon Alphin	.	.	3	.	.
Israel Meniard	1	.	3	.	.
Henry Harrell	1	.	1	1	1
Mary Smith	.	1	1	.	.
Henry Walton	1	2	4	2	4
James Hayes	3	3	4	1	4
James Jones	1	3	4	.	.
Abraham Riddick	1	1	6	.	.
Demsey Trotman	1	1	.	5	6
Priscilla Walton	.	.	1	1	6
Richard Bond	.	3	2	6	4

STATE CENSUS OF NORTH CAROLINA 1784-1787

Head of Household	WM 21-60 yrs.	WM under 21 & above 60	WF all ages	Blacks 12-50	Blacks under 12 & above 50
John Robbins	.	2	2	1	3
Samuel Harrell	1	2	5	2	2
William Lewis	1	3	1	1	3
Dionishus Minshew	1	1	5	.	.
Jacob Bagley	1	3	1	4	3
Lydia Spivey	.	1	3	1	4
Jane Hill	.	.	2	.	1
Jehordah Green	.	.	1	2	4
Jeremiah Jordan	1	2	2	.	.
William Kirbey	1	2	2	.	.
Charles Eure	1	3	3	5	3
Samuel Taylor	1	5	4	3	.
Stephen Eure	1	2	3	4	4
William Davidson	1	1	.	1	4
Isaac Langston	1	1	3	1	.
William Ellis	2	3	3	.	.
William Rutter	1	3	2	.	.
William Tryer	1	2	4	.	1
James Landing	1	4	3	.	.
Isaac Tryer	1	.	4	.	.
Demsey Langston	3	.	2	.	.
Job Umfleet	1	3	3	.	.
Josiah Harrell	1	3	3	.	.
James Keen	1	1	2	.	.
Thomas Piland	2	4	4	.	.
	452	690	996	789	941
Pg. 14					
David Umfleet	1	3	5	.	.
Lamuel Keen	1	.	3	.	.
John Parker	1	3	2	.	1
John Harrell	1	1	5	2	1
Samuel Harrell	1	1	2	.	1
James Eure	1	4	2	.	.
Uriah Eure	2	1	4	.	.
Reuben Sparkman	1	1	3	.	.
Lewis Sparkman	1	1	4	.	.
Willis Sparkman	1	1	1	.	.
Thomas Sparkman	.	1	3	.	.
John Eure	1	.	3	.	.
Benjamin Eure	1	3	3	.	.
Thomas Norriss	1	2	1	.	1
Samuel Green	1	2	4	.	.
Peter Harrell	2	1	8	.	.
Thomas Harrell	1	2	5	.	.
Mills Eure	1	2	1	.	.
John Carter	1	1	3	1	1
Frederick Farrow	1	2	1	.	.
Ann Piland	.	.	1	1	.
Ann Harrell	.	1	4	.	.
Darcase Vann	.	.	3	.	1
Milley Harrell	.	.	4	1	2
Sarah Hughes	.	.	1	.	.
Moses Jones	1	2	4	.	.
Levi Lee	2	4	3	.	.
Hezekiah Jones	1	1	1	.	.
William Morriss	2	4	2	.	.
William Crafford	4	3	3	6	4
Demsey Harrell	1	3	3	.	.
Daniel Ellis	2	.	4	.	.
James Parker	1	1	7	.	.
Samuel Thomas, Sr.	2	3	3	.	.
Samuel Thomas, Jr.	1	.	2	.	.
Pg. 15					
Isaac Carter	1	2	2	2	3
Aaron Harrell	1	1	5	1	.
Matthias Green	1	1	5	.	.
Jesse Warrell	1	1	4	.	.
Jesse Harrell	2	3	4	1	.
Samuel Browne	1	2	3	.	.
William Vann	1	2	2	.	.
Jonathan Cullins	1	2	5	.	.
Sarah Ellis	.	.	2	.	.
Richard Stallings	1	2	.	.	.
Josiah Stallings	1	1	1	.	.
	461	760	1126	798	954
pages	82	141	235	131	127
	543	901	1361	929	83

A true copy. Test. Law. Baker, G. C.

Sir:

Gates County, May 30, 1786.

The within & above is a list of the inhabitants of this County of Gates taken agreeable to the Act of Assembly for that purpose, the list was not returned until our May Court or should have transmitted to you sooner. I am,

Your Excellany's
Most obt. servant
Law. Baker

43

GRANVILLE COUNTY

"The number of Inhabitants in County Line district in the Year 1786".

Pg. 1

Head of Household	WM 21-60 yrs.	WM under 21 & above 60	WF all ages	Blacks 12-50	Blacks under 12 & above 50
James Yancey Jr.	1	.	.	.	.
Lewis Amis	1	2	1	2	.
Samuel Whitehead	1	3	6	1	1
William Easley	1	7	2	4	2
Drury Stovall	1	3	5	3	3
Luke Sanders	1	1	5	.	.
John Stovall	1	3	7	4	4
John Puryear	1	1	2	2	1
Ezikal Hendrickson	1	3	3	.	.
Aaron Pinson	2	3	3	1	.
Thomas Boswell	1	.	2	.	.
William Shepard	2	6	4	6	3
John Young	1	2	6	30	26
Richard Hailey	1	3	7	.	.
John Pomfrett	.	1	3	8	4
John Blackwell	1	5	3	6	3
Josiah Daniel	1	8	4	6	5
Chales [sic] Yancey	1	4	6	3	6
Ann Nuckcolls by Chal. Yancey	.	.	.	1	1
	19	55	69	77	59

Pg. 2

Head of Household	WM 21-60 yrs.	WM under 21 & above 60	WF all ages	Blacks 12-50	Blacks under 12 & above 50
William Knight	1	1	2	1	.
Thornton Yancey	1	8	1	3	3
Joel Chandler	1	6	3	7	7
James Hester	1	4	4	.	.
George Vaughn	1	.	.	.	.
William Puryear	1	.	1	1	5
Ransom Boswell	1	2	3	.	.
Joseph Hart	1	3	5	2	3
Robert Puryear	1	4	1	1	4
Philip Yancey	2	1	2	2	3
William Yancey	1	2	1	1	5
Jordon Whitlow	1	.	1	.	.
William Davis	1	.	3	1	2
Joseph Chandler	1	2	2	.	.
Daniel Chandler	.	1	2	.	.
John Chandler	1	2	3	.	.
John Boswell	1	2	2	.	.
James Millener	1	2	4	.	.
William Millener	1	6	2	.	.
	19	46	42	19	32

Pg. 3

Head of Household	WM 21-60 yrs.	WM under 21 & above 60	WF all ages	Blacks 12-50	Blacks under 12 & above 50
Lewis Yancey	2	1	2	6	9
John Hart	1	3	8	.	.
Gideon Crenshaw	1	1	4	2	.

Head of Household	WM 21-60 yrs.	WM under 21 & above 60	WF all ages	Blacks 12-50	Blacks under 12 & above 50
David Smith	1	5	5	3	3
William Royster	1	3	1	5	3
Samuel Harrison	1	.	3	.	.
William Bailey	1	.	1	.	.
William Stovall	1	1	5	2	1
John Reed	1	1	4	.	.
Samuel Crafton by James Hunt Jr.	2	1	.	2	1
James Yancey	1	2	1	10	28
James Yancey for Robert Boyd	.	1	.	2	3
James Downey Jr.	1	.	.	3	1
Josiah Farmer	1	1	6	2	.
William Royster by Archd Scarwood	1	2	2	6	2
Larkin Johnston	1	2	2	.	.
John W. Graves	1	3	2	6	2
Bat. Stovall	1	4	4	.	.
Abraham Crenshaw	1	3	5	2	3
Samuel Pittard	1	5	3	.	.
Henry Hester	1	5	4	.	.
	22	44	62	51	56

Pg. 4

Head of Household	WM 21-60 yrs.	WM under 21 & above 60	WF all ages	Blacks 12-50	Blacks under 12 & above 50
Thomas Mutter	2	1	3	17	10
Samuel Peace	1	1	4	2	4
M. Hunt	1	2	5	9	18
	4	4	12	28	32

A List of the Number of Souls in Nutbush District for the Year 1786.

Pg. 1

Head of Household	WM 21-60 yrs.	WM under 21 & above 60	WF all ages	Blacks 12-50	Blacks under 12 & above 50
Simon Williams	1	4	6	9	7
John Vandyke	1	3	2	.	.
John Wms. Daniel	2	1	3	5	6
Benjamin Johnstone	2	1	2	.	.
Bartholomew Strum	1	.	4	.	1
Joseph Burchit	1	.	4	4	.
John Hartgrove	1	2	5	5	7
Argill Hanks	1	.	2	.	.
William Berry	1	.	2	.	.
John Breedlove	1	3	6	.	.
Henry Wilson	1	3	3	.	.
Stephen Turner	1	4	5	3	5
Daniel Ellington	1	1	2	1	.
Charles Hammock	1	.	1	.	.
Simon Malone	1	2	4	.	.
William Todd	1	2	3	.	.

Head of Household	WM 21-60 yrs.	WM under 21 & above 60	WF all ages	Blacks 12-50	Blacks under 12 & above 50
David Mason	1	4	3	1	2
Robert Smith	1	5	3	.	.
Sherwood Sims Junr.	1	4	5	4	.
John Scott	1	1	5	.	.
Dennis Paschall	1	3	3	.	.
Saml Hammond Junr.	1	1	4	.	.
David Hammock	1	2	2	.	.
George Chapman	1	1	1	1	2
Peter Perry	1	2	1	.	.
Lend. Sims	1	4	3	11	14
Henry Freeman	1	2	3	.	.
Guilliam Norwood	1	2	5	1	3
Thos. Earls	1	2	7	.	.
Elisha Sims	3	5	4	3	6
William Dodson	1	2	4	5	1
Saml Hammond Senr.	1	.	2	1	.
William Sims	1	2	7	2	3
Charles Dodson	2	2	4	1	.
Elisha Paschall	1	6	3	.	.
Thos. Sartin	1	2	2	.	.
Lewis Parish	1	2	3	.	.
Mary Robinson	1	.	3	.	.
John Collins	1	2	3	2	5
David Adkins	1	2	2	.	.
Job Hammond	2	3	3	2	.
Thos. Cardwell	1	5	3	.	.
John Morgan	1	2	2	.	.
Joseph Lindsey	2	.	4	1	.
Pg. 2					
John Howell	1	3	1	1	.
Saml Manning	1	1	2	2	.
Benjamin Guy	1	3	4	.	.
Griffin Tuggle	1	.	2	1	1
Sherwood Sims Senr.	.	1	1	3	1
Archelaus Williams	1	2	3	.	.
James Burchet	2	2	2	.	.
Silas Paschal	1	4	3	.	.
Lend. Hen. Bullock	2	1	5	23	27
Thomas Sims	1	3	3	.	.
Robert Cook	1	2	1	.	.
John Cole	2	.	3	.	.
Thos. Kelly	1	1	4	.	.
Henry Lyne	.	1	3	26	21
Thos. Hilliard	1	1	1	2	1
Nathl. Robinson	1	7	3	2	6
Saml. Searcy	1	2	1	.	.
Lucy Searcy	.	6	4	4	.
William Moore	1	3	2	.	.

Head of Household	WM 21-60 yrs.	WM under 21 & above 60	WF all ages	Blacks 12-50	Blacks under 12 & above 50
Daniel Williams	2	6	5	12	15
Tho. Lanier	1	1	2	7	15
Howel Moorse	1	2	6	3	2
John Taylor	1	1	7	9	11
John Somerville	2	3	2	27	28
Benoni Hancock	1	2	2	1	.
Terisha Turner	1	.	1	2	3
Presley Thorn	1	.	2	1	2
Elisabeth Watkins	.	2	3	.	1
James Lyne	1	1	.	1	.
James Hutcherson	1	.	2	.	.
Permenas Williams	1	4	4	8	13
Askenas Williams	1	4	4	4	3
James Paskill	1	2	1	.	.
James Roper	1	.	1	.	.
Benja. Thomas	1	2	2	4	3
James Mathis	[no numbers]				
	[No Totals given]				

"The within List Taken by Howell Lewis J. P. August 9th 1786 - Total 382"

The Number of Souls in Island Creek District. (One page with two columns) (Column one)

Head of Household	WM 21-60 yrs.	WM under 21 & above 60	WF all ages	Blacks 12-50	Blacks under 12 & above 50
Dent Suit	1	3	8	.	.
Phisllestine Howel (?)	1	1	.	4	.
Joseph Akin	2	2	3	2	1
James Akin Jun.	1	1	1	.	.
William Byars	4	3	2	1	.
William Gober	1	4	3	.	.
Roland Terry	1	6	2	2	1
Vinkler Jones	1	4	4	15	8
Martha Gober	.	3	5	.	.
Jordan Norwood	1	3	4	3	4
John Glover	1	1	5	1	2
Daniel Glover	3	1	1	9	5
James Terry Senr.	1	3	3	3	3
Gidion Gooch	1	3	6	5	6
William Cak	.	2	2	3	4
Jarrot Wright	1	1	2	.	.
John Evans	1	.	.	.	.
James Terry Jur.	1	.	4	.	.
Roland Gooch	1	5	4	3	2

Head of Household	WM 21-60 yrs.	WM under 21 & above 60	WF all ages	Blacks 12-50	Blacks under 12 & above 50
Joseph Gooch	4	1	.	8	2
Robt. Crawley, Virgia	.	.	.	8	2
James Lewis	1	2	3	8	6
Batt Booth	1	1	2	.	.
Timothy Driskoll	1	3	5	1	.
Benja. Norwood	1	1	1	3	6
James Akin Sen.	1	2	9	.	1
James Akin	1	.	.	.	.
Field Reed	1	3	3	1	2
Frances Lewis	.	4	2	10	9
Nickolas Burch	.	1	2	2	3
Saml. Sneed	2	3	2	10	7
[written over]			3		
James West	1	6	5	.	.
John Taylor Esqr.	1	.	1	17	25
Robt. Lewis Estate	.	.	.	19	23
Lewis Lanier	1	1	1	2	1
Miles King Esqr.	.	.	.	6	4
George King	1	1	2	2	.
Column two					
Edward King	1	.	2	3	.
Robt. Malone	1	5	2	1	1
Christopher Harris	2	2	5	1	.
Jesse Harper	1	.	7	13	10
Mathew Crowder	1	2	2	.	.
John Robertson	1	.	.	.	.
John Butler	1	.	.	.	.
John Barnett	1	2	2	.	.
Isham Akin	2	3	3	2	1
John Tery	1	1	1	.	.
Daniel Scott	1	.	2	.	.
John Gomer	1	.	1	.	.
Thomas Goldsmith	1	.	3	.	.
Sarah C. Barnett	.	3	5	3	.
Thomas Kendrick	1	1	1	.	.
William Gober Jun.	1	.	.	.	.
Jesse Barnett	1	4	5	2	.
Nathaniel Parrot	1	1	1	.	.
William Gomer	1	1	1	.	.
Joab Glover	1	2	3	1	2
John Dellon	1	2	6	.	.
Stephen Terry	1	1	1	.	.
Thos. Robertson	1	.	.	.	.
James Satterwhite	1	4	3	1	1
Henry Melton or Milton	2	3	9	3	2
Absolem Davis	1	.	.	4	13
Solomon Davis	1	.	4	6	3

Head of Household	WM 21-60 yrs.	WM under 21 & above 60	WF all ages	Blacks 12-50	Blacks under 12 & above 50
Benjn. Scurry	1	.	4	1	.
Zachariah Hester	1	4	7	.	.
Howel Lewis Junr.	4	.	1	14	19
William Bullock	1	1	4	23	16
John Penn	3	.	.	39	31
James Woodal	1	3	4	.	.
	41	45	89	117	189

Number of Inhabitants in Dutch District.
(one page of two columns)

(Column one)	WM 21-60 yrs.	WM under 21 & above 60	WF all ages	Blacks 12-50	Blacks under 12 & above 50	Total
Robert Allison	1	4	3	1	.	9
John Adcock	1	4	8	.	.	13
Bowland Adcock	1	1	6	.	.	8
Frederick Beck	.	2	3	.	.	5
John Beck	1	5	4	.	.	10
Mary Byars	.	2	2	2	3	9
Michael Beck	1	.	1	.	.	2
John Bailey	.	2	3	.	.	5

[Name of Thos. W. Culverhouse crossed out; supplied by N. C. Geneology, pg. 2158]

	WM 21-60 yrs.	WM under 21 & above 60	WF all ages	Blacks 12-50	Blacks under 12 & above 50	Total
Joseph Baxter	1	4	2	.	.	7
Stephen Bailey	1	.	2	.	.	7
David Bundridge	1	2	5	.	.	8
Micajah Bullock	2	4	3	3	1	13
Henry Bagley	1	1	2	.	1	5
Thomas Bonner	1	3	3	.	.	7
Caleb Brassfield	1	.	2	4	5	12
Richd D. Cooke	1	3	4	5	3	16
Peter Cash	1	3	1	.	1	6
Benjamin Clark	1	2	3	.	.	6
Thos. W. Culverhouse	.	3	2	.	.	5
James Clackton	1	6	4	.	.	11
Edmund Carnes	1	3	3	.	.	7
Joseph Carnes	1	1	1	1	.	4
James Cash	1	.	2	1	1	5
Joseph Cash	2	3	2	1	.	8
Thomas Clement	1	3	4	4	3	15
Ephraim Emery	2	1	3	.	.	6
Gedeon Freeman	3	4	3	5	4	19
Moses Fuzel	1	1	5	1	.	8
Conrod Farmer	1	1	2	.	.	4
Futril Hall	1	1	2	.	.	4
William Hunt	2	.	.	4	3	9
Claboun Harris	1	4	3	.	.	8
David Harris Sr.	1	1	4	2	2	10
Joseph C. Hall	1	5	4	.	.	10

STATE CENSUS OF NORTH CAROLINA 1784-1787

Head of Household	WM 21-60 yrs.	WM under 21 & above 60	WF all ages	Blacks 12-50	Blacks under 12 & above 50	Total
Sam Harris	2	3	3	6	7	21
James Haskins	1	3	5	.	.	9
Jacob Huffman	1	1	2	.	.	4
John Hatcher	1	4	6	.	.	11
Robt. Harris	1	3	4	.	.	8
Thomas Jones	1	2	3	.	.	6
William Jones Jr.	1	5	3	.	.	9
David Lovitt	1	1	2	.	.	4
Joseph Landers	1	3	3	.	.	7
Abraham Lawrence	1	1	2	.	.	4
Thos. Longbottom	1	.	3	.	.	4
George L. Moore	2	4	5	.	.	11
James McLemore	1	3	2	.	.	6
John McLemore	1	3	1	.	.	5
[end of column]						
Benjamin Moore	1	.	2	.	.	3
William Merryman	1	1	5	.	.	7
Malachi Merryman	1	1	4	.	.	6
Chas. Merryman	1	1	3	.	.	5
Kimbrough Ogelviee	1	.	3	1	.	5
Smith Ogelviee	1	.	.	.	.	.
Joseph Okey	1	2	3	.	.	6
Harris Ogilvie	1	.	3	.	1	5
John C. Peak	1	4	5	2	.	12
Thomas Swiney	1	2	3	.	.	6
George Story	1	3	4	.	.	8
William Swiney	1	1	1	.	.	3
William Tatom	1	1	2	.	.	4
Charles Turner	1	1	8	.	.	10
Edward D. Tyler	1	1	2	.	.	4
John Tippitt	1	4	5	.	.	10
John Tuggle	1	.	2	.	.	3
John Tatom	1	1	1	.	.	3
Elijah Veasey	2	3	2	.	.	7
Jehu Williams	1	2	7	2	.	12
Benjamin Wheler	1	.	4	.	.	5
Ann Whelor	.	1	3	.	.	4
Nathl Waller	1	6	3	.	.	10
Thos. Wilbourn	1	5	3	.	.	9
Augt. Willard	1	2	2	.	.	5
Amey Wade	.	3	5	.	.	8
Wyat Wilkinson	1	2	4	1	3	11
William White	1	2	3	3	5	14

(Signed) Pr. Edmd. Taylor Jur.

Head of Household	WM 21-60 yrs.	WM under 21 & above 60	WF all ages	Blacks 12-50	Blacks under 12 & above 50	Total
Number of souls in Raglands Dist.						
Pg. 1						
Samuel Allen	1	3	5	1	1	11
John Brodie	2	3	3	5	7	20
Elizabeth Bristow	.	.	2	2	1	5
James Bishop	2	.	1	2	1	6
Edward Bass	2	4	5	.	.	11
Nathon Bass	1	3	5	.	.	9
Joshua Bell	1	2	5	.	1	9
Hugh Currin	1	4	3	.	.	8
Elizabeth Currin	.	1	7	3	4	15
James Crews	1	3	5	.	.	9
Thomas Crews	1	1	6	.	1	9
Gideon Crewes	"Not given in"					
Young Clerk	1	.	2	.	.	3
Jo Pomphry Davis	1	1	1	5	7	15
Denis Driskell	1	3	3	.	1	8
John Earl	1	1	3	1	.	6
John Earl Junr	1	2	2	.	.	5
Lemuel Goodwin	1	3	1	4	5	14
Edward Grisham	1	2	1	.	.	4
John Gilliam	1	4	9	3	5	22
Benja Grisham	1	3	1	.	.	5
Richard Glasgow	1	3	3	2	3	12
James Grisham	1	2	1	.	.	4
Henry Gilpin	1	.	3	.	.	4
Sherwood Harris	1	2	2	.	.	5
George Harris	1	3	3	.	.	7
Benjamin Hester	1	.	1	1	2	5
	27	65	83	29	39	131
Pg. 2						
William Hicks	.	2	3	5	4	14
Dinah Hicks	.	1	1	.	.	2
Samuel Jeeter	1	2	1	7	3	14
Drury Kimbal	1	5	3	4	3	16
Edward Loyd	.	2	5	.	.	7
William Loyd	1	.	2	.	.	3
Elisha Lindsy	1	2	1	.	.	4
Jarriot Loyd	1	.	3	.	.	4
John Major	1	2	3	.	.	6
John Morton	3	.	.	1	.	4
John Mize	1	2	2	.	.	5
do for Sam Clay	.	.	.	6	2	8
William Paskel	1	3	2	.	.	6
Charles Parrish	1	4	4	1	3	13
William Parrish	2	2	8	.	.	12
Wm. Parrish Junr.	1	2	2	.	.	5
Elizabeth Parrish	.	1	3	.	.	4
Drury Pettiford	1	1	2	.	.	4
David Parrish	.	3	5	.	.	8

Head of Household	WM 21-60 yrs.	WM under 21 & above 60	WF all ages	Blacks 12-50	Blacks under 12 & above 50	Total
Clayborn Parrish	1	2	3	.	.	6
George Pettiford	1	.	1	.	.	2
John Parrish	1	3	4	.	.	8
Sophe Plumer "N given" [Not given]						
Amy Ragland	.	1	1	6	4	12
Thomas Reekes?	.	2	1	8	3	14
William Ragland	1	4	5	1	1	12
Brumfield Ridley	1	1	4	11	15	32
Ransom Sutherland	1	2	3	11	13	30
John Sears	.	4	5	.	.	9
Dudley Sneed	1	.	.	.	.	1
William Thomason	1	1	2	.	.	4
Thomas Thompson	1	2	5	2	1	11
Drury Tayborn	1	3	2	.	.	6
Widow Traylor "N given"						
Peyton Wood	1	3	2	8	6	20
Charles Williams	1	5	4	.	.	10
	28	67	92	71	58	308

Pg. 3

Head of Household	WM 21-60 yrs.	WM under 21 & above 60	WF all ages	Blacks 12-50	Blacks under 12 & above 50	Total
Nathaniel Williams	2	4	3	.	.	9
John Wilson	2	2	7	1	.	12
Richard Wilkins	1	3	5	3	.	12
William Wilkins	1	.	1	.	.	2
John Wright	1	.	2	.	.	3
Thos. Whicker	1	1	3	.	.	5
Elizabeth Whicker	.	.	4	.	.	4
William Whicker	1	1	1	.	.	3
Thomas Norman	1	1	5	10	5	22
Ambrose Barker	2	2	6	2	3	15
	12	15	37	16	8	78

"E. [Errors] Excepted
A. Barker"

A list of souls taken by Zacharias Higgs in Fishing Creek district for the year 1786 Granville County.

Pg. 1

Head of Household	WM 21-60 yrs.	WM under 21 & above 60	WF all ages	Blacks 12-50	Blacks under 12 & above 50	Total
Sherwood Parrish	1	1	3	.	.	5
Benjamin Smith	1	.	2	.	.	3
Jonathan Kittrell	1	1	2	8	4	16
Isham Kittrell	1	.	.	.	1	2
Rowland Bryant	1	2	4	1	.	8
Henry Fowler	1	1	2	.	.	4
Henry Lankford	.	4	4	.	.	8
John Lankford	1	3	6	.	.	10
Jesse Lankford	1	.	1	.	.	2
Ezekiel Fuller	2	4	4	3	6	19
Justus Parrish	1	1	8	.	.	10
Henry Hays Junr.	1	.	2	.	.	3

Head of Household	WM 21-60 yrs.	WM under 21 & above 60	WF all ages	Blacks 12-50	Blacks under 12 & above 50	Total
Elijah Parrish	1	4	4	.	.	9
Wm. Parham Sen.	1	4	3	.	.	8
Leonard Clark	1	5	3	2	2	13
Isaac Hopkins	2	2	1	.	.	5
Jacob Byrum	1	.	2	.	.	3
Joshua Hutchinson	1	.	.	.	.	1
Jesse Parrish	2	1	7	.	.	10
Vallentine Tuder	1	.	2	.	.	3
Stephen Inscoe	1	.	.	.	.	1
Burgis Reeves	1	2	1	.	.	4
Allen Reeves	1	2	2	.	.	5
	25	37	63	14	13	152

Pg. 2

Head of Household	WM 21-60 yrs.	WM under 21 & above 60	WF all ages	Blacks 12-50	Blacks under 12 & above 50	Total
Thomas Newby	1	3	7	.	1	12
Parrish Lankford	1	2	1	.	.	4
Samuel Walker	2	1	2	7	4	16
John Dickerson Junr	1	2	5	3	.	11
John Parham	1	3	5	.	1	11
Joseph Peace	1	5	3	.	.	9
Cornelus Cooper	1	4	3	1	.	9
Henry Smith	1	1	5	.	.	7
Thomas Parham	1	.	2	.	.	3
John Cooper	1	.	2	.	.	3
William Weavour	2	.	4	.	.	6
Drury Hudson	1	.	1	.	.	2
John Peace	2	4	1	6	3	16
John Easter	1	.	1	.	.	2
Joshua Hays Senr.	1	1	4	.	.	6
Joshua Hays Junr.	1	1	3	.	.	5
Henry Hays Senr.	1	2	3	.	.	6
Avery Parham	1	2	5	.	.	8
William Wright	1	1	4	1	4	11
Isham Parham	2	5	9	.	.	16
Jonathan Johnson	2	1	1	4	4	12
Larrance Petiford	1	2	3	.	.	6
Jesse Garriot	1	.	1	.	.	2
Samuel Hicks	1	1	2	.	.	4
Carter Hudgpeth	1	2	3	1	.	7
Barnet Tatum	1	2	2	.	.	5
Nicholus Loyed	1	3	4	.	.	8
Gideon Johnson	1	1	2	.	.	4
Total [Actually 211]						207
Carried Forward						359

Pg. 3

Head of Household	WM 21-60 yrs.	WM under 21 & above 60	WF all ages	Blacks 12-50	Blacks under 12 & above 50	Total
Nathan Whitlow	2	2	4	.	.	8
Solomon Whitlow	1	.	.	.	.	1
Fedrick Reeves	1	1	3	.	.	5
Philemon White	1	.	1	.	.	2

Head of Household	WM 21-60 yrs.	WM under 21 & above 60	WF all ages	Blacks 12-50	Blacks under 12 & above 50	Total
Thomas Parham	1	.	2	.	.	3
John Guess	1	1	4	.	.	6
Elizabeth Tuder	.	3	5	.	.	8
William Hicks	1	2	3	.	.	6
Jacob Woodall	2	2	3	.	.	7
Thomas Parham Sen.	2	3	4	.	.	9
David Hicks	1	3	1	.	.	5
John Dunkin Senr.	1	2	3	2	.	8
Lewis Parham	1	2	2	.	1	6
William Parham Jun.	1	1	4	.	.	6
Mikajah Debruler	1	2	1	.	.	4
John Suite	1	1	3	.	.	5
James Fowler	1	3	2	.	.	6
Harris Mauldin	1	1	2	.	.	4
Joseph Hays	1	4	6	.	.	11
Ephram Parham	3	1	4	.	.	8
John Allison	1	.	.	.	.	1
James Allison	1	.	.	1	.	2
William Reeves	2	4	5	.	.	11
George Bristow	1	2	2	.	.	5
John Smith Jun.	1	.	3	.	.	4
James Smith	1	.	.	.	.	1
Joseph Smith	1	.	.	.	.	1
John Dunkin Jun.	1	.	2	1	.	4
Total						147
Carried Forward						506

Pg. 4

Head of Household	WM 21-60 yrs.	WM under 21 & above 60	WF all ages	Blacks 12-50	Blacks under 12 & above 50	Total
William Johnson	1	2	1	.	.	4
Moses Lankford	1	.	3	.	.	4
Joseph Rogers	1	1	6	2	2	12
Thomas McDaniel	1	2	4	.	.	7
Christian Thomas	.	1	3	1	6	11
Laban Haselip	1	1	2	.	.	4
William William	1	6	2	1	5	15
Thomas Peyton	1	1	1	.	.	3
Reubin Inscoe	1	3	6	.	.	10
Brissey Parrish	.	3	1	1	.	5
William Hunt	1	1	3	4	1	10
Isaac Kittrell	1	.	2	2	.	5
Nimrod Brummit	1	4	4	.	.	9
James Blackly	1	.	.	.	.	1
James Cardin	1	1	2	.	2	6
Ann Sneling	1	2	2	.	.	5
Lettiss Sneling	.	1	4	1	3	9
William Farrow	1	3	6	2	3	15
William Petaford	1	.	3	.	.	4
Reuben Bass	1	1	4	.	.	6
Hugh Sneling	1	4	3	2	5	15
William Chavis	1	.	1	1	.	3

Head of Household	WM 21-60 yrs.	WM under 21 & above 60	WF all ages	Blacks 12-50	Blacks under 12 & above 50	Total
William Dickerson	2	4	3	.	1	10
Bartlet Tyler	1	5	5	.	1	12
Stephen Hicks	.	6	2	.	.	8
Isaac Shemwell	1	2	5	.	.	8
James Shemwell	1	4	6	.	.	11
John Moss	1	.	1	.	1	3
William Lock	.	4	5	.	.	9
William Allison	1	.	.	.	.	1
Jonathan Lock	1	.	1	.	.	2
Total						227
Brought Forward						733

Pg. 5

Head of Household	WM 21-60 yrs.	WM under 21 & above 60	WF all ages	Blacks 12-50	Blacks under 12 & above 50	Total
Corbin Hickman	1	5	4	.	.	10
William Barton	1	4	4	1	2	12
Thomas Harp	1	3	3	.	.	7
Daniel Hunter	1	.	.	.	.	1
Sarah Guess	.	3	1	.	.	4
Ths. Parrish	.	1	1	.	.	2
James Jett	2	3	6	1	1	13
Robert Allison	1	.	3	4	.	8
[Wm. Parham Senr., crossed out]						
James Smith Senr.	1	2	3	.	.	6
Malichi Reeves	.	2	4	3	3	12
John Kittrell	1	6	2	.	.	9
Burrel Ivvins	1	3	3	.	.	7
Noel Johnston	1	3	4	.	.	8
James Bristow	1	.	.	.	.	1
Mary Pendergrass	.	.	2	.	.	2
John Smith Senr.	1	.	4	.	.	5
Zacharias Higgs	2	2	3	5	1	13
John Bristow	1	5	3	.	.	9
Solomon Thornton	1	1	3	.	.	5
Total						131
Brought forward						733
"The hole"						864

Fishing Creek District taken by Z. Higgs

Tara River District

Pg. 1

Head of Household	WM 21-60 yrs.	WM under 21 & above 60	WF all ages	Blacks 12-50	Blacks under 12 & above 50	Total
Thomas Philpot	1	2	1	5	2	11
Saml. Bradey	1	.	.	.	.	1
Thos. Bird	1	2	3	.	.	6
Blackmon Pardeu	1	1	3	.	.	5
Jno. Washington	1	.	1	2	5	9
Wm. Philpot	1	3	8	1	.	13
John Cragg	1	7	4	.	.	12
John Badget	4	4	4	1	2	15
Danl. Meadows	1	.	2	.	.	3

Head of Household	WM 21-60 yrs.	WM under 21 & above 60	WF all ages	Blacks 12-50	Blacks under 12 & above 50	Total
John Shearmon	1	2	4	2	3	12
James Meadows	1	1	2	1	.	5
Wm. Cocke	1	1	1	5	3	11
Michl. Meadows	1	1	1	.	.	3
Mishl. Shearmon	1	2	4	3	2	12
Thos. Oakley	2	6	4	.	.	12
Wm. Oakley	1	4	6	.	.	11
Jno. Williams	1	2	1	.	.	4
Geo. Reeves	1	1	3	.	.	5
John Thomason	1	4	6	2	2	15
Jos. Hester	1	1	3	1	1	7
Wm. Gill	2	.	3	3	6	14
Henry Nowland	1	1	2	.	.	4
Anthony Lumkin	1	7	5	1	3	17
Groves Howard	2	3	8	5	12	30
John Jones, Taylor [tailor?]	1	3	3	.	.	7
Shermon Goss	1	2	3	.	1	7
James Brinkley	1	3	2	.	.	6
Wm. Allin Leather	2	4	4	2	.	12
Jac. Slaughter Sen.	1	4	5	2	.	12
Harrison Dunkin	1	1	3	.	.	5
Geo. Dunkin	1	3	2	.	.	6
Jac. Slaughter Jun.	1	.	2	1	.	4
Jacob Slaughter, Taylor [tailor]	1	.	.	.	.	1
Allen Howard ?	1	.	.	.	2	3
John Thorp	2	1	2	3	6	14
Reuben Butler	.	.	.	3	1	4
Peter Brinkley	1	5	4	.	.	10
	44	81	109	43	51	328
Pg. 2						
Ishum Johnson	1	2	6	1	.	10
William Primrose	1	1	2	.	.	4
Francis Wilkerson	1	2	1	.	1	5
Phil. Lewis	1	5	8	2	5	21
Nathan Childs	1	2	1	8	2	14
Richd Fowler	1	4	5	.	.	10
David Webb	1	4	7	.	.	12
Ben Bass Jun.	1	2	4	.	.	7
Ben Bass Senr.	2	5	4	.	.	11
Elias Pettyford	1	.	2	.	.	(sic)
Miles Wells	1	8	4	.	.	13
Charles Long	1	.	2	.	.	3
Stephen Terry	1	1	2	1	.	5
Solomon Williams	1	.	3	.	1	5
Richard Brigs	1	1	2	.	.	4
Ephraim Frazer	1	4	3	1	.	9
Geo. Long	1	4	3	.	.	8

Head of Household	WM 21-60 yrs.	WM under 21 & above 60	WF all ages	Blacks 12-50	Blacks under 12 & above 50	Total
Robert Adcock	1	2	2	.	.	5
Amous Gooch	1	.	.	.	.	1
John Russel	1	6	5	2	5	19
John Hill	1	5	2	.	.	. (sic)
Thomas Person	7	2	9	64	58	140
John Landish	1	6	1	.	.	. (sic)
	74	147	187	122	127	634

Number of Inhabitants in <u>Goshen District</u> 1786.

Head of Household	WM 21-60 yrs.	WM under 21 & above 60	WF all ages	Blacks 12-50	Blacks under 12 & above 50
Pg. 1					
John Webb	1	3	5	7	8
William Palmer	1	4	2	7	.
John Kinnon	1	3	4	14	22
Robert Sandford	1	4	4	1	.
William Laseter	2	.	.	3	3
Richard Boyd	1	1	2	.	.
do for Charles Edwards	.	.	.	7	2
Lewis Ashman	3	.	2	.	.
George Melone	1	3	3	.	2
Stephen Beezley	1	.	.	.	.
do for Robt Beezley	.	.	.	3	7
Robert Bevel	1	1	3	.	.
Thomas LeMay	1	1	2	5	5
Dennis Obrian	1	2	2	.	.
Brazenton Jones	1	2	2	1	.
Shadrack Roberts	1	2	3	.	.
Rev. George Micklejohn	1	5	2	.	.
Robert Wade	1	.	2	3	.
Ambrose Jones	2	2	4	10	7
Richard Walden	1	.	.	.	.
James Warton	1	3	5	.	.
Seth Pettypool	2	4	6	.	.
John Pettypool Jun	1	.	3	.	.
William Glass	1	3	4	3	4
John Owen, Senr	1	.	3	4	7
John Owen, Junr.	1	2	4	3	.
James Winfree	1	3	6	1	1
Peter Bennet	1	2	5	2	6
Wm. Puryear, Junr	1	1	2	.	.
do for Thomas Aplin	.	.	.	3	3
Charles Harris	2	5	5	4	4
Joseph Chandler	1	4	5	.	.
John Heath	1	1	4	.	.
Thomas Edwards	1	4	4	3	1
James Chandler	1	.	.	.	1

Head of Household	WM 21-60 yrs.	WM under 21 & above 60	WF all ages	Blacks 12-50	Blacks under 12 & above 50
John Harris	2	3	5	4	5
Lewis Bennett	1	1	3	3	1
Thomas Pool	1	3	3	4	3
Henry Graves	1	.	.	2	.
Richard Deuty	1	5	4	4	3
Patrick Obrian	1	4	2	4	4
David Wilkerson	1	5	4	2	4
John Wilkerson	1	6	4	6	2
Josiah Mitchell	.	2	3	.	3
Andrew Samuel	1	.	1	.	.
Joseph Blanks	1	5	5	2	3
Chesley Daniel	2	3	5	16	30
(Total 505)	51	52	138	133	131
Pg. 2					
Timothy Chandler	1	.	4	.	.
Nimrod Ellis	1	4	2	.	.
Samuel Pointer	1	3	3	9	13
Edward Howard	2	4	3	1	.
Andrew Patterson	1	1	2	.	.
John Pettypool, Sen	2	4	6	3	4
Stephen Pettypool	1	.	1	.	.
John Knott	1	5	5	5	14
James Knott	1	1	1	1	1
David Knott	1	3	5	5	8
Michael Saterwhite	1	3	3	2	5
Charles Wade	1	3	3	4	5
Archibald Cambell	1	.	2	.	.
Bartley Greer	1	1	1	.	.
Milley Harison	.	.	3	.	.
Reubin Jones	1	2	2	.	2
Robert Hester	1	2	1	3	2
Thomas Owen	1	5	7	3	6
(Total 200)	19	41	54	36	60

Taken by Thomas Owen, J. P. F'd. 505
Total 705

Henderson Dist. August 1786.

Pg. 1	WM 21-60 yrs.	WM under 21 & above 60	WF all ages	Blacks 12-50	Blacks under 12 & above 50	Total
Travis Bowdon	1	6	2	.	1	10
Meriman Barns	1	4	7	.	.	12
John Mitchell	1	3	5	7	.	16
Ralph Neil	1	6	2	5	6	20
James Stark	.	4	4	2	2	12
William Gilliam	1	2	4	1	5	13
John Smith	1	.	1	.	1	3
Thos. Rowland	1	6	4	.	.	11
George Perdue	1	1	1	.	.	3
Richd. Stringfellow	1	2	3	.	.	6
John Weaver	.	1	2	.	.	3

Head of Household	WM 21-60 yrs.	WM under 21 & above 60	WF all ages	Blacks 12-50	Blacks under 12 & above 50	Total
John Harris	1	6	3	.	.	10
John Mabry	1	4	2	.	2	9
Richd. Grisham	2	3	4	.	.	9
Saml. Reavs	1	1	1	.	.	3
George Waif	1	.	4	.	.	5
George Brack	1	3	3	.	2	9
Saml. Brack	1	2	3	.	.	6
Thos. Satterwhite	2	2	3	13	15	35
John Rice	1	2	1	.	.	4
Wm. Rice	1	.	4	.	.	5
John Fleming	1	.	.	.	.	1
Oswell Byrum	1	3	2	.	.	6
Elizath Henderson	.	3	8	2	9	24(sic)
do for Polly Wms.	.	.	.	.	.	.
Isham Harrison	1	.	4	1	2	8
John Daniel for self						
& Mary Daniel	1	2	4	7	6	20
Reuben Daniel	1	.	4	1	.	6
Charnish Cox	1	1	4	.	1	7
(other records: Charnich Cox)						
John Spraburg	1	2	4	.	.	7
Jos. Spraburg	1	4	3	.	.	8
Pg. 2						
James Cooper	1	2	4	.	1	8
Ransom Smith	1	2	1	2	.	6
William Shears	2	3	8	1	.	14
						269

Number of Souls in Henderson Dist. by
Tho. Burton, J. P.

"A List of Souls, Nap of Reeds District, 1786".

Pg. 1	WM 21-60 yrs.	WM under 21 & above 60	WF all ages	Blacks 12-50	Blacks under 12 & above 50
Wm. Bennet	1	2	2	1	.
Hardiman Bennet	1	2	1	.	.
Jacob Brazlton	1	4	4	.	.
Jacob Cozart	2	4	4	1	1
Anne Cozart	.	2	3	.	.
David Cozart	1	1	3	.	.
Joshua Bulloch	1	2	1	1	2
Jere Bulloch	1	1	1	1	1
Saml. Adams	1	4	2	1	.
Zechry. Wilborn	1	2	3	.	.
Howell Mangum	1	2	3	.	.
John Wm. Manire	1	.	1	.	.
Henry Green	1	3	2	1	.
Wm. Ogilvie	1	3	4	2	.
John Bolling	2	4	6	.	.

Head of Household	WM 21-60 yrs.	WM under 21 & above 60	WF all ages	Blacks 12-50	Blacks under 12 & above 50
Joseph Mangum	1	5	6	.	.
Fredrick Rose	1	5	2	.	.
Alex. Moore	1	1	1	.	.
Amos Parker	1	2	3	.	.
Wm. Bolling	1	.	.	.	.
Absolem Foard	1	1	4	1	.
Israel Eastwood	.	7	7	.	.
Thos. Goss	1	1	4	5	4
Benj. Hopkins	1	3	6	.	.
Wm. Jones T. R.	1	4	3	.	.
Wm. Bennett T. R.	1	3	6	3	4
Wm. Eastis	2	2	5	4	6
Stephen Clement	1	.	4	2	.
Amos Tims	1	4	3	.	2
Wm. Jacob	.	1	2	.	.
John Clement	1	2	3	1	.
Obediah Clement	1	2	5	.	.
Saml Clement	1	.	.	1	.
Francis Bressie	1	2	3	3	6
	34	81	107	28	26
Pg. 2					
Samuel Jackson	1	.	1	3	1
Fowler Jones	1	2	2	.	.
Edmd. Partee	1	.	.	.	.
Howell Rose	1	.	.	1	.
Richd Hopkins	1	1	1	.	.
John Waller	1	5	3	.	.
Mary Walker	.	3	1	.	.
George Wright	2	5	3	.	.
James Custard	1	1	1	.	.
Jacob Stem	1	.	3	.	.
Wm. Cole	1	.	3	.	.
Job Green	1	3	2	.	.
Edwd. Jones	1	3	2	.	.
Joseph Okey Sr.	.	2	4	.	.
Jacob Holston	1	2	3	.	.
Ralph Williams	1	3	3	3	5
Howard Cash	1	2	3	1	1
Joel Perkinson	1	2	4	.	.
Jacob Ferribaugh	1	2	3	.	.
Charles Bullock	1	.	2	1	.
Joseph Eastwood	1	2	3	.	.
Wm. Rose	1	2	4	.	1

Head of Household	WM 21-60 yrs.	WM under 21 & above 60	WF all ages	Blacks 12-50	Blacks under 12 & above 50
Joel Chambless	1	1	4	.	.
Zephaniah Waller	1	4	7	.	.
Moses Jones	1	.	3	.	.
Benjn. Partee	1	1	1	1	.
Nathan Childs	1	2	2	.	.
Zebulon Veazey	1	4	2	.	1
Leonard Adcock	1	2	6	.	.
Rebecah Mangum	.	1	4	.	.
Chas. Patee	1	3	8	4	4
Stephen Meritt	1	3	8	4	4
Edward Adcock	1	3	3	.	.
Hezekiah Hobgood	.	3	8	.	.
	32	70	110	18	17
Pg. 3					
Thomas Hobgood	1	.	.	.	.
John Hobgood	1	.	.	.	.
Barnett Pullom	1	.	.	2	1
Jesse Meadows	1	2	3	.	.
Francis Griffon	1	.	2	.	.
Hollis Tims	1	2	3	.	.
Wm. Ashley	1	2	7	.	.
Zephaniah Clement	1	2	5	1	2
Simon Clement	1	1	.	.	.
Samuel Hancock	1	2	3	.	.
Wm. Jones Bigg	1	1	1	2	6
Micajah Okay	1	.	2	.	.
Wm. Webb	1	5	3	11	14
John Hawkings	1	2	3	4	4
Chas. Jones	1	3	5	.	.
Robert Hood Harris	1	.	.	.	.
Thos. Harris, dec'd	.	2	4	6	.
Joseph Waller	1	2	3	1	1
Robt. Harris, Esq. dec'd	.	.	1	4	2
John Manire	1	4	5	1	.
	18	32	52	27	30

Taken by John Manire, J. P.

Head of Household	WM 21-60 yrs.	WM under 21 & above 60	WF all ages	Blacks 12-50	Blacks under 12 & above 50
A list of number of Inhabitants in Abraham Plain's District, taken by Samuel Smith, J. P., Aug. 7, 1786.					
Pg. 1					
James Hunt	.	2	1	14	17
Samuel Smith	1	7	5	16	17
Lattiney Montague	1	1	6	4	5
John Smith	2	.	.	4	5
Jacob Mitchel	2	2	3	4	6
William Hagie	1	5	2	1	1
William Owen, Jurn	1	5	2	.	.
Henry Townes	1	2	1	2	1
Henry Graves	2	2	1	12	11
James Downey	1	1	3	11	7
Grant Alen	1	.	2	2	2
William Alen	.	1	1	2	4
Mary Graves	1	1	6	8	14
John Downey	1	.	3	4	12
Zacheriah Bevil	2	4	5	.	.
William Fraisyier [Fraser or Frazier; Ed]	.	4	4	4	4
John Raven	1	1	2	1	.
James Johnston	1	4	4	5	10
William Amis	1	2	4	4	1
Henry Montague	1	.	3	1	1
Anderson Smith	3	.	9	18	14
James Chavis	1	4	3	.	.
James Smith	2	.	2	5	10
John Raven, Junr	1	.	.	.	.
John Oliver	1	.	.	3	1
Peter Oliver	1	1	3	8	9
Mary Oliver	.	.	2	1	3
Robert Huckabee	1	1	1	.	.
Arthur Fraisyier	1	.	3	1	1
William Knight	2	3	4	4	6
Elisabeth Brasfield	.	1	3	3	4
Pg. 2					
Edward Leavel	1	4	5	3	.
Mary Hester	1	4	5	.	.
Thomas Berry	1	8	4	.	2
George Pettis	1	4	4	.	.
Wm. Owen, son of Jas	1	4	7	.	.
Jessee Scurry	1	2	4	1	1
Wm. Owen, Senr.	2	3	6	.	.
George Norman	1	5	5	1	1
Gideon Williams	1	5	3	.	.
John Whitlow	.	3	7	.	.
Jonathan Knight	1	4	4	1	.
James Owen	.	2	4	.	.

Head of Household	WM 21-60 yrs.	WM under 21 & above 60	WF all ages	Blacks 12-50	Blacks under 12 & above 50	Total
Fredrick Owen	1	.	5	.	1	
Rev. Henry Pattillo	2	9	3	6	6	
Buckner Syms	1	1	1	.	1	
Mary Butler	.	1	1	.	1	
Lovit Gates	1	3	2	1	.	
Lovit Reade	1	.	2	.	.	
Jessee Siddles	1	1	3	2	2	
Young Mountague	1	.	2	.	.	
William More	1	.	2	.	.	
John Howard	2	.	2	4	2	
Willis Roberts	1	2	4	.	.	
Sarah Fraisyier	.	5	8	.	.	
John Owen	1	.	3	2	2	
John Forsythe	1	4	4	.	.	
James Forsythe	1	2	1	.	.	
Benjan. Putman	1	7	3	.	.	
John Pittard	1	4	4	.	.	
Thomas Glaze	1	2	4	1	3	
Howel Lewis Jr.	1	2	3	37	34	
John Tinnin	1	.	1	.	.	
"A list of souls in Epping Forest District for the year 1786 taken by Charles P. Eaton, Granville Co.						
Pg. 1						
Berry Lewis	.	7	1	.	.	8
Dorothy Scribner	.	3	2	.	.	5
Wm. Spears, Senr.	.	2	.	1	2	5
Thomas York	.	7	8	2	2	19
Thomas Smith	1	4	5	.	.	10
Richard Thomasson	2	6	3	.	1	12
Charles Moore	.	3	6	.	.	9
Thomas Harp Sr.	1	4	4	.	.	9
Mark White	1	.	3	.	.	4
Wm. Floyed	.	3	3	.	.	6
John Dugger	1	4	4	.	.	9
John Askyou	1	.	1	.	.	2
Stirling Harding	1	1	5	.	.	7
Isaac Roberts	1	.	1	.	.	2
Thomas Loyed	1	2	1	.	.	4
John Harp	1	1	3	.	.	4
William Hornsby	.	3	7	.	.	11
Morris Floyed	1	3	3	.	.	7
Vallintine White	.	2	3	.	.	5
Thomas White	1	2	3	.	.	6
Bartlit White	1	2	4	.	.	7

Head of Household	WM 21-60 yrs.	WM under 21 & above 60	WF all ages	Blacks 12-50	Blacks under 12 & above 50	Total
Henry Fuller, Jr.	1	2	5	.	4	12
Joseph Mcdaniel	.	4	2	.	.	6
James Mcdaniel	1	.	.	.	.	1
Hilkiah Crowder	1	2	1	.	.	4
Wm. Spears	1	.	7	.	.	8
Wm. Rogers	2	.	1	.	.	3
						181
Pg. 2						
Charles Moore	.	2	1	.	.	3
William Loyed	1	3	4	.	.	8
Isaac Loyed	1	6	5	.	.	12
John Hunt	1	5	4	.	.	10
John Finch, Junr	1	3	3	.	.	7
John Haynes	2	7	7	.	.	16
Blanton Cook	.	1	.	.	.	1
John Larrance	1	.	1	.	.	2
Deborah Larrance	.	1	3	.	.	4
Benjamin Johnston	1	3	1	.	.	5
William Roberts	1	2	3	.	.	6
Henry Fuller, Senr	1	5	2	5	1	14
William Bobbit	1	5	3	.	.	9
William Cook	1	1	4	.	.	6
John Edwards	1	4	2	.	.	7
Benjamin Hays	2	.	4	.	.	6
Joseph Johnston	3	7	7	.	.	17
John Finch, Senr	1	1	3	1	.	6
Hezikiah Hifil [Highfield?]	1	1	1	.	.	3
Samuel Kittrell	1	5	3	4	6	19
Alexander Fowler	2	.	1	.	.	3
John Williams	.	2	1	.	.	3
Martha Williams	.	.	2	.	.	2
Sarah Hays	.	2	4	.	.	6
Joshua Kittrell	1	1	1	2	1	6
Nicoles Roberson	1	4	6	1	.	12
Phel Spears	1	1	1	1	.	4
John Dickerson	1	.	3	.	.	4
Leonard Higgs	1	2	2	.	1	6
						207
Pg. 3						
Williamson Finch	1	2	6	.	.	9
Jonathan Kittrell Jr	2	5	2	2	4	15
Samson Harp	1	1	3	.	.	5
John Jorden	1	4	3	3	2	13
Samuel Jones	1	4	3	.	.	8
Edward Harris	.	3	3	.	.	6
Margit Clapton	.	4	1	1	.	6
William Sloter	1	1	1	.	.	3
George Pearce	1	4	2	.	.	7
Sarah Cash	.	1	3	.	.	4
Samuel Fuller	1	5	2	8	10	26
Rosser Alley	1	1	4	.	.	6
Kannon Cooper	.	5	4	.	1	10
Thomas Devaun	.	1	.	.	.	1
Robert Ried	1	.	.	3	7	11
Ephram Vessels	1	.	4	.	.	5

E. [errors] Excepted

(signed) Charles P. Eaton, J. P.

"A list of Inhabitants of Oxford District, 1786, taken by R. Reed.

Head of Household	WM 21-60 yrs.	WM under 21 & above 60	WF all ages	Blacks 12-50	Blacks under 12 & above 50
Pg. 1					
Reuben Searcy, Esq.	3	7	5	5	3
James Bradie	2	2	5	.	.
Wm. H. Searcy	1	3	2	.	.
Thomas Howell	1	3	3	.	.
Samuel Johnston	1	4	8	2	6
Jonathan White	1	6	4	.	.
Thomas Williams	1	1	2	.	.
Jane Semple	.	4	2	.	.
Archd. Mitchell	1	9	3	.	.
Nathaniol Snipes	1	6	1	3	2
Solomon Walker	1	1	4	8	9
Charles Mitchell	1	.	1	7	1
Jeptah Parker	1	1	2	1	1
Henry Rarden	1	3	3	1	1
Caleb Croose	1	1	5	.	.
Francis Busshire	1	2	.	.	2
John Walker	1	.	1	9	1
Wm. Mallory	1	3	5	.	.
Reuben Tallie	1	4	2	4	5
Thomas Hicks	1	.	.	1	.
Gideon Crosse	1	3	4	.	.
James Wade	1	.	3	.	.
Isaac Butler	1	4	4	5	5
Joseph Hilliard	.	.	.	3	.
Thomas Butler	.	.	.	5	3
John Hunt	1	1	6	5	6
Jeremiah Frazer	1	5	2	2	2
John Locke	1	4	3	.	.
Sherwood Harris, Esq.	1	5	5	2	3
Wm. Heaster, T.R.	1	1	3	.	1
John Meaner	1	2	2	.	.
Wm. Upchurch	1	2	2	.	.
Nicholas Tallie	1	2	2	.	1

Head of Household	WM 21-60 yrs.	WM under 21 & above 60	WF all ages	Blacks 12-50	Blacks under 12 & above 50
Ruth Huddleston	.	1	3	.	.
Robert Curtis	1	.	1	.	.
John Huddleston	1	.	1	.	.
Benjamin Beardin	1	5	4	2	4
351	35	95	105	64	54
Pg. 2					
Lewis Anderson	.	.	.	3	13
John Sack	1	.	1	.	.
Cyrus Davis	1	.	3	.	.
William Walker	1	1	3	.	.
Francis Heaster	1	1	3	.	.
Constante Heaster	1	1	3	.	.
Philemon White, Jun	1	.	1	.	.
Henry Tuder	1	6	2	.	.
Robert Hicks Jr.	2	.	2	.	5
William Longmire	1	.	2	6	5
Edward Noling	1	2	2	.	.
Philemon Pettiford	1	.	.	5	3
Richard Searcy	1	2	5	.	.
George Hunt	1	2	2	3	6
Robert Lewis, Jun. B	1	.	1	11	10
John Mathews, T. R.	1	1	2	.	.
Richard Harris, T. R.	2	1	2	5	5
John Williams	1	.	3	.	.
John Potter, N. R.	5	4	4	19	26
William Currin, T. R.	1	.	.	.	.
Sarah Lindsay	.	1	5	.	.
Charles Harris	1	.	1	1	2
Samuel Parker	1	.	1	1	.
John Searcy	1	.	2	.	.
Augustine Davis	1	.	7	1	.
Robert Paul	2	.	.	.	.
Jonathan Parker	1	3	2	.	.
John Morris	2	6	2	3	.
Richard Harris, Jr	2	.	2	4	.
David Harris, Jr.	1	.	2	.	.
Thomas Thomeson	2	5	6	2	.
Mathew Hawkins	1	.	.	6	.
James Smith	1	3	4	.	.
William Coathen	1	4	4	.	.
George Bruce	.	1	1	17	.
John Boyd	1	3	4	.	1
Charles B. Eaten Esq	1	.	4	30	31
Richard Brinkley	1	3	5	.	.
Col. Edmond Taylor	2	2	4	37	.
Col. Joseph Taylor	2	2	4	56	.
Samuel Walker Junr.	1	2	5	.	.
Joseph Rend (?)	1	3	7	.	.
Zacharish Heaster	1	2	.	.	.
562	52	63	110	218	119

Total Oxford 913

Head of Household	WM 21-60 yrs.	WM under 21 & above 60	WF all ages	Blacks 12-50	Blacks under 12 & above 50	Total
Undesignated District						
Pg. 1						
Joseph Daniel	1	1	5	2	5	14
Thomas Critcher	1	.	1	4	3	9
Isham Harris	1	5	3	3	6	18
Newsom Harris	1	2	1	.	.	4
Ransom Harris	1	.	1	.	.	2
Nathaniel Cunningham Sr.	1	.	1	.	1	3
Elizabeth Henderson	.	.	3	2	1	6
John Williams Esq.	4	4	9	16	26	59
Phil. Hawkins, Esq.	2	6	9	17	21	55
Samuel Williams	1	3	4	2	3	13
William Hanks for self & father B	1	1	1	1	7	11
David Mitchel for L						
Mary Robertson A						
Manus Weaver N						
Henry Smith K						
Thomas Parrish	1	2	3	.	.	6
James Hill	1	2	3	.	.	6
Samuel Reves	(No souls given)					
Robert Burton	3	4	5	11	19	42
William Gray	1	4	3	.	.	8
Arthur Jordon	1	2	1	7	12	23
James Brame	1	6	3	5	8	23
						269
Pg. 2						
Samuel Morse	1	2	6	5	11	24
John Craft	1	7	3	4	1	16
Ben Denton	1	4	2	.	.	7
Sterling Yancy	1	.	2	2	2	7
Thomas Rice	2	4	5	.	.	11
William Frarrer	.	3	3	.	.	6
David Mitchel	2	4	3	18	14	41
Do in Caswell (County)	.	.	.	.	.	.
Stephen Sneed	2	3	1	3	3	12
Stephen Sneed &c	.	.	.	2	1	3
John (?) Keeling	1	.	.	.	.	1
Thomas Wiggins	.	1	1	3	2	7
Edward Weaver	1	.	8	1	.	10
William Weaver	1	1	3	.	.	5
Wm. Fleming	1	1	3	.	.	5
Jos. Godferry	.	1	.	5	.	6
Wm. Bowdon	2	4	3	2	.	11
Thos. Burden	.	1	1	2	2	6
Elijah Mitchel	2	2	2	7	8	21
Thos. Craft	.	3	4	3	1	11
Peter Fleming	1	5	5	.	.	10
Major Mitchel	1	1	3	2	1	8
John Chadwick	1	4	5	.	.	10

Head of Household	WM 21-60 yrs.	WM under 21 & above 60	WF all ages	Blacks 12-50	Blacks under 12 & above 50	Total
Wm. Smith	1	4	2	9	8	24
Harriss Rice	1	1	1	.	.	3
Danl Fleming	1	1	2	.	.	4
Obediah Earle	1	.	6	.	.	7
Rhody (?) Coal	1	1	1	.	.	3
John Fleming	.	4	4	.	.	8
Thos. Fleming	1	2	1	.	.	4
Wm. Valandingham	1	1	3	.	.	5
Edmond Smith	1	3	4	2	.	10
Wm. Tollan	1	.	2	.	.	3
Hugh Wyllie	.	2	.	.	.	2
Frederck Wigins	2	5	4	3	6	20
Reuben Moss	2	7	?	?	?	23

529 + 267 = 798

Pg. 2

Head of Household	WM 21-60 yrs.	WM under 21 & above 60	WF all ages	Blacks 12-50	Blacks under 12 & above 50	Total
(O?)bey Mayfield	1	3	5	2	.	11
---n(m?) Jeffers	4	5	4	.	.	13
George Leverston	2	2	3	.	.	7
Alexander Carter	1	4	4	.	2	11
Mary Megehe	.	3	3	.	.	6
--(k?)abod Carde(?)	1	4	3	.	.	8
Lewis Taylor(?)	1	3	3	13	12	32
Thomas Gowing	1	3	5	.	.	9
John Simmons	1	5	5	.	.	11
[Blurred]	1	.	.	.	.	1
Thomas Pledger	1	.	4	.	.	5
Tomas Carter	1	1	2	.	1	5
Jesse Carter	1	1	4	.	1	7
Coley White	1	.	1	1	1	4
Surrel White	1	.	2	.	.	3
Peter Vincent	1	3	6	.	.	10
Alexander Vincent	1	3	6	.	.	10
Jacob Vincent	1	3	3	.	.	7
John Campion	1	4	6	.	.	11
Robert Mills	1	3	4	.	1	9
John Bradford	1	4	4	2	1	12
Charles Hefflen	1	1	4	.	.	6
William Nailin	1	1	2	1	1	6
Abraham Jones	1	3	2	.	.	6
James Norrill	1	5	3	2	.	11
William Askew	(blank)					
Thomas Locklear	1	2	8	.	.	11
Thomas Carroll	1	2	3	.	.	6
Spencer Carroll	1	1	2	.	.	4
Joseph Parker	(blank)					
David Blaylock	1	.	4	.	.	5
Jeremiah Blaylock	1	.	1	.	.	2
Christopher Kittle	1	5	3	.	.	9

Head of Household	WM 21-60 yrs.	WM under 21 & above 60	WF all ages	Blacks 12-50	Blacks under 12 & above 50	Total
James Kittle	1	4	3	.	.	8
Robert Allison						
Major Moore						
John Massey						
William Gowing	1	4	2	.	.	7
Bird Driver	1	1	2	.	.	4
Elizabeth Nevels	.	2	4	.	.	6
[?]hen Hargraves	1	.	2	.	.	3
[? Stephen ?]						
Isaac Vincent	1	.	1	.	.	2
Richard Jones	1	.	9	.	.	10
John Dickerson Sr	2	2	2	25	24	55
	150	241	77	86	63	?
Harris Gillom	.	?	7	3	?	17
John Rust	2	5	4	5	7	23
John Peace, Junr	1	1	4	1	2	9
John Welch	2	2	4	1	.	9
George Preddy	2	1	7	.	1	11
Henry White	1	2	1	.	.	4
Wm. Byrum	1	5	2	.	.	8
Shem Cook Senr.	1	2	1	7	12	23
Philemon Bowers	.	1	.	2	3	6
William Cook	1	2	5	2	2	12
James Jenkins	2	.	6	2	2	12
William White	1	2	6	.	.	9
George White	2	4	2	5	6	19
John Rogers	1	1	7	.	.	9
Samuel Homes	2	1	5	.	.	8
George Rust	1	.	3	1	3	8
Nathan Megehe Sr.	3	5	2	.	.	10
Nathan Megehe Jr.	1	.	.	.	.	1
Benjamin Megehe Sr.	1	3	5	.	.	9
Joseph Megehe	1	2	5	.	.	8
Benjamin Megehe Jr.	1	1	4	.	.	6
William Mills	1	4	.	.	.	5
John Sutton	1	1	1	[blur]		
Wilson Rogers	1	2	2	.	.	5
Vaul Mayfield	1	4	4	.	.	9
Charles Knowling	1	1	2	.	.	4
Edward Going	1	1	3	.	.	5
William Minor	1	1	1	.	.	3
John Carroll	1	.	2	.	.	3
Robert Preddy	1	1	3	1	3	9
Thomas Preddy	1	2	3	1	2	9
(P?)omfrett Edwards	2	.	3	.	.	5
John Gowing	1	.	3	.	.	4
	47	65	147	38	44	

HALIFAX COUNTY

Head of Household	WM 21-60 yrs.	WM under 21 & above 60	WF all ages	Blacks 12-50	Blacks under 12 & above 50

"A List of the Number of White & Black Inhabitants in District No. One, Taken by Joseph Pearce, this 23rd day of February Anno 1786, Agreeable to an Act of the General Assembly.

Pg. 1

Head of Household	WM 21-60 yrs.	WM under 21 & above 60	WF all ages	Blacks 12-50	Blacks under 12 & above 50
Henry Joyner	2	2	5	4	9
Charnel Corbin	2	3	3	2	2
John Buck	1	1	3	3	3
John Lankford	1	2	2	1	.
Patrick Dwyre	1	.	.	4	3
Jesse Goodwin	1	.	.	3	3
John Pope	1	1	.	2	2
William Harrdin	.	3	5	2	3
John Moore	2	1	5	25	21
Josiah Goodwin	1	1	3	4	4
James Hardin	1	.	.	.	.
Robert Hulme	1	.	3	22	13
John Joyner	2	1	1	1	2
	16	15	30	73	65

Pg. 2

Head of Household	WM 21-60 yrs.	WM under 21 & above 60	WF all ages	Blacks 12-50	Blacks under 12 & above 50
Levi Lane	2	2	6	13	15
Tomes Pulley	1	1	4	.	.
Lasey Simmons	2	.	3	.	.
Fredrick Spellings	1	.	.	.	.
Bridgman Joyner	1	.	.	5	8
William Pearce	1	.	4	2	1
Isaac Ricks	1	1	3	10	10
Abraham Hanks	1	2	2	.	.
Theophelus Joyner	1	1	1	4	5
Peter Morgan	1	2	2	3	2
James Atkinson	1	3	6	.	.
Demsey Lasitor	1	.	5	.	.
Mathew Barnes	1	1	3	1	.
John Ricks	2	2	5	13	15
Richard Carney Esq.	.	1	2	9	9
Stephen Carney	1	.	1	4	.
Henry Tatom	1	.	.	.	.
Isom Scott	1	.	4	.	.
John Lawrence	1	.	2	17	27
Edward Crowell Sr.	.	2	3	5	10
Verdin Hill	1	.	.	.	.
Lane Copland	.	1	4	2	1
Charity Taylor	.	3	4	2	1
Famuth Lucas	1	.	.	.	.
David Lane	2	.	4	12	14
	25	22	68	102	118

Pg. 3

Head of Household	WM 21-60 yrs.	WM under 21 & above 60	WF all ages	Blacks 12-50	Blacks under 12 & above 50
Mathew Howell	1	5	3	1	.
Zacriah Lankford	1	2	5	3	.
John Daffin	1	1	3	1	3
Churchill Gibson	1	2	3	.	.
Nansey Scott	.	2	3	.	.
Henry Garland	1	.	.	.	.
William Cox	1	.	.	.	.
John Hickman	1	.	.	.	.
William Moore	1	.	.	.	.
Joseph Pearce	1	7	1	10	5
Edward Crowell Jr.	1	.	2	2	1
	10	19	20	17	9
Taken by Joseph Pearce	25	22	68	102	118
	16	15	30	73	65
	51	56	118	190	273

District No. 2, Taken by Francis Jones, Febry. 11, 1786.

Pg. 1

Head of Household	WM 21-60 yrs.	WM under 21 & above 60	WF all ages	Blacks 12-50	Blacks under 12 & above 50
Jesse Read	1	4	4	7	7
Saml. Mahanes	1	1	2	.	.
Francis Jones	1	1	7	5	3
William Hurt	1	2	3	3	5
Abraham Scott	2	4	7	.	.
Thomas Nevill	.	5	1	3	4
William Nevill	1	.	3	.	.
Benjn. Nevill	1	.	1	.	.
Miles Smith	1	2	4	.	1
Joseph Leadbetter	1	.	.	.	.
William Read	1	1	1	.	.
Joel Hurt	.	1	2	7	13
Thomas Cook	1	2	4	.	.
Thomas Hawkins	1	2	1	3	3
Jesse Daverson	1	5	3	1	.
John Partin	.	8	6	.	.
Hannah Stephens	.	3	2	.	1
[T by Compiler]	14	41	51	29	37

Pg. 2

Head of Household	WM 21-60 yrs.	WM under 21 & above 60	WF all ages	Blacks 12-50	Blacks under 12 & above 50
Moses Brewer	1	1	2	.	.
William Partin	1	.	.	.	.
Joseph Holt	1	2	3	.	.
Thomas Holt	1	.	1	.	.
James Daverson	1	.	4	.	.
Benjn. Nevill	1	5	5	3	2
Robt. Carstarphen	1	7	2	3	3
James Carstarphen	2	2	2	5	4

Head of Household	WM 21-60 yrs.	WM under 21 & above 60	WF all ages	Blacks 12-50	Blacks under 12 & above 50
Patiance Pace	.	1	5	1	.
James Winter	1	1	4	.	.
Joseph Seat	1	4	2	.	.
Arther Hewlin	1	4	2	.	.
James Winter	1	3	4	.	1
Thomas Holt	1	1	1	.	.
James Holt	1	1	1	.	.
Thos. Pasture	1	.	1	3	2
William Burt	1	1	7	4	6
John Partin	1	2	1	.	.
Mathuel Corbin	1	1	4	.	.
William Burt	1	5	2	.	.
John Powers	1	1	3	.	.
David Crawley	1	2	1	5	3
Absolam Powers	1	2	2	.	.
Jesse Powers	1	.	2	.	.
Elizabeth Edmonds	.	2	4	10	7
William Powers	1	2	1	.	.
Ephram Knight	2	7	2	8	6
Lewis Daniel	1	1	5	2	5
William Corbin	1	3	5	1	2
	29	61	78	49	47
Pg. 3					
Benjamin Hux	2	2	5	.	.
Henry Jones	1	.	3	.	.
Rebacah Hogg	.	6	5	.	.
Thomas Sanders	1	4	6	.	.
Daniel Green	1	2	3	.	.
Moses Read	1	1	6	1	1
George Green	1	1	2	.	1
William Hays	1	.	2	.	1
Thomas Crawford	2	4	6	13	21
Sarah Pritchett	.	5	2	.	.
Anderson Nunary	.	1	1	.	.
Sterling Daniel	1	1	4	.	.
John Saxon	1	2	3	4	3
William Heath	1	1	2	.	2
Thomas Smith	2	2	1	3	3
Benjn. Partin	1	4	3	.	.
Christian Sulivat	.	1	1	.	1
William Daniel	2	4	3	4	5
Thomas Marshall	1	1	2	2	3
John Dickens	1	2	2	2	1
Simon Jones	1	2	4	4	.
James Sikes	1	1	2	.	.
Benjn. Coats	1	3	2	.	.
William Iles	1	.	1	.	.
John Iles	1	2	6	1	.
William Sulivant	1	2	4	3	3
Randal Bull	1	.	1	1	.
[Total by Ed.]	27	54	82	38	45

Head of Household	WM 21-60 yrs.	WM under 21 & above 60	WF all ages	Blacks 12-50	Blacks under 12 & above 50
Total Dist. 2	70	156	211	116	129

District No. 3; taken by Lemuell Hogun 1st Febry. 1786.

Head of Household	WM 21-60 yrs.	WM under 21 & above 60	WF all ages	Blacks 12-50	Blacks under 12 & above 50
Pg. 1					
John Cook	1	1	5	.	.
John Drew	1	2	3	6	8
Thomas Drew	1	.	2	3	4
Solomon Drew	1	2	1	.	1
William Cane	.	1	1	.	.
Samuel Gayner	1	.	.	1	.
William Jackson	1	.	1	.	.
Ann Gayner	.	.	1	1	4
Joshua Drew	1	1	4	1	1
Hermon Strickland	1	1	4	.	.
Thomas Taylor	1	.	5	.	1
Harriss Taylor	1	2	2	.	.
James Hodges	1	4	4	.	.
Robert Hodges	1	.	1	.	.
Willie Hodges	1	1	4	.	.
John Carlile	1	1	3	.	.
John Kent	1	1	1	.	.
Thomas Good	.	1	1	.	1
Thomas High	1	4	5	.	.
Erastus L. Tippit	1	1	2	1	.
	17	23	50	13	20
Pg. 2					
Matthew Cartrite	.	4	2	.	1
James Alsobrook	1	4	2	.	2
Thomas Dew	1	4	2	.	.
Jesse Haynie	2	2	4	2	1
Benjn. Haynie	1	2	4	.	.
Ishum Hill	1	2	6	.	.
Caleb Rafield	2	2	2	.	.
William Spear	1	2	3	.	.
Marmaduke Young	1	5	2	5	7
Lewis Haynie	1	.	2	.	1
William Bynum Jr.	1	.	2	.	.
Nathan Spear	1	1	4	.	.
William Bynum Sr.	.	2	2	.	2
James Spear	1	.	.	.	.
William Kitchen	1	3	3	.	2
Phillip Rawls	1	3	5	.	.
Talbert Tucker	1	3	1	.	.
Robert Cotten	3	2	2	6	3
David Kauffmon	1	4	1	1	1
Lewis Brantley	1	7	3	.	.
Erastus Tippit	1	3	1	2	5

Head of Household	WM 21-60 yrs.	WM under 21 & above 60	WF all ages	Blacks 12-50	Blacks under 12 & above 50
John B. Cartrite	1	.	2	.	.
Mary Vick	.	1	7	.	.
Benjn. Dicken	4	3	5	9	9
Thos. Merritt	1	.	.	.	.
James Powell	1	1	3	.	.
Patience Hail	1	4	5	.	.
George Bell	1	2	4	2	1
	32	66	69	27	35
Pg. 3					
David Alsobrook	1	5	3	.	.
Marmaduke Norfleet	1	1	.	10	10
Absalum Merritt	1	4	5	7	5
Thos. Alsobrook	2	4	4	.	.
Edward Emmory	.	3	6	.	.
Sarah Merritt	1	3	6	4	5
Lamuel Hobgood	1	.	4	.	2
William Alsobrook	1	3	5	2	3
Edward Brantley	1	2	3	.	.
Martha Brantley	.	2	2	.	1
Thomas Brdley	1	4	3	.	.
Drewry Alsobrook	2	.	3	3	4
Jesse Alsobrook	1	1	1	.	.
John Alsobrook	1	2	3	3	3
Molley Ownsbey	.	.	3	.	1
William Cotten	1	1	2	3	4
Henneritter Hopson	.	1	2	.	1
Lamuel Bell	1	1	2	.	.
Eli Harriss	1	5	3	10	7
Willis Rawls	1	.	.	.	.
James Slater	1	3	3	10	6
Jacob O. Daniel	.	6	6	.	.
Benjn. Brantley	1	3	3	2	.
Benjn. Whitehead	1	3	5	1	1
Solomon Turner	1	1	4	2	2
Thomas Turner	1	.	.	1	.
John Chanel	1	6	2	.	.
Pg. 4					
James Cane	2	4	5	2	2
Mark Murrey	1	.	7	.	.
Mathew Packer	1	.	3	.	.
William Blackburn	1	.	3	.	.
Cloe Webb	1	.	3	.	.
James Braswell	.	5	4	.	.
Drew Braswell	1	1	3	.	.
Gibson Jackson	.	1	.	.	.
Hermon Strickland Sr.	.	1	2	.	.
John Strickland	1	1	2	.	.
Howel Alsobrook	1	5	4	.	.
James Alsobrook	1	.	3	1	.
Elijah Wilkins	1	4	2	1	1

Head of Household	WM 21-60 yrs.	WM under 21 & above 60	WF all ages	Blacks 12-50	Blacks under 12 & above 50
Elijah Hobgood	3	4	6	6	3
Clabrurn Alsobrook	.	1	.	.	.
	38	91	130	68	61
Pg. 5					
Mary Woller	.	2	4	.	.
Samuel Pass	1	.	2	1	2
John Butler	1	2	6	.	.
Nathanial Merritt	1	.	.	.	.
Lemuel Hogun	1	4	4	16	23
	4	8	16	17	25
Taken by Lemuel Hogun	17	23	50	13	20
	32	66	69	27	35
	38	91	130	68	61
	91	188	265	125	141

District No. 4, taken by Turner Mason, 17th Febry., 1786.

Head of Household	WM 21-60 yrs.	WM under 21 & above 60	WF all ages	Blacks 12-50	Blacks under 12 & above 50
Pg. 1					
Turner Mason	2	1	1	3	5
John Roach	1	3	2	.	.
Margery Hill	.	2	2	.	.
Joshua Jones	1	3	3	.	.
Henry Harper	1	3	3	1	.
Eliner Wood	.	3	3	.	.
Lucy Turner	1	3	2	6	9
Solomon Hawkins	1	4	3	.	.
Jordan Stafford	1	3	1	.	.
Bartlit Moorland	1	1	1	.	.
Isaac Harper	1	3	3	4	6
Benjamin Powell	1	1	2	2	3
Saml. Duffy	1	2	4	.	.
William Edmonds	1	.	5	.	.
William Grinstead	1	3	2	1	2
William Vaughn	1	1	1	2	1
James Perry	1	1	2	1	.
Christopher Hinton	1	1	2	1	.
Augustin Parrott	1	1	4	.	.
William Guthrie	1	2	4	1	.
William Smith	1	2	1	.	.
David Pugh	1	6	2	.	.
	21	49	59	22	26
Pg. 2					
Christopher Moss	2	1	2	6	9
Thomas Gill	.	4	3	.	.
Edward Hathcock	1	3	7	.	.
Mary Frances	1	2	3	.	.
Wm. Whitfield	1	4	5	2	1
Archabald Felts	2	1	2	2	1
Mical Hendrie	.	2	2	3	5

Head of Household	WM 21-60 yrs.	WM under 21 & above 60	WF all ages	Blacks 12-50	Blacks under 12 & above 50
Richard Howel	1	.	.	.	.
James Hays	1	.	.	.	.
William Ticker	2	5	2	.	.
John Rivald	1	4	2	.	.
Isam Hathcock	1	3	3	.	.
Vinson Harper	1	.	2	1	2
Joseph Perry	1	2	6	.	.
Edward Moorland	2	2	2	1	.
Richard Monford	3	5	3	.	.
William Downs	1	1	3	1	.
Joseph Parsons	1	.	.	7	8
Moses Smith	1	.	3	.	.
John Manders	1	.	2	.	.
Elizabeth Edmons	.	3	4	1	.
Wm. Williams	1	3	5	.	.
Ambros Harper	1	2	2	3	2
Thomas Neel	1	2	7	5	3
Sarah Corlew	.	3	7	.	.
Mary Wever	.	2	4	.	.
Frances Roberts	2	.	2	1	.
William Jackson	1	1	1	1	1
	30	58	84	34	32
Pg. 3					
Thorogood Demcy	1	4	5	.	.
Moses Batly/Batby	2	2	1	.	.
Elizabeth Weldon	.	1	3	17	16
Thos. Tabb, Esq.	3	.	1	24	33
Reuben Young	.	1	2	1	.
	6	8	12	42	49
No. 1	21	49	59	22	26
No. 2	30	53	84	24	32
No. 3	6	8	12	42	49
Turner Mason	57	110	155	98	67

District 5, taken by Giles Lang, 21st January 1786.

Pg. 1

Head of Household	WM 21-60 yrs.	WM under 21 & above 60	WF all ages	Blacks 12-50	Blacks under 12 & above 50
Ann Boregess ?	.	2	3	.	.
William Williams	1	3	6	.	.
William Cullen	1	4	5	.	.
Mathew Killingsworth	1	1	3	1	.
Nicholas Lewis	1	4	3	.	.
Sarah Rozar	.	2	2	1	1
Joseph Dicken	1	3	2	.	.
Elias Harris	1	4	5	2	.
Richard Blanton	1	2	3	.	1
Thomas Harlow	1	.	2	.	.
William Dicken Jr.	1	1	3	.	.

Head of Household	WM 21-60 yrs.	WM under 21 & above 60	WF all ages	Blacks 12-50	Blacks under 12 & above 50
Jacob Harper	.	3	3	.	.
Joseph Edmonson	.	1	2	.	.
John Purnal	2	4	5	1	.
William Brown	1	.	4	.	.
James Harwil (?)	.	4	1	.	.
Josiah Gardner	1	.	.	1	1
Philip Corlew	2	4	5	.	1
Richard Yarbrogh	1	3	4	.	.
	16	45	61	6	4
Pg. 2					
William Lovel	1	4	6	.	.
William Killingsworth	2	2	5	.	1
William Dicken Sr.	1	8	2	.	.
Daniel Crawley	1	2	4	.	.
Lucy Jones	.	2	2	2	1
Richard Richards	1	.	2	2	4
George Eubank	2	1	6	3	3
Joseph Eubank	1	.	3	3	1
William Crab	1	3	3	.	.
Henry Evens	2	1	4	.	.
John Wood	1	1	1	.	.
Mary Exum	.	2	2	.	.
John Allen	2	4	1	.	.
Isaac Harris	1	5	2	3	1
Geo Zollicoffer	1	4	3	7	13
Davis Bagby	1	2	6	1	1
Prissilla Barrot	.	6	2	1	2
Richard Bishop	1	2	1	4	2
Avis Haile	1	.	2	1	.
William Gillam	2	2	2	.	.
Jonathan Haile	1	5	5	.	.
William Gagby	1	.	1	.	.
William Smith	1	2	3	1	2
Williamson Haile	1	2	3	2	.
James Bloyse	2	.	4	.	.
Ann Potts	1	1	3	.	.
Jesse Roan	1	.	1	1	2
Sarah Taylor	.	2	3	1	1
Thos. Williams	1	2	2	7	12
[T by Compiler]	31	65	84	39	46
Pg. 3					
Heartwell Hyde	1	1	5	4	3
William Dubry	1	6	4	1	.
Theophilus Hayse	1	2	3	.	.
Clabern Waddle	1	3	2	.	.
Absalom Scott	1	2	2	.	.
John Roan	1	2	4	.	.
William Green	1	1	1	.	.
Robert Harris	1	2	3	.	.
Jesse Martin	1	1	1	.	.

STATE CENSUS OF NORTH CAROLINA 1784-1787

Head of Household	WM 21-60 yrs.	WM under 21 & above 60	WF all ages	Blacks 12-50	Blacks under 12 & above 50
Joseph Hawkins	1	3	2	.	.
David Hawkins	.	2	5	.	.
Henry Hawkins	1	.	1	.	.
Lucy Hawkins	.	.	3	.	.
Hannah Smith	.	1	2	.	.
Zechariah Smith	1	2	3	.	.
Joshua Stafford	1	1	1	.	.
John Hargrove	3	7	4	4	8
Sarah Hargrove	.	3	4	2	3
Elizabeth Bozeman	.	1	2	.	.
Richard Willis	1	3	2	.	.
Henry Hyde	2	3	3	8	10
Richard Thompson	1	5	5	.	.
Thomas Dicken	1	.	.	.	.
McCallister Vincent	1	3	3	.	.
Thomas Vincent	.	1	4	.	.
Willis Vincent	1	.	3	.	.
Giles Long	1	3	4	2	1
Sarah Green	1	1	3	1	1
	25	59	79	22	26
Total Dist. by Giles Long	72	179	125	67	76

Head of Household (Pg. 2)	WM 21-60 yrs.	WM under 21 & above 60	WF all ages	Blacks 12-50	Blacks under 12 & above 50
Edmund Irby	1	1	5	.	.
Elizabeth Denton	.	2	6	2	.
Elizabeth Boothe	.	.	1	.	.
Francis Mallory	3	1	1	4	8
Furnea Southall	1	1	3	2	1
Francis Coley	1	.	2	.	.
Frederik Lee	1	4	4	.	.
Francis Coley	1	3	3	.	.
Gilliam Newsum	1	1	1	2	4
George Pierson	1	2	5	.	.
Hubbard Perry or Terry	1	1	1	.	.
Henry H. Tucker	1	1	7	4	6
Hartwell Sledge	1	.	.	.	.
Henry Anselm	1	2	1	.	.
Hannah Coley	2	1	4	.	.
Job Garregus	1	.	1	.	.
James Carter	1	.	4	.	.
John Perry	1	3	2	.	.
John Gunn	1	2	1	.	.
James Shine	1	2	4	.	.
James Baker	1	2	6	2	.
John Ellis	1	1	2	.	.
John Toney	1	2	2	.	.
John Mallard	1	1	2	.	.
John Sledge	1	3	4	5	3
	26	39	72	21	23
[Correctly]		36			22

District 6, taken by Walter C. Ballard 16th Febry. 1786.

Head of Household (Pg. 1)	WM 21-60 yrs.	WM under 21 & above 60	WF all ages	Blacks 12-50	Blacks under 12 & above 50
Augustine Willis	1	.	3	10	6
Augustom Williams	1	.	1	.	.
Abraham Johnston	1	8	1	1	.
Archibald Sledge	1	3	3	4	2
Anne Pughe	.	.	1	10	10
Anne Coley	.	.	2	.	.
Agness Thompson	.	.	4	.	.
Anne Marlow	.	.	2	.	.
Benjamin Smith	1	.	2	.	.
Benjamin Bradey	1	2	2	.	2
Charles Hamlin	.	2	.	23	23
Charles Leath	1	5	6	4	3
Charles Carter	1	2	6	.	.
Charles Yarborough	1	4	1	.	.
Charles Wells	1	.	4	.	.
Charles Coley	2	6	14	.	.
David Owen	1	1	1	.	.
David Coley	2	.	5	.	.
Eldridge Clark	1	2	3	3	6
Edward Turner	1	.	.	.	.
	17	35	61	55	52

Head of Household (Pg. 3)	WM 21-60 yrs.	WM under 21 & above 60	WF all ages	Blacks 12-50	Blacks under 12 & above 50
John Story	1	2	3	.	.
John Justiss	1	7	5	4	6
Jonathan Carpenter	1	2	6	2	.
James Allen	1	.	.	2	.
James Coley	1	.	4	.	.
Jesse Carter	1	1	1	.	.
John Marlow	1	1	1	.	.
James Williamson	1	.	2	12	9
John Tucker	1	.	2	.	.
Jacob Carter	1	1	2	.	.
Jeffrey Coley	1	1	1	.	.
John King	1	.	.	.	.
John F. Jarrell	1	6	2	.	.
John Thompson	1	.	2	.	.
Keziah Coley	.	1	5	.	.
Lewis Johnston	1	.	1	.	.
Mark Rickman	1	4	3	.	.
Mary Ellis	.	1	5	5	3
Martha Wallis	.	2	2	.	.
Mary Clay	.	2	2	.	.
Mary Jolley	.	2	2	.	.

Head of Household	WM 21-60 yrs.	WM under 21 & above 60	WF all ages	Blacks 12-50	Blacks under 12 & above 50
Mary Hyde	.	.	3	3	1
Martha Still	.	.	2	.	.
Nancy Clark	.	2	3	2	2
Phillip Carter	1	1	2	.	.
Mary Smith	1	1	4	.	.
	18	37	65	30	21
Pg. 4					
Nathaniel Sledge	1	1	1	.	2
Nathaniel Hix	1	2	1	.	1
Phillip Morriss	2	2	6	.	.
Robert Carter	1	2	4	.	.
Robert Carter	2	4	3	.	.
Thomas Marshall	1	1	1	.	.
Thomas Graves	1	2	4	1	.
Thomas Poythress	1	1	2	.	.
Thomas Smith	1	.	1	.	.
Thomas Atkins	1	2	4	.	1
Vincent Vaughan	1	.	.	.	.
William Carter	2	2	5	3	6
William Ballard	1	.	1	2	1
Wm S. (T. ?) Ballard	1	.	.	4	4
William Pike	1	3	3	1	.
William Jenkins	1	4	5	2	1
William S. Carter	1	1	1	.	.
William Johnston	1	1	3	1	.
William Jones	1	.	3	.	.
William Thompson	1	.	3	.	.
William Smith	1	1	4	.	.
	24	29	55	14	15
Total	85	140	253	120	111

W. C. Ballard

District 7, taken by Shadrick Rutland
28 Jany. 1786.

Head of Household	WM 21-60 yrs.	WM under 21 & above 60	WF all ages	Blacks 12-50	Blacks under 12 & above 50
Pg. 1					
William Vaughn	2	4	1	2	3
John Young	1	1	3	2	5
Lucia Bryant	.	1	3	3	2
Thomas Davis	2	1	3	14	13
Thomas Merritt	1	1	5	2	4
Wm. Grimmer Sr.	1	2	5	.	.
John Grimmer	1	1	4	.	.
Elisha Howell	1	.	3	1	.
Wm. Whitehead Jr.	1	2	1	.	.
John Jones	1	3	2	.	.
Stephen Merritt	1	1	1	.	.
Drewry Merritt	3	5	5	2	1
Martha Vasser	.	1	4	.	.
Jesse Shute	1	.	1	.	.

Head of Household	WM 21-60 yrs.	WM under 21 & above 60	WF all ages	Blacks 12-50	Blacks under 12 & above 50
John Foort	1	5	1	20	14
Wm. Rogers	1	2	2	.	.
Mathew Joyner	1	2	5	1	.
Wm. Whitehead Sr.	1	4	3	4	6
Martha Edwards	.	2	5	12	9
Solomon Dawson	2	2	6	2	2
Barthw. Barnes	1	1	2	4	3
John Bell	1	1	2	2	1
Wm. Champion	2	1	3	1	3
	26	43	70	72	67
Pg. 2					
Jemmima Bryant	1	1	3	1	1
Jesse Edwards	1	1	3	1	1
Samuel Bradly	1	.	.	.	.
Mary Howell	.	1	5	.	1
James Jossy	1	3	5	5	8
Josiah Dixon	1	1	1	1	.
Jesse Dixon	1	.	4	2	5
Benjamin Pully	1	4	7	4	3
Brown Edwards	1	.	2	.	.
John Moore	1	.	6	4	3
James Parker	1	1	2	6	5
Elijah Pope	1	3	2	1	1
Henry Daffin	1	2	1	3	2
Lucia Patrick	.	.	4	.	.
John Edwards	1	1	3	.	1
Lemuel Watson	1	2	3	1	.
Patince Brown	.	.	3	7	2
Susanah Whitehead	.	.	4	4	3
Wm. Grimmer Jr.	1	.	2	.	1
Elias Foort	2	1	1	10	8
Sugans Foort	1	.	.	4	1
Sarah Champion	.	3	2	.	.
Ann Whitaker	.	1	3	3	4
Henry Hancock	1	.	1	1	1
James Smith	.	2	7	40	22
James Brantly	1	2	3	12	7
Jurdan Baker	1	.	1	.	.
Randell Robertson	1	3	4	.	1
Sarah Bell	.	1	2	3	1
Elisha Bell	.	2	1	5	6
	22	35	85	118	88
Pg. 3					
Hawkins Whitaker	1	1	3	.	.
Joshua Manning	1	3	2	.	.
Ann Baker	.	1	2	.	.
John Sutherland	1	2	6	.	.
Joshua Barker	2	2	4	1	2
Mary Barker	.	2	2	3	1
Elizabeth Jones	.	3	4	2	1

Head of Household	WM 21-60 yrs.	WM under 21 & above 60	WF all ages	Blacks 12-50	Blacks under 12 & above 50
John Williamson	1	.	.	.	.
David Terry (?)	1	.	1	.	.
Edward Whitaker	1	1	2	.	.
Lewis Brewer	1	3	2	.	.
Shad Rutland	2	1	3	5	6
	11	19	31	11	10

Feb. 20th. Taken by Shd Rutland

No. 1	26	43	70	72	67
No. 2	22	35	85	118	88
No. 3	11	19	31	11	10
	59	97	186	201	165

District 8, taken by William Branch Jr.
20 Febry. 1786.

Pg. 1

William Branch	.	5	3	9	7
James Flewellin	2	1	5	4	2
William Hill	1	1	3	1	.
Abraham Hill	2	2	3	.	.
William Dillard	1	2	5	1	.
William Flewellin	2	3	2	2	7
Henry Overstreet	1	2	4	6	.
Thomas Low	1	2	5	1	1
Daniel Wilburn	1	2	2	2	.
George Duncan	1	1	4	1	.
William Swett	1	.	3	.	.
Abraham Swett	1	2	5	.	.
Jeremiah Dawgitt	1	3	2	3	.
John Bradley	2	1	4	.	.
James Turner	1	1	2	.	.
William Turner	.	2	2	2	.
Thomas Wigins	1	1	1	.	.
Edwin Turner	1	1	6	2	5
John Morgin	1	3	4	.	.
	21	35	65	34	22

Pg. 2

Lovatt Burges	1	2	3	14	16
William Merett	2	2	3	.	2
William Duncan	2	5	5	.	1
Owin Dillard	1	.	1	1	2
Jonathan Garland	1	1	4	.	.
Burwell Smith	1	.	.	.	.
Isam Philips	1	3	3	.	.
Morgin Lewis	1	1	3	3	4
John Gaskins	1	2	3	.	.
Shadrack Meritt	1	.	5	1	2
Morgin Lewis	1	.	2	.	.
John Lewis	1	.	4	.	.

Head of Household	WM 21-60 yrs.	WM under 21 & above 60	WF all ages	Blacks 12-50	Blacks under 12 & above 50
Charlis Lewis	1	2	2	.	.
Fedrock Meritt	1	1	3	1	.
Robin Knight	1	3	1	.	.
Thomas Meritt	1	.	1	.	.
(M?)adrack Meritt	1	3	3	.	.
William Gulledg	1	.	4	.	.
Benjamine Crowell	2	.	.	4	3
Benjamine Pearce	1	3	4	2	1
Edward King	1	6	9	.	.
Joseph Eelbeck	3	.	.	9	17
Jane Eelbeck	1	1	3	3	1
Baxer Thrower	1	2	1	.	.
Will Cox	1	2	2	.	.
John Turner	2	.	2	.	.
George Wallice	1	3	5	4	.
Joel Dillard	1	1	1	3	1
	34	43	77	45	50

Pg. 3

Presillar Philips	.	5	3	.	1
Egbirt Haywood	1	4	4	12	7
Lewis Whitehead	2	3	6	1	1
John Meritt	1	4	2	.	.
William Turner	1	.	.	.	.
John Brickell	1	3	5	7	8
Henry Molley	1	.	.	.	.
George Wast (West?)	1	2	3	3	3
Daniel Thompson	1	.	4	3	.
John Ring	3	2	.	.	.
Thomas Ring	1	.	.	.	.
Moses Mathis	1	4	5	.	.
James Pipkins Slaus *	2	.	2	1	.
Feby Smith	.	.	5	2	3
Marthew Mitchell	.	.	2	.	1
Temprance Smith	.	2	3	.	.
John Mitchell	1	.	4	1	.
John Philips	1	4	1	.	.
Samuel Rolings	1	3	4	.	.
John Burtt	1	3	3	2	3
Hardy May	1	2	2	.	.
William Branch Jr.	1	.	3	.	.
John Clayton	1	5	3	2	2
	22	41	58	35	27
pg. 2	34	43	77	45	50
pg. 1	21	35	65	34	22
	78	123	193	116	101
			601		

*could be Slans, Staus or Stans ?

District 9; taken by Robert Freear, Dec. 24, 1785. Returned to Feb. Court 1786.

Pg. 1

Head of Household	WM 21-60 yrs.	WM under 21 & above 60	WF all ages	Blacks 12-50	Blacks under 12 & above 50
Nicholas Long	.	7	6	50	43
John Kelley	1	2	2	.	.
Peter Isabell	1	1	1	.	.
John Inglis	1	.	2	2	1
James Faucett	1	2	4	.	.
Andrew Miller	1	.	.	.	.
James Watson	1	.	.	.	.
William Muir	1	1	.	4	.
Robert Freear	1	2	3	6	3
Joseph Montfort	1	.	.	.	.
Jesper FitzGerrald	1	.	.	.	.
James Culfer	1	.	.	.	.
Patrick Martin	1	.	.	2	5
Anthony Hart	1	1	1	9	1
Mike Omally	1	.	.	1	.
Elizabeth Aron	.	1	2	.	.
Nicholas Gurley	1	.	2	.	.
Goodrum Davis	1	.	.	6	6
Archibald Davis	1	.	.	6	.
Richard Smith	.	3	2	.	.
John Watson	3	1	3	7	6
Peter Turner	1	.	.	2	3
Britain Jones	1	.	2	1	.
Samuel Marram	1	.	.	.	.
David Edwards	1	.	.	.	.
Josiah Sparks	1	2	2	2	.
John Faucett	1	.	1	.	.
John Ford	1	.	.	.	.
Georgia Bradley	1	.	.	4	9
John Coleman	1	2	3	1	.
Patrick McDonnald	1	1	1	.	.
William R. Davis	1	1	2	14	14
John B. Ashe	1	1	3	20	28
Robert Powers	1	.	4	2	2
John Marshall	1	1	1	2	4
John Eaton	1	2	1	9	2
Charles Pasteur	1	2	7	12	19
Peter Qualls	2	5	4	5	3
John Geddy	2	.	4	22	10
Robert Fenner	2	.	1	9	6
James Martin	1	1	6	18	18
William Gilmour	2	3	1	6	6
William Martin	1	2	5	23	21
Howell Tatum	1	.	.	.	.

Chas. Eads Ovr for

Head of Household	WM 21-60 yrs.	WM under 21 & above 60	WF all ages	Blacks 12-50	Blacks under 12 & above 50
J. Harvey	2	.	3	14	21
James Pasteur	1	.	1	10	9
John Kinchin	1	1	.	6	10
James Tatum	1	.	.	.	.
James W. Green	1	1	2	25	12
William Barksdale	2	1	.	6	4
Thomas Ferrell	1	.	.	1	2
	56	47	82	307	265

Pg. 2

Head of Household	WM 21-60 yrs.	WM under 21 & above 60	WF all ages	Blacks 12-50	Blacks under 12 & above 50
Gilmour & Hendric(?)	4	.	.	42	46
William Lowe	3	4	4	16	9
Jesse Reid	1	.	3	.	1
Montfort Eelbeck Sr.	3	.	8	8	4
Montfort Eelbeck Jr.	1	1	4	6	.
Thomas Hogg	1	2	1	6	12
John Poase	1	.	.	6	1
Jesse Rhymes	1	.	.	.	.
Daniel Pointer	1	4	2	3	.
Hance Bond	1	1	3	12	6
Willie Jones	1	2	4	55	45
Jean McClanahan	.	.	1	5	.
Benjamin McCullock	1	5	4	41	42
	75	66	116	507	431

R. Freear

District 10; taken by Samuel Crowell 22nd May 178-

Pg. 1

Head of Household	WM 21-60 yrs.	WM under 21 & above 60	WF all ages	Blacks 12-50	Blacks under 12 & above 50
Joseph Whelas	1	1	1	.	.
James Whelas	1	1	7	.	.
Matt^w. Rabun	1	1	7	6	7
James Grant	1	1	1	5	5
John Branch	2	3	5	11	12
John Bradford	2	2	9	10	18
Henry Bradford	1	1	2	4	4
Jesse Butts	1	3	3	.	.
Joseph Daniell	1	4	4	1	.
James Kneel	1	2	2	.	.
William Read Jr.	1	3	4	.	.
Joseph Willie	1	1	1	.	.
Wilie Grissel	1	.	2	.	.
Addam White	1	3	2	.	.
Joel Walker	1	.	3	4	2
William West	1	2	2	.	.
Thomas Drummon	1	5	2	.	.
John Smith	1	2	3	.	.
William Bradley	1	1	1	.	.

STATE CENSUS OF NORTH CAROLINA 1784-1787

Head of Household	WM 21-60 yrs.	WM under 21 & above 60	WF all ages	Blacks 12-50	Blacks under 12 & above 50
Mary Caple	.	.	2	.	.
	21	36	63	41	48
Pg. 2					
Jarrott Edward	1	.	4	.	.
Joseph Edward	.	4	3	1	2
Jonathan Lock	1	3	4	.	.
Sion Daniell	1	.	1	2	.
Peter Daniell	1	4	3	1	.
Luraney Herington	1	.	2	7	2
Israel West	1	.	2	6	10
Martha Wright	.	1	4	.	.
Robert Motley	1	3	5	.	.
John Lock	1	3	5	1	.
Anderson Graves	1	.	1	.	.
Ransom Edwards	.	2	5	.	.
William Harburt	1	1	2	1	3
John Read	1	2	5	1	.
James Baker	1	1	2	3	1
Thomas Rose	1	.	4	.	.
Jesse Everitt	2	2	2	4	5
Margrat Hillard	.	1	1	1	3
Solomon Turner	1	1	4	.	.
Caleb Morgan	1	4	2	.	.
William Batchelor	1	2	4	5	5
George Everage	1	1	4	.	.
John Tillery	1	.	.	2	.
William Wooten	1	2	2	4	8
John Marshell	1	3	3	5	6
Griffin Morris	1	2	3	.	.
Moses Butts	1	4	3	4	7
Jerimiah Turner	1	1	6	.	.
Henry Purkins Jr.	1	5	6	.	1
Thomas Purkins	1	2	1	.	.
Aaron Parker	1	1	6	.	.
Nathaniel Carlile	1	1	4	.	1
	51	92	106	89	102
Pg. 3					
Joseph Edward Jr.	1	1	4	2	1
Ambrose Daniell	1	5	3	.	.
Nathan Council	1	3	4	.	.
Jesse Morris	1	6	3	.	.
James Nichols	1	4	3	.	.
William Morran	1	3	7	.	.
Peter Kathorn	1	3	.	.	.
Samuel Morran	2	1	1	.	1
Jesse Pope	1	4	4	3	5
Hardy Whelus	1	2	3	.	.
William Purkins	1	2	.	.	.
Henry Purkins Jr.	.	1	2	.	.
Timothy Ives	1	1	5	.	.

Head of Household	WM 21-60 yrs.	WM under 21 & above 60	WF all ages	Blacks 12-50	Blacks under 12 & above 50
Charles Parker	1	3	5	.	.
Joseph Whelas	2	4	4	1	.
William Morran Jr.	1	.	.	.	.
Josiah Lock	2	1	4	.	.
William Hattaway	.	2	3	.	.
Thomas Locler(?)	1	2	4	.	.
Ladamon Shelton	.	3	4	1	4
Shadarack Wever	1	3	3	.	.
William Cummin	1	.	1	.	.
Allen Sweat	.	1	2	.	.
Adley Morres	1	.	2	1	.
Moses Purkins	1	1	1	.	.
Hezekiah Morres	1	4	5	.	.
Arthur Shuffell	1	4	4	.	.
Thomas Hynes	1	.	2	.	.
Exum Scott	1	5	3	.	.
Samuel Crowell	1	2	1	8	3
Bethlehem Turner	.	1	4	.	.
Holloway Morris	1	.	3	1	.
	81	166	260	106	115
Pg. 4					
Richard Sute	1	1	2	.	.
Trustram Drake	2	4	1	.	1
Luke Nichols	2	1	2	.	.
Frederick Man	1	2	2	.	.
Jas. Wollsey	1	1	3	2	3
	88	175	270	108	119

District 11; taken by Matt C. Whitaker, 9th Feby. 1786.

Head of Household	WM 21-60 yrs.	WM under 21 & above 60	WF all ages	Blacks 12-50	Blacks under 12 & above 50
Pg. 1					
Ambrose Pitman	2	2	2	4	4
William Barrow	1	4	3	23	22
John Bass	1	.	3	7	5
Joseph Carter	1	3	3	9	10
Robert Barrow	1	.	1	2	1
David Pulley	1	4	3	2	2
Thos. Applewhite	1	5	2	.	.
Robert Brantley	2	1	4	4	7
John Wyatt	1	4	3	.	.
Jesse Wyatt	1	2	2	.	.
John Dancy	2	.	1	5	4
William Brantley	1	2	6	1	.
Arthur Pitman	1	4	2	1	2
Elisha Pitman	1	4	7	4	6
John Denton	1	1	2	1	1
Peter Bird	1	2	3	3	2
Arthur Speer	1	4	2	1	2
Arthur Whitehead	1	4	5	2	2
Samuel Speir	1	2	4	.	.
	22	48	58	69	72

Head of Household	WM 21-60 yrs.	WM under 21 & above 60	WF all ages	Blacks 12-50	Blacks under 12 & above 50
Pg. 2					
Sanuel Foreman	1	4	6	2	2
Allen Fort	2	4	3	8	1
Richard Russel	1	2	3	5	2
William Merritt	1	.	3	1	2
Elias Fort	1	.	.	.	.
Robert Ward	1	1	4	2	1
Lewis Wyatt	1	3	2	.	.
William Davis	1	2	4	.	.
George Kerkly	1	.	2	.	.
Barrum Sands	1	3	2	5	6
William Jackson	1	1	1	3	.
William Jackson Jr.	1	.	1	.	.
David Hyatt	1	2	4	1	1
Samuel Pitman	1	4	5	4	5
Benjn. Rowell	1	3	3	4	8
John Steptoe	1	1	3	1	1
Arthur West	1	.	1	2	1
Arthur West Jun.	1	2	2	1	4
John Desnall	1	1	1	.	.
Xpher Haynes	1	.	1	3	4
Willis Fort	.	1	1	2	3
James Wyatt	1	.	2	.	.
	22	34	54	44	41
Pg. 3					
Rhodham Rawlings	2	2	2	8	4
John Whitaker	1	5	5	10	7
William Noblin	1	1	2	3	3
William Bass	2	1	2	2	3
Cary Whitaker	1	.	2	8	9
Sarah Jones	.	1	3	2	2
Elizabeth Lane	.	2	3	9	8
John Wooten	1	2	2	1	2
Richard Whitaker	1	2	3	8	9
James Ward	1	4	4	4	1
Thomas Howell	.	3	2	4	6
Lewis Whitehead	2	3	6	1	1
Matt C. Whitaker	2	.	.	16	14
	14	26	37	86	69
No. 1	22	48	58	69	72
No. 2	22	34	54	44	41
No. 3	14	26	37	86	69
	58	118	149	199	182

District 12; taken by Thomas Harvey, 12 February 1786.

Head of Household	WM 21-60 yrs.	WM under 21 & above 60	WF all ages	Blacks 12-50	Blacks under 12 & above 50
Pg. 1					
Thomas Bull	1	3	5	3	3
Thomas Williams	.	1	2	1	.
Moses Gains	1	4	5	.	.

Head of Household	WM 21-60 yrs.	WM under 21 & above 60	WF all ages	Blacks 12-50	Blacks under 12 & above 50
David Matthis	1	2	3	.	1
John Lee	2	4	5	4	4
Richard Mathis	1	6	3	4	1
Lovick Worley	1	1	2	.	.
John Broom	.	1	1	.	.
John Cleaves	1	5	6	.	1
Edward Jordán	1	3	3	.	.
Rubin More &c.	1	1	8	.	.
Richd. Fleweling Junr.	1	2	4	.	.
Isham Pulley	1	1	5	1	.
Jos. Jordan	1	2	3	.	.
William Jorden	1	4	2	.	.
Taylor Fleweling	1	2	2	1	1
Jno. Cone &c.	2	2	2	3	4
Saml Porter	1	3	6	1	6
Saml Yarbour	1	1	6	4	6
Jno. Worley	1	1	4	.	.
Charles Studavant	1	.	1	.	.
	21	49	78	22	27
Pg. 2					
Burrel Broom	1	4	2	.	.
Phil Vinson	1	4	4	.	.
Jos. Birt	2	7	6	7	4
Benj. Doles	2	1	3	2	2
Jno. Pritchett &c	1	5	4	1	.
Jesse Doles	1	1	4	.	.
Go. Angell	1	2	3	1	3
Moses Winter	1	2	4	.	.
William Fuqua &c	1	3	4	.	.
Francies Taylor	1	3	4	.	.
Shadrack Roggers	1	.	3	.	1
William Bruce	1	2	2	.	.
Francies Weaver	.	3	10	.	.
Lucy Broom	.	1	1	.	.
Richd Fleweling Sr.	.	2	2	.	.
Sarah Hopkins	1	3	3	.	.
John Long	2	3	3	2	1
Isham Davis	1	6	4	3	4
Wm. Pritchett &c	1	1	6	1	2
Wm. Pearman (?)	1	5	3	.	.
Saml Williams	1	2	5	.	1
Jno. Stevens	1	3	3	.	.
Wm. Sentel	1	1	2	.	.
Jas. Conner	1	3	6	1	.
Thos. Hervey Senr	2	4	5	8	11
Elijah Humphris	1	1	2	4	5

Head of Household	WM 21-60 yrs.	WM under 21 & above 60	WF all ages	Blacks 12-50	Blacks under 12 & above 50
William Hervey	1	4	3	.	.
Jno. Chappel	1	3	3	4	8
Christopher Pritchett	1	3	2	2	3
Saml Smith	1	2	7	4	4
Isaack Kirk	1	2	5	4	6
Edmon Raines &c?	3	2	5	3	5
JoS. JnO. Worley	1	3	3	.	.
	34	88	125	47	60
Pg. 3					
William Slautter &c	2	1	1	4	6
Elisha Hurt	1	1	3	1	6
Val. Garner	1	1	7	.	.
Peter Edwards	1	2	5	3	4
Tig Dameron	1	1	6	1	.
Capt. JnO. Powers	1	4	4	5	5
William Gilbert Sr.	1	1	3	1	.
Gab. Gilbert?	1	2	3	1	1
Jas. Gilbert	1	.	3	.	.
Saml. Williams	2	.	2	.	.
Abraham Brinkley	1	2	2	4	1
Jos. Williams	1	1	2	.	.
Jery Matthis	1	4	3	3	2
Jery Sulavant	1	4	5	.	.
Archbl. Gaulden (?)	1	1	2	.	.
Jas. Mathis, Esq.	1	5	4	6	3
Wm. Brinkley Sr.	1	2	.	2	4
Robert Grigs [No figures returned]					
Jno. Grigs	1	1	2	13	21
Richd. Birt [No return]					
Wm. Holt	1	.	4	.	.
Thos. Cavanah [No return]					
David Matthis [No return]					
Jas. Daniel [No return]					
Jos. Williams Esq.	2	2	5	14	11
Jas. Matthis	2	.	.	10	9
Mrs. Ann Hunt Alston	.	1	3	11	10
JoS. Alston	2	.	.	6	4
Gideon Alston	.	1	.	6	6
Jas. Parker [No return]					
Saml. Hawkins	1	.	.	.	.
Thos. Roggers	1	4	4	.	.
William Wood	1	.	1	.	.
Benj. Richardson	1	5	6	.	.
Abner Fleweling	1	2	2	3	4
	32	47	81	94	110

Head of Household	WM 21-60 yrs.	WM under 21 & above 60	WF all ages	Blacks 12-50	Blacks under 12 & above 50
Pg. 4					
Wm. Richardson [No return]					
Thos. Grigs [No return]					
Jas. Weever	1	1	2	.	.
Charles Jonston [No return]					
Jno. Hervey	1	.	.	.	.
Isham Rawser	1	2	3	.	.
Saml. Matthis	1	3	3	1	.
	4	6	8	1	.
Taken by Thos. Harvey	21	49	78	22	27
	34	88	125	47	60
	32	47	81	94	11
	91	190	292	164	98

District 13; taken by Gideon Harris 20th day of Febry. 1786.

Head of Household	WM 21-60 yrs.	WM under 21 & above 60	WF all ages	Blacks 12-50	Blacks under 12 & above 50
Pg. 1					
Gideon Harriss	1	2	8	8	1
David Hardy	1	4	4	4	3
Edward Good	.	7	5	.	.
Francis Williams	1	1	2	2	1
Robert Green	2	3	2	2	3
Burril King	1	5	4	.	.
James Gill	1	1	4	1	3
John Corlew	.	2	2	.	2
John Green	1	4	3	.	.
William Good	1	1	3	.	.
Thomas Miles	.	2	4	.	.
George Morris Sr	1	4	3	7	11
Joshua Sikes	1	2	2	.	.
William Morris	1	.	.	1	.
Dunston Morris	1	1	8	.	.
John Stafforo	1	.	4	.	1
Charles Blanton	.	2	2	2	.
Joel Sikes	1	5	6	.	.
Benjamin Williams	1	.	1	4	3
Roe Harris	3	.	1	6	2
George Morris Jr.	1	1	1	.	2
	20	47	69	37	32
Pg. 2					
William Mehone	1	2	5	2	1
Henry Dauson	1	4	2	4	.
Littlebery Green	1	3	4	3	1
Jacob Sikes	1	.	1	.	.
Joab Sikes	1	.	2	.	.
Phillip Adams	1	.	3	.	1

Head of Household	WM 21-60 yrs.	WM under 21 & above 60	WF all ages	Blacks 12-50	Blacks under 12 & above 50
Mary Solomon	.	4	2	.	.
John Linsey	2	4	6	13	10
Hoolman Southall	1	1	4	3	3
Joshua Gamons	1	3	4	.	.
John Brown	1	4	2	.	.
James Wright	1	.	1	1	1
Matthias Gariguss	1	3	2	.	.
Edward Elams	1	2	4	.	.
Jese Brown	1	4	2	.	.
William Turner	1	2	3	.	.
John Roaper	2	.	7	2	2
Richard Stevans	1	5	6	.	.
Joel Davis	1	.	2	.	.
Richard Stevens Sr.	.	1	1	.	.
Samuel Madix	1	2	4	.	.
Willis Alston	2	4	6	19	20
Charles Ash	2	5	3	.	.
William Coats	1	1	4	.	.
Molton Carter	1	2	4	.	.
Gray Tucker	1	1	1	.	.
Antoney Edwards	.	2	6	.	.
Thomas Tucker	1	2	3	.	.
Wintrup Hillton	1	1	5	.	.
	30	62	99	47	39
Pg. 3					
William Mehonee	2	4	6	2	1
John Mehona(d?)	2	.	3	.	1
Sarah Williams	.	.	3	.	1
Lamuel Sikes	1	.	7	.	.
Mary Leathco	.	2	4	.	.
	5	6	23	2	2
	30	62	99	47	39
	20	47	69	37	32
Total amt.	55	115	191	86	73

In obedience to the Worshipful Cort [Court] of Halifax County in the State North Carolin(a), I have taken the above list of the souls of those that hath given in the list of themselves familys in &c.

Gideon Harris
Febry 24th, 1786

District 14; taken by John Drew, 1st February 1786.
Pg. 1

Head of Household	WM 21-60 yrs.	WM under 21 & above 60	WF all ages	Blacks 12-50	Blacks under 12 & above 50
James Myhand	1	3	1	3	2
Frances Allen	3	2	.	3	2
Elisha Williams	1	4	4	12	8

Head of Household	WM 21-60 yrs.	WM under 21 & above 60	WF all ages	Blacks 12-50	Blacks under 12 & above 50
Jeremiah (D?)ems	1	.	.	.	.
Joab Cotton	1	7	4	14	21
Francis Boil	1	.	.	.	.
Elijah Johnson	1	.	.	.	1
Thomas Logan	1	.	.	.	.
Garrod Young	1	1	2	4	2
James Duke	1	1	3	3	4
Joshuay Hill	1	.	.	.	.
Jonathan Joiner	1	.	.	1	.
Thomas Shields	1	.	.	4	3
Arther Smith	2	3	3	28	32
Blount Whitmill	1	3	3	4	4
Jacob Barrow	1	1	4	4	4
Joshua Barker	.	2	.	3	4
Joel Joiner	1	2	7	7	8
Dolph Young	1	1	5	5	8
James Griffin	1	1	3	2	1
Jeremiah Nelms	1	1	6	10	9
Henry Hoge/Hage	1	5	2	3	4
Henry Joiner	1	.	.	1	.
Cley Joiner	1	1	1	1	.
Blount Joiner	1	.	2	5	10
Benj. Sils	1	2	3	.	.
William Wiggins	1	2	1	5	3
William Adkinson	1	1	1	1	1
John Doles	1	1	3	1	.
	31	44	58	124	131
Pg. 2					
John Addams	1	1	4	3	1
Sarah Doles	.	2	3	1	.
Isom Sils	.	1	4	.	.
Jesse Brewer	1	2	5	.	1
Robert Spencer	1	2	3	2	3
Henry Hunter	1	.	1	3	5
Samuel Simson	1	.	1	.	.
James Farrow	1	3	3	.	.
Martha Applewhite	.	.	2	4	6
Isom Scott	1	2	3	.	.
Fill Jones	.	1	3	.	.
John Thomas	1	5	3	5	10
Moses Bisshop	1	.	1	1	.
Asabil Griffin	.	3	1	3	7
Amos Hoke	1	.	.	.	.
Sarah Bisshop	.	2	3	3	2
William Bryant	1	1	2	5	6
Moses Barrow	2	.	1	3	2
Thos. Boyakon	1	.	.	8	7
William Boyken	1	.	.	6	6

STATE CENSUS OF NORTH CAROLINA 1784-1787

Head of Household	WM 21-60 yrs.	WM under 21 & above 60	WF all ages	Blacks 12-50	Blacks under 12 & above 50
John Bisshop	1	2	3	1	.
Benj. Fourmon	1	3	2	6	4
Elexr. Loid	1	2	2	.	.
John Young	1	.	2	3	4
Lewis Willifred	1	.	2	.	.
Josiah Duke	1	1	2	5	4
Elexr. McComb	1	1	1	.	.
Thos. Jones	1	1	3	1	.
Arch^s. Young	1	.	.	.	.
Thos. Young	1	2	6	3	5
Benj. Blackburn	1	5	1	.	.
Norfleet Harriss	1	.	.	10	7
John Drew	1	2	3	26	10
	28	44	70	102	111
	31	44	58	124	131
	59	88	128	226	242

District 15; taken by Thomas Pace 10th
Feby. 1786.
Pg. 1

Head of Household	WM 21-60 yrs.	WM under 21 & above 60	WF all ages	Blacks 12-50	Blacks under 12 & above 50
Jesse Sturdevant	1	6	3	1	2
John Winfield	.	1	1	1	2
Stphen (?) Samson	1	.	1	.	5
Adam Heath	1	2	2	2	4
Mathew Harris	1	1	3	2	4
William Heath	1	.	.	.	.
Thomas Hill	.	1	2	49	36
Joseph Ward	1	1	4	1	.
Mason Thrower	1	.	2	3	3
Thomas Rock	1	2	2	.	.
William Harris	1	1	3	.	3
John Richason	.	4	1	.	.

[Page wrinkled when laminated, thus obliterating two surnames below]

Head of Household	WM 21-60 yrs.	WM under 21 & above 60	WF all ages	Blacks 12-50	Blacks under 12 & above 50
Joseph [----]	1	1	7	.	.
Phillip [----]	.	1	.	.	.
Benjamin Thrower	.	1	3	.	.
Thomas Thrower	.	3	1	4	5
William Etheredge	1	1	.	.	.
Aaron Etheredge	.	1	2	2	.
Henry Restore Jones	1	3	4	2	7
Aaron Clark	1	4	3	.	.
Caleb Etheredge Jr	1	1	2	.	.
	14	35	46	67	68

Pg. 2

Head of Household	WM 21-60 yrs.	WM under 21 & above 60	WF all ages	Blacks 12-50	Blacks under 12 & above 50
Caleb Etheredge Sr	.	3	2	1	1
James H(ee?)th	1	.	2	2	2
Jesse Williams	1	2	3	7	8
Robert Clark	.	1	.	.	.
Eley Williams	1	2	6	2	2
Saml. Scarborough	1	1	5	.	.
Joshua Butt	1	3	7	.	2

Head of Household	WM 21-60 yrs.	WM under 21 & above 60	WF all ages	Blacks 12-50	Blacks under 12 & above 50
Robert Etheredge	1	2	2	1	1
Willis Powel	1	6	2	.	.
S(usan?) Troughton	.	1	1	.	.
Samuel Smith	1	.	.	2	1
James Judge	.	1	2	3	2
Joseph Cogbun	.	1	.	.	.
William West	1	.	1	4	4
Thos. Lent Hall	1	.	3	1	3
Benjamin Hines	1	.	3	1	1
Elizabeth Heath	.	1	2	1	3
John Heeth	1	.	.	.	.
Moses Heeth	.	1	.	.	.
Jesse Heeth	.	1	.	.	.
John Burgde(?)	.	2	2	.	.
Mornin Evens	.	2	2	.	.
Ellender Evens	.	1	1	.	.
Cornelas Clark	.	1	.	.	.
Lamuel Nicholson	.	1	2	4	3
Joseph Nicholson	1	2	3	9	4
William Hill	1	.	1	7	4
Nanny Pitts	.	3	5	2	4
Mark Pitts	1	3	2	2	3
Lewis Pitts	.	.	.	2	4
Henry Pitts	.	1	.	2	4
Rebeckah Parham	.	3	6	3	1
William Sikes	1	1	3	.	1
	16	46	68	56	57

Pg. 3

Head of Household	WM 21-60 yrs.	WM under 21 & above 60	WF all ages	Blacks 12-50	Blacks under 12 & above 50
James Wiatt	1	2	4	2	.
John Guttery	.	1	2	.	.
Richard Hill	1	5	8	5	7
William Laws	.	2	.	2	1
Randolph Scoot	1	1	3	.	.
Richard Heeth	1	2	6	3	.
Sarah Heeth	.	.	2	2	3
John Wright	1	6	2	4	8
Lawrance Mooney	.	1	.	.	.
William Pulley	1	4	5	3	2
Radford Butt	.	1	.	.	.
Henry Robertson	.	1	1	.	.
Bennit Wood	.	4	2	4	8
Young Davis	.	1	.	.	.
Charles Anderson	.	2	2	1	.
William Davis	.	1	2	1	.
Ambress Hadley	.	2	3	3	4
Samuell(torn) Smith	.	1	3	.	.
Aaron [---] (torn)	.	4	1	.	.
John Blunt	.	1	.	.	.
Henry Drury	.	1	.	.	.

69

Head of Household	WM 21-60 yrs.	WM under 21 & above 60	WF all ages	Blacks 12-50	Blacks under 12 & above 50
Arthur Davis	1	4	6	5	3
Thomas Bridgers	.	1	.	.	.
Joseph Hadley	1	2	3	1	2
Prier Gardner	.	3	3	1	3
Mary Passmore	.	4	8	2	4
Arthur Long	.	2	3	.	.
Totals by Ed.	8	59	67	45	45
Pg. 4					
Joseph Garges	.	1	1	.	.
Stephen Marsal	.	2	4	.	.
William Marshall	.	1	.	.	.
Josiah Hancock	.	1	.	.	.
Thomas Matthis	1	4	7	.	.
Isaac Dean	1	4	3	1	.
Robert Worley	1	.	3	.	.
Wilaba Sycks	.	1	4	.	.
Henry Sycks	1	.	.	.	.
Nathaniel Sycks	1	2	3	.	.
William Tucker	1	4	4	.	.
James Cleveland	.	2	2	.	.
William Hall	1	.	.	.	.
Jessee Cristee	1	4	4	.	.
Luke Senter	.	2	1	.	.
Thomas Pace	1	3	4	15	15
Moses Mathis	.	1	2	1	1
Majr. John Williams	1	1	8	10	16
Benjamin Ward	.	1	1	3	4
Hardy Wall	.	1	.	.	.
Benjaman Williams	.	1	.	.	.
Howel Williams	.	1	.	.	.
Abraham Dean	.	1	2	.	.
John Jones	1	5	5	13	?
Est. Wm. Walker deceased	.	3	2	3	3
William F. Ellem(?)	1	2	2	3	4
Abasalom --------	1	1	1	.	.
John McCornack or McComack(?)	1	.	1	6	1
	20	111	116	84	99
	14	35	46	67	68
The Hole (sic)	16	46	68	56	57
amount of souls	60	192	230	207	224

District 16; taken by Ptolem Powell 2nd Jany. 1786.

Head of Household	WM 21-60 yrs.	WM under 21 & above 60	WF all ages	Blacks 12-50	Blacks under 12 & above 50
Pg. 1					
Ptolem Powell	1	4	3	7	2
Adam Hamell(?)	1	8	4	3	2
William Smith	.	1	2	.	1

Head of Household	WM 21-60 yrs.	WM under 21 & above 60	WF all ages	Blacks 12-50	Blacks under 12 & above 50
William Martin	2	4	5	4	.
Charles Moore	1	1	3	5	1
William Powell	1	3	5	4	.
Uriah Smith	1	2	3	2	.
James Easley	1	2	1	4	2
Nathanel Glover	1	.	1	.	1
Thomas Jones	1	.	.	.	.
Fredrick Spann	1	.	.	1	.
Ephrim Merritt	1	.	.	.	.
Elisha Rose	1	1	4	3	3
John Powell	1	.	1	.	.
Peter Smith	.	2	1	6	3
John Nasworthy	1	2	3	2	2
Richard Taylor	1	5	1	2	2
Benjamin Green	1	1	2	.	.
James Killey	.	3	4	.	.
Bryant Edmondson	1	2	2	.	.
Jann Edmondson	.	.	1	.	.
Totals by Ed.	18	41	46	43	19
Pg. 2					
Jarrott Wallice	2	.	.	6	7
Richard Norwood	1	.	.	4	1
John Jones	1	2	4	.	.
William Sikes	1	2	2	.	.
Willis Spann	1	.	.	.	2
James Spann	1	.	.	1	1
William Carpenter	2	2	4	.	.
Richard Spann	1	.	.	.	1
Thomas Lyall	1	4	5	.	10
Thomas Killey	1	1	4	.	.
William Killey	1	.	.	.	.
David Arnold	1	1	1	1	2
Wormley Rose	.	1	.	2	1
Zachariah Powell	1	2	5	1	.
Hannah Green	.	2	2	1	2
William Downs	.	2	4	.	.
William Martin	1	1	2	.	.
Robert Ivey	1	1	3	1	1
Joseph Winter	1	2	3	.	1
Samuel Norwood	.	1	3	5	6
Pennelope Weldon	.	1	2	4	7
David Downs	1	.	.	.	.
Mary Taylor	.	2	4	2	.
Elizabeth Doe	.	1	2	.	.
Young Heathcock	1	1	3	.	.
Rebeacah Morriss	.	.	4	.	.
John Heathcock	1	.	.	.	.
Totals by Ed.	21	29	57	28	42

Head of Household	WM 21-60 yrs.	WM under 21 & above 60	WF all ages	Blacks 12-50	Blacks under 12 & above 50
Pg. 3					
Mark Morgan	1	.	.	.	.
William Edmondson	1	.	1	.	.
John Smith	1	.	.	.	.
William Yarbrough	1	.	.	.	.
James Shaw	1	2	3	1	2
Thomas Shaw	1	2	2	1	2
James Hocaday	1	.	1	2	1
Worick Hocaday	1	2	1	.	.
Samuel Bumpuss	1	1	1	.	.
Nathan Sikes	1	.	2	.	.
James Prothriss	1	2	2	.	.
George Powell	1	.	2	.	.
Emanuel Scott	1	1	3	.	.
Phillip Gill	2	.	1	.	.
William Powell	1	3	7	2	3
Aaron Powell	1	.	1	.	.
Moses Smith	1	5	2	2	2
Anna Harriss	.	1	4	.	.
John Jones Sr.	.	3	3	.	.
William Rose	1	1	2	2	4
James Moore	1	1	1	3	1
William Orange	1	1	1	.	.
Lewis Roan	1	3	4	.	.
Robert Bumpess	1	2	4	.	.
James Adams	2	1	8	.	1
Totals by Ed.	25	31	56	13	16

Head of Household	WM 21-60 yrs.	WM under 21 & above 60	WF all ages	Blacks 12-50	Blacks under 12 & above 50
Pg. 4					
Thos. Hill	2	1	1	2	.
George Person	1	2	4	.	.
James Shaw	1	.	1	.	.
Hannah Shaw	.	3	2	.	.
John Shaw	1	.	.	.	.
Gardner Harvill	2	1	1	11	12
Geo. Yarbrough	1	4	3	.	1
Total on microfilm	72	112	171	97	90
				542	
	18	41	46	43	19
	21	29	57	28	42
	25	31	56	13	16
	8	11	12	13	13
	72	112	171	97	90

HYDE COUNTY

Number of Inhabitants in Capt. Cason Gibbs' District, Feb. 1786.

Pg. 1

Head of Household	WM 21-60 yrs. & above 60	WM under 21	WF all ages	Blacks 12-50	Blacks under 12 & above 50
Jesse Harris	1	3	4	.	.
John Selby	4	5	2	4	5
Joseph Sirman	1	3	4	.	.
William Hudson	.	1	3	.	.
Alexander Benson	1	1	2	.	.
Jane Benson	1	.	1	.	.
William Boomer	1	1	3	.	.
Joseph McGown	1	5	4	.	.
William Carrowon	1	3	6	1	.
William Harris	1	2	3	.	.
Mary Fisher	1	4	4	.	.
William Berry	1	2	5	.	.
Daniel Murry	2	2	3	.	.
Caleb Swindell	1	3	2	.	.
Peter Carter	1	2	1	.	.
Jacob Gaskill	1	3	1	2	1
Mary Tooly	.	.	4	1	1
Thomas Brooks	1	2	2	.	.
John O'Neal	1	1	3	.	.
Robert Gray	2	.	.	.	.
William Neal	1	.	3	.	.
John Turner	1	1	2	.	.
Mitchel Rose	2	.	2	.	.
Elisha Harris	1	.	3	.	.
	28	44	67	8	7

Pg. 2

Head of Household	WM 21-60 yrs. & above 60	WM under 21	WF all ages	Blacks 12-50	Blacks under 12 & above 50
James English	2	2	2	.	.
Salathiel Lairy	2	.	1	.	.
James Mason	1	4	1	.	.
Andrew Wise	1	.	5	.	.
Solomon Baker	1	.	1	.	.
James Watson	1	.	3	.	.
Job Sirman	1	1	4	.	.
Elisabeth McLin	.	.	3	.	.
Major Newton	1	4	1	.	.
John Harris	1	.	4	.	.
Thomas Harris	1	2	4	.	.
Robert Henry	1	2	2	.	.
Caleb White	1	3	3	3	5
Elisabeth Spring	1	4	4	.	.
Charles Cuthrell	.	4	1	.	1
John Dixon	1	2	6	2	3
Susannah Carrowon	.	2	1	.	.
William Albert	1	.	.	.	.

Head of Household	WM 21-60 yrs. & above 60	WM under 21	WF all ages	Blacks 12-50	Blacks under 12 & above 50
John Carrowon	2	4	4	.	.
Thomas Bridgman	1	1	4	.	.
Francis Creedle	2	5	3	.	.
William Gibbs	1	2	1	2	1
Nathan Selby	1	1	3	1	1
William Selby	1	.	2	2	2
Joseph Jennett	1	2	2	.	.
Aaron Spring	3	.	2	.	.
Thomas Gibbs	1	.	4	5	7
	30	45	70	15	20

Pg. 3

Head of Household	WM 21-60 yrs. & above 60	WM under 21	WF all ages	Blacks 12-50	Blacks under 12 & above 50
Massey Benson	1	.	5	.	.
John Benson	1	2	3	1	.
Bridget Green	.	.	5	.	.
Samuel Selby	1	3	2	3	.
Robert Gibbs	1	2	4	3	2
Abram Jones	2	2	2	5	5
Stephen Brooks	2	2	5	2	.
John Farrow	1	3	5	1	1
Ezekiel Turner	1	1	2	.	1
Timothy Murry	1	1	1	1	1
William Williams	1	3	5	.	.
Solomon Jones	2	3	4	4	5
Peter Sirman	1	.	2	.	.
Maurice Jones	1	1	3	1	.
David Green	1	2	4	.	.
Carson Gibbs	1	1	5	5	6
Ann Sirman	.	2	1	.	.
William Watson	2	2	5	1	.
Richard Jones	1	2	3	.	.
Ignatius Herbert	1	3	2	.	.
Edward Crickman	1	.	2	.	.
Henry Jones	1	1	2	.	1
Leah Linton	.	1	2	.	.
Samuel Linton	1	1	2	.	.
Laurainah Hicks	.	1	1	.	.
Abraham Jones	1	1	2	3	1
Robert Maccay	1	.	.	.	.
Samuel Barber	1	.	.	.	.
(sic)	28	38	79	29	29
Total	86	127	217	42	40

Test.   Caleb (illegible)

(One page of two columns)

Head of Household	WM 21-60 yrs. & above 60	WM under 21	WF all ages	Blacks 12-50	Blacks under 12 & above 50
Seth Hovey	3	1	3	1	2
Bethuel Baily	2	2	7	.	.

Head of Household	WM 21-60 yrs.	WM under 21 & above 60	WF all ages	Blacks 12-50	Blacks under 12 & above 50
Tahliel Smith	2	2	2	1	3
Lazerous Foreman	1	.	5	2	1
Benjamin Foreman	1	.	.	1	.
George Barrow Sr	1	2	2	5	5
Samuel Daily	1	1	1	3	2
John Right (Wright)	1	1	2	.	.
Joseph Cocks	1	1	3	5	2
Seth Kipps	1	1	4	.	.
Ezekel Chambers	2	2	4	1	.
Thomas Mallerson	1	.	.	.	.
Homes Pairtree	1	5	5	.	.
John Webster	1	1	3	2	1
Joseph Keech	1	2	1	.	.
James Baily	1	3	3	.	.
Jasper Keech	1	2	3	.	.
John Mark Harvey	1	2	6	.	.
Thomas Baily	1	1	2	1	5
Simon Baily	1	1	2	1	.
Caleb Chambers	1	1	2	1	1
William Cording	3	.	2	3	3
Hosea Martain	1	1	5	5	6
Jesse Latham	1	.	2	4	2
Ann Fortiscue	.	1	2	.	.
Noah Pairtree	1	.	.	.	.
	33	33	71	35	33
Thomas Right	2	4	2	.	.
Mary Chambers	.	.	2	.	.
William Right	1	1	5	.	.
Joel Gerganous	1	2	2	.	.
Dorcas Gilbert	.	3	1	.	.
Henry Moor	1	5	1	.	.
Thomas Jordan Sr	2	3	6	6	2
Cosimo Medecei	1	.	.	1	1
James Capps	2	1	6	.	.
Sarah Burges	.	1	4	.	.
John F(illegible)ar	1	1	5	.	.
Cason Capps	1	4	2	.	.
Dianah Baily	1	2	2	.	.
Sarah Cording	.	5	2	3	1
William Cording	1	.	1	.	.
Ann Adams	.	2	2	.	.
Mary Martain	.	1	2	3	5
James Robins	1	2	3	1	4
George Barrow Jr.	1	.	3	1	.
Ebenezor Harris	1	.	.	.	.
Joseph Eckols Sr.	1	1	2	.	.
Abner Eckols	1	1	2	.	.
Joseph Eckols	1	1	1	.	.
Patrick Wilkins	1	4	1	5	9

Head of Household	WM 21-60 yrs.	WM under 21 & above 60	WF all ages	Blacks 12-50	Blacks under 12 & above 50
Burrage, H. Silby	1	5	5	10	7
Joshua Baily	2	3	5	.	.
	24	50	66	30	29
	33	33	71	35	33
Total 404	57	83	137	65	62

"A List of the Inhabitince of Capt. Capps
Company of White & Blacks"
(one page of two columns)

	WM 21-60 yrs.	WM under 21 & above 60	WF all ages	Blacks 12-50	Blacks under 12 & above 50
William Lee	1	.	3	.	.
Joshua Foreman	1	3	2	.	.
Charles Herrenton	1	2	2	.	.
John Vick	1	.	2	.	.
Benjamin Cording	1	3	3	.	.
Gidien Simons	1	.	.	.	.
Benjamin Wilkins	1	1	.	1	4
Jacob Conner	1	.	3	1	.
David Baily	1	2	2	.	.
Mikel Foreman	1	2	2	1	.
Abraham Jordan	1	2	2	.	2
Richard Slaughter	1	.	2	.	.
Ednea Hancock	.	1	5	5	3
Ephram Elsbre	.	1	1	.	.
Richard Capps	1	1	2	1	3
Zeanas Ebonne	1	2	3	3	2
Fredrick Barrow	1	4	4	4	4
	15	24	38	16	18
John Cannon	1	.	1	.	.
Lazerous Gilbert Foreman	1	3	4	.	.
Nathan Harvey	2	.	3	.	.
John Abrams	1	2	2	.	.
Jasper Harderson	2	2	5	.	.
Daniel Harris	1	.	1	.	.
Joseph Feltier or Febtier(?)	1	.	2	.	.
Thomas Wilkins	1	2	4	3	1
Baas Hamond	1	.	4	.	.
Richard Russel	1	1	2	.	.
Thomas Cording	1	.	2	.	.
Kendrel Bosty	1	2	1	.	.
Peter Harris	.	2	4	5	4
Easter Thurrigood	.	1	2	1	.
John Capps	1	1	4	.	.
Zacheriah Barrow	1	1	7	5	14
Stephen Chambers	1	2	3	.	.
Test	18	20	53	16	21

Caleb Foreman, Clk." Returned to February
Hyde Inferior Court 1786".

Head of Household	WM 21-60 yrs.	WM under 21 & above 60	WF all ages	Blacks 12-50	Blacks under 12 & above 50
"The No. of White and Black Inhabitants in Capt. Joseph Gibbs Company, Mattamaskeet, 1786.					
Pg. 1					
Robert Jennett	1	1	2	11	4
Sarah Jennett	.	2	2	2	5
Mary Bonner	.	1	2	3	2
Richard Saunderson	1	5	4	2	4
John Gamewell	.	1	2	.	.
Samuel West	1	1	2	.	.
John Jennett	1	2	3	.	.
Samuel Sadler	1	1	3	.	.
Edward Spencer	.	6	3	6	7
Robert Gibbs Sr	.	4	1	11	.
William Rascow	1	3	4	.	.
John Bray	1	3	4	.	.
Joseph Jennett	1	3	2	.	.
Richard Spencer	1	5	3	.	.
Benjamin Gibbs, Minr.	1	1	3	1	.
Daniel Cuthrel	2	2	2	1	.
Daniel Lenton	1	.	3	.	.
Thomas Carrow	2	4	2	.	.
Ezekiel Harress	1	4	4	.	.
William Coffey	1	2	4	.	.
Zedekiah Swendell	1	3	2	.	.
William Thoronton	2	1	3	.	.
Samuel Wormington	1	1	6	6	4
Benjamin Spencer	1	2	5	2	1
Thomas Hall	1	1	2	.	.
Nathan Spencer	2	5	6	1	1
Christopher Spencer	1	4	5	.	.
Paul Sparrow	1	4	4	6	5
	27	70	80	52	41
Pg. 2					
Selby Gibbs	2	1	7	6	4
Wm. Cohoun Coffey	1	1	2	2	.
Joel Swendell	1	2	1	.	.
John Brinn	1	2	1	.	.
Wm. Spencer Sr	1	4	6	3	3
John Spring	1	2	1	.	.
Benjaman Mason	1	1	3	.	.
Caleb Mason	2	3	1	.	1
James Daniels	1	2	2	.	.
Thomas Thoronton	3	3	2	.	.
Zephfenias Sawer	1	4	2	.	.
Thomas Daniels	1	.	1	.	.
Richard Brinn	1	1	4	.	.
Nicolas Brinn	.	1	2	.	.
Richard Sadler	1	2	3	.	.
Joseph Williams	2	1	3	.	.
Hopkins Williams	2	1	4	.	.
George Williams	1	.	5	.	.
Samuel Sadler	1	2	3	.	.
William Sanders	1	.	2	.	.
Benjaman Cuthrell	1	1	1	.	.
James Carpender	1	.	.	.	.
John Davis	1	2	5	.	.
Charles Mooney	.	4	3	.	.
Lemuel Cartright	1	1	1	.	.
James Daverson	2	2	3	.	.
Jesey Thomas	1	4	4	.	.
John Moore Sr	1	2	4	.	.
Joseph Cuthrell	1	2	1	1	.
James Hall	1	2	6	.	.
Mallacha Jolley	1	2	1	.	.
Joseph Gibbs Jr	1	2	2	2	5
James Reed	1	6	1	.	.
Hugh Henry	2	2	3	.	.
David Spencer	1	1	3	1	.
John Swendell	1	1	3	.	.
Andrew Sanders	1	.	4	.	.
	43	65	100	15	13
Pg. 3					
George Hopkins	1	.	2	.	.
Margret Hopkins	1	2	2	.	.
Joseph Gibbs Sr	2	3	4	5	12
Joab Daniels	1	4	2	.	.
Joseph Swendell	1	1	2	.	.
Samuel Saunderson	1	.	.	.	.
Josiah Swendell	1	3	4	.	.
Elizabeth Boomer	1	2	1	.	.
Thomas Mason	1	1	1	.	.
Evan Maulbern	1	.	4	.	.
George Esdoll	1	1	3	.	.
Josiah Swendell	2	2	6	.	.
Nathan Cason	1	.	2	.	.
Caleb Swendell	1	.	3	.	.
William Porter	1	1	.	.	.
Benjamin Gibbs Jr	1	3	2	1	.
William Spencer Jr	1	1	1	1	.
William Smith	1	5	3	.	.
John Clayton	1	2	1	2	.
William Smith (then written over with Harress)	1	3	2	.	.
Josiah Huffmire	1	2	1	.	.
Abraham Jones, Mir.	1	2	2	3	1
Henry Gibbs Sr	1	2	4	2	7
Josiah Gibbs, Mir.	1	2	3	5	1

Head of Household	WM 21-60 yrs.	WM under 21 & above 60	WF all ages	Blacks 12-50	Blacks under 12 & above 50
Jesse Cox	1	2	3	2	.
Isaac Swendell	1	4	6	.	.
Benj[n]. Gibbs Sr.	1	1	7	4	6
Francis Duke	1	.	2	.	.
	30	49	73	25	27
Pg. 4					
Salathiel Caps	1	3	2	.	.
John Moore Jr.	1	1	3	2	.
David Cuthrell	1	3	2	.	.
John Lenton	1	2	1	1	1
John Ensly	1	4	4	.	.
Samuel Henry	1	4	2	.	.
Elizabeth Spencer	1	1	4	5	2
Benjaman Neel	1	.	5	.	.
William Gibbs Sr.	1	2	4	3	.
Henry Carrow	1	3	4	.	.
John Williamson	1	1	1	.	.
Solomon Swendell	1	1	1	.	.
Henry Williamson	1	2	4	.	.
[Samuel West entered but struck out]	1	1	2	.	.
	14	28	39	11	3
Total 814	114	213	300	103	86

Test, William Spencer.
Retd. to Feby. Inferr. Court 1786
Test, Caleb Foreman, Clk.

"A List of the Inhabitants of Capt.
Thomas Smith's District.
Pg. 1

Head of Household	WM 21-60 yrs.	WM under 21 & above 60	WF all ages	Blacks 12-50	Blacks under 12 & above 50
Eliz[th] Jasper	1	1	4	8	10
Ebenezer Slade	1	2	1	1	.
Nathan Slade	1	1	3	.	.
Jessey Slade	1	3	4	.	.
Simon Leary	2	3	3	3	.
Lovey Dawes	.	1	2	2	1
Thos. Henderson	1	3	1	2	.
William Russell	2	4	2	7	3
Ben Russell	1	6	4	6	4
Henry Tuley	1	3	3	4	1
Rich[d]. Jordan	1	1	4	2	5
James Clevess ?	1	.	4	2	2
Jessey Allen	1	1	2	.	.
John Allen	2	2	2	.	.
Isaac Allen	1	2	3	.	.
Ben Elliss	1	1	1	1	.
Thos. Hussey	1	.	3	2	1
Sam[l]. Davis	1	2	4	2	1
Frances Melison	1	.	2	.	.

Head of Household	WM 21-60 yrs.	WM under 21 & above 60	WF all ages	Blacks 12-50	Blacks under 12 & above 50
Abraham Bell	1	2	5	1	.
Daniel Tyson	.	5	4	5	5
A. Wilkenson Jr	1	.	2	.	.
Darkass Easter	.	3	2	.	.
Ruben Slade	1	.	1	2	1
William Beechum(?)	1	5	3	.	.
Isack Wood	.	2	.	.	.
Adam Richards	1	1	1	1	.
Keeling Whitehead	1	2	2	.	.
Widow E. Slade	.	.	5	.	.
Rich[d]. Richards	.	2	2	.	.
Watson Bell	1	2	1	.	.
William Fortescue	1	.	.	1	.
Rubin Baster (?)	1	.	.	2	.
Jeremiah Alen	2	.	2	.	.
Lydia Ethridge	.	3	3	1	2
Margrett Smith	.	2	2	3	2
Malica Burgess	1	1	2	2	.
Lam. Palmer	1	1	1	1	1
Thos. Smith	1	3	3	2	2
Joacam Ebern	1	2	2	.	2
John Russell	2	1	1	3	1
Sarah Witney	.	1	4	4	5
John Tyson	1	2	2	1	2
Total 326	39	73	103	71	40

Retd to Feby. Hyde Infer Court 1786
Test. Caleb Foreman, Clk.
List of Hyde Co. No. 17   3424

"A List of the Inhabitants of Capt.
Gaylard's District, N. Carolina, Hyde
County, 1786."
Pg. 1

Head of Household	WM 21-60 yrs.	WM under 21 & above 60	WF all ages	Blacks 12-50	Blacks under 12 & above 50
William Hollowell	3	3	4	.	1
Capt. S. Gaylard	1	2	4	2	.
Isaac Wilkison	1	.	2	2	1
Mapel Windly	.	.	1	2	2
Sarah Windly	.	4	1	1	1
Michael Windly	1	.	2	1	.
John MDowell or McDewell or McDowell	1	.	.	.	.
Jonathan Gurganus	1	3	6	1	.
Fran[s]. Egleton	.	1	3	.	.
Churl. Windly	1	.	.	.	.
John Philips	1	2	2	.	.
George Condre	1	1	4	.	.
James Ratliff	1	.	2	.	.
Frances Galoway	.	3	1	.	.

Head of Household	WM 21-60 yrs.	WM under 21 & above 60	WF all ages	Blacks 12-50	Blacks under 12 & above 50
Wm. Campbell	.	.	.	.	.
Joel Davinport	2	1	1	.	.
Phin[s]. Latham	1	5	2	3	9
Thos. Gaylard	1	1	2	.	.
Dewel Bilbre	1	1	5	.	.
Benj. Flinn	2	2	3	1	4
Jacob Wilkison	1	1	2	2	2
Elizabeth Wilkison	.	1	1	6	3
Rebecca Flinn	.	2	3	.	.
Baley Benton	1	1	3	.	.
Wm. Gurganus	1	.	4	.	.
Wm. Eborn	1	1	2	2	.
James Eborn	3	3	3	6	7
Vin[rd]. Campbell	1	2	2	1	2
John Egleton	1	2	1	.	.
Edward Hobs	1	3	.	.	.
Pg. 2					
Noe Egleton	1	.	4	.	.
Thos. Gaylard Sr.	.	2	1	2	.
James Gaylard	1	2	4	.	.
E. C. Slone	1	1	2	.	.
Benj[n]. Gaylard	1	.	3	2	1
John Loyd	1	5	4	.	.
Margret Hollowell	.	2	3	3	3
Ira Hollowell	2	.	.	.	.
Epharim Eborn	1	2	4	1	.
Thos. Windly	2	.	1	.	.
Jahu Eborn	1	.	.	.	1
Jacob Durden	2	.	2	.	.
Robert Barnet	1	2	4	.	.
Casen Stiren	2	.	.	.	.
Nathaniel Eborn	2	1	3	.	.
Sam[l]. MDewell (McDewell)	2	1	4	.	.
Henry Eborn	2	2	3	6	7
Henry Scott	1	1	5	.	.
James Smith	1	.	1	.	.
Elisabeth Shabner	.	2	1	.	.
James Windly	1	.	.	.	.
Thos. Windly	1	.	.	.	.
Wm. Harvey	1	.	3	.	.
Wm. Gurganus	.	2	1	.	.
Wm. Howard	2	1	5	.	.
Jere[h]. Gaylard	1	2	7	1	.
John Gaylard	1	2	3	.	.
Thos. Toping	1	2	2	.	.
Zachariah McSwain	1	.	1	4	3
Joseph Smith	1	2	4	.	.

Head of Household	WM 21-60 yrs.	WM under 21 & above 60	WF all ages	Blacks 12-50	Blacks under 12 & above 50
Edward McSwain	1	1	3	3	2
John Allen	3	1	.	12	3
J. Satchwell	1	2	2	5	10
Caleb Forman	1	3	4	5	10
Henry Scott	1	3	4	4	6
	69	89	160	76	72

J. Satchwell
"Return[d]. to feby Hyde Infer[r]. Court 1786."

The Number of White and Blacks in Capt[n]. Will[m]. Satterthwait's Co. Jany. 8th, 1786.

Pg. 1	WM 21-60 yrs.	WM under 21 & above 60	WF all ages	Blacks 12-50	Blacks under 12 & above 50
Jonathan Philips	1	1	7	.	.
Thomas Addams	1	3	4	1	.
James Wilkerson	1	2	3	2	2
Will[m]. Hogges Slade	1	.	4	1	.
Richard Winfield Jr	1	1	1	.	.
Welhta Winfield	.	1	5	2	1
Abraham Gallowell	1	2	4	1	1
Jesse Winfield	1	.	4	.	.
Bryan Winfield	1	.	.	.	.
Charles Banks	1	1	6	.	.
Capt[n]. Will[m]. Satterthwait	1	1	2	3	3
(torn) Davis Senr.	1	.	1	.	.
(torn)h Satterthwaite	1	.	2	.	.
(torn)ul Winfield	1	1	2	.	.
William Davis	1	3	5	1	2
Peter McWilliams	1	3	4	.	.
Jacob Paul	1	3	4	.	.
John Wilkerson	1	1	2	.	.
John Davis Junr.	1	1	2	.	.
Margaret Smith	1	1	2	.	.
Joseph Mesick	1	3	2	.	.
George Dukes	.	1	2	1	.
Moses Banks	1	.	4	.	.
William Bushop	1	.	3	.	.
William Morriss	1	.	.	.	.
Stephen Roggers	1	.	1	.	.
Jeremiah Johnson	1	2	2	.	.
Mary Powell	.	1	3	.	.
Lamuel Morress	1	3	3	1	.
Richard Harvey Senr	1	2	1	4	4
Jonathan Satterthwait	1	4	6	.	2
John Winfield Senr	.	3	1	5	3

Head of Household	WM 21-60 yrs.	WM under 21 & above 60	WF all ages	Blacks 12-50	Blacks under 12 & above 50
George Carter	1	2	4	.	.
Ezekiah Stilley	1	.	2	.	.
John Arthur	1	1	2	.	.
John Winfield Junr	1	1	2	.	.
William Satterthite Jr	1	1	2	.	.
Pg. 2					
William Satterthwaite Senr.	.	2	4	.	.
James Chambers	1	2	2	.	.
Henry Jerman	1	.	.	.	.
Richard Winfield Junr	1	.	4	3	.
George Davinport	1	5	2	.	.
John McWilliams	.	3	4	.	.
Samuel Slade	1	5	3	.	.

Head of Household	WM 21-60 yrs.	WM under 21 & above 60	WF all ages	Blacks 12-50	Blacks under 12 & above 50
Thomas McWilliams	1	3	2	.	.
Aaron Gurganus	1	4	3	.	.
Jesse Wilkerson	2	3	4	2	1
Stephen Smith	1	4	4	2	3
Solomon Smith	1	2	1	.	.
Mary Mason	.	.	2	.	.
Rich^d. Harvey Junr.	1	.	3	.	.
Major Clark	1	1	2	12	7
Abraham Wilkinson	1	6	1	3	5
Abraham Satterthwaite	1	3	3	.	.
John Bushop	1	.	1	.	.
Shaderick Roggers	1	.	.	.	.
Elisha Roggers	1	.	.	.	.
	53	101	149	44	35

Returned to Feby. Hyde Inf. Court 1786.
Test. Caleb Foreman, Clk.

76a

JOHNSTON COUNTY

A list of the names taken by me.
Jesse Tiner in Capt. Whitley's Comp.

Pg. 1

Head of Household	WM 21-60 yrs.	WM under 21 & above 60	WF all ages	Blacks 12-50	Blacks under 12 & above 50
Joseph Ingram	1	2	3	6	5
John Davis	1	3	2	.	.
Sander Burnet	1	4	7	.	.
Nicholas Thompson	1	2	4	4	1
John Whitley	1	5	2	3	4
Druary Muselewhite	1	.	5	.	.
William Roberts	1	1	2	.	.
William Davis	1	3	1	.	.
Arthur Davis	1	.	.	.	.
Nathan Adkinson	1	2	4	7	16
Benja. Sellars	1	.	7	.	.
Benja. Parnal	1	6	2	.	.
John Phillips	1	2	1	.	.
Needham Powell	.	1	2	3	5
Jeremiah Powell	1	.	.	4	1
William Farmer	2	4	2	2	8
Britten Smith	1	.	3	3	.
William Bridgers	1	1	2	5	6
John Allen	1	2	3	5	6
Isaac Powell	1	5	5	5	2
Abraham Gamalian	1	7	1	12	9
Thomas Cradick	1	1	5	1	4
Lewis Jernigan	1	3	6	3	5
Jasper Jernigan	1	1	1	7	5
Richard Warren	1	.	2	5	2
Solomon Pranie/Prance	1	3	2	.	.
William Roberts	1	3	1	.	.
Jarrot Thompson	1	2	5	1	.
	28	63	80	76	79

Pg. 2

Head of Household	WM 21-60 yrs.	WM under 21 & above 60	WF all ages	Blacks 12-50	Blacks under 12 & above 50
Jacob Daves	1	1	1	.	.
Davis Strickland	2	1	3	.	.
George Collins	1	4	7	.	.
Thomas Gwing/Gueing	1	3	6	.	.
Uriah Strickland	1	.	2	.	.
Eligah Thompson	1	1	2	.	1
William Ewell	1	3	1	.	.
Sarah Bryan	.	3	2	27	22
Nathan Powell	1	.	.	1	5
Eligah Warren	1	1	3	2	5
Daniel Dees	1	5	1	4	.
Thomas Chambers	1	.	1	.	.
Deal Collins	1	3	3	.	.
David Overbey	1	3	4	.	.

Head of Household	WM 21-60 yrs.	WM under 21 & above 60	WF all ages	Blacks 12-50	Blacks under 12 & above 50
John Prance	1	.	2	.	.
Jacob Stallings	1	1	2	1	.
John Battin	1	3	2	.	.
Joshua Lynch	1	1	2	.	.
John Hatcher	1	.	1	1	3
Jesse Purvis	1	3	2	.	.
Needham Whitley	1	2	2	6	4
Mary Medlin	.	.	2	.	.
Jesse Tiner	1	4	2	2	6
John Pool Senr.	1	3	7	.	.
Edward Blurton	1	3	5	2	.
William Litleton	1	2	4	.	.
Charles Litleton	1	.	3	.	1
Rebeckah Stevens	.	.	1	1	3
Etheldred Willis	1	1	1	.	.
	55	111	154	123	129

"Capt. Isaac Hinton's District. Names of Persons who gave the following lists of their families. 24th Feby. 1787.

Pg. 1

Head of Household	WM 21-60 yrs.	WM under 21 & above 60	WF all ages	Blacks 12-50	Blacks under 12 & above 50
Thomas Avera	1	3	5	3	1
Amos Atkinson	1	1	3	.	.
William Branan	1	2	3	.	.
Thomas Branan	1	2	2	.	.
Lewis Bryant	1	3	4	.	.
James Bawcom	1	2	2	.	.
Daniel Brown	1	1	4	.	.
George Cooper	1	1	4	.	.
Henry Collum	1	3	3	.	.
Jacob Delk	1	3	3	.	.
Timothy Duck	1	4	3	.	.
Moses Eason Senr	4	3	6	.	.
William Earp	1	3	3	6	5
Jesse Green	1	3	5	.	1
John Green	1	1	3	.	.
William Green	1	1	2	.	.
Joseph Garner Sr	2	3	7	.	.
John Garner Junr	1	.	3	.	.

Pg. 2

Head of Household	WM 21-60 yrs.	WM under 21 & above 60	WF all ages	Blacks 12-50	Blacks under 12 & above 50
Patience Gale	.	1	4	.	.
Mead Gulley	1	2	3	.	.
John Garner Senr.	1	4	4	.	.
Robert Gulley	1	1	3	1	1
John Hayles Senr.	1	2	5	.	.
Sarah Hinton	.	2	2	1	1
Isaac Hinton	1	1	2	5	5
Malachi Hinton	2	4	4	7	10

Head of Household	WM 21-60 yrs.	WM under 21 & above 60	WF all ages	Blacks 12-50	Blacks under 12 & above 50
William Hinton	2	.	.	3	7
Shadrack Hill	1	5	2	.	.
Henry Hayles	1	3	1	1	2
James Holliman	1	4	4	.	.
Joseph High	.	6	3	.	.
Joseph Irwin	2	.	4	1	1
Freeman Killingsworth	1	4	4	.	.
Isles King	1	1	4	1	.
John Lee	1	2	3	3	3
Bryan Lee	1	3	2	2	1
Edward Lee, given in per father William Lee	1	1	2	2	3
Moiles Langley	1	4	4	.	.
John Moore	1	2	4	.	1
Hardy Miles	1	2	2	.	.
John Nowel	1	2	5	.	.
Isham Oneil	2	2	3	.	.
Richard Pope	1	3	6	.	.
Jeremiah Parnal	1	5	4	.	.
Demsey Perry	1	2	5	.	.
Drury Rawlins	1	1	4	.	.
James Shaw	1	4	6	.	.
Samuel Slater	1	4	3	.	.
					167

Pg. 3

Head of Household	WM 21-60 yrs.	WM under 21 & above 60	WF all ages	Blacks 12-50	Blacks under 12 & above 50
Joseph Spicer	1	4	6	.	.
James Spicer	1	.	1	3	.
Aquila Searcey	[No figures]				
George Searcey	1	3	1	.	.
William Searcey Sr	.	1	2	.	.
John Searcey	1	1	2	.	.
William Snipes	1	4	4	.	.
Col. Samuel Smith	1	4	4	23	23
Elisha Thomas	1	4	3	4	8
Josiah Taylor	1	1	5	.	.
William Wilder	1	2	4	.	.
Samuel Wilder	1	4	3	1	1
Matthew Wilder	1	4	5	1	1
Jesse Wall	1	2	4	.	.
William Wall	1	2	2	.	.
Jesse Wootten	1	3	3	1	2
Malachi Wimberley	1	1	4	.	.
John Watson	1	4	3	4	4
Elisha Woodard	1	2	2	5	7
William Walker	1	1	2	.	.
Herod Williams	1	4	1	.	.

Head of Household	WM 21-60 yrs.	WM under 21 & above 60	WF all ages	Blacks 12-50	Blacks under 12 & above 50
James Jordan	1	.	3	.	.
Jeremiah Price	1	2	3	.	.
John Abbet	1	.	.	.	.
Lewis Liles	2	3	2	.	.
William Hocutt Jr	1	1	2	.	.
Robert Birch	1	1	2	.	.
Thomas Proctor	.	1	2	.	1
Thomas Hill	1	4	1	.	.
					243

Pg. 4

Head of Household	WM 21-60 yrs.	WM under 21 & above 60	WF all ages	Blacks 12-50	Blacks under 12 & above 50
Richard Holt	1	3	5	.	.
Chapman Hayles	1	1	2	.	.
John Vinson	1	.	.	1	.
Samuel Holleman Sr. 79 yrs. of age	.	1	.	.	.
James Parnal	1	.	3	.	.
Seth Holliman	1	.	1	.	.
Mason Harn	1	3	3	.	.
William Smith	1	.	3	.	.
Mary Vaughan	.	.	5	.	.
Major Walker	2	2	1	.	.
Mileah Atkinson	.	1	8	.	.
John Hayles Junr.	1	1	2	.	2
					276

"Capt. Isaac Hinton's Dist., Johnston County, for the year 1787.

"A List of the Inhabitants of Johnston County for the Year 1787. Rec'd. March 16th 1787. A list of the number of inhabitants of Capt. John Bryan of Every Sect. and Condition."

Pg. 1

Head of Household	WM 21-60 yrs.	WM under 21 & above 60	WF all ages	Blacks 12-50	Blacks under 12 & above 50
John Ballinger	1	2	3	1	.
Joseph Bridgers	1	2	6	.	.
Charles Russel	1	5	2	.	.
George Kean	1	4	1	.	.
James Baker	1	3	5	.	.
Moses Johnson	1	2	5	.	.
Isaac Ingram	1	.	1	.	.
Ichabod Blackman	1	1	2	2	1
Ruebin Hobbey	1	3	5	.	.
Etheldred Harrell	1	1	4	.	.
John Blackman	1	4	8	1	.
William MClohon (McClohon)	1	1	3	.	.
Arthur Blackman	1	.	2	.	.
John Willson	1	1	2	.	.
Ruebin Barber	1	1	4	.	.

Head of Household	WM 21-60 yrs.	WM under 21 & above 60	WF all ages	Blacks 12-50	Blacks under 12 & above 50
Borzillai Blackman	1	2	3	.	.
Thomas Altmon	1	2	3	.	.
Theophilus Harrell	1	1	2	.	.
Joshua Johnson	1	4	4	.	.
Shadrick Jones	1	3	6	.	.
James Lee Sr.	1	1	1	.	.
Demcey Baker	1	4	5	.	.
George Field	2	2	5	.	.
Demcey Linch	1	.	.	.	.
Pg. 2					
Margrit Bailes	.	.	4	.	.
Roman Adkinson	1	4	4	.	.
David Williams	2	4	5	.	.
Willebey Hooks	1	1	6	.	.
Miles Williams	.	3	8	.	.
Nathan Allin	1	.	.	1	.
James Allin	1	4	8	4	1
Mary Lee	.	1	3	2	3
Noah Barfoot	1	.	2	.	.
Duncan Murrey	1	1	2	.	.
Noah Barfoot Junr.	.	1	3	.	.
James McClenney	1	3	3	.	.
Nathan Vick	1	.	3	.	.
Cato Lee	1	2	1	.	.
Joseph Langston Sr.	.	3	2	.	.
Joseph Langston Jr.	1	1	1	.	.
John Jackson	.	1	1	.	.
Samuel Eldridge	.	2	2	3	6
Henry Blaelock	1	1	4	.	.
Willis Wiggins	1	2	4	6	1
Simon Trent	1	3	2	.	.
Samuel Smith	2	2	3	9	9
Josiah Barnes	1	1	4	1	2
Nicholas Farmer	1	2	4	2	1
David Lee	1	3	3	3	1
William Durham	1	.	3	2	4
William Ballinger	1	.	.	1	.
Mary Ballinger	.	.	3	3	.
Pg. 3					
Thomas Linch	.	2	5	.	.
John Vanpelt	1	2	4	.	.
William Lee	1	2	5	.	.
John Lee	1	1	2	1	.
Dickson Faile	1	4	2	2	.
John Procter	1	2	3	.	.
Francis Demint	.	1	2	.	.
James Bell	1	5	3	.	.
William Morgan	1	.	.	.	.
John Morgan	1	1	3	.	.

Head of Household	WM 21-60 yrs.	WM under 21 & above 60	WF all ages	Blacks 12-50	Blacks under 12 & above 50
George Mills	1	4	7	.	.
Mathew Mathis	1	.	3	.	.
Lamuel Lee	1	3	2	1	.
Thomas Simpson	1	4	5	.	.
John Faile	1	4	4	6	2
Stephen Lee	1	1	1	1	.
William Bryan	1	2	1	.	.
John Bryan	1	1	5	1	.
Assa Bryan	1	1	3	1	.
Sampson Sellers	1	2	1	.	.
William Haregroves	1	2	3	.	.
Lamuel Taylor	3	1	2	.	.
Thomas Mills	1	.	.	.	.
Jeremiah Lee	1	.	.	.	4
Bryant Adams	1	3	1	.	.
James Lee Sr.	1	.	2	1	1
Drewry Binom	1	2	2	.	.
William Huel (?)	1	3	1	.	.
John Rhodes	1	4	4	.	.
Shadrick Ingram	1	2	5	2	.
Pg. 4					
William Gooding	1	2	.	.	.
Moses Adkinson	.	2	4	.	.
Benjamin Williams	.	1	2	2	3
Francis Harrell	1	4	6	.	.
Ann Lohon ?	.	3	4	.	.
Jacob Scott	.	.	.	2	4
Nathan Williams	1	3	2	22	19
	80	169	262	83	65

"A List of the Inhabitants of Capt. Fishes Dist. in Johnston Co. for the year 1787. Rec'd. March 16, 1787.

Pg. 1					
John MCullers	1	.	.	6	4
William Sanders	1	.	2	1	3
John Smith	1	.	3	.	.
William Blunt	1	4	3	1	.
Hen. Johnston	2	3	3	3	1
Mos. Johnston	2	.	2	.	1
Amos Johnston	1	1	1	.	.
James Landon	1	1	4	.	3
John Carrell	2	2	4	.	.
William Gowers	1	1	6	.	.
Richard Whittenton	2	3	5	.	.
John Gower	1	3	3	.	.
Clate Sowel	1	.	2	.	.
John Stepeson	2	3	3	.	.
Starling Johnston	1	.	1	.	.
Elizabeth Johnston	.	1	6	.	.

Head of Household	WM 21-60 yrs.	WM under 21 & above 60	WF all ages	Blacks 12-50	Blacks under 12 & above 50
William Brasel	1	.	5	1	1
John Snipes	1	.	6	.	5
Travis Pate	2	1	2	.	.
John Williams	1	1	3	.	.
Amos Johnston	1	3	2	.	.
Etheldred Johnston	1	4	2	.	.
John Terry	1	1	2	.	.
Lucey Hobby	.	1	1	.	.
Cordy Pate	1	.	1	.	.
Sarah Elen	1	.	4	.	.
William Mercer	1	2	1	.	.
Fedrick Reaves	1	1	2	.	.
Marting Johnston	1	1	2	.	.
Charles Steward	1	5	3	2	4
John Smith	1	4	1	5	1
Jese Page	3	6	4	.	.
Sion Right	1	1	2	.	.
John Girden	1	.	1	.	1
Pg. 2					
Elizabeth Smith	.	1	3	.	.
Jos. Delk	2	.	3	.	.
Solomon Stephenson	.	1	4	.	.
Joel Johnston	1	3	6	.	.
Samuell Right	1	3	3	.	.
James Stephenson	1	1	4	.	.
John Yong	1	3	2	.	.
Brigirs Freeman	1	.	2	.	.
Jorge Parrish	1	.	.	.	.
Jestus Parrish	1	1	8	.	.
Solomon Cotes	1	.	3	.	.
Travis Johnston	1	2	4	.	.
Bly Barber	2	3	4	.	.
Jacob Flowers	1	8	5	.	.
James Clements	1	1	2	.	.
John Austern	2	4	2	.	.
James Conner	1	1	1	.	.
Hardy Morgan	1	1	4	.	.
Edward Stephenson	1	5	2	6	5
Mathers Jones	1	6	3	3	2
James Baget	1	.	2	.	1
William Taylor	1	2	3	3	.
Liewas Calf	1	6	4	.	.
Samuell Carr	1	1	1	.	.
	65	105	167	31	32

Signed by William Taylor

"A List of the Inhabitants of Capt.
William Bryant's Company.

Pg. 1					
John Beningfld. Sr	1	2	5	1	.

Head of Household	WM 21-60 yrs.	WM under 21 & above 60	WF all ages	Blacks 12-50	Blacks under 12 & above 50
Zadok Stallins	1	1	1	2	5
John Turner	1	3	4	.	.
Nicolas Farrel	1	1	2	.	.
Jacob Farrel	1	3	7	.	.
Littletun Fuller	1	2	1	.	.
James H. Casle	1	2	2	.	.
Charles Kelly	1	1	3	.	.
Cornealus Ferrel	1	.	.	.	.
John Ellis	1	.	.	.	.
William Copland	1	.	3	.	.
John Kelly	1	1	3	.	.
John Brit	1	2	5	.	.
Francis Weding	.	1	1	.	.
John Beningfld. Jr.	1	3	2	.	.
Isaac Jones	1	2	2	3	1
Arthur Bryant	1	1	3	5	5
Mary Garland	.	1	2	.	.
Abner Sauls	1	3	3	3	3
Abner Jerdin	1	2	2	.	.
John Tinsley	1	2	4	.	.
Charles Copland	1	1	2	.	.
Charles Copland Sr	1	.	1	.	.
Pg. 2					
John Kellensworth or Killingsworth	2	2	3	.	1
John Snipes	1	1	1	.	.
Etheldred Grigory	1	6	2	3	3
Sill Jonston	1	2	2	.	.
John Hinton	2	1	4	3	1
Carter Smith	1	4	2	.	.
Danil Avrit	2	1	1	2	4
William Bryant	1	.	4	2	1
Edwd. Penny	1	.	2	.	.
Elisabeth Penny	.	.	2	.	.
William Looper	1	2	5	.	.
Drury Masse	2	3	2	.	.
Daniel Rogers	1	4	3	.	.
John Gulley Jr.	1	.	3	.	.
John Price	3	2	3	.	.
Benjamin Smith	1	2	3	.	1
Willm. Snipes	1	.	.	.	.
Nathan Gulley	1	1	1	.	.
John Gulley Sr.	1	9	2	.	.
William Jonston	1	2	3	.	.
Noel Jonston	.	2	1	.	.
Needum Smith	1	.	2	.	.
Lewis Wilmon	1	.	.	.	.
James Lockhart	1	7	3	5	6
Richard Rivers	1	1	6	.	.

Head of Household	WM 21-60 yrs.	WM under 21 & above 60	WF all ages	Blacks 12-50	Blacks under 12 & above 50
Savery Kelly	.	1	2	.	.
John Dodd	1	5	4	.	.
Math^w. Carter	1	5	5	4	5
Caleb Penny	1	4	5	1	.
Sander Redin	1	2	1	.	.
Pg. 3					
Absilum Jonston	1	3	8	.	.
Sollomon Willobey	1	.	2	.	.
Willm. Elis	1	.	.	.	.
	56	108	143	34	36
Matt^w. Carter					
"Capt. William Talton Company"					
Pg. 1					
Everitt Pearcie	1	.	4	4	5
Mathew Walk(er?)	1	1	6	?	.
John Killingsworth	1	.	.	.	.
Samuel Godwin	?	6	2	.	.
John Gaerald	1	2	2	.	.
John Richardson ?	1	5	5	.	.
Samson Johnson	1	8	5	.	.
William Horn	.	2	2	.	.
Caleb Horn	1	.	.	.	.
William Brown	1	4	5	.	.
Jesse Brown	1	.	1	.	.
James Watson	1	.	1	.	.
Elisabeth Watson	.	1	2	.	.
Nathan Batten	1	7	6	.	.
Jesse Brown	1	1	2	.	.
John Thorn	1	2	6	.	.
John Hollimon	1	.	2	.	.
Robert Bagley	1	3	4	.	.
David Watson	2	7	5	.	.
William Garner	1	.	2	.	.
Charles Wilkinson Sr	.	3	2	.	.
William Bailey	2	2	3	.	.
Micajah Bailey	1	1	1	.	.
Jesse Watson	2	6	3	.	.
Jesse Batemon	1	3	3	.	.
Robart Johnson	1	1	1	.	.
Thomas Godwin	1	4	3	.	.
William Starling	1	2	5	.	.
William Sasser	1	2	5	.	.
Abil Sasser	1	1	1	.	.
Arthor Sasser	1	.	2	.	.
Pg. 2					
Michajah Willkison	1	.	.	.	.
Arthor Pearce	.	2	3	3	3
Elkanah Wilkinson	1	.	2	.	.

Head of Household	WM 21-60 yrs.	WM under 21 & above 60	WF all ages	Blacks 12-50	Blacks under 12 & above 50
Adam Starling	1	3	4	.	.
Thophilus Pearce	1	.	2	2	.
Edmond Godwin	1	3	3	.	.
Frederick Rains	1	.	3	.	.
Ambrose Rains	1	3	3	1	.
William Hinnant Jr	1	2	1	1	1
William Hinnant Sr	1	2	6	2	.
James Hinnant	1	1	6	1	.
Thomas Faulk	1	4	2	.	.
Ezekel Watson	1	2	4	.	.
Thomas Woodard	1	3	5	.	.
Levin Watson	1	2	1	.	.
Noel Rentfree	1	3	4	.	.
Thomas Boyet	1	.	2	.	.
John Odum	1	2	3	4	5
Jacob Yelverton	.	1	.	.	.
Charles Wilkinson Jr	1	1	3	.	.
Sasser Keen	1	1	2	.	.
John Keen	1	.	3	.	.
Sarah Boyet	.	3	2	.	.
Reuben Wilkinson	1	3	2	.	.
John Newsom	1	1	5	2	6
Shadrack Yelverton	1	3	2	.	.
Pg. 3					
Simon Pearce	1	.	.	2	.
Richard Pearce Sr	.	1	3	3	2
Thomas Cockrell	1	6	3	.	.
Charels Wellons	1	.	2	.	.
James Odom	1	.	.	.	.
Aaon Tison	1	.	.	.	.
Gidden Yelvenston	1	.	2	.	1
Moses Johnson	1	2	4	.	.
David Brewer	1	1	2	.	.
Lewes Grice	2	.	3	.	2
Jonathan Bateman	1	2	1	.	.
William Bateman	1	.	2	.	.
Simon Watson	1	.	2	.	.
Sollimon Watson	1	1	2	.	.
Nathen Smith	1	.	1	.	.
Sollimon Boykin	1	1	4	.	.
Sadock Yelventon	1	3	2	1	1
Jesse Pearce	1	5	2	2	1
Jesse Register	1	.	3	.	.
Isack Parrell	1	.	2	.	1
Stephen Godwin	1	.	2	.	.
Mathew Bruer	.	1	1	.	.
Joel Horn	1	1	4	.	.
Jesse Cearby	1	2	3	.	.
Joshua Corbit	1	1	3	.	.
Apslom Curley	1	2	2	.	.

Head of Household	WM 21-60 yrs.	WM under 21 & above 60	WF all ages	Blacks 12-50	Blacks under 12 & above 50	Head of Household	WM 21-60 yrs.	WM under 21 & above 60	WF all ages	Blacks 12-50	Blacks under 12 & above 50
Pg. 4						James Holt	1	2	3	.	.
Dellah Avis	.	.	.	4	.	Bryan Linch	1	1	2	.	.
Solomon Watson	1	2	3	.	.	William Medlin	1	.	2	.	.
Ephram Watson	1	1	3	.	.	Bryan Medlin	.	1	1	.	.
Hardey Tallton	1	1	3	.	.	Jacob Daughtry	1	2	1	.	.
William Talton	1	1	1	1	.	Saray Gurley	.	1	1	.	.
William Muselwhite	1	?	4	.	.	William Tarlton Sr	2	1	2	.	.
Ephram Perce	1	.	3	1	.	Phillip Pearce	1	1	3	2	.
Richard Perce Jr	1	3	2	?	.	Urier Mushlewhite	1	.	2	.	.
Aaron Spyvey Jr	1	2	3	.	.	Jacob Braswell	1	.	4	.	.
John Spyvey	1	1	3	.	.	Jacob Mills	1	.	2	.	.
Francis Evans	1	1	1	.	.	Leonard Mushelwhite	1	1	2	.	.
John Pearce	1	1	1	1	.	Maray Lohnhon	.	3	1	.	.
Edward Wadell	1	5	2	.	.	John Whuse	1	5	4	.	.
Josiah Barns	1	.	2	.	.						
James Watkins	1	3	5	.	.	Pg. 2					
Aaron Spyvey Sr	.	1	3	.	.	James Tallon/Talton	1	3	1	.	.
Joh Folck	1	1	1	.	.	John Corbit	1	2	2	.	.
James Folck	1	?	.	.	.	Benjamin Strickling	1	3	3	.	.
Obdiah Watson	1	.	.	.	.	Jacob Edwards	1	.	.	.	.
Luke Woodard	1	?	3	.	.	William Caps	1	1	1	.	.
Moses Johnston Jr	1	?	2	.	.	Marthew Caps	1	.	.	.	.
	97	174	264	39	26	William Caps Sr.	.	2	4	.	.
						Mikel Edwards	1	3	5	.	.
"A List of the Inhabitants of Johnston Co.						John Gurley	1	2	3	.	.
Co. 1787. Rec'd. March 16th 1787.						John Olliver Sr.	2	4	3	.	.
Pg. 1						Isick Stallons	1	.	.	1	.
Joseph Boon Jr.	1	3	3	4	8	Phillip Raiford, Esq.	1	3	4	6	5
Joseph Boon Sr.	.	1	1	5	8	Ambrus Rains	1	1	1	3	.
Charles Stevens	1	3	4	2	.	Ann Rains	.	.	1	.	.
Jesse Watkins	1	2	5	1	.	Aurther Pearce	1	1	1	2	.
Benjamin Simes	1	.	.	1	.	Benjamin Crawford	1	.	3	2	1
Thomas Wise	1	.	2	.	.	Shadrick Pearce	1	.	1	.	.
Patiance Simes	.	5	1	1	1	Joshua Battain	1	3	6	.	.
Benjamin Woodard	1	2	2	.	.	Mikagar Hicks	1	2	1	.	.
Rachel Bulls	.	.	4	.	.	Joshua Creech	1	5	2	.	.
Cornelas Linch	1	2	3	.	.	Nicolas Tiner	2	1	3	.	.
Charles Hood	1	.	.	.	.	William Tommas	1	1	2	.	.
Benjamin Tiner	1	2	2	.	.	Joseph Edwards	1	.	4	.	.
Ann Gurley	.	1	2	.	.	Elizabeth Edwards	.	1	3	.	.
Aurther Gurley	1	.	.	.	.	Elizabeth Masse	1	3	1	.	.
Benjamin Bridgers	1	4	6	1	1	Maray Gurley	.	1	4	.	.
Joseph Harp	1	.	4	.	.	John Olliver Jr.	1	1	2	.	.
James Patterson ?	1	1	2	1	1	Milley Davis	.	1	2	.	.
Jesse Hayse	1	2	6	3	2	Edwards Gurley	2	2	4	.	.
William Bulls	1	1	2	.	.	Maray Gurley	.	.	2	.	.
Henry Bulls	.	2	.	1	1	Hester Ballard	.	.	1	.	.
Jesse Tiner	1	1	1	.	.	Winnifurd Worley	.	.	1	.	.
Barnabath Bulls	1	3	1	.	.	Doll Burnett	.	2	1	.	.
James Linch	1	.	1	2	.	Whole amount			383		
						J. Boon					

"A List of inhhettants of Capt. Houlder's Company, 1787. The persons that give ther Numbers of Famaleys to Fred. Hollimon."

Pg. 1

Head of Household	WM 21-60 yrs.	WM under 21 & above 60	WF all ages	Blacks 12-50	Blacks under 12 & above 50
James Houlder	1	4	2	3	4
Samuel Oneal	1	1	1	.	.
Henry Baley	1	3	3	2	3
Arthur Baley	1	.	.	.	.
Mary Hinton: widow	1	1	6	.	.
Cloe Baley: widow	.	1	2	.	.
Patrick Oneal	1	1	6	.	.
William Hatcher	1	2	6	.	.
Applewhite Richardson	3	2	4	2	1
Moses Oneal	2	3	2	.	.
Mathew Parker	1	6	3	.	.
Jesse Hatcher	1	.	.	.	.
Lewis Price	1	1	3	.	.
Randol Moore	1	1	1	.	.
Thomas Jones	1	1	5	.	.
William Richardson	1	4	2	1	2
William Bryan	.	3	4	.	.
Zacharius Price	1	2	3	.	.
Ailsebeth Oneal-wid.	.	2	5	2	1
Isham Oneal	1	2	1	1	1
	20	40	59	11	12

Pg. 2

Head of Household	WM 21-60 yrs.	WM under 21 & above 60	WF all ages	Blacks 12-50	Blacks under 12 & above 50
Thomas Driver	.	6	2	.	.
Henry Finch, Esq.	1	3	3	.	.
John Stanssel Sr.	1	3	4	3	2
John Stanssil	1	.	1	.	.
William Baley	1	3	3	.	.
Benjamin Oneal	2	2	4	.	.
Benjamin Crumpler	1	2	3	.	.
Thomas Pender	1	1	3	2	.
Dixon Price	.	1	3	.	.
Rice Price	1	4	3	.	.
Etheldred Price	1	1	1	.	.
Thomas Hollimon	1	2	6	1	2
Saml. Hollimon Jr.	1	.	2	.	.
Nathanel Lewis	2	1	3	.	.
Harbord Gilmon	1	.	1	.	.
Burrel Johnston	1	1	1	.	.
Nathan Price	1	.	5	.	1
Daniel Searsey	1	3	3	.	.
Mathew Harris	1	.	.	.	.
Jethro Woodard	1	3	5	.	.
Gabril Parker	.	4	4	1	3
Julon Tommas, wid.	.	1	1	.	.
John Price	1	1	6	.	.

Head of Household	WM 21-60 yrs.	WM under 21 & above 60	WF all ages	Blacks 12-50	Blacks under 12 & above 50
Thomas Eateman	1	1	1	.	.
William Oneal Jr.	2	5	3	1	2
David Baley	2	4	1	.	1
Arthur Pope Jr.	1	3	4	.	.
Arthur Pope Sr.	.	2	2	.	.
Zachariah Oneal	1	2	5	1	.
William Hollimon	1	3	6	.	.
Amos Oneal	1	2	1	1	.
William Oneal Sr.	1	2	6	.	.
Frederic Holmes	1	2	2	.	.
James Price Jr.	1	2	1	.	.
	53	111	157	21	23

Pg. 3

Head of Household	WM 21-60 yrs.	WM under 21 & above 60	WF all ages	Blacks 12-50	Blacks under 12 & above 50
Benjamin Wilkinson	1	2	3	.	.
John Edward	1	.	.	.	.
Arthur Baley Johnson	1	.	1	.	.
Richard Price	1	2	1	.	.
James Price Sr.	1	2	3	.	.
Wm. Walker ?	1	.	1	.	.
Ezekel Tomberlinson	1	4	2	.	.
Lucy Bryan - harlot	.	1	2	.	.
Edward Price	1	1	1	.	.
Solomon Johnson	2	3	4	.	.
Bashford Morphus	1	.	3	.	.
William Hoccot	3	1	4	.	.
Henry Jorden	1	4	5	.	.
William Hackney	1	.	1	5	6
Fred Hollimon	1	2	2	1	1
William Johnson	1	.	.	.	.
	71	133	190	27	30

"A List of the Inhabitants of Capt. Houlder's Company for the year 1787. Received this 16th March 1787".

"A List of the Inhabitance within the District of Capt. Alexander Hobbys Company for the year 1787. Both white and black of Every Demonanation."

Pg. 1

Head of Household	WM 21-60 yrs.	WM under 21 & above 60	WF all ages	Blacks 12-50	Blacks under 12 & above 50
William Dodd	1	5	4	.	.
Thos. Tomlinson	2	4	5	2	.
Nathan Norriss	1	3	3	.	.
John Norriss	.	3	3	.	.
John Coats	1	2	3	2	.
Emely Vinson	.	.	1	2	1
Charles Parrish	1	?	6	.	2
James Purvis	1	1	1	.	.
Elizabeth Hathcock	.	2	4	.	.

Head of Household	WM 21-60 yrs.	WM under 21 & above 60	WF all ages	Blacks 12-50	Blacks under 12 & above 50
James Norriss	1	1	7	.	.
Sollomon Gail	1	.	.	.	.
James Ogborn	1	.	.	.	.
Bretian Robards	1	.	3	.	.
Charles Royals	.	.	?	.	.
John Pool	1	4	3	.	.
John McCullers	1	4	3	.	.
Hardy Bryan	1	4	2	9	4
David Beel	2	3	1	2	.
Jacob Avera	2	3	7	.	.
Alexd\u02b3. Avera	2	5	5	.	.
Lewis Avera	1	.	.	.	.
Mary Whittington	.	1	4	.	.
John Bryan	1	1	1	10	3
Nehemiah Smith	1	.	1	.	.
Henry Blurten	1	1	3	1	1
Robart Whittington	1	2	4	.	.
Mathew Durham	.	1	.	.	.
David Charles Craft	1	1	1	.	.
Wm. Durham	1	.	.	.	.
Wm. Cannada	1	5	3	.	.
Nahor Norris	1	.	2	.	.
Abram Smith	1	.	1	.	.
John Lewis	1	1	6	.	.
John Smith	1	.	2	.	.
Pg. 2					
Mary Avera	.	2	5	.	.
Richard Willoughby	1	3	3	.	.
Jesse Breet	1	3	4	.	.
Sollomon Serbord	1	.	2	.	.
David Prince	1	5	2	.	.
Moses Rainwater	1	6	4	.	.
Jacob Giles	1	.	.	.	.
Sam. Durham	1	5	5	.	1
Arther Taylor	1	.	.	.	.
Samuell Baulding	1	.	5	.	.
Drewry Peoples	1	1	2	.	.
Alexd\u02b3. Hobby	1	7	3	.	.
Alexd\u02b3. Avryt	1	3	4	1	.

Head of Household	WM 21-60 yrs.	WM under 21 & above 60	WF all ages	Blacks 12-50	Blacks under 12 & above 50
Drewry Vinson	1	2	4	5	.
John Eason	1	.	2	4	4
James Rosser	1	6	3	3	1
Blake Bryan	1	1	1	5	2
Jonathan Smith	1	1	4	14	10
Aaron Vinson	2	2	7	6	7
John Brady	.	2	3	1	.
Salathiel Holston	1	2	1	.	.
Mary Sanders	.	2	4	7	10
Sollomon Staton	1	2	8	2	.
David Smith	1	3	3	.	.
James Butler	.	1	4	.	.
John Gewin	1	3	4	1	.
Nathaniel Giles	1	2	3	.	.
Steven Powel	1	5	6	.	.
Thomas Price	1	1	1	.	.
William Ward	1	3	2	14	11
Abnor Peoples	1	.	2	.	.
Obed Johnston	1	5	3	.	.
James Renn	1	.	2	.	.
John Talton	1	1	2	1	1
Ezekiel Stallings	2	.	.	.	.
Wm. Youngblood	1	.	.	.	.
Alexd\u02b3. Smith	1	.	3	6	2
Pg. 3					
Howel Addoms	1	3	5	.	.
Malcum Gillis	1	.	.	.	.
Malcum Mun	1	.	.	.	.
Richard Brown	1	2	1	.	.
Wm. Avera	1	2	5	5	3

Taken by Wm. Avera

"Of the Inhabitants of the County of Johnston & in Capt. Alex. Hobbys Dist. for the Year 1787 & Received March 16th 1787."

Head of Household	WM 21-60 yrs.	WM under 21 & above 60	WF all ages	Blacks 12-50	Blacks under 12 & above 50
"A list of the White and Black Inhabitants in Jones County as returned by the Several Justies (Justices) Appointed by the Court of said County to Receive the same Heads of families names".					
Pg. 1					
1. Lemuel Hatch Jr	1	2	3	7	11
2. John Hatch	1	2	3	5	7
3. Lamuel Hatch Sr.	1	4	4	1	3
4. John Gregory	1	.	.	5	1
5. John Goslin	1	1	6	.	.
6. Mary Ammyet	.	2	1	.	.
7. John Taylor	1	1	3	.	.
8. Wm. Norment	1	.	.	.	.
9. David Ventress	1	1	2	.	.
10. Richard Crotchfield	1	1	2	.	.
11. Philip Crotchfield	1	.	1	.	.
12. Cornelius Taylor	1	1	.	.	.
13. Eurebious Crotchfield	1	2	2	1	.
14. N(i?)lany or Vilany Allcock	.	3	4	.	.
15. Ann Crotchfield	.	1	2	.	.
16. John Alliver	2	2	2	.	.
17. Durent Hatch	1	.	1	6	7
18. Edmund Hatch	1	.	1	6	7
	16	23	37	31	36
Pg. 2					
19. Peter Andrews	2	5	3	.	.
20. Adam Andrews	1	4	5	2	.
21. Jabez Bump	.	1	1	.	.
22. John Burnet	1	2	6	.	.
23. John Harrison	1	.	.	.	.
24. William Harrison	1	.	.	.	.
25. Vincent Amyet	1	5	3	1	.
26. David Ventress Sr	1	2	5	.	.
27. Wm. Lipsey	1	4	5	.	.
28. Arthur Lipsey	2	3	3	.	.
29. James McDaniel	1	4	5	.	.
30. Rossko Lipsey	1	3	5	1	4
31. James Pollock	1	.	.	.	.
32. Peter Steel	2	2	5	.	1
33. John Eubank	1	4	3	.	.
34. Mark Bogue	2	.	4	.	.
35. Josiah Bogue	1	1	4	.	.
36. Josiah Parrisher	1	.	2	.	.
37. Borden Stanton	1	1	1	.	.
38. Daniel Eubank	1	1	1	.	.
39. Penelope Reynolds	.	3	3	2	3
40. Tho. Morris	2	.	5	.	.
	41	70	105	37	44
41. Sugar Dulin/ Dewlens	2	.	2	.	.
42. Adkin Broxen/ Brocksons	1	2	3	.	.
43. Emanuel Simmons	2	2	3	7	7
44. Jacob Foy	1	1	1	4	5
45. Geo. Ventress	1	1	3	.	.
46. Thos. Philips	1	2	5	.	.
47. Martin Callahan	1	1	1	.	.
48. Nathen Gregory	1	3	3	13	13
49. Richd. Williamson by Edwd. Whitly, Esq.	1	3	2	.	.
50. John Granade	.	2	3	2	1
51. John Saunderson	1	2	2	.	.
52. Robert Grimes	3	3	5	4	3
53. John Tillman	1	2	3	1	.
54. George Eubank	1	4	3	.	.
55. Mary Eagerton	1	1	5	3	2
56. Elijah Eubank	1	.	4	.	.
57. John Eagerton	1	1	2	.	.
58. Benj. Brockitt	1	.	.	2	3
59. Danl. Cobern	1	.	.	.	.
60. Thos. Sanderson	1	1	4	.	.
61. Danl. Simmons	1	2	2	5	8
	62	103	161	79	86
Pg. 4					
62. Wm. Taylor	1	2	3	.	.
63. John Burton Lee	1	2	2	.	.
64. Esther Ramsey	.	.	4	.	.
65. Isaac Williams	1	3	4	.	.
66. David Williamson	1	2	4	5	5
67. Elizabeth Simmons	.	1	3	1	1
68. James Jones	1	.	2	.	.
69. John Jones	1	.	3	.	.
70. Joseph Kinsey	2	.	2	1	.
71. Peter Smith	3	2	3	.	.
72. James Smith	1	.	.	.	.
73. Geo. Whitehead	1	.	.	.	.
74. James Smith	.	2	2	.	.
75. Elizabeth Kinsey	1	.	3	.	.
76. Ann Simmons	2	1	1	7	3
77. George Simmons	1	.	1	5	3
78. John Bender	1	3	3	.	.
79. Joseph Granade	1	4	6	.	.
80. John Mundine	1	3	3	.	.
81. Eliza. Stevens	.	2	2	.	.
82. Kitterill Mundine	1	3	3	.	1
83. Levi West	1	1	1	.	.
	84	132	213	108	108

The next 14 pages (microfilm) of names were duplicated on other pages, sometimes showing a variation in spelling. Both lists are shown below with the discrepancy in parenthesis.

Head of Household	WM 21-60 yrs.	WM under 21 & above 60	WF all ages	Blacks 12-50	Blacks under 12 & above 50
Pg. 5					
84. John West	1	.	1	.	.
85. Kedar Knight	1	2	2	2	1
86. Enas Harrald	1	4	5	.	.
87. Ann Foy	.	.	4	5	9
88. Dudley Cahoon	1	2	3	.	.
89. Wilson Deas/Dias	1	1	3	.	.
90. Levi Sanders	1	.	3	.	.
91. William Skinner	1	.	2	.	.
92. Edmund Hatch Esq	1	3	3	16	16
93. Edward Whitty Esq	1	3	3	1	2
94. Wm. George	2	4	1	1	.
95. John Kinsey	1	3	2	.	.
96. Rebekah Market (or Merkert)	1	4	3	.	.
97. Wm. Griffith	1	3	2	.	.
98. Moses Watson	1	4	1	5	3
99. Tho. Tice(or Lee)	1	3	5	.	1
100. Anthony Barns (or Barnes)	1	3	3	.	.
101. Coleson Johnson	2	3	5	.	.
102. John Littleton	1	3	2	.	.
103. Wm. Clarke	1	1	1	6	4
104. Stephen Yates	1	3	4	.	.
105. Micajah Frazer	1	3	4	7	10
	107	184	275	151	155
Pg. 6					
106. Mary Hill	2	2	3	88	75
107. Joseph Sanderson	1	.	.	1	.
108. Thomas Foy	1	.	.	15	12
109. George Stevens	1	5	3	1	.
110. James Mundine	1	1	1	.	.
111. Isaac Gipson Jr (or Gibson)	1	.	1	1	2
112. Nathan Ball	1	.	1	.	1
113. James Lipsey	1	.	3	.	.
114. Ephraim Stilly (or Stilley)	1	3	1	.	.
115. Thomas Littleton	.	1	3	.	.
116. Sinah Littleton	.	.	1	.	1
117. Stephen Wallis	1	2	1	.	.
118. Jer^h. Watson	.	2	2	2	6
119. Mary Sanderson	1	2	4	6	1
Ret^d. by T. Harget Esq.					

Head of Household	WM 21-60 yrs.	WM under 21 & above 60	WF all ages	Blacks 12-50	Blacks under 12 & above 50
120. Frederick Harget	2	4	5	6	6
121. Henry Jones	1	2	1	.	.
122. Jno. Williamson Jr.	1	1	4	.	.
123. Risdon McDaniel	1	2	4	.	.
124. Edmund Taylor	1	2	2	.	.
125. John McDaniel	1	2	4	.	.
126. John Williamson	.	3	4	.	.
	128	218	321	274	255
Pg. 7					
127. Wm. Harrison	1	3	6	9	14
128. Nehemiah Randal	2	2	5	.	.
129. Benj. Pickrun	1	3	3	.	.
130. John Perry	2	3	4	.	.
131. Richard Pate	2	3	.	.	.
132. Abraham B. Simmons	1	5	8	1	2
133. Benjn. Lavender	1	.	.	.	.
134. Lewis Bryan	2	8	13	13	11
135. Reuben Small	1	2	1	.	.
136. Betsey Kelly	4	4	.	.	.
137. John Bryan	1	3	2	10	26
138. Edwd. Bryan	1	.	1	4	8
139. John H. Bryan	2	.	2	6	6
140. Arthur Blackman	1	.	.	2	.
141. Nathan Womble	1	3	4	.	.
142. Matthew Stevenson	1	4	5	.	.
143. Hugh Stanaland	1	1	2	.	.
144. John Pickren or Pickrun	1	.	1	.	1
145. Gabriel Pickron or Pickrun	1	1	1	.	.
146. Tobias Miller	1	5	2	.	.
147. James Taylor	1	.	2	.	.
148. James Brown	1	.	2	.	.
149. Aaron Pickron or Pickrun	1	4	5	.	.
	159	271	390	319	324
Pg. 8					
150. Thomas Thornton	1	1	2	.	.
151. Caleb Busick	1	1	3	.	.
152. Wm. Spencer	1	.	2	.	.
153. Sabra Johnston	.	1	1	.	.
154. Holladay Packet or Holiday Parker	1	4	2	.	.
155. Southey Sanders	1	.	1	.	.

Head of Household	WM 21-60 yrs.	WM under 21 & above 60	WF all ages	Blacks 12-50	Blacks under 12 & above 50
156. Daniel Perry or Parry	2	3	3	1	2
157. Joseph Gilbert	1	.	.	.	.
158. Henshie Killibrew or Hinchey Kilbrew	1	2	3	.	.
159. James Mashburn	1	3	4	.	.
160. Nathl. Kellum or Kelham	1	2	1	.	.
161. Elijah Kellum or Kelham	1	1	3	.	.
162. Richd. Jelks	1	1	3	.	.
163. Dorcas Alligood	.	2	6	.	.
164. John Adams	1	1	3	.	.
165. William Adams	1	1	1	.	.
166. Nathan Bryan	1	1	4	.	.
167. Joseph Saunders	1	.	5	.	.
168. James Busick	1	4	3	1	.
169. Daniel Koonce	1	3	2	.	.
170. Chas. Saunders	1	1	5	1	1
171. Henry Mainn/ Mainer	1	2	2	.	.
	160	305	448	322	327
Pg. 9					
172. Elizabeth Hall	.	.	2	.	.
173. Wm. Morris	1	2	2	4	.
174. John Freeman	1	.	1	.	.
175. John Saunders or Sanders, Tuckahoe	1	2	5	.	.
176. Alexr. Blackshear	.	1	3	3	2
177. Abraham Black-shear	1	2	4	1	1
178. John Gilbert	2	3	1	2	3
179. Wm. Busick Sr.	1	1	3	.	.
180. John Gilbert Jr.	1	1	1	1	1
181. Benj. Wilcock/s	1	1	1	.	.
182. Joan/Jean Mackey. or Milton	1	.	3	.	.
183. Arthur Smith	1	1	7	.	.
184. Vincent Branson	2	.	1	.	.
185. Philemon Morris	1	4	2	.	.
186. John Saul/s	2	4	7	.	.
187. Wm. Pollard	1	1	4	.	.
188. Robert Humphrey	1	2	1	.	.
189. Wm. Brown Sr.	2	1	2	2	.
190. Tucker Malden or Maulden	1	2	3	.	.
191. Henry Maulden or Maulden	1	2	2	.	.
192. Joshua Melton/ Milton	1	.	3	.	.
193. John Perry Jr. or Parry	1	2	3	.	.

Head of Household	WM 21-60 yrs.	WM under 21 & above 60	WF all ages	Blacks 12-50	Blacks under 12 & above 50
194. Robert Perry or Parry	.	2	3	.	.
	203	340	530	334	335
Pg. 10					
195. John Johnston	1	3	2	.	.
196. John Lavender Jr	1	2	4	1	1
197. Thos. Miller	1	5	2	.	.
198. Samuel Bradshaw	1	3	1	.	.
199. Nancy Conner	.	.	1	.	.
200. John Saunders/ Sanders	.	.	1	.	.
201. Wm. Stevens/ Stephens	1	1	2	.	.
202. Jenny Hobson/ Hopson	.	1	4	.	.
203. Wm. Tippet	1	1	2	.	.
204. John Tippet	.	4	1	.	1
205. James Tippet	1	4	1	.	.
206. Charles King	1	3	5	.	.
207. Jesse Freeman	1	1	1	.	.
208. Edward Bryan or Brown	1	6	3	.	.
209. John Harrison	1	1	4	3	3
210. James Green	1	4	3	3	2
211. Moses Blackshear	1	2	2	.	.
212. Hugh Bradshaw	1	1	5	.	.
213. John Lavender	1	3	5	.	.
214. Christian Spock or Ipack	1	2	2	.	.
215. Samuel King	1	3	6	.	.
216. Danl. Shine	3	4	3	7	5
217. Robert Wilson/ Wilton	1	.	1	1	.
	224	395	593	350	348
Pg. 11					
(Note: Numbers drop by 100)					
118. John Shine	1	.	4	4	.
119. John Still	1	1	1	.	.
120. Wm. Busick Jr.	1	2	2	.	.
121. Rice Dulin	3	3	3	1	1
122. Michl. Smith	1	1	2	.	.
123. Noah Messer	1	2	3	.	.
124. Richd. Pickren/ Pickrun	1	2	6	.	.
125. John Gunter	1	4	5	3	8
126. Thomas Dulin	1	2	4	.	.
127. Jeduthan Gibson	3	.	3	.	.
128. Daniel Harrison	1	2	1	3	.
129. John Frank/Franck	1	1	1	5	4
130. Edwd. Frank/Franck	1	.	.	5	3
131. Wm. Randal	2	.	2	9	10

Head of Household	WM 21-60 yrs.	WM under 21 & above 60	WF all ages	Blacks 12-50	Blacks under 12 & above 50
132. Jordan Pittman	1	.	1	.	.
133. Benj. Messer	1	.	2	.	.
134. John Normant/ Norman	1	.	1	.	.
135. Wm. Jirman/ Jerman	1	1	3	.	.
136. Tobias Murray/ Murry	.	1	1	.	.
137. Jas. McDaniel	1	3	5	.	.
138. Rich^d. Griffin	1	1	3	.	.
139. Solomon Sanders	1	1	2	.	.
140. Ann Pittman	.	3	1	.	.
141. John Tarleton Harrison	1	.	5	.	.
	251	425	654	380	373
Pg. 12					
142. George Becton	1	3	5	5	3
143. John Isler	1	3	3	20	19
144. Mich^l. Becton	1	2	4	4	5
145. Fred^r. Metts/ Mitts	1	2	2	.	.
146. John Becton	1	2	3	5	2
147. George Metts/ Mitts Sr.	.	1	1	.	.
148. Benjn. Cox	1	2	1	.	.
149. Abner Cox	1	.	3	.	.
150. Geo. Metts/ Mitts Jr.	1	2	2	.	.
151. Elisha Cox	.	1	1	.	.
152. George White	1	1	1	1	2
153. John Hawkins Cox	1	1	.	.	.
154. Philip Mew	1	2	3	.	.
155. John Skean	1	1	1	.	.
156. William Ipock	1	.	1	.	.
157. Jesse Skean	2	2	6	.	.
158. John Moye	1	4	3	.	.
159. Zenas Swelly	1	1	5	.	.
160. Thos. Allen	.	1	2	.	.
[numbers skiped]					
170. Alex^r. Hicks	1	.	3	3	2
171. Mary Field/Fields	.	1	3	2	1
172. Joseph Kinsey	1	3	5	.	.
	270	460	712	418	407
Pg. 13					
173. Jacob Rhem	1	6	3	6	10
174. Aaron Gooding	3	1	3	1	3
175. Gershom Stanly or Standley	1	2	4	.	.
176. Elisha Atkinson	1	4	2	.	.
177. Lemuel Lavender	1	.	2	1	.
178. Wm. Dean	1	1	4	.	.
179. Aron/Abron Cox	1	1	4	.	.
180. Charles Gregory	1	.	2	.	1
181. Benjn. Davis	1	3	6	.	.
182. James Jones	1	5	5	.	.
183. Wm. Morgan	1	4	2	.	.
184. John Conner	1	7	5	.	.
185. Mark Conner	1	4	4	.	.
186. Joseph Brock	1	4	4	5	2
187. Clement Prichard	1	.	.	2	5
188. Bazel Prichard	1	.	2	5	6
189. Thomas Fern	1	1	7	.	.
190. Peter Harget	1	3	5	5	5
191. Hester Isler	.	1	4	4	4
192. Benj. Stanly or Standland	1	1	2	.	.
193. Martha Koonce	.	5	3	.	.
194. John Edwards	1	.	.	.	.
	292	513	785	447	443
Pg. 14					
195. Philip McQuillen	1	1	5	.	.
196. Andrew Antwine or Aortwine (?)	1	2	3	.	.
197. Simon Spight	1	4	3	6	11
198. Philemon Pate	1	.	2	1	3
199. Sharpe Reynolds	1	3	3	1	.
200. John Koonce Sr.	1	.	3	2	5
201. Thos. Askew	2	3	7	.	.
202. John Charles	1	.	3	1	1
203. Geo. Koonce Sr.	1	3	4	.	.
204. Christian Koonce	1	.	3	.	.
205. Daniel Harget or Hargit	1	.	2	3	3
206. Eliza. Koonce	.	4	2	4	10
207. Robert Jerman or Jarman	1	2	5	2	.
208. Benj. Stanly or Standland	4	2	3	.	.
209. Rich^d. Reynolds	1	2	6	2	3
210. Martin Stanly or Standland	1	2	2	.	.
211. Abraham Bailey or Baley	1	1	3	.	.
212. James Bailey/ Baley	1	1	3	.	.
213. Priscilla Gilbert	1	3	4	.	.
214. Benj. Fordham	1	3	7	.	.
215. Jacob Lee/Leigh	1	3	8	.	.
216. Howel Brown	1	1	4	.	.
217. Edward Kinsey	1	1	4	.	.
	278	553	873	469	480
Pg. 15					
217. David Wilcocks	1	.	3	.	.
218. John Jackson	1	3	3	.	1
219. John Acton Brice	1	.	3	1	.
220. Samuel Kent	1	1	3	.	.

Head of Household	WM 21-60 yrs.	WM under 21 & above 60	WF all ages	Blacks 12-50	Blacks under 12 & above 50
221. Wm. Jones	1	.	2	.	.
222. Wm. Allen	1	2	2	.	.
223. John Davis	1	2	5	.	.
224. Abraham Little	1	4	4	.	.
225. Wm. Knox	1	3	3	.	.
226. Aron/Aaron Wood	1	2	5	.	.
227. Hardy Jones	1	1	2	.	.
228. Mary Bradshaw or Bratcher	.	3	2	.	.
229. Idolet Gilstrap	1	3	2	.	.
230. Geo. Koonce Jr	1	4	6	1	4
231. Rich^d. Brown	1	1	3	.	.
232. James Blackshear	2	4	2	12	19
233. Wm. Bush	1	1	1	4	4
234. John Koonce Jr	1	4	2	1	1
235. Wm. Connerly	1	2	5	1	.
236. James Stanly or Stanley	1	3	6	.	.
237. John Koonce	1	.	1	.	.
238. Elisha Blackshear	1	2	8	2	.
	300	597	946	490	509
Pg. 16					
239. Benjn. Westbrook	1	6	1	.	.
240. Hannah Everet or Hanah Everet	.	1	6	3	6
241. Sarah Ives	.	1	1	.	.
242. Nathan Bryan by Wm. Orme, Esq.	1	3	4	9	6
244. Israel Gray	1	4	4	.	1
245. Jesse Ricketson	1	.	1	.	.j
246. Joseph Cox Gray	1	1	2	.	.
247. John Shelford or Shelfer	1	5	5	1	.
248. Ben. Gray	1	.	.	.	.
249. John Mallard	1	4	5	.	.
250. Mary Mallard	.	.	2	.	.
251. Zadoc Snead	1	1	1	.	.
252. Sarah Nelson	.	.	3	.	.
253. John Richard	1	1	4	.	.
254. Wm. Herbert/ Harbert	1	.	1	1	.
255. Henry Smith	1	3	3	.	.
256. Edwd. Frost	.	1	3	.	1
257. John Calvet or Colvert	2	3	7	.	.
258. Joshua Collins	1	1	1	1	.
259. Isaac Huggins	1	1	2	.	.
260. Wm. Smith	1	2	2	.	.
	317	635	1004	503	522

Head of Household	WM 21-60 yrs.	WM under 21 & above 60	WF all ages	Blacks 12-50	Blacks under 12 & above 50
Pg. 17					
261. Francis Blount	.	3	4	1	.
262. Joseph Reasonover or Risenover	1	3	1	2	1
263. Joseph Hudler	2	3	2	.	.
264. John Berry or Barrey	1	.	.	.	.
265. John Smith	1	3	4	.	.
266. John Andrew	2	3	6	1	.
267. Sarah Gray	1	1	3	1	2
268. Robert Messer	1	5	4	.	.
269. Gershom Wood or Gershom Woods	1	4	4	.	.
270. John Tracey or Traisey	1	.	5	.	.
271. Huggins Williams	1	.	.	.	.
272. John Hudler	1	.	1	.	.
273. Aaron Lambert	1	4	3	1	1
274. Danl. Mallard	1	2	4	.	.
275. Benj. Williams	1	1	2	.	.
276. Wm. Williams	.	3	2	.	.
277. Oldfield Chance	1	2	4	.	.
278. James Huggins	1	2	5	.	.
279. Wm. Kenaday or Kenaday	1	.	2	.	.
280. Saml. Stevenson	1	1	1	1	1
281. Simon Foscue [Fortescue]	1	2	5	7	1
282. Matthew Moore	1	3	2	2	1
	339	680	1066	519	538
Pg. 18					
283. Hezekiah Merrit or Merrett	1	3	5	1	1
284. Isaac Tillman	1	.	1	.	.
285. John Hudler	1	.	1	.	.
286. Wm. Williamson	1	1	2	.	.
287. James Harrison	2	2	3	.	.
	345	686	1078	520	539

Total 3168

345 white males 21-60 yrs.
686 D^o under 21 & over 60
1078 D^o females of every age
520 Blacks of every sex 12-50 yrs
539 D^o under 12 & over 50
3168 Total amount of white & Black Inhabitants

Returned 30th Sept. 1786.
Lew. Bryan, C. C.

MARTIN COUNTY

"A List of the Inhabitance in District No. 5. Taken pr Micajah Mayo. List of Inhabitants to June Ct. 1787."

Head of Household	WM 21-60 yrs.	WM under 21 & above 60	WF all ages	Blacks 12-50	Blacks under 12 & above 50	Head of Household	WM 21-60 yrs.	WM under 21 & above 60	WF all ages	Blacks 12-50	Blacks under 12 & above 50
Pg. 1						Wm. Hyman	1	1	2	1	.
Nathan Mayo	1	5	4	7	8	Edward Jackson	1	7	5	.	.
John Lewelling	1	2	6	12	8	John Barfell	.	5	3	.	.
Barris ? Summerlin	1	.	3	.	.	James Diel/Deel	1	2	1	.	.
William Bland	1	3	4	.	.	Richard Taylor	1	.	7	.	.
Jno. Rainor	1	1	1	.	.						
Wm. Edmondson	1	1	3	.	.	**Pg. 3**					
Thos. Edmondson	1	3	3	.	.	Luke Scott	1	3	2	.	.
Chas Phillpott	1	3	5	.	.	Richard Harris	2	4	4	.	.
Wils[n] Howard	1	.	2	1	.	Thomas Grimes	1	4	6	2	5
Sam[l] Gater	1	1	3	.	.	George Jackson	.	2	2	.	.
Robt. Savidge Sr.	1	1	1	2	4	Wm. Barfell	1	.	.	.	.
Jno. Edmondson	1	2	2	.	.	James Southerling	2	4	2	1	2
Aba[m] Johston	1	2	2	.	.	William Wallace	1	4	3	2	1
John Oweins	2	1	5	.	.	Henry Cross	.	5	3	.	.
Richard Knight	1	3	3	.	.	Milecha Manning	1	3	1	.	.
Isaac Hill	1	6	5	5	2	The Estate of Wm. Crisp	1	.	1	4	8
George Cockburn	1	2	4	1	1	Ezekiel Crisp	1	1	1	.	.
Britain Savidge	1	2	2	4	7	Jesse Crisp	1	1	3	1	1
Robert Savidge Jr	1	1	1	.	.	Nathan Pippen	1	.	1	.	1
Lewis Purvis	1	2	2	.	.	John H. Jones	1	2	5	3	5
						Mary Wiggins, widow	.	.	1	.	.
Pg. 2						Micajah Little	1	2	5	.	1
John Jones	1	3	3	7	4	William Rainor	1	.	1	.	.
Jethro Howell	1	6	3	3	2	John Garrot	1	2	1	.	.
Mariom Manning	1	3	5	1	1	Charles Barfell	1	3	4	.	.
Jams. Jones	1	2	2	2	.	Demsah Smith	1	1	.	.	.
Thos. Best	1	3	6	8	10		**70**	**144**	**200**	**83**	**78**
John Best	1	.	.	.	1						
John Taylor	1	1	1	.	.	**District 3:**					
Thos. Taylor	1	.	.	.	.	**Pg. 1**					
Fredrick Jones	1	.	.	1	.	William Slade	2	3	2	17	6
Richd. Taylor	1	2	3	1	3	Joel Cherry	1	.	3	.	1
Jos[h] Taylor Jr.	1	.	4	1	.	Joab Cherry	1	3	4	.	.
Charles Counsill	1	5	4	4	2	James L. Wilson	1	1	2	2	.
Joseph Taylor Sr.	1	1	2	.	.	Thos. Fones	1	.	.	.	.
Sam[l] Harrell	1	2	6	.	.	Amos Travis	1	2	1	.	1
Hez[h] Staton	1	.	3	.	.	Sam[l]. Virgin	1	2	3	.	.
Ezekiel Staton	1	4	4	1	5	Wm. Archdeacon	1	1	2	1	.
David Taylor	1	.	6	.	.	Thos. Hunter	4	5	2	18	16
Arthur Staton	1	1	3	1	1	James Nowell	1	1	5	.	.
Jesse Staton	1	5	2	.	.	Henry Hunter	1	1	4	4	8
Nem[h] Staton	1	1	4	.	.	Joseph Bryan	2	3	6	11	10
Benj[n]. Crisp	1	1	3	1	.	Wm. Davis	1	1	2	1	.
Jas. Averitt	1	2	6	.	.	James Powers	1	2	4	.	.
John Smith	2	4	5	5	2	John Ward	1	7	4	4	5
Wm. Jones	1	1	.	1	1						

Head of Household	WM 21-60 yrs.	WM under 21 & above 60	WF all ages	Blacks 12-50	Blacks under 12 & above 50
Jesse Cherry	2	2	3	1	.
Job Cherry	1	5	6	2	3
Ben^a. Burroughs	1	3	5	.	.
Faithfull Cherry	1	2	4	5	.
Benjamin Wheatley	1	2	.	4	3
Nathl J. Magruder	1	1	2	.	.
Daniel Frizle	2	.	4	.	.
James Biggs	1	2	3	.	.
Wm. Biggs	1	2	3	1	1
William Pierce	1	.	4	.	.
Allen Barnes	1	.	.	.	.
Thos. Nicholson	1	1	1	2	2
Miles Hatfield	2	2	3	4	4
Ben^a. Carter	1	6	2	.	.
Timothy Jenkins	1	2	5	.	.
William Garlenton	1	1	3	.	.
Thos. Beaman	1	1	3	.	.
Wm. Jenkins	.	4	3	.	.
Robert Brewer	1	1	2	5	.
Francis Anderson	1	1	1	.	.
John Jenkins	1	.	.	.	.
Ogburn Jenkins	1	2	5	.	.
John Morriss	1	2	5	.	.
Ephraim Wiott	1	2	3	.	.
Rich^d. Williams	1	1	3	.	.
Matthew Yarrell	1	3	5	3	2
Solomon Wiott	1	3	4	.	.
Francis Hodges	1	1	3	.	.
William Sowell	2	1	3	.	.
George Fowler	1	1	3	.	.
Pg. 2					
Obediah Bullock	1	2	2	.	.
William Pulley	1	1	4	3	.
Jesse Woollard	1	.	1	.	.
Zilpah Saunders	.	.	3	.	.
Josiah Nowel	1	.	2	.	.
William Burnett	1	1	1	.	.
Jesse Rawls	1	3	3	.	.
Joshua Rawls	1	4	3	.	.
John Fones	2	2	4	.	.
James Simmons	1	3	2	.	.
Joseph Biggs	.	2	2	1	.
Francis Rawls	.	1	2	.	.
Isaac Phillips	2	.	2	.	.
David Smithwick	1	3	3	.	.
Wm. Spellar Wards	2	5	1	1	6
Levi Swinson	1	.	.	3	2
John Summers	1	2	5	.	.
John Cherry	1	.	1	.	.

Head of Household	WM 21-60 yrs.	WM under 21 & above 60	WF all ages	Blacks 12-50	Blacks under 12 & above 50
James Rawls	1	.	2	.	.
Jeremiah Hassel	1	1	1	.	.
William Brogdon	1	1	2	.	.
John Watts	1	2	3	2	.
Wm. McKenzie	1	2	1	8	8
Dixon Williams	1	1	4	.	.
Thos. Swanner	1	4	2	.	.
Kedar Biggs	1	3	2	.	.
Marcom Short	1	3	5	1	.
John Day	2	1	6	.	.
Mary Cake	.	1	3	1	.
John Kennedy	1	3	5	.	.
William Martin	1	2	.	1	.
John Griffin	1	1	3	.	.
Joseph Warren	1	2	1	.	.
John Leggitt	1	2	3	.	.
Hezekiah Leggitt	1	2	3	.	.
William Ward	2	1	2	.	.
Jesse Mitchell	1	1	1	.	.
Thos. Beach	1	4	2	.	.
William Bagley	1	2	2	.	.
Pg. 3					
Joseph H. Warren	1	2	7	.	1
Amos Hudnal	1	.	.	.	.
Isaac Kennedy	2	.	2	.	.
Nicholas Gilbert	1	.	3	.	.
William Gilbert	1	2	1	.	.
Southy Haselep	1	2	1	.	.
Hardy Wheatley	1	3	6	.	.
Fred^k. Haselep	1	2	2	.	.
Edwd. Bird	2	2	7	5	8
Charles Hooks	.	4	5	.	.
Joseph Lilley	1	1	6	.	.
James Bennett	1	4	2	2	3
William Lanier	1	3	.	.	.
John Lanier	2	4	4	4	.
Thos. Holladay	2	3	6	1	5
William Wynns	1	4	5	5	5
Henry Robason	1	2	1	2	5
Steven Bland	1	4	2	.	.
William Hooks	1	4	5	5	5
Levi Holloway	1	2	1	2	.
William Mobley	1	4	2	.	.
Edward Mobley	1	.	1	.	.
Giles Webb	3	.	4	.	.
Alse Waters	1	1	1	.	.
Wm. Anderson	1	1	2	.	.
Burwell Mitchell	.	2	2	.	.
Saml. Leggett	1	3	3	1	.

Head of Household	WM 21-60 yrs.	WM under 21 & above 60	WF all ages	Blacks 12-50	Blacks under 12 & above 50
Andrew Anderson	1	4	2	.	.
Samuel Saunders	1	3	4	.	.
Joshua Cherry	1	2	3	.	.
Bena. Leggitt	1	1	2	.	.
John Bland	1	.	2	.	.
John Price	1	2	3	.	.
Mary Hudnall	1	1	3	.	.
Jesse Askew	1	.	2	.	.
Arthur Wheatley	2	.	5	.	.
Amy Hagan	2	2	4	.	.
Zach. Lilley	1	.	1	.	.
Harrell Cherry	1	.	2	.	.
Isaac Byrd	1	2	2	.	.
James Mizell	1	2	5	.	.
Wm. Mizell	1	4	1	3	4
Pg. 4					
Elijah Price	1	.	6	3	.
William Rawls	1	3	2	.	.
Joseph Biggs	1	.	2	.	.
Josiah Hedgpeth	1	1	1	.	.
	145	240	345	135	112
(signed) Ebr. Slade					
Pg. 1; 1st col.					
William Hyman	2	1	5	2	1
David Cooper	1	3	4	.	.
Nathan Edmanson	1	.	2	.	.
Simon Butler	1	1	4	7	6
Elisha Horten	1	1	3	.	.
Jacob Strictlain	.	1	2	.	.
Robert Hunter	1	.	.	.	.
Timothy Ward	1	.	.	2	.
William Cooper	1	4	2	.	.
Elijah Vance	1	.	1	.	.
John Vance	1	.	1	.	.
William Purvis	1	2	4	.	.
John Baker	1	1	1	.	.
Ephraim Kiff	1	2	4	.	.
John Price	1	6	4	.	1
Micael Carter	2	3	5	.	.
William Evritt	2	2	2	.	.
Thomas Spellers	1	2	1	2	2
David Horten	1	1	1	.	.
Mathew Griffin	1	2	1	.	.
William Curch	1	2	4	.	.
John Butler	1	3	1	3	3
	24	43	52	16	13
Pg. 1; 2nd col.					
John Drake	1	4	1	.	.
Henry Clark	2	8	2	.	.

Head of Household	WM 21-60 yrs.	WM under 21 & above 60	WF all ages	Blacks 12-50	Blacks under 12 & above 50
Jesse Johnson	1	3	4	.	.
Micajah Hord	1	3	4	.	.
Benjamin Griffin	1	2	6	.	.
Silas Ballard	1	2	1	3	8
Jacob Brayboy	1	2	3	.	.
Daniel Wood	1	1	1	.	.
Mordica White	2	1	2	.	.
Jonas Wood	1	.	2	.	.
Thomas Joiner	1	2	7	4	4
James Counsil	3	.	5	.	1
Isack Boyt	1	1	3	.	.
Lewis Sharrod	1	1	1	4	5
William McDaniel	.	1	2	.	.
William Duggan	1	4	6	1	.
Thomas Pinniwell	1	.	1	.	.
Epenetus Griffin	3	1	1	3	1
Elijah Strawbridge	1	.	.	.	.
Joseph Hansil	2	.	.	.	.
James Little	1	2	2	1	2
John Hansel	1	3	2	1	1
	28	33	56	17	22
Pg. 2; 1st col.					
Wm. Outterbridge Esq	2	1	2	5	4
Eliazar Hyman	1	2	3	3	1
Jesse Pearce	1	2	2	4	3
Randol Sharrod	.	1	.	1	.
John Evrett	1	.	.	.	.
Robert Sharrod	1	4	6	3	3
Ephraim Hoox	1	2	1	.	.
Elias Price	1	.	3	.	.
John Banks	1	2	3	.	.
Etheldred Andrews	1	1	7	5	5
George Forris	1	.	.	.	.
Thomas Davis(,)Carpn.	1	.	.	.	.
Thomas Davis	1	.	.	.	.
John Hortin	1	1	6	.	.
Cloanah Slade	.	6	3	6	4
James Ballard	1	2	3	2	1
Arthur Barden	1	2	2	4	8
John Evritt, Esq.	1	.	2	7	6
Edward Wills	1	.	.	.	.
William Evritt	.	1	.	3	1
Estate of James Evritt &c	.	.	.	3	3
John Bennet	1	1	3	6	5
Mary McGaskey	.	4	3	5	3
	19	32	49	57	46
Pg. 2; 2nd col.					
John Wheatley	1	5	3	1	2

92

Head of Household	WM 21-60 yrs.	WM under 21 & above 60	WF all ages	Blacks 12-50	Blacks under 12 & above 50
	24	43	52	16	13
	28	33	56	17	22
	19	32	49	57	46
	71	113	167	90	83

(signed) William Barden

District 7

Pg. 1

Head of Household	WM 21-60 yrs.	WM under 21 & above 60	WF all ages	Blacks 12-50	Blacks under 12 & above 50
John Parker	1	2	2	.	.
Bena. Sinclear	1	.	3	.	.
Wm. Collins	1	4	2	1	.
John Pettey	1	1	5	.	.
John Cook	1	1	6	.	.
John Lambert	1	2	2	.	.
Saml. Jackson	1	2	5	.	.
Thos. Savage	2	.	2	.	.
Henry Medfort	1	2	1	.	.
John Medfort	1	3	1	.	.
John Rhodes	1	3	1	.	.
James Medfort	1	2	4	.	.
James Howell	1	1	4	.	2
Edward Harrell	1	3	6	.	.
Needham Bryan	1	2	2	4	2
Elias Ballard	.	1	3	.	.
Lewis Bryan	1	3	2	.	.
Thos. Baggett	1	2	2	.	.
Wm. Watson	1	1	3	.	.
Hugh Hyman	1	.	2	1	.
Hester Harrell	.	2	3	2	.
Thos. Watson	1	4	4	1	2
Robt. Bryan	1	3	4	2	1
Abner Brown	1	2	3	2	1
Wm. Freeman	1	2	5	.	.
Elias Ballard Jr.	1	.	1	.	.
John Staford	1	1	5	.	.
Allen Baggett	1	1	1	.	.
Jacob Parker	1	7	2	.	1
Mathew Birnett	1	1	3	.	.
Thos. Baggett	1	.	.	.	.
Thos. Weathersbee	1	.	4	1	2
Thos. Hyman	1	2	2	.	.
Widow Booth	.	.	3	1	.

Pg. 2

Head of Household	WM 21-60 yrs.	WM under 21 & above 60	WF all ages	Blacks 12-50	Blacks under 12 & above 50
Henry Linch	1	1	2	.	.
John Weathersbee	1	.	.	1	1
Thos. Davis	1	1	3	.	.
Jeremiah Culpeper	.	1	.	.	.
Hardy Bryan	1	2	3	.	.
Elisha Ballard	1	2	2	3	4
Wm. Blackwell	1	.	3	.	.
Richd. Jones	1	.	2	.	.
Solo. Boyt	1	1	8	.	.
Jesse Lynch	1	.	2	.	.
Widow Weathersbee	.	4	1	.	.
Jonathan Drake	1	2	4	.	.
Jesse Ballard	1	.	.	.	.
Steven Cross	1	1	2	.	.
John Hines	2	.	4	.	.
Andrew Pearce	1	.	.	.	.
Lovick Pierce	1	2	3	.	.
Phillip Pearce	.	1	2	.	.
John O(')Cain	1	.	.	.	.
Thos. Barnes	1	.	3	.	.
Wm. Kent	1	.	1	.	.
Elias Bryan	1	.	3	5	2
John Hyman	2	2	4	1	2
Ephraim Birnett	1	.	3	.	.
Thos. Bland	1	1	4	.	.
Jonathan Cherry	2	2	4	.	.
William Watson	1	.	2	.	.
Jacob Watson	.	3	2	.	.
Aquilla Long	1	3	2	1	.
James Birnett	1	4	4	.	.
Christopher Hynes	1	4	3	.	.
John Taylor	2	1	4	11	5
Isaac Mitchell	2	4	3	.	.
John Burnett	1	1	8	4	3
Wm. O(')Cain	1	2	2	.	.
Joshua Johnson	1	3	4	.	.
James Kiff	1	.	3	.	.
Wm. Davis	1	.	.	.	.
Steven West	1	1	2	.	.

Pg. 3

Head of Household	WM 21-60 yrs.	WM under 21 & above 60	WF all ages	Blacks 12-50	Blacks under 12 & above 50
Thos. Boyt	1	2	2	.	.
Wm. Weathersbee	.	1	2	.	.
Joseph Cooper	1	3	5	.	.
Lott Harrell	1	4	6	4	9
Zachariah Harrell	1	.	2	.	.
George Etheringane	1	1	2	1	2
John Carter	1	1	3	1	.
Leml. Jackson	1	.	1	.	.
Ann Belflour	.	4	2	.	.
Whitll. Hill	2	3	3	130	32
Isum Nowel	.	1	.	.	.
Wm. Price	2	.	4	.	.
James Brown	1	6	4	2	2
Zachariah Archer	3	1	4	.	.
Thos. Price	1	.	.	.	.

Head of Household	WM 21-60 yrs.	WM under 21 & above 60	WF all ages	Blacks 12-50	Blacks under 12 & above 50
Saml. Williams	1	2	5	43	47
Jacob Brown	1	.	1	1	.
Wm. Price Jr.	1	.	.	.	.
Varnell Adams	1	.	1	.	.
Daniel Rogers	1	.	4	.	.
Lem^l. Wiggins	1	4	4	6	11
Mich^l. King	2	1	3	11	6
Joel Harrod	2	.	.	.	.
Wm. Sinclear	1	.	.	.	.
Hodges Moore	4	.	2	9	15
Thos. Carnall	2	1	2	7	6
Wm. Guy	1	8	2	3	1
Henry Guy	1	.	.	.	.
Lewis Watts	2	1	2	.	2
John Guy	1	.	.	.	.
Blake B. Wiggins	1	4	5	12	17
Joshua Taylor	1	4	4	11	4
Samson Mahoon	1	.	.	.	.
Thos. Brewer	1	4	4	.	.
Timothy Collins	1	1	5	1	2
Jos. Redding	1	1	3	5	3
Thos. Andrews	1	1	3	5	3
John Wiggins	.	3	.	2	1
Widow Bayless	.	.	4	1	1
Wm. Williams	1	3	2	20	22
	117	165	259	318	211

"Agreeable to an Order of the Worshipfull Court of Martin County to me directed to take the list of Inhabitants of District No. 1 the under mentioned is a true list taken by John Stewart June 16th 1787".

Pg. 1; col. 1

Head of Household	WM 21-60 yrs.	WM under 21 & above 60	WF all ages	Blacks 12-50	Blacks under 12 & above 50
Shubal Claghorn Sr.	1	2	3	.	.
Shubal Claghorn Jr.	1	2	3	.	.
Haws Claghorn	1	1	1	.	.
John King	1	1	1	.	.
William Carkeett	2	2	4	.	1
Henry Olivant	1	.	2	.	.
James Hardison	2	.	.	.	.
Thomas Hardison	1	.	5	3	2
James Mackay	1	.	.	.	.
John Smithey	1	2	1	2	1
Benjamin Demeret	1	.	1	.	.
Richard Hardison	1	1	5	1	.
Thos. H. Hudson	1	2	4	.	.
Nathl. Everett Sr.	1	3	5	3	6
John Stewart	2	2	6	23	8
Willm. Hinson	1	1	3	.	.

Head of Household	WM 21-60 yrs.	WM under 21 & above 60	WF all ages	Blacks 12-50	Blacks under 12 & above 50
Jeremiah Gerkin	1	3	4	.	.
Thos. Browning	1	1	1	.	.
Rebekah Morris	.	3	4	.	.
David Hardison	1	2	2	.	.
Abagail Ange	.	2	1	.	.
Darcus Harrison	.	1	3	.	.
Mich^l. Melon	1	.	2	.	.
Hannah Seals	.	1	7	.	.
Mary Hudson	.	2	3	.	.
Frances Ange	1	3	1	.	.
Sarah Moss	.	.	2	.	.
Mary Moss	.	1	1	.	.
Drury Narn	1	.	2	.	.
Ben. Blount	1	3	2	.	.
John Collins	1	3	4	.	.
Stevens Fagan	1	.	3	.	1
William Hardison	2	4	4	1	1
Rich^d. Fagan	1	3	4	.	.
Salvanus Buttrey	1	3	4	.	.
Charles Vernitson	.	2	3	.	.
Charles Vernitson Jr	1	1	2	.	.
Joseph Hardison	1	3	4	4	3
John Buttrey	1	3	4	.	.
Benjamin Moss	1	3	5	.	.
John Philps	.	1	1	.	.
Addison Watson	1	.	2	.	.
	37	68	122	37	22

Pg. 1; col. 2

Head of Household	WM 21-60 yrs.	WM under 21 & above 60	WF all ages	Blacks 12-50	Blacks under 12 & above 50
Mary Watson	.	2	3	.	.
Henry Hooton	1	1	3	1	.
Willm. Hooton Sr.	.	1	2	6	6
Charles Hooton	1	2	5	4	.
Willm. Hotton Jr.	1	1	1	4	3
Aaron Demerit	1	1	4	.	.
Sarah Cobb	.	.	4	.	.
William Moss	1	1	4	.	.
John Griffin	1	1	5	.	.
Sarah Crooley	.	.	5	1	.
Mich^l. Stealy	1	1	1	.	.
David Broun	1	1	1	.	.
James Garrett	1	1	2	.	.
John Middleton	1	.	2	3	2
Edwd. Cooper Sr.	2	.	5	.	1
Henry Cooper	1	.	4	.	.
Edwd. Cooper Jr.	1	.	2	.	.
Locatan Cooper	1	1	2	.	.
John Smith	1	1	4	.	.
Willm. Smith	1	.	3	.	.
Rebekah Hardison	.	2	1	.	.
Job Ready	2	.	1	.	.

Head of Household	WM 21-60 yrs.	WM under 21 & above 60	WF all ages	Blacks 12-50	Blacks under 12 & above 50
Thomas Ames	1	2	3	.	.
David Griffen	1	2	1	.	.
Arch^d. Simpson	1	4	2	.	.
Luke Mezell Sr.	.	2	.	4	6
Edwd. Mezell	1	3	3	1	.
John Mezell	1	2	6	2	1
Willm. L. Mezell	1	.	.	1	.
James Mezell Jr.	1	4	2	.	.
Maurice Moore	2	2	1	5	3
John H. Hudson	1	3	6	1	.
Robert Warbritton	1	.	3	3	.
Thomas Brown	1	2	2	1	.
Willm. Philps	1	4	5	.	.
James Stubbs	1	2	4	.	.
Caswell Hassell	1	1	5	.	.
Joshua Hardison	.	4	3	4	4
James Mezell Sr.	1	3	1	.	.
Josiah Smith	1	3	3	4	1
John Hardison	1	3	2	.	.
Frances Ward	1	.	5	15	17
	38	63	121	60	44
	27	68	122	37	23

613 Souls

[This list undesignated, but in same handwriting as District No. 7]

Pg. 1

Head of Household	WM 21-60 yrs.	WM under 21 & above 60	WF all ages	Blacks 12-50	Blacks under 12 & above 50
William Griffin	2	1	.	6	6
John Ross Sr.	1	4	4	2	3
Daniel Cockburn	1	.	2	.	.
Ezekiel Cockburn	1	.	1	.	.
Abner Cockburn	1	1	3	.	.
Zach. Pinket	1	.	3	.	.
Francis Cockburn	1	4	2	1	1
Jonas Mayo	1	3	3	.	.
Benj. Morriss	1	.	.	.	.
Joseph Moore Jr.	2	2	4	1	.
Martin Joyce	1	2	5	.	.
Malachi Smith	1	1	3	2	2
James Brewer	1	1	6	.	.
John Whitfield	1	1	3	.	.
John Brewer	.	3	4	.	.
John Ross Jr.	1	2	3	.	.
Joseph Ross	1	1	5	.	.
Wm. Harrill	1	2	.	.	.
John Joyce	.	2	1	1	3
Stapleton Bonner Jr.	2	2	2	.	.
Griffin Cockburn	1	.	.	.	.
Alex^r. Phillips	1	3	4	.	.
Luke Matthews	1	2	1	.	.

Head of Household	WM 21-60 yrs.	WM under 21 & above 60	WF all ages	Blacks 12-50	Blacks under 12 & above 50
Jesse Cone	2	1	1	1	.
Neal Cone	1	1	7	.	.
Willis Whitfield	1	.	3	.	.
John Cockburn	1	1	2	.	.
Thos. Ross	.	1	1	.	.
Silas Ballard	1	1	3	2	2
Ephraim Kennedy	4	1	4	.	.
Robert Johnson	2	2	3	.	.
Cloe Hurst	1	3	2	.	.
David Vance	1	2	5	.	.
Isaac Glisson	2	.	.	.	.
George Cockburn	.	4	5	2	.
Thos. Smith	1	2	3	.	.
Wm. Cone	2	5	4	.	.
Elizabeth Whitley	.	.	2	.	.

Pg. 2

Head of Household	WM 21-60 yrs.	WM under 21 & above 60	WF all ages	Blacks 12-50	Blacks under 12 & above 50
Joseph Moore	1	3	4	.	.
John Warbutton	1	.	2	.	.
James Smith	1	3	1	.	.
Willis Belch	1	1	4	.	.
James Brogdon	1	2	4	.	.
John Collings	8	3	6	.	1
John Summerlin	1	1	3	.	.
William Kelley	1	1	2	.	.
Vincent Page	1	1	2	.	.
Francis Martin	2	3	4	.	.
Samson Taylor	1	1	2	.	.
Caleb Joyce	1	2	6	.	.
Hugh Ross	3	6	9	1	1
James Cross	1	3	1	.	.
Stapleton Bonner	1	1	.	2	.
Nathan Ross	1	5	2	.	.
Jacob Morriss	2	2	4	.	.
Hezekiah Mchoon	1	1	3	.	.
George Roebuck	1	1	3	.	.
John Thomas	1	3	5	.	.
Wm. son (of) John Ross	1	.	2	.	.
Alex^r. Brown	1	2	4	.	.
Amelia Blount	.	.	2	1	.
Prue M'Hoon	.	.	2	.	.
John Powell	1	.	1	.	.
Jesse Ellisson	1	4	5	.	.
Jehu Griffen	1	.	2	.	.
Thomas Currell	1	4	1	2	4
George Cader	1	.	2	.	.
Edward Balentine	.	2	4	1	3
Nehemiah Balentine	1	.	3	.	.
John Cockburn Sr.	2	2	8	.	.
William Ross	1	1	2	.	.

Head of Household	WM 21-60 yrs.	WM under 21 & above 60	WF all ages	Blacks 12-50	Blacks under 12 & above 50
William Moore	1	1	4	.	.
John Cobb	1	6	5	.	.
Pg. 3					
Levi Rogers	1	1	5	.	.
William Page	1	1	3	.	.
John Page	1	1	2	.	.
James Ross Sr.	2	1	1	.	.
Sampson Taylor	1	1	4	.	.
James Barkhill	1	3	3	.	.
Starling Rogers	1	4	4	.	.
William Gatlen	1	.	1	.	.
William Whitfield	1	.	6	.	.
Jethro Collins	1	.	2	.	.
Ephraim Bullock	1	3	2	.	.
Hannah Hurst	.	2	1	.	.
Lucreasy Moon	.	.	3	.	.
Leavy Cone	1	.	2	.	.
John Griffen	1	.	1	4	5
Benja. Blount	1	.	1	.	.
Jesse Cooper	1	1	3	.	.
William Warbutton	1	1	6	.	.
John Ballard	2	1	7	2	4
	98	145	275	37	35

[Undersignated list, but same handwriting as District No. 7]

Head of Household	WM 21-60 yrs.	WM under 21 & above 60	WF all ages	Blacks 12-50	Blacks under 12 & above 50
Pg. 1					
Robert Lanier	1	3	3	2	1
David Rogers	1	5	4	.	.
William Smithwick	1	1	3	2	.
Josiah Lilley	1	3	1	.	.
John Sones	2	3	4	.	.
Sarah Lanier	1	5	2	1	3
Elizabeth King	3	3	4	.	.
Whitmel Reddick	.	3	1	2	.
John Jones	2	1	.	.	.
David Carraway	2	3	3	2	3
James Swain	1	2	.	2	2
John Lanier	1	1	2	1	2
Burrell Mitchell	1	4	2	.	.
Winburn Jenkins	1	2	2	.	.
Luelling Leggitt	1	.	4	.	1
Mills Eason	1	1	2	.	.
David Leggitt	1	4	1	.	.
William Mattocks	1	1	2	.	.
William Swain	3	.	1	.	.
Timothy Lilley	3	3	2	.	.
James Campbell	1	2	2	.	.

Head of Household	WM 21-60 yrs.	WM under 21 & above 60	WF all ages	Blacks 12-50	Blacks under 12 & above 50
Kedar Lilley	1	1	4	.	.
Phillip Williams	1	1	2	.	.
Hardy Stallings	1	2	6	.	.
William Robason	2	3	4	.	.
Joshua Robason	1	1	5	2	5
James Robason	1	5	7	.	.
Jesse Manning	1	3	4	.	.
David Robason	1	.	2	.	.
Edwd. Griffen	1	2	1	2	.
William Griffen	.	2	2	.	.
Saml. Gardner Sr.	1	1	4	.	.
Isaac Gardner Sr.	1	1	2	.	.
Thomas Gardner	1	3	1	.	.
Hardy Hollady Hudson	1	1	2	.	.
John Hardison	1	1	3	2	4
Bentley Manning	1	3	3	.	.
Mary Eason	.	1	6	3	2
Aaron Duggan	1	3	4	2	.
Joseph Wetherington	1	2	2	1	.
Pg. 2					
Richd. Woollard	2	2	5	.	.
Thos. Bennett Jr.	1	2	6	.	.
James Daniel	1	.	2	3	.
James Robason	1	2	3	.	.
George Godward	2	1	3	.	.
William Warren	1	1	7	.	.
John Williams	1	.	1	.	.
Luke Mizell	1	1	4	.	.
Martin Griffen	1	5	3	.	.
Mark Mizell	.	2	5	1	.
Edmund Smithwick	1	3	4	6	8
Saml. Gardner	2	2	4	.	1
Isaac Gardner	2	4	3	.	.
Cathrine Slaughter	.	1	3	.	.
Joseph Price	1	3	2	.	.
William Bennett	1	5	3	3	4
Thos. Bennett Sr.	.	2	1	3	2
John Cory	2	6	2	.	.
James Woollard	1	1	2	.	.
John Woollard	1	.	1	.	.
Benja. Woollard	2	2	4	.	.
Jacob Tyce	1	5	2	.	.
William Ross	1	3	4	1	4
Martin Ross	1	2	3	1	4
Christian Reddick	2	2	4	3	3
Elizabeth Swain	.	2	3	.	2
John Reddick Jr.	1	.	3	.	.
David Reddick	1	3	5	.	.

Head of Household	WM 21-60 yrs.	WM under 21 & above 60	WF all ages	Blacks 12-50	Blacks under 12 & above 50	Head of Household	WM 21-60 yrs.	WM under 21 & above 60	WF all ages	Blacks 12-50	Blacks under 12 & above 50
John Reddic Sr.	1	6	1	2	2	Rich^d. Taylor	1	.	1	1	.
William Duggan	1	2	3	1	1	Thos. Sparkman	1	.	3	.	.
Edwd. Smithwick, Esq.	1	4	5	5	10	Saml. Smithwick, Esq.	2	5	4	13	9
Luke Smithwick	1	.	1	1	.	David Robason Sr.	1	2	5	.	2
Edwd. Smithwick Jr.	1	1	1	1	.	John Bennett	1	1	2	.	1
George Moore	2	4	6	.	.	John Robason	1	2	2	.	.
Charlton Clemmons	1	3	5	1	1	Daniel Robason	1	1	1	.	.
						William Perry	1	1	1	.	.
Pg. 3						William Daniel	1	1	5	2	.
Jesse Davis	1	1	2	2	2	John Griffen	2	4	6	.	.
John Smithwick Sr.	2	1	3	3	3	John Perry, Esq.	2	?	5	3	5
Saml. Smithwick Jr.	1	1	2	.	.	John Peal	1	1	2	.	.
Simon Daniel	1	.	3	1	3	John Backus	1	1	3	.	.
John Smithwick Jr.	1	1	3	1	.		105	196	280	80	84
William Gardner	1	4	4	.	.						

MONTGOMERY COUNTY

"State North Carolina, Montgomery County. Dist. No. 2. In obedence to an order of The County Court of Montgomery And Agreeable to an act of the General Assembly I have Numbered the Inhabebtence In the above Districk As(?) wearther Extend & Certified." This 3rd Day of July 1787.

James Butler."

[On back of this list is: "Dist. No. 2 - "this List Contains the Number of the inhabatans in Dist. No. 2".

Pg. 1

Head of Household	WM 21-60 yrs.	WM under 21 & above 60	WF all ages	Blacks 12-50	Blacks under 12 & above 50
Rasha Sugg	2	1	3	.	.
William Jordan	1	[blur]	.	.	
Ruben Jordan	1	[blur]	.	.	
Jas. Runels (?)	1	4	4	.	.
Thomas (M?)oras	1	.	3	.	.
David Boling	1	1	5	.	.
Jesse Hurt	1	1	2	.	.
John Boling	1	2	1	2	2
Joseph Nicoles	1	2	2	.	.
Joshua Butler	1	1	5	.	1
William Osher (?)	1	3	2	.	.
William Holtom	1	4	2	.	.
William Holtom	.	1	1	2	.
George Archer	1	3	5	.	.
Edmon Nicoles	.	2	2	.	.
Henery Stephens	1	.	2	.	.
John Stephens	2	3	1	.	.
Spencer Holtom	1	4	4	.	1
George Gilbord	1	2	2	.	.
James Stephens	1	5	3	.	.
Edmon Nicoles	1	3	2	.	.
Tapely Tullus	1	3	3	.	.
Thomas Hayes	1	1	?	.	.
George Stogner	1	?	?	.	.
William Nicoles	1	2	1	.	.
John Harden	1	1	3	.	.
John Boling	1	2	1	.	.
Joseph Holtom	1	1	2	.	.
	28	55	73	4	4

Pg. 2

Head of Household	WM 21-60 yrs.	WM under 21 & above 60	WF all ages	Blacks 12-50	Blacks under 12 & above 50
John Ussery	1	.	2	.	.
James Sanders	[blur]	2	.	.	

Head of Household	WM 21-60 yrs.	WM under 21 & above 60	WF all ages	Blacks 12-50	Blacks under 12 & above 50
John Nicoles	1	3	3	.	.
Ishum Smith	1	2	4	.	.
Benager Ransdle(?)	1	1	6	.	.
Richard Green	1	3	5	.	.
John Humble	1	.	2	.	.
Jafery Sanders	1	.	2	.	.
John Stogner	1	1	2	.	.
Haton Moris	1	4	4	.	.
Leus Bishop	1	1	2	.	.
John Moris	1	.	3	.	.
Haton Moris	1	.	1	.	.
William Boling	1	2	2	.	.
Jacob Humble	.	6	4	1	.
John Gibens(?)	1	1	3	.	.
Joseph Wade	2	3	5	.	.
Ruben Holdness	1	2	5	.	.
Johnson Ransdle	1	3	1	.	.
Joseph Hurt	1	1	4	.	.
Nathan Smith	1	.	.	.	.
Henery Jackson	?	5	5	.	.
James Simmons	1	?	3	.	.
Thos. Jenkins	1	2	3	.	.
Thos. Ward	1	.	4	.	.
Danel Hix	1	.	2	.	.
	54	107	156	5	5

Pg. 3

Head of Household	WM 21-60 yrs.	WM under 21 & above 60	WF all ages	Blacks 12-50	Blacks under 12 & above 50
George Sugg	1	2	5	.	.
Elija Ussery	1	?	?	.	.
Jasse McClendon	1	4	2	4	4
John Davidson	1	.	.	.	.
John Cheek(?)	.	.	.	1	.
William Morgin	1	1	7	.	.
Thomas Mason	1	2	5	.	1
Isham Williams	1	.	4	1	1
Jonathan Williams	.	1	1	.	.
Samuel Williams	1	5	2	.	.
James Scarbrough	1	4	1	.	.
Nimrod Crosswell ?	1	1	1	.	.
Henry Fraser/Frazer	1	.	.	.	.
Amos Williams	1	.	.	.	.
Eliseth Liley	.	2	1	2	2
Benje Handcock	1	5	4	.	.
Job Benten	1	2	4	.	.
John Butler	.	3	2	.	1
Collin(?) McCray	1	6	2	1	.

STATE CENSUS OF NORTH CAROLINA 1784-1787

Head of Household	WM 21-60 yrs.	WM under 21 & above 60	WF all ages	Blacks 12-50	Blacks under 12 & above 50
Aleck Sander McCray	2	1	2	.	.
Charles Campbell	1	2	1	.	.
William Barnes	1	3	7	.	.
John Scarbrough	.	3	3	3	2
Solomon Williams	1	1	?	.	.
James Smith	1	1	?	1	.
Joseph (Hall?)	1	3	4	.	.
Benjamin Stogner	1	2	2	.	.
John Ballard	1	4	5	.	.
Joshua Usery	1	1	2	.	.
	79	166	235	17	15
Pg. 4					
Elasebeth Ussery	.	3	2	.	.
Mary Farcloth	.	.	.	1	3
Mathew Bassherd (?)	.	1	2	.	1
Hanson Quin	1	3	4	1	.
Stephen Williams	1	2	3	.	.
Thos. Williams	1	.	10	.	.
Seth Williams	1	7	1	1	2
Mathew Bassherd(?)	1	3	3	.	1
James Bassherd(?)	1	.	.	.	.
Sias(?) Billingsley	1	5	3	.	.
Randle Cheek	1	4	2	.	.
Charles Spencer(?)	1	.	1	.	.
David Fowler	1	.	.	.	.
Nevil Benet	1	3	2	.	.
Jesse More	1	1	5	.	.
David Dumes	1	7	3	5	7
William Bergis (?)	1	3	3	.	.
Thos. Megginson	1	4	4	3	1
James Williams	1	2	3	1	.
Mathew Harril	1	.	3	.	1
James Enet(?)	1	2	1	.	.
John Thomson	1	2	4	.	.
Henery Debry	1	5	4	1	.
Martin Hill	1	.	.	.	.
Nichles Christen	?	3	4	1	2
John Boyed	?	?	2	.	.
David (C?)orgie					
Marthy Willson	1	2	2	2	2
Corneales Roberson	1	3	3	1	8
	105	233	315	42	43
Pg. 5					
Charles Roberson	1	.	.	2	.
Colba Randle	1	3	3	1	1
John Hill	1	4	3	.	.
Edmon Liley	1	.	.	3	1
Elias Butler	1	3	1	.	1

Head of Household	WM 21-60 yrs.	WM under 21 & above 60	WF all ages	Blacks 12-50	Blacks under 12 & above 50
Thos. Butler	1	1	3	.	.
Richard Tilman	1	3	3	3	.
John Lightfoot	1	2	3	2	.
Thomson Haris(?)	1	1	3	1	.
Thos. Prichard	.	1	2	.	.
John Kimbrough	1	1	4	.	.
Ed. Chambers	1	3	5	2	.
Carey Prichard	1	2	3	4	.
Wm. Pearse	1	2	2	.	.
Roger Williams	1	4	3	.	.
Aron Lancaster	1	.	1	.	.
James Butler	1	2	4	.	.
	121	269	360	60	46

Taken 3rd Day July 1787 by James Butler

The remaining seventeen pages of Montgomery County have been marked by the North Carolina Department of Archives and History as "Very very Poor Material."

District No. 4
Pg. 1; column 1
1. George Davidson   1 4 5 7 5
2. Jasiah Davidson
3. William Randle
4. Ephrim A----
5. John ----
6. Richard ----
7. Majr. Jno. ----
8. Joseph (Smith?)
9. Sarah Davidson
10. George Shankel
11. Abraham Shankil
12. Geo. Shankil J. (Jr. ?)
13. Jacob Shankil
14. John Swearingen
15. Zedekiah ----   (#15 & #16 have)
16. Hannah (Lockett???) (same last name)
17. John Cheek
18. Jacier(?) Colley (on 1790 census as Joyee Coley)
19. Phillip Linch
20. Vallentin Vanhoose
21. Jas. Loe (Lee?)
22. Edmd. Randle
23. Phil Mabery

99

24. Joseph N(or V?) ----?
25. Josies (Josier?) A(?)----?
26. Wm. John---?
27. Danl. Cat---? (A Daniel Cato 1790 Census)
28. Jos. Johnson
29. George Ren---?
30. Gabril Davis
31. Isaac Davis
32. Nich^s. (Baescom or Baylom?
    on 1790 Census as Boyeom;
    probably Baucom?)
33. Sarah Mabry
34. John Johnson

Pg. 1; column 2
35. Robert (Forrist??)
36. Wm. (Barnes?)
37. Thos. Simpson
38. Wm. Rice
39. Saml. Kelly
40. (Joseph?) Cheek
41. Thos. ----
42.
43.
44. Alexr. (F---- or T----)
45. Jno. Randle (Sr. ?)
46. Wm. Woolley
47. Jno. Scharbrough (?)
48. Joseph Bennett
49. Thos. Noble
50. Wm. Horton
51. (Sanct? or Sarah?) Cox
52. Andrew Rankin
53. Jno. Curtis
54. Joshua Carter
55. Benja. Fincher
56. Thos. Roland
57. Jno. (W or F?)aning
58. Jona. (?) Fincher(?)
59. Pern---? ----
60. Jno. ? ----
61. Wm? ----
62. Jas. Ma---?
63. Thos. Ha--- (or Hu---?)
64. Jno. Cox
65. Jno. Morris
66. Robert Walker
67. James Cox
68. Jno. Tankesley
69. Benja. Comings(?)

Pg. 2; column 1
70. Fedrick Rogers
71. Chas. Meriman
72. Chas. Lewis
73. Saml. Carter
74. James Rodgers
75. Peter Ware
76. Saml. P----?
77. Roland ----
78. Jno. H----
79. Isaac ----
80. Saml. C----
81. James Herne(?)
82. Kinchen Penington
83. Danl. McLester
84. Moses Curtis
85. Littleton Fisher
86. Andrew Harrison
87. Saml. Bowen
88. Joseph (B or R----)
89. Robert ----
90. Jno. Thomas
91. Dority Fox
92. Jno. Dunn
93. Simson Noble
94. Nich^s. Meriman
95. Jno. Martin
96. Bredy (?) ----
97. Jacob ----
98. Abner (N?----)
99. Hez--- ----
100. Bartlet Mc----?
101. Wm Mc(Grice?)
102. Thos. Sugg
103. Wm Miller Esqr.
104. David Gray
106. Neddy Penington
107. Ephraim Carter
108. Wm. Noble (Sr. or Jr. ?)

Pg. 2; column 2
109. Thos. Vandyke
110. Mich^l. Wever
111. David Noble
112. Richd. Tindall
113. Fedrick Earles
114. Samson B----
115.
116.
117.

118. Howel ----
119.
120.
121. West (Har(ris?)
122. Robert ----
123. Abraham ----
124. Wm. Kendal
125. Charles Jones
126. Isaac Strowd
127. John F. Smith
128. Joshua Carter
129. Isaac Brown
130. Wm. Noble (Sr. ?)
131. John Robbins(?)
132. Hartwell ----
133. John Kirk
134. Robert Moss
135. Mark Allen
136. Thomas Durham

State of North Carolina, Montgomery Co.
"In Obediance to an Order [of] the Court
of sd County and an Act of the Genl.
Assembly I have Take the Number of the
Inhabitants in District No. 4
       Qalified p me
          Thos. Durham   J. P. "

District No. 5 - 1787
(1 sheet - 2 columns on front, an
endorsement on back)
1. John ----
2. Moses ----
3. John ----
4. Geo. W----
5. John (Allen?)
6. Eperphero(?) ----
7. Richard Almoad
8. John Hamblett
9. Wm. Irbey
10. Edward ----
11. Isaac ----
12. Isaac ----
13. James ----
14. James ----
15. Benjamin ----
16. Thos. Mat---?
17. Hudson (Taylor?)
18. Edmond (Taylor?)
19. Jessee Gilbert

20. James Bankston
21. Wm. Wever
22. Spener ----
23. Henry (Taylor?)
24. James ----
25. Wm C----?
26. David ----
27. Hil--? ----
28. Shad--- ----
29. Hezekiah ----
30. Wm----
31. Thos. (Almond?)
32. Geo. Cal---?
33. Augustin (Roland?)
34. Thos. Reg(ister?)
35. Wm Mc----
36. Joel ----
37. Shearwood ----
38. Cha$. ----
39.
40. John ----
41. Wm ----
42. Thos. Landram (?)

      Pg. 1; column 2
43. Medellin Poole(?)
44. Bryant (Austen?)
45.
46. John (C?)oop(er?)
47.
48.
49.
50. John Cheek
51. John (Rogers[on?]?)
52. Paul Daniel
53. Nimrod (Taylor?)
54. George Whitley?
55. Francis(?) ----
56.
57.
58.
59.
60.
61. Luke ----
62. Anthony (Hol?)land
63. Barton(?) Daniel(?)
64. Tyree Roberson
65. Wm Johnson
66. Alexander ----

101

67. Gideon
68. Wm (Polk Sr. ?)
69. Thos. ----
70. Robert ----
71.
72.
73.
74. Edmond ----
75. David (Nisbet?)
76.
77. Reuben (Hildreth?)
78. James (Fletcher?)
79. Peter ----
80. (James?) ----
81.
82.

(Unidentified list)
Pg. 1
---- Mask
James McDaniel
John Saow(?)
Robart Levintt(?)
Edwen Ingrum
Callup Tuchstone
Edward McCollum
John Smith Sh.
Isaac Armstrong
Wm Sowell
Wm Hogwood
Grifen Hogwood
Elisabeth Hogwood

Pg. 2
Samuel Persons(?)
Randolph Blake
Jasse(?) Wallis
David(?) ----
Elisabeth (S?)immons
Thos. Ussery
Joseph Allin
John Ward
Benjamin Page
John Simons
Wm Right
John Persons
Mary Deton
Thomas Ward
Abraham Cockrum

---- Luckus?
Jonathan Carpender
James Cotten
Thos. Cotten
Joseph Smith
---- Smith
(Richard?) Ellkins

Pg. 3
Marg(?) Caskill
Sion ----
Swain McIn----?
Little John MCaskill
Wm Frishore(?)
Normond MCloud
Daniel Battin
Malcom MCafee
Alexander MClandon
Malcom Chism
Steth Pemberton
Thomas Cottrell
Donkin (MCloud?)
John ----
---- ----
Steven Tuchstone
John McDonnald
Petter Batton?

Pg. 4
(illegible, except for what looks like
John Sugg?)

(Unidentified list) (Many names illegible)
Pg. 1
James McDonald Jr. ?
Gordon Gu----?
John Macklemore
James Maclemore
Jacob Redwine
William Ashford?
John Morris
John Taylor
William Taylor
John Taylor
Thomas Tolbart?
George ----
Joseph ---- (These two have same last
Walter ---- (names [Reaves???]

Allexander Goodwin
Samuel ----
Simon ----
Thomas (Ussry?)
Robt. Lax
Casper(?) Friddle(?)
Stephen Hearne
William Stewart
Josiah Hurley
Georg Sugg?
Simon Hankok?

Pg. 2
John Davis
Jos. Hurley
John Russel
James Harris
Wm? Monday
Arthur Harris
Michel ----

Pg. 3
Moses Curtis
Benjamin Bell
John Bell
Richd. Bell
Ransom (Williams?)
John ----

Axom ----rter?
Jesse Clifton
Wm Clifton
Philemon Edwards
John Harris
Henry Colthorp
Turner Harris
Gadwell (Doarke?)
Thos. Williams
Jesse Harris
Brantley Harris
Wm Morgan
Christopher Chapel
John Psalmer?
Arthur Harris
John Barnet
John Dixen
George Monroe
Joel M--ley?
George Williams
John Harris
John (Baker?)
Mark Bennet Esqr.
Drury(?) Bennet
---- Bennett
Nathaniel Edwards
James McDonald

NEW HANOVER COUNTY

Head of Household	WM 21-60 yrs.	WM under 21 & above 60	WF all ages	Blacks 12-50	Blacks under 12 & above 50
A Return of the Inhabitants of Black River District, April the 1st 1786. Pg. 1					
James Devane	1	2	2	5	2
Peter Poitevint	1	.	.	1	.
Timothy Wilson	2	1	3	1	.
James Bloodworth	1	7	3	11	7
Ben Robinson	1	3	3	19	20
Edmond Hawes	3	2	3	1	.
Nicholas Richards	1	2	2	.	.
Thos. Devane, Esq.	1	.	3	8	7
Maurice Fennell	1	.	3	1	1
John Herring	1	1	3	4	4
John Henry	4	.	1	.	3
Hezekiah Howard	2	3	7	.	.
Anne Newton	3	2	6	.	.
Elizabeth Rogers	2	.	5	3	1
Thomas Rogers	1	1	2	2	2
John Sykes	1	1	5	.	.
Elizabeth Bennerman	1	2	7	.	.
Archibald McCalep	1	2	4	.	.
Robert Cook	1	2	2	.	.
Daniel Carr	2	1	3	.	.
Wm. Robenson	1	1	6	.	.
Solomon Lee	1	4	5	1	.
David Bailey	1	2	6	1	2
Edward Spearman	3	.	2	5	5
Nicholas Fennell	2	1	2	.	.
Isaac Poitevint	3	1	1	1	2
Samuel Poitevent	1	.	.	1	.
Timothy Bloodworth	1	2	7	5	2
John Bloodworth	1	1	2	1	2
James Bland	1	2	3	.	.
Thomas Corbett Sr.	3	1	1	6	4
Thomas Corbett Jr.	1	2	3	.	.
Arthor Baker	1	3	1	.	.
Pg. 2					
John Sellars	1	1	5	1	.
Daniel Highsmith Sr.	4	1	5	1	.
Daniel Highsmith Jr.	1	2	2	.	.
Thomas Lee	1	4	2	.	.
Wm. Herringtine	1	3	2	.	.
George Devane	2	.	3	4	1
Mary Robenson	.	.	4	.	.
John Carr	1	2	1	.	.
James Smith	1	2	4	.	.

Head of Household	WM 21-60 yrs.	WM under 21 & above 60	WF all ages	Blacks 12-50	Blacks under 12 & above 50
Josiah Lee	1	2	2	.	.
Jacob Powell	2	3	7	1	.
Archibald Kelsaw	.	1	3	.	.
Robert Murphy	1	.	4	1	.
Thomas Devane Jr.	1	1	2	9	13
Margaret Devane	.	.	1	4	8
Thomas Devane Sr.	2	.	1	8	9
John Munrow	1	2	2	.	.
John Devane, Esq.	3	.	4	17	10
Richard Henecy	1	.	3	.	.
William Sloan	3	5	3	.	.
John Roan	1	.	2	.	.
Willis Wood	1	.	2	.	.
John Heneey	1	.	2	.	.
Bennet Smith ?	1	5	2	.	.
John Henecy	1	2	5	.	.
James Smith	1	1	2	.	.
	83	83	190	122	92

N. Hanover County, April Term 1786,
Tho. Maclaine, Clk.

"A Return of the Number of Souls as given in by them selves in the Head of the Sound District". [On BACK of list: "Inhabitants in upper Sound District, April Term 1786". "New Hanover, No. 5, 5092 [9 not clear]

[Three additional columns given in this list—
Col. 6: Mulatto Males 21-60
Col. 7: Mulatto Males under 21; over 60
Col. 8: Mulatto Females all ages

Head of Household	WM 21-60 yrs.	WM under 21 & above 60	WF all ages	Blacks 12-50	Blacks under 12 & above 50
Pg. 1					
Thomas Davis	3	1	8	11	13
John Jones	1	3	3	.	.
Abraham Jones	1	1	4	.	.
Edward Russell	1	2	3	2	.
Wm. Felley or Filley	1	2	2	.	.
James Downing	1	.	4	.	.
Thomas Looper	1	2	2	2	2
Thos. Cunninghame Jr	1	1	.	2	4
William Mosely	1	1	3	41	1
Frances Hennery	1	.	5	.	.
Jesse Atkins	1	.	3	.	.
Elizabeth Boatwright	.	4	8	.	.
Thomas Robison	.	.	.	.	2 3 5
Elizabeth Johnson	.	.	.	.	1 2
John Hunt	.	.	.	.	1 . 2

Head of Household	WM 21-60 yrs.	WM under 21 & above 60	WF all ages	Blacks 12-50	Blacks under 12 & above 50			
Wannie McLamy	1	3	3	5	6			
Caleb Thomas	1	.	1	.	.			
John Edins	1	1	1	1	.			
Sanders Rowse	2	2	2	3	1			
Miles Knight	1	1	.	.	.			
Catharine Nichols	.	2	1	1	1			
John Vaine	1	2	2	.	.			
Anne Nichols	.	1	4	.	.			
Edward Robeson	.	.	.	.	.	1	1	1
John Nichols	1	6	5	3	4			
Jacob Stokely	1	2	5	.	1			
Adam Williamson	1	2	5	.	.			
John Morriss	2	3	2	.	1			
McNight Chadwick	2	2	3	.	.			
Thomas Peavey	.	.	.	.	.	1	.	3
James Erwen	1	.	.	2	.			
	28	44	79	79	33	5	5	14

Pg. 2

Head of Household	WM 21-60 yrs.	WM under 21 & above 60	WF all ages	Blacks 12-50	Blacks under 12 & above 50
Jane Erwen	.	.	1	4	7
Mr. Ferrell	1	1	1	.	.
Charles Ward	1	.	.	.	.
Daniel Bernard	1	2	1	.	.
Estate of Wadman Bishop by Jno Nichols	.	.	.	3	1
Daniel Bennet	1	.	2	.	.
Charles Bishop	1	1	2	.	.
Joshua Peavey	.	.	.	.	.
John Roling	1	1	5	.	.
George Stimere	2	2	5	.	.
Benj^m. Mott?	1	4	4	4	5
Elizabeth Bowan	1	1	3	.	.
John Hust	1	1	2	.	.
Peter Smith	1	1	2	.	.
Rebecca Green	.	2	3	1	.
Thomas Johnson	1	2	3	.	.
Fred^k. Jones Jr.	1	.	1	22	16
Thomas Howe	1	1	4	12	8
Yarrington Buford	1	.	.	.	.
Alex^r. McCulloch	1	.	1	4	2
William Henry	1	.	3	.	.
John Erwin	1	.	4	3	3
James Harper	1	1	1	4	4
William Rutledge	1	.	5	1	.
	49	64	132	138	79

A Return of the Inhabitants of the Welch Tract District, April 4, 1786 by D. Williams, Cap.

73	120	179	153	138

By Wm. Wright, Capt., April Term 1786

93	182	246	44	49

Long Creek Company, April Term 1786

54	74	134	119	109
2	1	5	20	8
1	1	3	22	12
1	.	1	5	1
5	3	7	71	46
63	79	150	237	176

Cap. James Lakin's Company

District of New Topsail.
N. Hanover County, April Term 1786.
Tho. Maclaine, Clk.

49	80	127	104	84
3	1	3	4	3
1	.	3	.	.
1	.	.	31	41
2	2	3	12	15
56	83	136	151	143
1	2			
57	83	138	151	143

District of Upper Sound

Thos. Cragg	1	.	.	1	.
Lewis Cragg	1	.	5	2	.
Benj. Cragg	1	.	2	3	.
	3	.	7	6	.

Wilmington District:

152	97	250	488	335

April 1, 1786
by Mars. Rob. Willkings
"1322 People in all"

Thos. Maclaine, Clerk
New Hanover County
The Amount of the whole given in
4963. T. M.

STATE CENSUS OF NORTH CAROLINA 1784-1787

NORTHAMPTON COUNTY

A List in Capt. Winborne's District:
(List undated)
Pg. 1

Head of Household	WM 21-60 yrs.	WM under 21 & above 60	WF all ages	Blacks 12-50	Blacks under 12 & above 50
Jacob Parker	1	4	3	.	.
Joseph Parker	2	2	3	.	.
Jno. Grant	1	1	7	.	.
Marthew Graff	1	2	3	.	.
John Jutthre	.	1	2	.	.
Jesse Blanchet	1	2	2	.	.
Abram Gums	2	1	4	8	.
Jno. Mills	1	1	4	.	.
Elias Hays	1	2	3	.	.
Daniel Jackson	1	1	3	2	2
James West	1	2	5	.	.
Wm. or Win. ? Boon	1	2	3	2	2
John Hass	1	2	4	.	2
Nat. Vallentine	1	3	2	.	.
Jno. Macklamore	1	2	2	.	1
Hicklan Leak	1	2	3	5	3
Nathan Gums	1	.	.	.	1
Wm. Grant	1	2	.	1	.
Thos. Vaughan	1	3	6	.	.
Henry Lutin	1	2	6	.	.
Lewis Sumersett	2	3	2	.	11
Knowel Dukes	1	.	6	.	.
Thos. Bryan	1	.	1	5	6
Fredk. Jones	2	.	4	1	.
Wm. Howell	1	1	4	.	3
Henry Murrell	1	2	.	.	.
Arther Griffen	4	6	3	.	3
Mandew Goodson	2	2	.	.	.
Wm. Powell	3	2	2	.	.
Jesse Powell	3	2	2	.	3
Obediah Plumley	1	3	.	.	.
Wm. Willet	2	1	1	.	2
Edwd. Streter	3	1	2	.	3
David James	2	3	.	2	.
Sampson Hass	2	3	2	.	.
Saml. Parker	2	3	3	.	1
Humphrey Morgan	1	1	6	.	.
	57	75	103	20	43
Pg. 2					
Henry Stevins	1	1	1	1	.
Eliphaz Lewis	3	2	3	.	.
Siot(?) Jones	3	3	3	.	.
John Lewis or Lowes or Servis (?)	1	.	3	.	.

Head of Household	WM 21-60 yrs.	WM under 21 & above 60	WF all ages	Blacks 12-50	Blacks under 12 & above 50
Wm. Wenborne	6	1	3	.	2
Fed. Hathcock	1	3	4	.	.
Jesse Powell	1	2	3	.	.
Richd. Grant	5	3	.	.	.
Merrett Murrell	1	.	.	.	.
Jonl. (?) Miller	1	1	3	.	.
Elisha James	1	1	3	.	.
Jesse James	4	4	.	.	.
Elias Winborne	1	.	.	.	.
Charles Gibson	4	3	2	.	.
Wm. Horn	1	.	1	.	.
John Waldin	3	4	.	.	.
Charles Byrd	4	3	.	.	.
Phillip Byrd	2	.	2	.	.
Mike Waldin	1	2	1	.	.
Solomon Byrd	1	.	4	5	.
John Branch	4	4	.	26	5
Solomon [blank]	1	3	2	3	2
Robin Bell	4	1	1	.	.
Wm. Pace	1	.	1	11	.
John Bryant	1	.	1	7	.
Elijah Daughtry	2	3	1	.	5
Shadrack Boyt	4	3	3	.	1
Bryant Winborne	3	2	5	.	2
Caleb Taylor	3	5	6	2	1
Benjamin Bryom	2	2	.	23	.
Wm. Pater	1	1	.	13	2
Hardy Pace	4	3	2	19	4
Aar. Parker	1	4	4	3	1
John Low	2	.	1	.	.
Thos. Boon	6	7	5	3	1
Nickloss Boon	2	2	1	.	.
A. Jones	3	.	5	60	50
Dempsey Taylor	1	3	5	5	2
	90	76	90	181	78
Capt. Lashley's District: Pg. 1					
Henry King	.	.	4	6	.
John Rook	2	2	3	5	.
Robert Tutor	1	2	3	.	.
William Jones of Wm.	2	3	4	8	9
Richard Jones	1	.	1	5	4
William Thrift	1	.	1	2	2
Nathaniel Thrift	1	.	1	.	.
Atho. Tucker	1	3	3	7	3
Churchwell Andrew Jr	1	3	3	1	1

Head of Household	WM 21-60 yrs.	WM under 21 & above 60	WF all ages	Blacks 12-50	Blacks under 12 & above 50
Benjn. Rook	1	.	2	2	3
Burwell Gilliam	.	2	3	5	3
John King Sr.	1	2	2	3	6
William Fulks	1	8	4	2	3
John Brooker	1	1	.	.	.
Christopher Williams	1	4	3	1	1
Charles Williams	1	2	3	1	.
Howel Lashley	2	1	4	4	2
Sarah Rook	.	2	3	1	2
Theoderick Hall	1	4	3	13	1
Richard Jackson	1	2	5	.	.
James McDougal	1	.	.	.	.
John King Jr.	1	.	.	.	.
Mark Clanton	1	.	2	5	4
William Clements	1	2	4	26	27
John Cowthon	1	3	4	12	18
John Moore	1	3	4	7	6
William Edwards	1	1	2	1	1
Drury Tucker	1	3	5	.	.
	28	53	72	103	93
Pg. 2					
Francis Hatton	2	7	5	3	4
Thomas Owen	1	1	3	2	.
Isham Harrison	1	3	3	8	8
Thomas Jinkins	2	1	.	9	11
John Norwood	2	1	3	.	.
George Norwood	1	2	6	1	1
Thomas Day	2	.	2	1	3
Benjamin Moody	1	1	6	5	3
Edward Harris	1	3	4	.	.
Lewis Day	1	2	3	.	.
Vaughan Johnson	1	4	5	.	.
Hardy Short	1	1	7	.	.
William Jones Tug ?	1	1	5	3	5
Simon Woodward	1	.	2	.	.
Curle Tucker	1	1	3	1	1
Surrel Moody	1	4	3	.	.
Gilliam Moody	1	3	1	1	1
Samuel McDougal	1	.	.	.	.
Roger Squire	1	1	3	.	.
David Day	1	.	.	.	.
Benj. Williamson	1	1	.	11	7
Priscilla Williamson	.	.	5	16	23
John Holloway	2	1	.	2	.
Benjn. Edwards	2	1	1	12	15
William Eaton	2	2	3	25	20
Joshua Dubry	1	2	5	.	.
Lewis Jones	1	.	.	13	7

Head of Household	WM 21-60 yrs.	WM under 21 & above 60	WF all ages	Blacks 12-50	Blacks under 12 & above 50
Joshua Vinson	1	2	4	1	1
	62	98	154	217	204
Pg. 3					
John Goldson	2	3	5	3	5
Zachariah Thompson	1	4	2	1	1
John Hogwood	3	1	4	.	.
Uriah Brock	.	4	3	1	2
Howel Hobbs	2	2	2	6	1
	70	112	170	220	209

Capt. Lashley's District.

Capt. William's District:

Head of Household	WM 21-60 yrs.	WM under 21 & above 60	WF all ages	Blacks 12-50	Blacks under 12 & above 50
James Roy	1	.	1	1	.
Paten Maughan	1	2	1	3	.
William Maughan	1	7	4	1	.
Edmond Jeter	1	.	2	2	1
Martha Stanback	.	1	3	.	1
Seth Peebles	1	.	2	3	3
Burwell Lucy Sr.	.	1	.	.	.
Phebe Bass	.	1	2	.	.
John Hathcock	1	2	8	.	.
John Mitchel	1	5	1	2	.
William Mitchel	2	2	1	.	1
Jesse Collier	1	1	1	.	.
Mary Lockhart	.	2	4	1	1
David Scott	1	2	4	.	.
William Mitchel Jr	1	.	2	2	.
William Jean	1	1	3	2	.
John Morgan Sr.	1	.	4	.	.
Michael Morgan	1	3	2	.	.
William Horton	1	6	5	1	2
	16	36	50	18	9
Pg. 4					
Thomas Severett	1	.	.	.	.
Joseph Collier	1	1	4	.	.
William Norton	1	2	2	.	.
Oadom Poytress	1	3	4	.	.
Numan Hathcock	1	.	2	.	.
John Morgan Jr.	1	3	1	.	.
Henry Lee	1	3	1	.	.
Starling Rachel	1	.	3	.	.
Thomas Williams	1	1	7	.	.
James Norton Jr.	1	3	1	.	.
James Norton Sr.	.	1	3	.	.
Isham Norton	1	.	2	.	.
Jesse Mitchel	1	6	.	5	7
William Norwood	1	6	5	4	10
Natthal. Norwood	1	5	3	8	8

Head of Household	WM 21-60 yrs.	WM under 21 & above 60	WF all ages	Blacks 12-50	Blacks under 12 & above 50
William Love	1	1	1	1	.
Ransford Flowers	.	1	2	4	6
Robert Malone	1	4	4	2	.
Robert Crittenden	1	.	2	6	7
Edward Capel	1	6	4	4	1
Jesse Roper	1	3	5	.	.
Saml. Wornum	1	5	1	2	2
John McGrigger	2	3	5	8	2
Lemmond Land	1	1	.	.	.
Allen Glover	1	.	.	.	.
Thomas Maughan	1	.	.	.	.
Nathan Harris	1	3	2	1	.
	42	92	114	63	62
Pg. 5					
James Crew	1	4	1	.	.
William Smith	1	1	2	.	.
William Hathcock Sr	1	1	2	.	.
Hardymon Poytress	1	2	2	.	.
John Rieves	1	1	3	11	8
Simon Harris	1	4	1	1	2
John Harden	1	6	3	2	1
George Brewer	1	1	1	1	2
Stephen Scott	1	2	1	.	.
William Garner	2	3	5	4	8
Andrew Crew	1	4	2	1	.
John Benford	1	.	1	.	.
Jones Glover	2	1	3	1	1
Matthew Hey or Key	1	4	1	.	.
Henry Williams Jr	1	.	1	.	.
Henry Williams Sr	.	1	1	.	.
Bartholomew Ellis	1	1	3	.	.
Rowland Ellis	1	2	6	.	.
Joshua Collier	1	.	1	2	1
William Norsworthy	1	2	3	.	.
Also Collier	1	2	3	1	1
Richard Justice	2	2	3	1	.
Isham Johnston	1	7	2	2	3
Thomas Love	2	2	7	2	1
Mary Chapmon	.	1	4	.	.
Mary Mason	.	1	2	19	14
John Lee	1	.	2	.	.
	68	147	181	111	99
Pg. 6					
Burwell Lucy	1	.	2	.	.
William Sturdifant	2	2	3	5	9
Thomas Ammons	1	.	3	.	.
Henry Meacham Sr.	.	1	2	.	.
William Kemp	1	1	2	.	.

Head of Household	WM 21-60 yrs.	WM under 21 & above 60	WF all ages	Blacks 12-50	Blacks under 12 & above 50
Henry Meacham	1	.	3	2	1
Thomas Hodges	1	4	4	1	.
William Maughan Sr.	.	1	1	.	.
Elisabeth Wornum	.	.	2	1	1
William Hudson Sr.	2	.	.	20	21
William Hathcock Jr.	1	3	2	.	.
Thomas Collier	.	1	1	.	1
William Glover	1	.	.	.	.
Allen Chapmon	1	.	1	.	.
Frederick Collier	1	.	2	.	.
William Collier	1	.	.	.	.
Cuthbert Stafford	1	1	1	1	.
Thomas Brown	1	1	2	.	.
Richard Moore	.	1	6	4	5
Banks Meacham	1	4	5	5	.
James Bradley	1	.	.	.	.
Samuel Lockhart	1	5	5	11	18
Samuel Revis	1	.	1	5	7
Eaton Haynes	3	1	4	26	21
	91	173	234	192	178

Capt. William's District

Capt. Vincent's District:

Head of Household	WM 21-60 yrs.	WM under 21 & above 60	WF all ages	Blacks 12-50	Blacks under 12 & above 50
Pg. 7					
Josias Crump	2	2	4	15	13
David Edloe	1	.	2	.	.
James Short	1	.	.	2	2
Judith Short	.	.	1	1	1
Sally Short	.	.	1	1	.
Mary Short	.	.	1	1	1
Benjamin Peebles	1	.	1	2	1
John Epps	1	2	2	.	.
Jesse Thompson	1	.	.	.	.
Morris Floyd Jr	1	1	2	.	.
William Epps	1	1	3	.	1
James Connellow	1	.	3	.	.
Benjn. Coker	1	6	6	.	.
John Kay (?)	1	.	.	.	.
William Carr	1	3	3	3	4
Josiah Smith	1	.	.	2	.
John Manders	1	3	3	.	.
John Stokes	1	3	3	.	.
Robert Ellis Sr.	1	4	2	2	2
Robert Ellis	1	1	3	2	.
James Step	2	2	4	1	1
John Richards	2	3	1	1	4
William Sparks	1	2	3	.	.

Head of Household	WM 21-60 yrs.	WM under 21 & above 60	WF all ages	Blacks 12-50	Blacks under 12 & above 50
Thos. Barrett Jr.	1	.	.	3	3
Charles Williams	1	2	4	.	1
James Collins	1	.	1	1	1
William Amis	2	1	4	12	12
	28	36	57	48	47
Pg. 8					
William Richards	1	1	3	3	5
William Eves	1	1	3	.	1
John Ellis Sr.	1	3	4	.	.
John Ellis	1	1	3	.	.
Thomas Barrett Sr.	.	2	2	9	8
Charles Thompson	2	1	3	1	2
William Thompson Jr.	1	1	4	.	.
Mary Tarver	.	4	1	.	.
Buckner Floyd	1	3	1	.	.
Jiles Davis	1	.	2	1	.
Phillip McClanan	1	1	3	.	.
Michael Waldrif	1	3	2	.	.
John Patterson	1	.	3	2	.
David Merrymoon	1	5	3	1	.
William Patterson	1	2	4	.	.
Joseph Patterson	.	2	1	.	.
John Merrymoon	1	.	2	.	.
William Patterson	1	.	3	.	.
Ezekiah Merrymoon	1	.	2	.	.
Elisabeth Patterson	2	.	1	4	1
William Patterson	1	3	2	1	.
David Patterson	1	1	2	.	.
Benjamin Patterson	1	2	3	1	.
Joseph Patterson	1	3	5	1	.
Isaac Edwards	1	4	4	.	.
Andrew Prince	.	4	3	1	.
Arthur Smith	1	1	1	2	1
John Edloe	.	1	1	.	.
	53	84	128	75	65
Pg. 9					
William Carpenter	1	.	2	.	.
Jeremiah Reams	1	4	7	.	.
Natth[l]. Dobey	1	2	3	2	1
Wm. Reams	.	1	2	.	.
Charles Gee	.	3	2	3	6
Martha Seat	.	1	3	.	.
Anne Curvin	.	2	1	.	.
Noel Waddel	1	2	3	.	.
William Gee	1	.	2	1	1
Robert Merrymoon	1	1	2	.	.
Peter Merrymoon	1	2	8	.	.
Francis Merrymoon	1	2	3	.	.
Hartwell Harriss	1	2	5	.	.

Head of Household	WM 21-60 yrs.	WM under 21 & above 60	WF all ages	Blacks 12-50	Blacks under 12 & above 50
William Flanders	1	1	3	.	.
Morriss Floyd	1	1	1	1	1
Wm. Williams	1	.	2	.	.
Anne Capel	.	6	2	1	3
Henry Vincent	1	.	.	.	.
John Mitchel	1	2	5	.	.
Kinchen Hines	1	.	2	6	1
Frederick Stanton	1	.	.	3	2
Miles Thweat	1	.	.	.	.
Kinchen Peterson	1	1	1	7	1
James Cureton	1	4	4	9	8
John Short	1	1	2	13	9
James Vincent	2	3	4	8	6
James Benford	.	2	3	8	16
John Peterson	2	1	2	12	11
John M. Benford	1	1	3	7	9
	78	132	204	156	140
Pg. 10					
Sterlin Peebles	1	.	.	6	1
Henry Thompson	2	2	4	.	.
John Melton	1	1	5	6	11
Ath[o]. Moore	1	3	4	2	10
Henry Moore	1	2	4	1	1
Balaam Emmory	1	2	1	1	2
John Smith	1	2	1	4	1
William Smith	1	2	1	1	.
Robert Peebles	1	2	3	6	2
Buckner Williams	1	2	1	.	.
George Pace	1	.	.	.	1
David Short	1	1	2	11	9
William Pace	1	.	2	5	4
Jonas Hale	2	1	1	3	6
Elias Massey	1	.	1	.	.
Howel Gee	1	.	.	1	.
David Woodrowffe	3	2	8	.	.
John Medlin	1	4	2	.	.
Mary Webb	.	2	4	6	3
Lewis Edwards	1	.	.	5	1
Benjamin Tarver	1	1	2	1	.
James Seat	1	1	4	2	.
Jarrott Seat	1	3	4	.	.
James Gee	1	.	1	1	1
Benj[n]. Cheatom	1	4	2	2	2
Col[o]. Edmonds	.	.	.	5	8
Mary Smith	.	2	2	2	3
John Braddey	1	1	1	.	.
Benj[n]. Hall	1	4	3	.	.
Wm. Thompson Sr.	.	2	1	3	5
Matthew Pitmon	1	2	4	.	.

Head of Household	WM 21-60 yrs.	WM under 21 & above 60	WF all ages	Blacks 12-50	Blacks under 12 & above 50
Drury Gee	1	.	1	5	4
Anne Roper	3	.	3	.	.
	113	180	276	235	215
Pg. 11					
Capt. Elisha Webb's District:					
Elisha Webb	1	.	5	1	.
Judith Freemon	.	2	.	1	.
William Jones	.	1	8	.	.
James McDoughall	1	2	2	.	.
Michael Fulgam	1	3	5	10	7
Jesse Goodson	1	2	2	.	.
William Ellis	1	.	3	.	.
Peter Smith	1	.	2	.	.
Harwood Jones	1	.	.	26	23
John Jones	1	.	.	6	7
Thomas Glover	1	1	1	2	2
Robert Jones	1	1	.	7	11
William Powel	1	2	2	.	.
Eper Kilbey	1	.	1	1	.
Epaphro[s]. Kilbey	1	1	2	1	4
Matthew Buffellow	1	3	5	.	.
Jesse Webb	1	6	2	1	.
Martha Lewis	.	1	1	.	.
Lucy Rowell	.	2	2	.	.
Bernaby Murrell	1	1	7	1	.
Samuel Tarver	1	1	.	2	3
James Tarver	1	.	4	.	1
Lucy Tarver	.	3	2	2	3
Henry Hill	1	2	2	4	3
Hermon Hill	1	.	1	3	3
Martha Lewis	.	1	1	3	6
James Lewis	1	2	3	2	1
Benja[n]. Tarver	1	2	1	.	.
Humphry Revel	1	3	2	.	.
Thomas Harriss	1	3	1	8	5
John Jones	1	1	3	1	.
	25	50	66	81	79
Pg. 12					
Patience Wheeler	1	1	1	.	.
George Braswell	1	.	2	.	.
Isham Jones	1	.	1	.	.
Robert Snipes	1	4	3	3	1
Mary Burnet	.	2	1	.	.
Mary Rowell	.	1	2	2	3
William Burke	1	.	3	.	3
Mary Burke	.	.	1	3	2
Jean Vaughan	.	1	7	.	.
Laurance Smith	1	2	3	14	14
Warren Hart	1	1	1	3	.

Head of Household	WM 21-60 yrs.	WM under 21 & above 60	WF all ages	Blacks 12-50	Blacks under 12 & above 50
Isaac Edwards	1	1	2	.	.
Joseph Vasser	1	2	6	4	3
James Vasser	1	1	1	1	1
John Hart	1	3	2	4	5
Patience Griggs	.	2	2	.	.
Swan Prichard	1	2	4	.	3
Billison Tarver	1	2	4	1	.
John Wheeler	1	3	2	4	3
Henry Gay	1	2	3	.	.
John Webb	1	3	3	2	.
Mary Chapel	.	2	2	.	.
John Seet	1	2	2	1	1
James Dancey	2	1	.	15	13
Antho. Moore	1	1	1	2	.
Joseph Exum	1	1	1	5	5
William Exum	1	.	2	7	2
Anne Exum	.	1	2	5	5
John M. Holland	1	2	2	1	2
Mosis Barns	1	1	2	.	.
Thomas Parker	1	1	3	11	8
Leonard Hall	1	1	1	3	1
Jepthan Atherton	1	1	4	18	17
	52	97	142	150	147
Pg. 13					
Capt. Sike's District:					
John Wade	1	2	7	4	.
William Parkes	1	1	4	.	.
Jesse Gay	1	4	2	.	.
Solomon Gay	1	.	1	1	1
Thomas Tadlock	1	5	5	.	.
John Underwood	1	2	3	.	.
John Underwood Jr.	1	3	3	1	.
Etheldred Martin	1	6	3	1	.
John Pierse	.	1	1	.	.
William Coplin	1	1	1	.	.
Thomas Mann	1	2	3	2	6
Elisha Pierse	1	5	3	.	.
John Mortin	.	3	5	1	2
William Bridgers	1	2	2	.	.
David Parker	1	.	.	.	.
Thomas Robertson	1	.	1	.	.
Catharine Parks	1	2	5	.	.
Mary Sikes	.	2	6	.	.
Jacob Pierse	1	2	4	.	.
Jesse Allen	1	3	3	.	.
Hardy Powell	1	4	5	.	.
Joseph Johnson	1	1	4	1	.
Silas Johnson	1	.	1	.	.
Catharine Parks Jr.	.	.	1	.	.

Head of Household	WM 21-60 yrs.	WM under 21 & above 60	WF all ages	Blacks 12-50	Blacks under 12 & above 50
Joseph Bridgers	2	1	3	.	.
M. William Mann	1	1	2	.	.
Edward Davis	.	4	4	.	.
Benjn. Garris	1	4	5	.	.
John Taylor	1	1	3	.	.
Rhoda Barkley	1	1	1	1	2
Edward Davis Jr.	1	.	1	.	.
Saml. Edwards	1	8	2	1	.
	28	72	92	13	11
Pg. 14					
Jonathan Gay	1	2	4	1	1
John Edwards	1	5	1	.	.
Anne Sikes	.	1	6	3	2
John Allen	1	1	2	.	.
Andrew Parks	1	.	.	.	.
James Parks	1	.	.	.	.
William Parks	1	.	.	.	.
James Parks	.	2	6	.	.
Thomas Sikes	1	.	2	5	5
James Conner	1	.	.	.	.
Joseph Spence	1	.	.	.	.
George Barkley	1	4	4	.	.
Thos. Underwood	1	1	2	.	.
Francis Tisdal	.	2	1	.	.
James Sikes	1	3	6	9	11
Fancis Deloach	1	2	3	4	4
Hezekiah Hough	3	2	6	3	3
Lewis Daughtrey	1	2	3	.	.
Solomon Hays	1	2	4	2	.
Jesse Underwood	1	2	1	.	1
Solomon Deberry	1	2	4	2	3
John Garrus	1	4	5	.	.
Newit Harris	1	.	3	9	18
James Lassiter	1	2	2	1	.
Jethro Sikes	1	.	3	.	.
Michael Deloach	1	1	6	3	.
Thos. Davis	1	2	4	.	.
Joseph Taylor	.	3	4	.	.
Joseph Taylor	1	5	2	.	.
John Wheeler	1	2	3	.	.
Henry Garrus	1	1	1	.	.
	57	125	180	41	59
Pg. 15					
John Parker	1	4	4	.	.
John Fiveash	1	6	1	.	.
James Parkes	1	4	3	.	5
Thomas Tadlock	.	2	2	2	1
Thomas Skinner	1	.	2	.	.
Absalom Mann	1	4	7	.	.
Henry Warren	1	.	3	.	.
	63	145	202	43	61

Capt. Sike's Dist.

Head of Household	WM 21-60 yrs.	WM under 21 & above 60	WF all ages	Blacks 12-50	Blacks under 12 & above 50
Capt. Bennet's District:					
Owing Breene or Brune or Burn or Bunn	1	1	1	3	1
Wm. Breene or Brune or Burn or Bunn	.	4	2	.	.
Benjamin Turner	1	3	5	.	.
Solomon Smith	1	3	3	.	.
Josiah Davis	1	2	1	.	.
Mandew Daughtrey	1	3	3	.	.
Abraham Wall	1	3	6	.	.
Isaac Vick	.	1	.	.	.
Joseph Johnson	.	2	1	.	.
Sampson Morgan	1	1	4	.	.
Jacob Powel	.	2	7	1	5
Arthur Stevenson	.	2	2	1	1
Abraham Stevenson	1	2	2	1	2
William Stevenson	.	1	1	.	.
Martha Vick	.	.	2	.	.
Elisabeth Wall	.	.	2	.	.
John Bryant	1	.	2	1	2
Benjamin Boon	1	.	4	2	.
Daniel Johnston	1	3	4	.	.
Hardy Suiter	1	2	4	.	1
Millison Smith	.	4	3	.	.
John Stancil	1	2	2	.	1
Nathan Stancil	2	.	7	2	.
John Watkins	1	1	3	4	2
	16	42	71	15	14
Pg. 16					
Martha Parker	.	.	2	.	.
John McCoone	1	2	4	.	.
Benjn. Johnston	.	1	3	2	4
Jonathan Pope	2	3	2	2	3
William Bennet	1	1	2	5	4
Boeng Bennet	1	.	2	2	3
Jiles Suiter	1	2	3	.	.
Harwood Fasson	1	2	4	3	4
William Allen	1	1	1	7	8
Elphenston Carey	2	.	2	.	2
Winkfield Robertson	1	.	.	.	.
Benjn. Binson	1	2	2	.	.
Elisha Robertson	1	4	4	.	.
Cloy'd Clifton	1	3	5	.	.
Tabitha Parks	.	.	1	.	.
Joseph Johnson Jr.	1	1	4	1	3
Abraham Massengale	1	3	5	.	.
Jacob Boon	2	.	3	1	1
Jacob Boon Jr.	1	2	5	.	.
Jesse Briton	1	3	4	.	.
Jacob Burne	1	1	1	2	.

111

Head of Household	WM 21-60 yrs.	WM under 21 & above 60	WF all ages	Blacks 12-50	Blacks under 12 & above 50
Joseph Woodward	.	3	3	.	.
John Davis	1	4	1	.	.
Kinchen Martin	1	.	1	1	1
Elijah Johnston	1	1	3	1	.
Samuel Hays	.	1	1	3	3
Elisabeth Hayes	.	2	1	.	.
Sarah Hayes	.	2	2	2	1
Winifred Bottoms	.	1	1	.	.
Henry Deberry	2	.	.	12	18
William Fason	1	1	2	1	1
Booth Nusom	.	.	.	1	2
Anna Wells	.	.	.	1	3
Sarah Cornet	.	.	.	1	.
Sarah Scott	.	.	1	3	.
Solomon Jones	.	.	1	1	.
Martha Jones	.	.	.	2	.
Theney Warrick	.	.	.	1	2
	43	88	147	70	77

Capt. Bennet's District

Pg. 17
Capt. Dupree's District:

Head of Household	WM 21-60 yrs.	WM under 21 & above 60	WF all ages	Blacks 12-50	Blacks under 12 & above 50
Col. Howel Edmonds	1	1	2	11	13
Drury Deberry	2	.	2	10	9
Benjamin Branch	1	.	2	13	7
Martha Turner	.	.	1	9	5
Edmon Turner	1	.	.	6	3
Solomon Dawson	1	1	.	4	.
Thomas Williams	1	2	4	4	3
Joseph Rogers	2	2	5	2	1
William Sturgeon	1	.	.	.	.
Maj. James Vaughan	1	.	6	6	6
Abraham Joyner	.	4	4	4	2
Mark Phillips	1	1	2	5	1
Abraham Lumbly	1	.	4	1	2
William Davis	1	.	.	5	.
Bythel Haynes	1	2	2	.	2
Mary Williams	.	1	1	6	5
John Davis	1	.	2	3	.
Arnold Morgan	1	3	3	1	.
Robert Murrel	1	2	2	.	1
Jesse Brittle	1	2	3	3	4
Timothy Morgan	1	2	3	1	.
Rowland Brittle	1	1	4	.	.
Thomas Westbrook	.	4	3	.	.
Sarah Brittle	.	2	2	2	2
Solomon Deloach	1	1	2	3	3
Edmond Nicholas	1	.	2	.	.
William Nicholas	1	1	3	.	.
Antho. Armistead	1	.	4	4	4

Head of Household	WM 21-60 yrs.	WM under 21 & above 60	WF all ages	Blacks 12-50	Blacks under 12 & above 50
Samul. Monger	1	1	4	2	6
William Stricklin	1	.	1	.	.
William Phillips	.	2	3	.	.
Mary Nicholas	.	1	1	1	2
	27	36	78	98	83

Pg. 18

Head of Household	WM 21-60 yrs.	WM under 21 & above 60	WF all ages	Blacks 12-50	Blacks under 12 & above 50
William Munger	1	3	3	1	.
Epps Broom	1	5	5	5	4
Haley Broom	1	5	2	4	3
Henry Hast	1	2	3	4	1
Newet Edwards	1	2	2	.	.
Thomas Doles	1	1	3	3	.
Henry Suiter	1	2	3	2	3
William Cobb	1	.	1	.	.
Jesse Joiner	1	1	4	3	1
Aaron Howel	1	5	2	1	1
Edward Sorrow	1	.	4	4	6
John Cook	.	2	1	.	1
Moses Newsom	.	.	.	9	7
Amos Newsom	.	.	.	4	4
Nathan Byrd	.	.	.	4	4
Drury Tan	.	.	.	3	2
Lemmon Kinchen	.	.	.	2	1
Mickleberry Williamson	.	1	.	.	.
Henry Howel Sr.	1	2	2	4	4
John Jones	1	1	3	.	1
Elisabeth Harris	.	2	4	1	3
Benjan. Howel	1	1	2	1	.
Anne Taylor	.	.	3	5	6
Sarah Howell	.	1	1	.	5
Mary Artis	.	.	.	.	1
Arthur Hallowmon	.	2	1	2	2
Arthur Bird	.	.	.	4	2
Thomas Nicholas	1	1	1	.	.
John Williamson	1	.	.	.	.
Byrd Cornet	1	1	2	.	.
	24	76	130	165	145

Pg. 19

Head of Household	WM 21-60 yrs.	WM under 21 & above 60	WF all ages	Blacks 12-50	Blacks under 12 & above 50
Absalom Joyner	1	2	4	9	9
Henry Howel Jr.	1	.	1	2	1
James Newsom	.	.	.	5	5
Arthur Allen	.	.	.	2	4
Jerry Andrews	.	.	.	1	4
Daniel Demroy	.	.	.	4	8
Micajah Demory	.	.	.	1	.
James Sweat	.	.	.	1	.
Baley Munger	1	.	.	.	.
John Munger	1	2	6	.	.
Mark Murrel	1	1	4	.	.

Head of Household	WM 21-60 yrs.	WM under 21 & above 60	WF all ages	Blacks 12-50	Blacks under 12 & above 50
John Sorrow	1	.	1	1	.
Peter Deberry	1	1	2	3	5
Absalom Deberry	1	.	3	4	2
Elisabeth Hart	.	.	2	4	6
John Edwards	.	1	.	.	.
James Camel	1	.	.	.	.
Thomas Holland	1	.	.	.	.
Henry Sorrow	1	3	5	5	2
Jeremiah Grizzard	1	2	2	2	.
Jiles Joyner	1	2	4	2	2
Jesse Dupree	1	4	2	2	2
William Bank	.	.	.	3	4
Nehemiah Long	2	1	2	11	6
Benjamin Deberry	1	1	3	6	6
Jesse Boon	1	5	2	2	3
	42	101	173	238	214

Pg. 20
Capt. Andrew's District:

Head of Household	WM 21-60 yrs.	WM under 21 & above 60	WF all ages	Blacks 12-50	Blacks under 12 & above 50
Matthias Speed	1	2	5	9	.
John Edmunds	1	.	3	6	7
Elisha Fly	1	3	5	.	.
Moses Odum	1	3	4	.	.
Nathan Gardner	1	3	4	.	.
Randolph Madrie	1	1	3	1	1
John Butler	1	.	1	.	.
John Olliver	1	3	2	.	.
Rich^d. Gray	2	2	4	.	.
Benjn. Liles	1	6	5	.	.
Thos. Liles' Estate	.	.	2	5	1
Robert Turner	1	2	3	.	.
Celey Rochel	.	1	2	.	.
Jesse Liles	1	4	2	.	.
Benjn. Strickling	1	4	4	.	.
Micajah Woodward	1	2	4	.	.
William Madrie	1	3	2	1	.
Redman Hacket	3	2	.	2	.
Joseph Ellis	1	.	.	.	.
Ezekiel Benson	1	3	3	.	.
Arch^d. Warren	1	3	2	.	.
Zachariah Morrel	1	2	2	.	.
Henry Sowsberry	1	.	2	2	.
William Fly	5	.	2	.	.
Daniel Massengale	1	4	5	.	.
Rich^d. Andrews	2	.	2	4	.
James Wilson Coker	1	1	2	.	.
David Jenkins	1	1	6	1	.
James Davis	1	3	3	1	1
Abraham Stephenson	1	.	2	7	7
Arch^d. Warren Jr.	1	.	1	.	.

Head of Household	WM 21-60 yrs.	WM under 21 & above 60	WF all ages	Blacks 12-50	Blacks under 12 & above 50
James Washington	1	.	.	.	.
Robert Davis	1	1	.	.	.
John Warren	1	1	5	.	.
John Woodward	1	1	2	.	.
John Parke	1	.	.	.	.
	42	59	90	39	7

Pg. 21

Head of Household	WM 21-60 yrs.	WM under 21 & above 60	WF all ages	Blacks 12-50	Blacks under 12 & above 50
William Tiner	1	2	2	.	.
Charles Stepherson	1	.	3	4	1
Jesse Warren	2	4	3	3	2
John Fly	1	4	3	.	.
Drury Strickling	1	.	2	.	1
James Boon	1	.	.	.	.
John Tyner	1	5	2	13	.
Elisabeth Tyner	.	.	4	.	.
Nicholas Tyner	1	2	2	7	1
Wm. Frankling	.	1	3	.	.
Wm. Frankling Jr.	1	.	2	.	.
Christopher Cook	1	.	.	.	.
William Sherrod	2	.	2	3	.
Benjn. Morrell	1	1	2	1	1
Nathl. Madrie	1	3	1	.	.
Benjn. Clifton	1	.	1	3	5
James Judkins	1	1	1	1	1
Mary Judkins	.	4	3	2	4
Josie Long	.	1	5	8	6
Warsden Pulley	1	.	2	.	.
Joseph Strickling	1	4	4	.	.
Sarah Taylor	1	.	3	.	.
William Strickling	1	2	3	.	.
Edward Jiggets	2	2	2	2	2
Thomas Boon	1	.	3	2	1
Wm. Boon	2	1	4	1	.
Joseph Boon	1	1	2	.	.
Cadar Butler	1	1	1	.	.
John Boon	1	1	4	2	3
Mary Sherrod	.	.	2	4	2
Absalom Cobb	1	1	2	5	5
John Cobb	1	3	3	2	3
Wm. Munley, Mullato					
Judith Inman	.	2	2	.	.
	31	44	78	63	38

Pg. 22

Head of Household	WM 21-60 yrs.	WM under 21 & above 60	WF all ages	Blacks 12-50	Blacks under 12 & above 50
Stephen Scott	1	2	3	5	5
Littleberry Spain	1	1	1	.	2
Littlebury Spain p[er]	.	.	.	24	13
Wm. Ruffin's Estate					
Elias Hillard	2	1	5	11	12
Priscilla Wells	.	1	4	.	.

Head of Household	WM 21-60 yrs.	WM under 21 & above 60	WF all ages	Blacks 12-50	Blacks under 12 & above 50
Kindred Carter	1	1	3	4	1
John Hillard	1	1	4	7	10
Thomas Sarrock	1	10	2	1	1
Thomas Gausland	1	.	.	.	.
Charles King	1	3	4	.	.
John Granberry	1	.	2	8	9
William Granberry	1	4	5	9	9
John Edwards	1	.	1	.	.
James Cotton	1	.	.	3	2
John Josey	1	1	1	5	3
William Wilkison	1	.	2	.	.
John Norsworthy	2	3	5	5	9
James Madrie	2	4	4	6	3
William Horn	1	.	1	3	1
Henry Cotton	.	2	.	3	10
Trinity Flaner	.	.	3	.	.
Elisabeth Leedum	.	.	1	.	2
Daniel Jarrott	1	1	4	.	1
Benjn. Biggers(?)	1	.	1	.	.
James Watts for Jno. Dawson	1	.	.	8	12
Elisabeth Sherrod	1	.	4	.	.
Nathan Wheeden	1	.	1	.	.
Jeremiah Brittle	1	.	1	.	.
Wilie Boddy & Thos. Wells	1	1	.	3	8
John Brittle	1	3	8	7	4
Councill Bass	1	2	1	2	1
Jethro Bass	1	1	2	3	1
Demsey Bass	1	.	1	1	2
Moses Hall	1	1	1	.	.
	32	43	75	26	121
Pg. 23					
Thomas Knox	.	1	2	1	.
Willis Bridgres	1	1	.	.	4
Arthur Wooton	1	1	1	.	.
Tabitha Lancaster	.	1	2	.	.
William Williams	1	.	2	1	5
Jesse Newby p[er] Simon Jeffers	.	2	.	9	13
Josiah Granberry	1	1	3	6	5
Abraham Durden	1	.	.	.	.
Isaac Marshall	.	1	2	1	.
James Carter	1	2	4	.	.
Jethro Peelle	1	2	4	.	.
James Horn	1	2	7	.	.
William McKinney	1	1	.	.	.
Elizabeth Fraim	.	2	2	.	.
Jesse Daughtrey Jr.	1	.	.	.	.

Head of Household	WM 21-60 yrs.	WM under 21 & above 60	WF all ages	Blacks 12-50	Blacks under 12 & above 50
Alason Bryant	1	3	1	.	.
William Dollerson	1	5	1	.	.
Jiles Randolph	1	4	2	5	10
Elizabeth Daughtrey	.	.	3	1	2
Laurance Daughtry	1	1	1	.	.
Jesse Daughtry	1	3	2	3	1
Watson Rutland	1	2	2	4	3
Clerky Bryant	1	2	2	1	2
James Lamboson	1	3	3	.	.
Elisha Daughtrey	1	4	3	.	.
Barbara Mitchner	.	2	5	.	.
Jean Bryant	.	.	3	.	.
Abraham Baggot	.	3	4	.	.
Joseph Laurance	1	2	6	2	1
Thomas Horn	2	1	2	.	.
Hardy Bagot	1	1	4	.	.
William Brittle	1	1	5	.	.
Tamer Wilkens	.	1	2	.	.
	24	55	80	34	42
Pg. 24 Capt. Horn's District:					
James Moore	1	.	3	1	.
Blake Rutland	1	1	2	8	2
Charity Rutland	.	2	1	1	2
James Moore Sr.	1	.	4	2	2
William Campbel	2	2	2	.	.
James Bryant	.	1	1	.	1
Jason Bryant	1	1	2	.	.
John Knox	1	5	4	1	.
Moore Stephenson & Wm. Steven.	2	2	2	4	10
William Lightfoot	1	4	4	3	3
Thomas White	1	1	4	11	11
Joseph Wood	2	.	3	10	14
Robert Armistead	2	.	1	8	12
Henry A. Wood	1	.	1	7	6
Zachariah Baron	1	1	1	.	.
John Laurance and Jno. Duke	1	7	4	13	17
Robert Laurance	1	3	3	4	2
Bryan Daughtrey	1	3	4	2	1
Christopher Manuel	1	1	3	.	.
Henderson Parker	1	1	2	1	1
Young Patterson and M. Thomas	1	4	3	12	3
Robert Burgess	1	3	2	1	.
John Peele	1	2	3	8	5
Edmund Peele	1	2	3	1	1
Wilson Rutland	1	2	2	1	3

Head of Household	WM 21-60 yrs.	WM under 21 & above 60	WF all ages	Blacks 12-50	Blacks under 12 & above 50
Martha Rutland	.	.	2	.	2
Thomas Rutland	1	.	.	1	.
Samuel Parker	1	1	2	1	1
Randolph Rutland	1	.	.	.	.
William Rutland	.	3	4	.	2
Mesheck Rutland	1	4	2	.	.
Isaac Hillard	.	1	.	10	9
Charles Laurance	2	3	2	.	.
Willis Council	1	1	.	.	.
Henry Dawson and Elisha Boles (?)	2	.	.	8	8
Thomas Outland	1	2	2	2	1
William Bridgers	1	3	4	16	9
William Bridgers	.	2	.	5	14
	38	68	82	134	135
Lawrence's District: Pg. 25					
Joseph Benthal	.	3	1	3	.
James Wood	.	1	4	14	11
Lamuel Parker	1	.	2	1	2
James Dickinson	1	1	3	9	11
Winifred Dickinson	1	1	.	.	.
Susanna Parker	1	.	1	2	4
Jean Barns	.	2	3	.	.
Ephraim Blanchett Sr.	.	3	1	2	5
Ephraim Blanchett	1	.	3	.	.
James Rose	1	1	3	.	1
Jonathan Blanchett	1	.	.	.	.
Jacob Jacobs	2	2	6	.	.
Robert Combs	1	.	3	.	.
Benjamin Hare	1	1	.	10	9
Jonas Wood	1	2	2	13	13
Benjamin Bala	1	1	1	.	.
Josiah Outland	1	5	2	3	4
Joseph Jordan	.	1	.	2	3
Nicholas Washington	1	4	1	6	4
Britain Long	2	.	3	4	3
Arthur Williams	1	2	4	1	1
Joel Sherrod	1	.	1	.	.
Joseph Hays	2	.	.	2	.
Samuel Cryer	1	2	7	2	5
Joel Futral	1	.	4	1	1
William Rix	8	3	1	2	3
Demsey Rix	1	1	1	.	.
Ollive Warde	.	1	4	.	.
Barnaba Johnston Sr.	1	2	5	4	1
Thomas Boon	1	3	2	.	.
John Dickinson Sr.	.	3	.	13	12

Head of Household	WM 21-60 yrs.	WM under 21 & above 60	WF all ages	Blacks 12-50	Blacks under 12 & above 50
Robert Griffin	1	1	4	.	.
Reddick Darden	1	2	1	2	2
William Gatlin	1	1	4	.	.
Esther Roberts	.	1	1	4	3
John Futral Sr.	.	5	3	4	4
James Griffin	.	1	3	.	.
	30	56	84	104	102
Pg. 26					
Cordey Hogans	1	2	4	4	1
John Futral	1	2	3	.	.
William Snipes	1	.	.	.	.
Joseph Lasator Jr.	1	3	7	.	5
Joseph Lassator	1	5	4	2	.
Sanders Futral	1	5	4	1	.
James Vinson Sr.	1	3	4	3	.
Thomas Futral	1	2	6	1	1
Jesse Lassetor	1	1	1	.	.
Henry Vinson	1	.	2	.	.
John Fryer	1	1	3	.	.
William Futral	1	1	3	3	1
Benjamin Futral Sr.	.	1	4	1	.
Benjn. Futral Jr.	1	.	3	.	.
Etheldred Futral	1	3	2	.	.
Winborn Jinkins	1	3	2	3	4
James Sherrod	1	.	3	.	.
John Vaughan	1	2	6	.	.
James Vinson Jr.	1	1	3	.	.
Hardy Vinson	1	.	1	.	.
Naman Mills	1	1	3	.	.
Henry Futral	1	.	1	.	.
Demsey Futral	1	2	6	.	.
Nathan Futral	1	1	1	.	.
John Mann	.	1	.	.	.
Morning Benn	1	1	3	7	6
Burwell Conner	1	1	1	.	.
Nathan Baggett	1	.	2	.	.
William Mann	1	5	2	.	.
John Futral Jr.	1	2	4	3	1
Richd. Mann	1	2	4	.	.
Thomas Bowers	1	.	2	.	.
Benjn. Haley	.	.	1	3	1
William Brown	1	.	4	1	1
John Bullock	1	2	2	.	.
Saul Parker	1	2	3	.	.
Joseph Boon	1	2	3	.	.
James Ozburn	.	2	1	1	.
	34	62	108	33	28

Head of Household	WM 21–60 yrs.	WM under 21 & above 60	WF all ages	Blacks 12–50	Blacks under 12 & above 50
Pg. 27					
Ephraim Futral	1	2	1	1	.
Demsey Futral	1	1	4	1	5
David Futral	1	1	5	1	.
Josiah Oadham	1	3	5	.	.
Joseph Smith	1	1	2	.	.
Elijah Lassator	1	.	.	.	.
Jacob Oadham	1	3	3	.	.
Moses Oadham	.	1	2	1	5
James Lassator	2	3	1	.	.
John Nelson	.	2	.	.	.
Joseph Stewart	1	2	2	.	.
Abraham Nelson	1	6	7	.	.
Francis Parks	1	1	4	1	.
John Clifton	1	.	2	.	1
Shadrack Lassator	1	.	5	.	.
Anne Fennel	.	1	3	1	2
Thomas Woodward	1	2	3	1	.
Aaron Oadham	1	.	.	.	.
Abraham Rogers	1	3	3	1	.
James Oadham	1	2	5	.	.
Thomas Adkison	1	.	1	.	.
Duke Moore	1	.	1	.	.
Sarah Sumner	1	3	6	4	.
Benjamin Johnson	1	1	2	.	.
Etheldred Woodward	1	1	1	.	.
Mathew Powel	1	6	3	3	.
Elizabeth Powel	.	.	1	1	.
William Benthal	1	.	1	1	1
Elias Turner	.	1	2	.	.
Francis Parker	2	2	6	.	.
Martha Lewis	.	.	1	.	.
Oliver Woodward	1	1	1	3	2
Joseph Futral	.	2	3	.	.
Kindred Skinner	1	.	7	5	10
John Dickison Jr.	1	2	5	6	3
John Norflet	.	1	.	.	.
Lamuel Laurance	1	2	5	8	6
	32	56	103	39	35

Head of Household	WM 21–60 yrs.	WM under 21 & above 60	WF all ages	Blacks 12–50	Blacks under 12 & above 50
Pg. 28					
Dardan Johnston	1	.	4	.	2
Sumner Tadlock	1	.	.	.	.
Stewart Pippin	1	2	2	4	2
Ephraim Shuffel	1	2	1	.	.
Jacob Simons	.	4	3	.	.
Barnaba Johnston Jr.	1	1	1	.	.
Charles Thompson	2	2	3	4	5
Francis Mabrey	2	1	2	.	.
Jesse Williams	2	6	5	7	7
James Vinson	1	1	2	.	.
Richard Jordan	1	.	2	2	.
	13	19	25	57	16

"A List of the White & Black Inhabitants in Northampton County, No. 4. 7043"
1786

ONSLOW COUNTY

"The Number of Souls in the Sound District. Taken in by me, May 24th 1786."
John Spicer, Junr.

Head of Household	WM 21-60 yrs.	WM under 21 & above 60	WF all ages	Blacks 12-50	Blacks under 12 & above 50
Pg. 1					
Benjamin Averitte	1	4	3	1	.
James Edens	1	2	2	.	.
John Jenkens	1	.	1	.	.
Mary Averitte	.	2	7	2	1
Alexander Gun	1	3	3	.	.
Leven Cambel	1	1	2	.	2
William Grace	2	.	1	.	.
James Wilson	1	4	4	.	.
Onesephorous Hunt	1	1	5	.	.
Robert Sinkler	1	.	2	.	.
Gabril Hardison	1	.	3	.	.
John Howard	2	1	2	.	.
Absolom Johnson	2	.	2	.	.
Benjamin Beesley	1	3	4	.	.
Henry Jenkens	2	4	3	.	1
John Parry (sic)	2	.	3	.	.
Thomas Parry	1	.	1	.	.
Jane Waltom	.	3	2	.	1
Elisabeth King	.	.	4	5	5
John King Jr.	1	.	1	1	.
Henry Ruarke	1	1	6	.	.
William Finsinger	1	3	6	.	.
Robert Sage	1	2	6	3	6
Robert Hare	1	1	1	6	.
James Lane Sr.	1	2	1	.	.
	27	37	75	18	16
Pg. 2					
John Burnet	1	1	2	.	.
John King Sr.	1	1	2	1	1
John Coston Jr.	1	5	2	.	.
Thomas Coston	1	1	1	1	.
Aaron Sigley	.	1	2	.	.
Andrew Fullwood	3	1	2	.	.
William Fullwood	1	1	2	1	.
Joshua Jenkens	1	1	2	.	.
Shadrock Hall	2	1	3	1	.
Peter Burges	1	.	1	.	.
Richard Mason	1	1	2	.	.
Nathaniel Ennett	1	1	1	.	.
Joseph Ennett	1	4	2	2	3
Benjamin Gill	1	.	1	.	.
William Wetherley	1	.	1	.	.
John Coomes	2	.	3	.	.
George Burges	1	.	2	.	.
George Devall	1	3	3	.	.
Joshua Devall	1	.	1	.	.
Rusel Prescote	1	.	3	.	.
Alexander Fuller	2	.	2	.	.
George Adams	1	1	1	3	.
William Red	1	2	1	.	.
Samuel Clegg	1	1	.	21	23
Benaja King	.	1	1	.	3
	28	27	43	30	30
Pg. 3					
John Wilkens	1	1	3	2	4
Peter Jones	1	1	3	.	.
Richard Barber	1	2	3	.	.
John Hansley	1	5	2	2	.
William Dudley	1	.	.	.	.
Chearles Hardison	1	4	1	.	.
Ezekiel Edens	1	.	.	.	.
Simon Hobbs	1	2	1	.	.
Thomas Edens	1	.	4	.	.
Francis Coston	1	1	2	.	.
Febe Coston	.	.	2	.	.
John Coston Sr.	1	5	3	.	.
Laben Justis	1	3	2	.	.
William Hill	1	4	1	.	.
Stephen Coston	1	3	2	1	.
James Lane Jr.	1	1	3	.	.
Absolom Carmon	1	4	3	.	.
James Cranford	.	4	.	.	.
Robert Williams	2	.	2	.	.
John Yopp	3	1	2	1	.
Jinkin Averitt	1	.	.	2	.
Abner Goodwine	1	2	3	.	1
Henderson Briess/Briefs?	1	.	.	.	.
William Hansley	1	.	1	2	.
	24	44	43	10	5
Pg. 4					
Asa Hatch	.	1	1	6	10
Cornelous Briefs	1	3	1	.	.
Francis Coston Jr.	1	2	1	.	.
George Curtis	1	2	3	.	.
Margreat Taylor	.	1	5	.	1
Mary Cranford	.	.	1	.	.
Winney Spicer	.	1	2	.	2
Sarah Simmons	.	1	1	.	.
John Waltom	1	1	4	.	.

117

Head of Household	WM 21-60 yrs.	WM under 21 & above 60	WF all ages	Blacks 12-50	Blacks under 12 & above 50
John Dixson	2	1	1	.	.
James Hobbs	1	.	1	.	.
Rebeca Reiles	.	.	2	.	.
John Spicer Sr.	2	1	1	11	13
Jeremiah Fonvielle	1	2	2	14	8
Sarah Haney	.	2	1	.	.
Edward Pilsher	1	.	3	.	.
Whitaker Red	1	2	1	.	.
Lucy Fonvielle	.	.	1	1	4
Mary Ogdon	.	1	2	1	1
John Atkinson	1	.	4	1	.
John Spicer Jr.	1	3	3	5	7
	14	24	41	39	46

Edwd. Ward's District

Head of Household	WM 21-60 yrs.	WM under 21 & above 60	WF all ages	Blacks 12-50	Blacks under 12 & above 50
Peter Carpenter	1	.	1	3	1
Jos. Tow (Tone?)	1	3	3	.	.
Benj. Simmons	1	.	.	.	.
Stephen Hadnot	1	.	3	1	.
James Towe	1	3	5	.	.
Solomon Burnet	2	1	2	.	.
Elias Cragg	1	1	1	.	.
John Edwards	1	1	3	3	6
Thos. Edward	1	1	1	1	1
Handcock Nichols	1	1	1	.	.
Mathew Carey	1	1	2	1	.
Seth Ward	1	4	6	11	12
Richard Collans	2	1	2	.	.
John Peirson	1	1	5	1	.
Edmond Howard	1	2	3	1	.
Wm. Gibbs	1	1	2	1	1
Thos. Peirson	2	1	2	1	.
Rich^d. Cannedey	1	.	3	.	.
Benj. Ward	1	2	3	2	2
Jo^s. Ward	1	.	3	1	2
Henery Simmons	2	.	2	.	.
Tho. Dulany	1	4	2	.	1
Nathaniel Handcock	2	3	6	1	.
Steven Midelton	1	3	2	.	.
Jams Powars	1	2	3	.	.
Jams Smith	.	1	1	.	.
Sarah Roberson	.	1	2	.	.
George Hegman	1	.	3	.	.
Samuel Everton	1	.	1	.	2
John Harte	1	2	1	.	.
David Roas	1	1	3	.	.
Wm. Hall	2	3	3	12	12

Head of Household	WM 21-60 yrs.	WM under 21 & above 60	WF all ages	Blacks 12-50	Blacks under 12 & above 50
Mrs. Mary Cray	.	.	3	3	1
Thos. Handcock	2	2	1	.	.
Robert Snead	1	2	2	6	2
Obediance Hadnot	1	3	3	8	5
Johnathan Erexson	1	1	1	.	.
Jean Weaks	.	1	2	.	.
Nanney Sallar	.	1	1	.	.
Wm. Hadnot	1	2	2	.	.
David Ward	1	.	6	5	6
	44	55	107	62	60

Head of Household	WM 21-60 yrs.	WM under 21 & above 60	WF all ages	Blacks 12-50	Blacks under 12 & above 50
Edwd. Ward	4	2	3	15	7
John Jarott	1	1	6	.	.
Caleb Smith	2	1	3	.	.
	7	4	12	15	7

"A List of the Number of souls of the uper N. E. District of the Yeare of Lord one thousand Seven hundred & Eighty Six. Taken by me   Richd. Jarrot.

Head of Household	WM 21-60 yrs.	WM under 21 & above 60	WF all ages	Blacks 12-50	Blacks under 12 & above 50
William Cray	1	4	2	6	5 18
Richard Ward	1	1	2	2	1 7
John Farr	1	3	3	4	2 13
John Hawkins	1	1	2	.	. 4
Anthony Chalcraft	1	1	1	7	. 10
Jane Charlcraft	1	.	2	2	. 5
Dempsey Butler	1	.	2	1	. 4
Benjn. Melton	1	2	1	.	. 4
John Miles	1	.	2	.	. 3
Mary Wards	.	2	1	.	. 3
Margaret Wartress	.	1	1	.	. 2
Rich^d. Jarrot	1	5	1	3	1 11
Edward Ward Jr	1	.	2	2	1 6
Obediah Haskins	.	1	1	.	. 2
[could be Hawkins or Perkins]					
Mary Melton	.	4	2	.	. 6
Eliza Simmons	1	4	1	2	. 8
John Bowing	.	1	1	.	. 2
John Bowing Jr.	1	3	1	.	. 4?
Thos. Cook	1	4	1	.	. 6
Geo. Chalcraft	2	1	4	2	2 11
Alexander Willey	8	2	2	2	1 15
Stephen Chalcraft	1	1	2	1	. 5
Willis Johnston	2	1	5	.	. 8
Zachariah? Littlethon	1	1	2	.	. 4
James Edmondson	1	.	5	.	. 6
Willm. Edmondson	1	.	.	.	. 1
Thos. Farnel	1	2	1	1	1 6

STATE CENSUS OF NORTH CAROLINA 1784-1787

Head of Household	WM 21-60 yrs.	WM under 21 & above 60	WF all ages	Blacks 12-50	Blacks under 12 & above 50
Bishop Dudley	1	2	4	9	8
	27	47	54	44	22

A List of the souls in the Upper N. East District by D(anl.) Ambrose (Esqr.)
Pg. 1

Head of Household	WM 21-60 yrs.	WM under 21 & above 60	WF all ages	Blacks 12-50	Blacks under 12 & above 50
Edward Howard	1	4	1	4	8
Thomas Johnston	1	5	4	4	1
James Orrell	1	.	1	.	1
Josiah Edwards	1	3	5	7	4
James Wren	1	2	4	1	.
John Johnston	1	2	3	1	.
Daniel Ambrose	1	6	2	2	3
James Strange	1	.	3	2	2
Samuel Bradey	1	1	.	6	8
John Elax Willey	2	.	3	2	2
Martin Hammond	3	1	2	.	1
William Shiver	1	1	2	1	.
West Hadnot	1	3	3	2	1
Edward Hammond	2	4	3	1	3
Joseph Hawkins	1	1	5	1	.
John Hackit	1	1	4	.	.
Ruth Strange	.	4	5	.	1
Charles Chaires	1	.	2	.	.
Fracis Venters	1	.	3	.	.
Thomas Orrell	1	1	3	1	.
Richard Farr	2	2	5	1	3
Solomon Lingr	1	1	3	.	.
John Taylor	1	5	3	.	.
Sarah Haslip	.	.	3	.	.
Mary Godley	1	2	3	1	.
Daniel Yeates	1	3	6	19	17
John Ballard	.	3	3	2	6
Joseph Ballard	1	1	4	.	.
Mary Ann Ambros	.	2	4	.	,
John Green	1	2	4	.	.
Benjamin Green	1	1	2	.	.
Joseph Chairs	1	1	1	.	.
Zachariah Barrow	1	1	4	4	.
Abra^m. Barrow	1	.	1	1	.
Nathan Askey	1	3	3	.	.
Sarah Wood	.	1	2	.	.
Susana Wiley	.	2	5	.	.
Jones(?) Mezick	.	1	1	.	.
Charles Thompson	1	1	4	2	3
No. 1	37	71	119	65	54
Abram Barrow	1	1	3	2	2
John Godley	1	.	2	1	.
John Murrell	1	.	2	.	.

Head of Household	WM 21-60 yrs.	WM under 21 & above 60	WF all ages	Blacks 12-50	Blacks under 12 & above 50
Wm. Murrell	1	2	2	1	5
Joseph Lovit	1	.	.	.	.
Camp Murrell	1	2	1	.	1
Abner Haslip	1	.	2	.	.
Joseph Beryman	.	1	6	.	.
Joshua Mezick	.	1	1	.	.
Thomas Jarmon	1	.	3	1	1
Benjamin Yates	1	1	3	.	.
Silvy Morriss	.	1	1	.	.
John Smith	1	.	6	3	4
Enoch Godfrey	1	3	5	2	.
Wm. Barnap	1	.	2	.	.
No. 2	12	12	39	10	13

Daniel Ambrose, J. P.

"A list of soles of the Upper So. W. Dist. Taken by me the 4th of April 1786. Errows Excepted."   D. Shepard
Pg. 1

Head of Household	WM 21-60 yrs.	WM under 21 & above 60	WF all ages	Blacks 12-50	Blacks under 12 & above 50
Philip Aman	1	5	3	1	.
Banester Lester	1	3	4	3	2
Jno. Aman	1	2	6	.	1
Abr. Haney	1	2	2	.	.
Jas. Cason	2	2	3	1	.
Zack. Gerganas	1	1	6	1	.
Geo. Sumner	1	.	.	.	.
David Turner	1	5	3	4	4
Tobitha Ogdon	.	.	2	2	4
Wm. King	1	5	3	.	.
James Foyldes	1	2	3	1	.
Thos. Waltom	1	3	1	.	.
Jno. Bond	1	3	1	.	.
Thos. Cummins	1	.	1	.	.
Jno. Jones	1	2	4	.	.
Thos. Loyd	1	3	1	3	1
Jno. Brinson, Esqr	1	1	1	.	.
Wm. Shepard	2	3	3	.	.
Drury Dun	1	3	2	2	.
Geo. Shepard	1	5	4	.	.
Jacob Lee	1	.	1	.	.
Jno. Lee	2	1	4	1	2
Isaac Brinson	1	1	3	1	2
Mary Gerganas	.	.	1	1	.
Jacob Aman	1	4	2	1	.
Wm. Weeb	1	.	2	.	.
Henry Mashborne	1	1	4	3	2
Benj^a. Shepard	3	.	3	.	.
Wm. Bennett	1	.	2	.	.
Zack Roger	1	.	.	.	.

Head of Household	WM 21-60 yrs.	WM under 21 & above 60	WF all ages	Blacks 12-50	Blacks under 12 & above 50
Pg. 2					
Dennis Aman	.	1	.	.	.
Thos. Kimmey	1	1	4	.	.
Jesse Weeb	1	1	3	.	.
Saml. Weeb	1	1	2	.	.
Zekl. Allexandre	.	1	3	.	.
Jos. Allexandre	1	1	1	.	.
Geo. Brinson	1	1	2	3	6
Gause Brinson	1	3	1	2	.
Jno. Hidleburge	1	3	5	1	2
Benja. Mashborne	1	1	2	2	5
Thos. Mashborne	1	2	5	1	2
Lewis Jenkins	1	5	2	2	1
Thos. Franklen	.	1	1	.	.
Thos. Franklen Jr.	.	2	1	.	.
Benja. Jones	1	.	4	.	.
Wm. Runnels	1	3	5	.	.
Mason Johnston	1	5	2	.	.
Jno. Evan	1	.	2	.	.
Chas. Nixson	1	1	3	1	.
Sarah Evan	1	1	3	.	2
Mathw. Brinson	1	.	2	.	1
Jas. Waltom	1	1	2	.	.
Jonathn. Brian	1	2	5	1	1
Jos. Shepard	1	3	3	.	.
Lany Lary	2	4	3	.	.
Thos. King	1	2	2	.	.
Mark Wood	1	.	2	.	.
Jas. Wilson	1	.	.	.	.
Jonathn. Dixson	1	5	3	.	.
Nathn. Murray	1	1	2	.	.
David Alphin	1	1	3	.	.
Jno. Hatch	1	.	1	4	3
Pg. 3					
Adam Brinson	1	2	2	.	1
Micaga King	1	2	1	.	.
Jos. Skipper	.	1	.	.	.
Nathn. Skipper	1	2	3	.	.
Sesse Engrom	1	2	3	.	.
Saml. Walker	2	.	2	1	3
Jno. Stiles	1	2	4	.	.
Thos. Horne	1	1	2	.	.
Thos. Henderson	1	3	2	1	.
Woodhs. Rhodes	1	1	3	3	2
Jacob Brown	1	4	2	.	.
Moses Barfield	1	2	5	1	.
Nathnl. Smith	.	3	2	.	.
Nick Gerganas	1	3	5	1	1
Henry Manor	2	2	1	.	.

Head of Household	WM 21-60 yrs.	WM under 21 & above 60	WF all ages	Blacks 12-50	Blacks under 12 & above 50
Robt. Nixson	1	1	3	5	3
Wm. Jones	1	2	2	1	1
Thos. Barber	1	2	2	.	.
Wm. Alphin	1	1	1	.	.
Isaac Brinson Jr.	1	1	3	.	.
Jas. Evan	1	.	.	.	.
Asa Hunter	1	.	2	.	.
Danl. Shepard	1	.	4	.	1
	84	140	192	40	50

"A list of the number of white & black inhabitants & the free Citizens of every age sex & condition in Captain Daniel Newton's district."

Head of Household	WM 21-60 yrs.	WM under 21 & above 60	WF all ages	Blacks 12-50	Blacks under 12 & above 50
Pg. 1					
G. Mitchell	1	4	4	17	12
B. Mitchell	.	2	4	.	.
N. Simons	.	2	4	.	.
J. Morgan	2	3	3	3	5
H. Marshell	1	1	2	.	.
J. Haskins	1	3	1	.	.
E. Simons	1	4	6	.	.
J. Simons	1	3	4	1	.
M. Simons	.	1	4	2	3
A. Nillson(?)	1	2	2	.	.
J. Cooper	1	.	7	1	.
L. Russell(?)	1	1	5	.	.
J. Row	2	.	2	.	.
M. (?) Yewell	2	2	3	.	.
M. Littleton	.	2	1	.	.
J. Hewet or Hewlet ?	1	.	2	.	.
E. (?) Farnell (?)	.	3	1	1	.
K. Roberts	1	1	2	7	7
? Hamell(?)	2	1	.	2	1
W. W. or Wm. Taylor	1	3	2	4	2
D. Moore	1	4	4	.	.
J. Watters or Walters	1	5	6	.	.
B. Henderson	2	1	1	.	.
Thos. Morres	2	1	3	.	.
? Henderson	1	3	2	.	.
J. Cooper Sr.	1	.	1	.	.
J. (?) Chalcraft	1	1	5	.	.
A. (?) Ball	1	2	2	.	.
P. Wood	2	7	3	.	.
J. (?) Frazor	1	1	1	.	.
J. (?) McKenney (?)	1	4	4	.	.
? Howard	2	1	4	.	.
J. (?) Barns(?)	1	1	3	.	.
J. Yewell	1	.	2	.	.
E. Milton	1	1	6	.	.

STATE CENSUS OF NORTH CAROLINA 1784-1787

Head of Household	WM 21-60 yrs.	WM under 21 & above 60	WF all ages	Blacks 12-50	Blacks under 12 & above 50
S. Haskins	1	.	1	.	.
W. Trott	.	2	2	.	.
N. Huggins	.	1	1	.	.
J. Milton	1	3	2	.	.
	40	76	109	38	33
Pg. 2					
J. Marshell	3	2	1	.	.
D. Bender	1	1	1	5	5
D. Newton	1	1	7	1	.
E. Newton	.	2	1	1	2
Elj. Newton	1	1	4	2	.
R. Causton	1	3	4	.	.
W. Haskens	1	4	2	.	.
W. Howard	1	4	2	.	.
? Howard	1	.	2	.	.
J. Biddle	1	.	1	.	.
M. Barber	1	3	5	.	.
Chr. Row	1	1	1	.	.
Kiah Row	1	1	4	.	.
M. Loyd	.	2	2	.	.
S. Cummons	.	1	2	.	.
R. Burke	.	.	4	.	.
J. Morton	1	2	3	.	.
Rd. Morton	1	1	3	.	.
J. Morris	1	1	1	.	.
P. Lemott ?	2	?	4	.	.
J. Yates	1	4	2	.	.
J. Ward	1	4	3	.	.
J. Morton Jr.	1	.	2	.	.
J. Morton	1	2	3	.	.
W. Simpson	1	3	4	.	.
C. Henderson	1	1	1	.	.
J. Huggins	1	3	4	1	.
T. Barber(t?)	1	2	2	1	.
Dec s. (?) Littleton	1	4	3	.	.
	28	59	78	13	8

Geo. Mitchell, 11th April 1786

Hugh Thompson's District; updated
"Pepals Names"
Pg. 1

Head of Household	WM 21-60 yrs.	WM under 21 & above 60	WF all ages	Blacks 12-50	Blacks under 12 & above 50
Jams Foy, Esqr.	1	5	2	5	3
Stephen Rock	.	6	2	3	1
Hanna Gray	1	2	4	1	.
Maray Thomson	.	2	2	.	.
Sarra Chanler	.	1	2	.	.
Contant Stoot	.	.	2	.	.
Daved Jural (?)	1	1	4	.	.
Jassay Bootler	1	.	2	.	.
Gorg Jankines	1	.	3	.	2

Head of Household	WM 21-60 yrs.	WM under 21 & above 60	WF all ages	Blacks 12-50	Blacks under 12 & above 50
Thos. Thompson	1	.	.	.	.
Charls Grasen	1	.	2	.	.
Robrt Hecks	1	1	1	1	1
Isaack(?) Jarrot(?)	1	1	3	5	4
Jams Thompson	1	2	7	5	3
Abraham Jarrot	1	2	2	?	.
Darby Laray	1	4	4	.	.
Staven Hadnot	1	1	2	1	.
Wm. Stocks	1	.	2	3	6
Hanna Murro	.	1	2	3	.
Robrt Hays	.	.	2	.	.
John Bootler	1	1	2	.	1
Maray Whathoust	.	4	4	1	1
Salman Ward	1	3	4	.	1
John Watrs	1	3	2	.	.
Ziffera or Zifferd Ward	2	.	.	1	5
	21	40	62	31	28
Pg. 2					
John Haws	1	2	2	1	.
John Shaperd	2	1	7	1	2
Thos. Loyd Sr.	.	1	1	.	.
Wm. Loyd Sr.	.	1	3	.	.
Johnnathon Murro	1	3	3	2	3
Abraham Gadins	1	1	3	1	.
Jonathan Pee(?)	1	.	1	.	.
Jassay Gurganas	1	3	6	.	.
Icaack(?) Jonston	1	.	1	.	1
Robrt. Dason(?)	.	3	.	.	.
James Gurganas	1	2	3	.	.
Abraham Sutlef	1	.	.	1	5
William Jonston	1	.	5	.	2
Jams Landan	1	.	3	.	.
Johnathan Coutler (?)	1	.	2	.	.
Robert Bootler	1	2	3	.	.
Wm. Jankences	1	2	3	.	.
Elabeth Rhodes	.	1	3	.	.
Wm. Loyd Jr.	1	1	4	.	.
Thos. Avery	1	1	2	1	2
John Hicks	1	3	1	1	4
Willeby Sheperd	1	.	1	.	.
Smith Shaperd	1	2	1	1	1
Wm. Landen Sr.	1	4	3	.	.
Richard Sempson	1	1	4	2	.
Thos. Turner	1	.	.	.	.
Thomas Fullerd	1	3	2	.	1
Jams Thomson Jr.	2	.	3	.	.
William Pallok	1	4	2	4	3
William Whhelar	1	1	3	.	.

Head of Household	WM 21-60 yrs.	WM under 21 & above 60	WF all ages	Blacks 12-50	Blacks under 12 & above 50
Hugh Thompson	1	.	5	1	.
	24	43	80	16	20

"List Soles So W District" July 3, 1786.
Amos Love.

Head of Household	WM 21-60 yrs.	WM under 21 & above 60	WF all ages	Blacks 12-50	Blacks under 12 & above 50
Jas. Dunn	1	1	3	1	2
Jno. Rhodes	2	.	3	1	2
Peton Pettiway	2	.	1	.	.
Thos. D(?)---ers	1	.	1	.	.
Daniel Humphrey	1	.	2	4	1
Zachah. Fields	2	.	1	.	.
Aaron Barfield	1	.	1	.	.
Arthur Avritt	3	1	3	6	4
Benjn. Williams	2	3	3	5	3
Jas. Ballard	1	3	1	.	1
Wm. Screws	1	.	.	.	.
Wm. Montfort	1	3	4	28	15
Jas. House	3	1	4	3	5
Elijah Norman	1	2	4	.	.
Amos Love	2	1	3	.	6
	26	15	34	38	39

The number of souls in Onslow County 1st Febry 1787.

Head of Household	WM 21-60 yrs.	WM under 21 & above 60	WF all ages	Blacks 12-50	Blacks under 12 & above 50
The Sound, "Sump S Dist."	93	132	203	97	97
H. Thompson	50	83	142	47	48
D. Shepard	84	140	192	40	50
A. Love	26	15	34	38	39
D. Ambross	49	83	158	75	67
R. Jarrot	27	47	54	44	22
G. Mitchell	68	135	187	51	44
Edw. Ward	51	59	119	77	67
White Oak	68	135	187	101	120
Shackelford	49	83	158	75	67
	625	912	1434	645	621

Total: 4, 237

Bishop Dudley's family	1	2	4	9	8

PASQUOTANK COUNTY

A list of the Inhabitants in District No. 3 taken by Samuel Swann Agreeable to an order passed last December Court 1785.

Pg. 1

Head of Household	WM 21-60 yrs.	WM under 21 & above 60	WF all ages	Blacks 12-50	Blacks under 12 & above 50	Total
1. Thomas Relfe	2	1	4	4	6	17
2. John Sawyer	1	2	3	6	9	21
3. John Trueblood	1	2	3	.	.	6
4. Thomas Russel	1	1	1	3	3	9
5. Malachi Norris	1	1	2	2	1	7
6. Dorcas Relfe	1	1	2	6	5	15
7. Joseph Relfe	1	1	1	.	.	3
8. Devotion Davis	1	1	1	.	.	3
9. Abraham Davis	1	4	4	.	.	9
10. Andrew Brothers	1	5	3	3	1	13
11. Daniel Trueblood	1	.	1	6	10	18
12. Martha Cartwright	.	.	1	1	2	4
13. Mary Pharoh	1	.	1	2	1	5
14. Milison Reding	.	.	3	3	3	9
15. Joseph Reding	1	3	5	8	15	32
16. Mary Templeman	.	.	3	13	14	30
17. Samuel Swann	1	.	.	9	4	14
18. Thomas Swann	.	1	.	2	10	13
19. Job Carver	1	4	3	4	5	17
20. Elias Alberson	1	.	1	3	2	7
21. William Barber	1	.	.	.	.	1
22. Robert Reding	2	2	1	1	1	7
23. Archibald Davis	1	5	3	2	.	11
24. John Crocker	3	1	1	1	1	7
25. Hezekiah Cartwright	.	2	2	1	.	5
26. Jehu Cartwright	1	2	5	.	.	8
27. Robert Hall	1	1	4	6	1	13
28. Jean Sawyer	.	3	3	.	.	6
29. Micajah Chaney	.	2	1	1	.	4
30. Job Brothers	1	1	3	.	.	5
	27	46	65	87	94	319

Pg. 2

Head of Household	WM 21-60 yrs.	WM under 21 & above 60	WF all ages	Blacks 12-50	Blacks under 12 & above 50	Total
31. Joseph Palin	1	.	.	.	2	3
32. William Monday	1	1	4	1	.	7
33. Rufus Williams	1	.	2	.	.	3
34. Richard Brothers	1	4	4	.	.	9
35. Elizabeth Gipson	.	2	2	1	.	5
36. Miriam Conner	.	1	1	.	.	2
37. Thomas Reding	1	4	5	4	9	23
38. John Pendleton	1	2	2	3	2	10

Head of Household	WM 21-60 yrs.	WM under 21 & above 60	WF all ages	Blacks 12-50	Blacks under 12 & above 50	Total
39. Samuel Brothers	1	.	1	.	.	2
40. Arnold White	1	.	1	.	.	2
41. John Evans	1	1	2	.	1	5
42. Demsey Caps	1	1	4	.	.	6
43. Joseph Scott	.	4	3	11	6	24
44. Thomas Becks ?	1	.	1	.	.	2
45. John Brothers	1	2	4	.	1	8
46. Thomas Brothers	1	.	.	.	.	1
47. William Pool	1	2	3	1	.	7
48. Lemuel Massaga	1	.	1	.	1	3
49. Jonathan Brothers	1	.	2	.	1	4
50. Jethro Kelly	1	1	2	.	.	4
51. William Brothers	1	2	2	.	.	5
52. Miles Brothers	1	.	1	1	.	3
53. Micajah Elliott	.	1	1	1	4	7
54. William Barrow	1	1	1	.	.	3
55. Lemuel Linton	1	2	4	1	.	8
56. Ann Kermott	.	.	2	.	.	2
57. Free Rachel	.	.	.	3	3	6
58. John Swann Sr.	1	1	2	5	5	14
59. Benjamin Pritchard	1	2	2	1	1	7
60. Thomas Palin Jr	1	2	4	6	5	18
61. Abraham Gordan	1	.	.	1	2	4
62. Thomas Palin Sr	3	1	1	5	4	14
63. Thomas Howard	3	2	5	10	13	33
64. William Jordan	1	2	3	4	4	14
	59	97	137	146	158	587

Pg. 3

Head of Household	WM 21-60 yrs.	WM under 21 & above 60	WF all ages	Blacks 12-50	Blacks under 12 & above 50	Total
65. David Bowls	1	3	3	.	.	7
66. Willis Palmer	1	1	4	.	.	6
67. Malachi Palmer	1	2	3	1	.	7
68. Martha Clark	.	2	3	.	.	5
69. Thomas Simpson	1	2	4	.	.	7
70. Mrs. Aytchardson	.	.	.	7	8	15
71. William Fentress	1	2	3	.	.	6
72. Aaron Trueblood	1	.	1	.	.	2
73. Robert Simpson	1	5	5	1	.	12
74. Edward Tadlock	1	5	3	1	1	11
75. John Needham	1	2	4	.	.	7
76. Evan Wood	1	.	.	.	.	1
77. Abell Stott	1	2	6	1	.	10
78. William Statt	1	4	2	2	1	10
79. Sarah Pavey	.	.	.	2	2	4
80. Samuel Davis	1	.	4	4	10	19
81. Benjamin Pike	1	1	2	.	.	4

Head of Household	WM 21-60 yrs.	WM under 21 & above 60	WF all ages	Blacks 12-50	Blacks under 12 & above 50	Total
82. Alexander McClean	.	.	.	3	4	7
83. Malachi Brothers	1	3	5	.	.	9
84. George Love	1	1	1	1	1	5
85. Same Price	.	.	.	2	.	2
	75	122	190	171	185	743
86. John Smithson	1	2	3	3	4	13
87. James Griffin	1	1	2	.	1	5
88. John Fennell	1	2	2	.	.	5
	78	127	197	174	190	768
District No. 2						
1. Thomas Harvey	1	3	2	13	12	
2. William Boyd	1	.	.	2	1	
3. Joseph Pendelton Junr.	1	1	7	2	5	
4. Joseph White	1	.	2	.	.	
5. Zachariah Jackson	1	.	6	.	.	
6. Thomas Palmer	4	3	4	.	.	
7. Jacob Lister	1	2	1	1	.	
8. John Commander	1	.	3	2	1	
9. Samuel Nichols	1	3	2	.	.	
10. Samuel Overman	1	2	3	.	.	
11. Lemuel James	1	2	1	.	.	
12. John Ward(s?)	1	3	3	4	.	
13. Ann Pendelton	.	3	2	2	5	
14. Nathan Pearson	1	2	4	1	.	
15. Abraham Symons	1	.	.	.	.	
16. Robert Bailey	1	2	4	7	8	
17. Aaron Morris Sr.	2	6	5	.	.	
18. John Overman	1	1	7	3	5	
19. Roan Howett	1	3	1	7	5	
20. John Steavenson	1	1	1	4	6	
21. Joseph Banks	1	.	1	1	.	
22. Thomas Pendelton	1	1	3	1	.	
23. Noah Parr	1	.	2	.	.	
24. Sarah Pendelton	.	1	2	.	.	
25. Samuel White	1	2	3	1	1	
26. Thomas White	1	.	1	.	.	
Pg. 2						
27. John Copper	1	7	3	1	.	
28. Elisha Lister	1	4	4	1	.	
29. Joseph Davis	1	1	4	1	.	
30. Aaron Morris Jr.	2	3	6	13	14	
31. Elizabeth Beck	.	.	1	.	.	
32. Joseph Clarke	1	4	4	.	.	
33. Lemuel Pendelton	1	3	2	1	.	
34. Devotion White	1	1	3	.	.	
35. Mulrain & Keegin	2	.	.	.	.	
36. Benjamin Pritchard	1	.	1	.	1	

Head of Household	WM 21-60 yrs.	WM under 21 & above 60	WF all ages	Blacks 12-50	Blacks under 12 & above 50
37. William Overman	1	.	4	1	1
38. Nicholson Wressell	1	2	3	1	.
39. Nohn Meeds	1	2	3	1	1
40. Caleb Pendelton	1	3	2	4	4
41. Thomas Trueblood	1	2	2	2	.
42. James Overman	1	.	2	2	1
43. Joseph Commander	1	1	.	4	.
44. John Hosea	1	2	1	4	3
45. James Jimson (?)	1	1	1	1	.
46. James White	1	1	3	.	2
47. William Luffman	1	3	2	1	1
48. Joseph White Sr.	1	.	6	.	.
49. Nathen Denbey	1	2	2	.	.
50. Jonathen Twedy	1	2	3	.	.
51. John Mackell	1	1	3	1	2
52. Onias Overman	2	.	.	.	.
Pg. 3					
47. Joseph Morris	1	4	6	.	.
48. Henry Lancaster	1	1	2	4	2
49. Mathew D. Greevs	1	3	5	6	5
50. John Morris	1	2	4	.	.
51. William James	1	.	1	.	.
52. Joseph Pool	1	1	4	.	.
53. Joseph Overman	1	2	5	.	.
54. Thomas Commander	1	1	1	1	3
55. Mary Meeds	.	2	2	.	.
56. John Low	1	1	3	.	1
57. Benjamine Morris	1	.	1	.	.
58. Mordica Morris	1	6	3	4	.
59. Joseph Commander Sr.	1	4	4	1	.
60. Jonathan Boyd	2	.	.	3	4
61. Grace Evins	.	2	3	.	.
62. John Symons	3	3	7	7	.
63. John Modlen	1	4	4	.	.
64. Joshua Arnol	1	.	7	.	.
65. Fisher Trueblood	1	5	2	1	.
66. Lemuel Stone	1	5	1	1	2
67. Zachariah Morris	1	.	2	1	.
68. William Harvey	1	2	2	10	7
69. Joseph Pendelton Senr.	1	1	1	3	6
70. Thomas Pritchard	2	1	3	10	10
Pg. 4					
77. Thomas Boyd	1	.	.	1	.

Head of Household	WM 21-60 yrs.	WM under 21 & above 60	WF all ages	Blacks 12-50	Blacks under 12 & above 50
78. Hepzebeth Pointer	.	4	1	1	.
79. Mathew Church	.	.	2	.	.
80. Mathew Poynter	.	.	1	1	1
81. Joshu Markam	1	1	2	4	.
82. Christopher Nicholson	1	4	3	1	2
83. Enuck Relfe	1	2	1	9	6
84. Winiferd Ashbe	.	2	1	.	.
85. Thomas Hill	2	1	1	.	1
86. Fru Sawry (?)	.	.	.	1	5
87. Anthony Markham	1	1	2	5	8

[Districts No. 5 and No. 4 not yet located. Ed.]

A List of the Inhabitants of District No. 1 agreeable to law. March 17th Day 1786.

Pg. 1 — Head of Household	WM 21-60 yrs.	WM under 21 & above 60	WF all ages	Blacks 12-50	Blacks under 12 & above 50
1. David George	1	2	5	9	4
2. John Winberry	1	2	3	.	.
3. John Bundy	1	4	1	.	.
4. Ch^S. Keel	1	.	5	.	.
5. Ch^S. Delon	1	2	2	.	.
6. Demsey Gardner	1	2	3	.	.
7. Samuel White	1	.	.	.	.
8. Stephen Keaton	.	1	.	.	.
9. Zach Keaton Sr	1	1	.	1	1
10. Thomas Meeds	.	1	1	.	.
11. Thaddeus Freshwater	1	.	4	5	5
12. Ditto Negro Rose	.	.	.	1	.
13. William Gordon	.	1	.	.	.
14. Joseph Gordon	1	1	3	.	.
15. Othniel Overman	1	.	1	.	1
16. John Wilson	1	1	2	1	.
17. David Palmer	.	.	1	3	1
18. Samuel Guin	.	1	.	.	.
19. Clement Cartright	1	4	2	6	10
20. Thomas Brosher	.	1	.	.	.
21. Stephen Wilcox	1	3	4	.	.
22. Isaac Jinnings	.	1	1	5	7
23. Joseph Jinnings	1	.	.	.	.
24. John Jinnings	.	1	.	.	.
25. William Snowden	1	2	1	5	1
26. Ruth Bundy	.	3	3	.	.
27. Jonathan Bundy	1	.	.	.	.
28. David Bundy	1	.	.	.	.
29. Oziass Overman	1	.	.	.	.
30. William Morris	1	1	1	.	.
31. John Daley	1	.	2	.	.

Pg. 2 — Head of Household	WM 21-60 yrs.	WM under 21 & above 60	WF all ages	Blacks 12-50	Blacks under 12 & above 50
32. William Wooten	1	.	4	.	.
33. Joseph Nichols	1	.	2	.	.
34. Charles Wooton	1	.	.	.	.
35. Thomas Teague	1	3	2	.	.
36. Jonathan Banks	1	3	3	10	5
37. Joseph Palmer	1	3	5	4	3
38. Ditto Negro Tom	.	.	.	2	2
39. Caleb Cartright	1	5	3	2	3
40. Oliver Thacary	.	1	3	.	.
41. Thomas Markam	1	4	4	.	1
42. Charles Markam	1	4	4	.	1
43. Mary Lowry	.	3	5	.	.
44. Joseph Fox	1	1	2	.	.
45. Jessea Cartright	1	3	4	3	4
46. William Palmer	.	.	.	5	.
47. Isaac Jordan	1	3	3	5	.
48. James Banks	1	.	2	.	.
49. Joseph Keaton Jr.	1	2	3	.	.
50. Partrik Keaton	1	.	2	2	1
51. Richard Sanders	2	3	3	4	6
52. Samuel Overton	.	.	.	.	3
53. Joseph Cartright	1	4	4	4	3
54. John Rose	1	1	4	.	.
55. Nathan Overman	1	2	2	.	.
56. Thomas Overman	1	2	2	?	.
57. James Barms	2	.	.	3	3
58. Thomas Tweedy	1	.	4	.	.
59. Hezekiah Cartright	1	3	3	.	1
60. Joseph Keaton Sr	1	2	5	5	7

Pg. 3 — Head of Household	WM 21-60 yrs.	WM under 21 & above 60	WF all ages	Blacks 12-50	Blacks under 12 & above 50
61. John Guin	1	.	.	.	.
62. William Webber	.	1	.	.	.
63. Robert Pool	1	1	3	1	2
64. James Pool	1	3	2	1	1
65. Hez. Woodley	1	3	3	.	.
66. John Cox	1	2	1	2	4
67. Silvenus Turner	.	.	.	2	5
68. Ch^S. Turner	.	.	.	2	3
69. Jos. Scarff	1	2	3	.	.
70. James White	1	1	3	.	.
71. Miriam White	.	.	1	.	.
72. Lemuel Jinnings	1	3	4	.	1
73. Cont. Luton	1	1	4	3	.
74. Ann Cory	.	.	3	.	.
75. Henry Keaton	1	1	5	1	3
76. Thomas Gaskins	1	1	8	5	9
77. Jabez Nichols	1	1	1	1	2
78. Timothy Meeds	1	1	1	.	1
79. John Wootton	1	.	.	.	.

Head of Household	WM 21-60 yrs.	WM under 21 & above 60	WF all ages	Blacks 12-50	Blacks under 12 & above 50
80. William Davis	1	3	2	2	3
81. John Keaton	1	3	2	.	1
82. Obediah Small	1	.	1	.	.
83. Demsey Palmer	.	1	.	.	.
84. Sarah Palmer	.	1	1	.	.
85. Lemuel Hall	.	.	.	2	1
86. Demsey Turner	.	.	.	1	.
87. Demsey Jinnings	1	3	4	4	2
88. Joseph Pendleton	1	1	2	.	2
89. Thomas Pendleton	1	1	2	.	2
90. Emanuel Knights	1	.	.	.	.
91. Allexander Mattox	1	3	4	.	.
Pg. 4					
92. Abel Palmer	.	.	.	1	.
93. William Freshwater	1	1	1	.	1
94. Rebecca Wilson	1	2	2	.	.
95. Sarah Keaton	.	.	1	.	.
96. Zachariah Keaton Jr	1	.	.	.	.
97. Job Morgan	1	2	3	.	.
98. Davison Cory	1	2	3	.	.
99. Jessea Moor	1	1	3	.	.
100. Joseph Sanders	1	2	2	4	2
101. Evan Sanders	1	.	2	.	1
102. Hackt. Williams	1	2	3	.	.
103. Robert Cartright	1	2	4	.	1
104. John Blackstock	1	.	2	11	28
105. Sidney Sampson	.	.	.	2	3
106. Levy Davis	.	.	.	2	.
107. Ann Baptist	.	.	5	4	9
108. Mary Lancaster	.	.	1	6	3
109. John Pool	1	.	1	1	.
110. William Keaton	1	.	.	.	.
111. Thomas Duncan	1	1	2	.	.
112. Asea Williams	1	.	2	.	.
113. Trimigan Williams	1	.	1	.	.
114. Elkh. Williams	1	3	1	.	.
115. William Sawyer	1	2	2	.	.
116. Thomas Barns	1	1	.	4	3
117. Mary Foster	.	.	1	2	.
118. Ann Barco	.	1	1	.	2
119. Kelly Casson	1	2	2	.	.
120. Joseph Henley	1	4	5	6	2
121. Elizabeth Winslow	.	1	4	.	1
122. Alexander Brown	1	3	2	1	.
123. Jesse Hill	1	.	1	.	.
124. Edwd. Everigin Esq	1	.	.	14	14
125. Watson Henderson	1	.	2	.	.
126. John Fountain	1	.	6	.	.

Head of Household	WM 21-60 yrs.	WM under 21 & above 60	WF all ages	Blacks 12-50	Blacks under 12 & above 50	Total
A List of Citizens in District No. 6						
Pg. 1						
Thomas Tempel	2	2	4	4	3	15
Mordick Smith	2	2	5	1	2	12
Caleb Koen	1	2	6	3	3	15
William Wormiston	1	2	1	.	.	4
James Blunt	1	5	2	.	.	8
Willis Sixto(n)	1	3	5	.	.	9
James Forehand (?)	1	2	3	.	.	6
John Rich	1	1	3	.	.	5
John Coalk or Coabk?	1	3	3	.	.	7
Demcey Sawyer	1	1	4	.	.	6
Rabrt Gray	1	.	2	2	3	8
Timothy Burnham	1	2	3	.	.	6
Thomas Leake	1	1	1	.	.	3
Jasoph Spence	1	2	1	1	.	7
James Spence	1	2	2	.	.	5
Jacob Tempel	1	3	5	.	.	9
Adom Baume	1	.	5	.	.	6
Thomas Hor(t?)on	1	3	5	.	.	9
Nancey Alson	1	.	3	.	.	4
John Jones	2	2	2	.	2	8
Danil ? Richardson	1	2	1	.	.	4
Caleb Coop(er?)	1	2	3	.	.	6
Isaac Wood	1	.	2	.	.	3
Obediah Rich	1	.	2	.	.	3
Moses Vardin	1	3	2	.	.	6
James Tempel	2	.	2	1	4	9
David Spence	1	.	1	.	.	2
Edward Williams	1	1	1	5	.	8
Willam Caright	1	2	3	.	.	6
Lamell Forehand	1	1	2	.	.	4
Pg. 2						
Sarah Gray	.	3	2	.	.	5
Jael (Joel?) Leake	1	.	.	.	.	1
Edward Halastred	1	3	2	.	.	6
Samuell Halstead	1	.	1	.	.	2
Frederick Davis	1	4	3	1	6	15
Anthoney Davis	1	2	5	1	.	9
Josiah Sexton	1	1	1	.	.	3
Jeremiah Leek	2	1	4	1	3	11
Willess Varden	.	1	.	.	.	1
Isaac Spence	1	.	.	.	.	1
John Leek	1	1	1	.	.	3
Jarvis Halsted	1	.	.	.	.	1
David Williams	1	1	3	2	.	7
Richard Hastings	1	.	.	.	.	1
Elisha Prichard Jr	1	.	2	.	.	3

Head of Household	WM 21-60 yrs.	WM under 21 & above 60	WF all ages	Blacks 12-50	Blacks under 12 & above 50	Total
Lazarus Lufman	1	.	6	.	.	7
Solomon Temple	1	.	3	.	.	4
Thamer Cherry	.	1	1	.	.	2
William Hastings	1	.	3	.	.	4
David Varden	1	.	.	.	.	1
Jeams Jons	1	1	2	.	.	4
Isaac Cartight	1	2	1	.	.	4
Robard Cartright	1	.	2	.	.	3
Caleb Cartwight	1	.	.	.	.	1
Mary Williams	.	1	2	.	.	3
William Woard(?)	1	.	2	.	.	3
Pg. 3						
Isaac Burnham	1	2	2	.	.	5
John Cartwright	.	1	1	2	3	7
Lot Sawyer	1	1	2	.	.	4
Thomas Richardson	1	.	3	1	2	7
John Sawyer	1	.	4	.	.	5
Letisha Spence	.	.	2	.	.	2
Bethier Nickles	.	2	4	.	.	6
Daniel Williams	1	2	4	4	5	16
William Sikes	1	2	2	.	.	5
Malsey Cooper	1	.	2	.	.	3
Peter Baum	1	.	.	.	.	1
John Walmslay	1	1	.	4	1	7
Mark Sexton	1	.	.	.	.	1
Daniel Koen	1	7	4	1	.	13
John Koen	1	2	3	1	1	8
Bengamin Cartwright	.	1	3	.	.	4
Caleb Koen	1	1	3	.	.	5
John Baum	1	3	3	.	.	7
Nathanel Gray	.	2	3	.	.	5
Anthoney Gray	1	2	7	.	.	10
Cortne Cartwright	.	.	3	.	1	4
Willes Cartwright	1	.	.	.	.	1
Simon Cartwright	1	.	3	.	.	4
Mark Spence	1	.	1	.	.	2
Joseph Stokley	1	2	1	3	5	11
Samuel Spence	1	.	2	.	.	3
Pg. 4						
Jesse McPhasion	1	1	3	.	.	5
John Gray	1	1	2	2	2	8
Eleazer Beth Varding	.	1	2	.	.	3
Silvester Varding	.	2	.	.	.	2
Abraham Harson	1	2	1	.	.	4
David Forehand	1	6	2	.	.	9
Caleb McDaniel	.	1	3	.	.	4
Peter McDaniel	1	3	1	.	.	5
Joseph Tempel	1	4	5	2	2	14
Isaac McDaniel	1	1	1	.	.	3

Head of Household	WM 21-60 yrs.	WM under 21 & above 60	WF all ages	Blacks 12-50	Blacks under 12 & above 50	Total
Samuel Forhand	1	.	3	.	.	4
John Cright	1	3	3	1	.	8
Jarves Jones	1	7	2	2	.	12
Elizabeth Sawyer	1	.	1	.	.	2
Jessey Harrison	1	.	2	.	.	3
Solomon Sawyer	1	1	1	.	.	3
Patsh(or?;it?) Griffth	.	.	3	.	.	3
Elisha Prichers	1	4	2	.	.	7
Joseph Drsor(?)	1	.	3	.	.	4
James Spence	1	2	1	.	.	4
Renchey Spence	1	4	2	.	.	7
Owen Williams	1	3	1	1	.	6
District No. 7						
Pg. 1						
Jean Bailey	.	1	2	.	1	
Thomas Wood(?)	1	2	3	.	.	
Samuel Spence	1	3	1	1	2	
Sarah Pool	.	4	2	1	.	
Benjamin Morgan	1	4	3	.	.	
Seth Morgan	1	3	3	.	.	
Thomas Overmon	1	2	4	2	.	
Samuel Staford	1	2	2	.	.	
Aaron Low	1	3	3	.	.	
John White	1	2	2	.	.	
Noah Lowry	1	2	2	.	.	
Jesy Symons	1	4	3	.	.	
Frances Fletcher	1	4	3	1	1	
William Price	1	3	2	2	1	
David Davis	1	3	2	4	3	
Sarah Bailey	.	1	1	.	.	
Abraham Symons	1	1	7	4	6	
Timothy Trublood	1	2	.	1	1	
Thomas Damron	1	2	.	2	.	
James Linwwrd	1	.	.	1	.	
Susanir Shannonhous	2	1	9	.	1	
Jerimiah Gilbert	1	4	4	.	.	
David Tatom	1	1	2	1	.	
Patrick Bailey	1	2	2	.	.	
Devotion Davis	1	.	1	2	4	
Ann Bailey	.	4	1	.	.	
Calob Mackie/Mackee	1	2	3	.	.	
David Bailey	1	1	2	.	.	
William Bruer	2	.	.	3	1	
Daniel Watson	3	2	2	1	1	
Benjn. Hicks	1	2	1	4	4	
James Overmon	1	5	5	.	.	
John Low(?)	1	.	6	.	4	
Devotion Benton	1	2	1	.	.	

Head of Household	WM 21-60 yrs.	WM under 21 & above 60	WF all ages	Blacks 12-50	Blacks under 12 & above 50
Jeen Mackneel	.	3	2	.	.
John Macknight	1	.	.	.	.
Pg. 2					
Thomas Ackess	2	.	3	2	.
Solomon Pool	1	.	3	5	3
Mark Delong	1	4	3	.	.
Joseph Brothers	1	4	6	1	.
Eleany Benton	1	.	2	.	.
Jonathon Morris	1	2	1	.	.
Mary Morris	.	2	3	.	.
Thomas Jirdan	2	2	4	1	.
Wilson Emverson	1	.	2	1	.
Charles Best	1	.	1	.	.
Nathon Morris	2	4	2	1	.
Symon Mondin	1	.	.	.	.
Cornelor Repir	1	3	4	.	.
Abraham White	3	2	2	.	1
Thomas Brothers	1	2	6	1	2
Benj. Bony(?)	1	.	2	.	1
Grabril Cosand	1	5	4	2	1
Joseph Wood	.	1	.	.	.
Grabril Ellot	1	.	1	.	1
Thomas Wolden	1	.	3	.	.
John Price	1	5	2	.	.
Jonathon Price	1	2	2	1	.
John Sanders	.	1	2	4	3
Patrick Pool	1	1	.	.	.
Charls Overmon	1	5	3	1	1
Honor Low	.	.	2	.	.
Patrick Pool	1	4	4	.	1
John Ward	1	3	3	.	.
Janes(?) Morgin	1	3	4	.	1
Francis Albertson	1	1	1	.	.
Jerden White	1	1	2	.	.
Joseph Giffin	1	2	6	1	.
Joshua Griffin	1	.	3	.	.
Caleb Davis	1	2	2	.	.
Pg. 3					
Aaron Twidy	1	4	2	.	.
Tillon(?) Jackson	1	1	4	.	.
Henery Jones	1	.	4	.	.
Oberdiah Small	1	4	3	1	.
John Symons	1	1	3	.	1
Jerimiah Symons	1	.	.	3	2
Benjamin Leonard	1	1	3	2	2
Joshua Jackson	1	3	3	2	9
Joseph Wilson	3	2	4	4	3
John Brown	.	.	.	3	1

Head of Household	WM 21-60 yrs.	WM under 21 & above 60	WF all ages	Blacks 12-50	Blacks under 12 & above 50
William Low	.	1	1	1	3
Robert Lowry	1	2	2	8	6
David Bailey	1	.	.	4	7
Spencer Williams	1	1	.	3	.
Samuel Trublood	1	.	1	.	.
John Lowry	1	.	.	.	.
Sarah Boswell	.	1	2	.	.
Thomas Trublood	1	.	1	.	.
John Low	1	1	1	2	2
Tamar Low	.	2	2	.	.
Elizabeth Cocks	.	1	1	.	.
John Henby	1	1	2	.	.
Josiah Pery	1	3	3	2	3
John Raper	1	1	2	.	.
Nathon Ellot	1	.	1	1	.
Benjamin Raper	1	1	2	.	.
Peny Adams	.	.	2	.	.
Lemuel Morgin	1	1	3	.	.
Sarah Griffen	.	.	1	.	.
Samuel Small	2	1	1	1	.
Hosey Gregry	1	2	4	.	.
John Mondin	1	.	2	.	.
Benjamon Mondin	1	1	2	.	.
Benjamin Morris	1	3	1	.	.
Mary Bright	.	3	2	.	.
Pg. 4					
Aaron Morris	1	2	6	1	7
Solomon Pool	1	3	1	.	.
James Neuby	1	1	3	.	.
John Taylor	1	1	6	.	.
Daniel Taylor	1	3	3	.	.
Benjamin Overmon	1	1	3	1	.
John Royall	1	2	1	.	.
Peter Mondin	1	2	2	.	.
Jacob Neuby	1	2	4	.	.
Sarah Small	.	3	2	.	.
Joseph Neuby	.	1	1	.	.
William Lane	1	3	3	4	1
Shadrick Taylor	2	1	4	.	.
Joseph Boswell	2	2	5	.	.
Miriam Bundy	2	3	2	.	.
Caleb Bunday	1	.	1	.	.
Benjamin Bundy	1	.	2	.	.
Demsey Bundy	2	4	2	.	.
Joshua Rankhorn	1	4	3	.	.
Thomas Mondin	1	1	1	.	.
Aaron Lin---(?)	1	2	4	1	4
John Erls	1	3	2	2	1

Head of Household	WM 21-60 yrs.	WM under 21 & above 60	WF all ages	Blacks 12-50	Blacks under 12 & above 50	Head of Household	WM 21-60 yrs.	WM under 21 & above 60	WF all ages	Blacks 12-50	Blacks under 12 & above 50
William Scott	1	1	1	1	1	Joseph Overman	1	2	1	.	.
Benjamin Fellops	1	.	1	.	.	Patrick Pool	1	.	2	.	.
James Wynn	1	1	2	.	.	Devotion Davis	2	6	4	9	7
Thomas Wiley	1	1	2	.	1	Benjamin Wood	1	.	1	.	.
Charles Colmon	2	1	3	1	.	John Croakham	1	.	1	1	.
John Miller	1	1	2	.	.	John Bailey	1	.	1	.	.
Lurany Stevonson	.	.	2	.	.						

PERQUIMANS COUNTY

Head of Household	WM 21-60 yrs.	WM under 21 & above 60	WF all ages	Blacks 12-50	Blacks under 12 & above 50
"A List of the number of Inhabitants in the Durants Neck district. Taken Oct. 1786 by Wm. Reed."					
Pg. 1					
Moses Stone	1	2	2	.	3
Joseph Mullen	1	3	3	12	16
Isaac Mullen	1	.	.	.	.
Estate Richard Williams	.	.	.	1	2
Jos. Bedgood	1	.	.	.	.
Abm. Howitt	1	1	3	5	9
Enoch Raper	1	.	1	.	1
Jos. Barclift	1	3	3	9	.
Est. Benjamin Weeks	.	.	1	1	.
Jos. Mackee	1	.	.	.	.
Pg. 2					
Jno. Turner Jr.	1	1	5	.	.
John Morgan	1	1	2	.	.
Richdson Morrs	1	.	3	.	.
Jos. Turner, the yunger	1	.	.	1	1
Caleb Ward	1	1	5	.	.
Thos. Stevenson	1	.	1	9	5
Hugh Stevenson	1	.	1	6	8
Tulle Godfree	1	.	.	.	.
Sam Week	1	3	2	.	.
Rebeckah Wood	.	.	1	.	.
Thos. Turner	1	.	1	.	2
Pg. 3					
Henry Raper Sr.	1	1	2	.	1
Luke Raper	1	.	2	.	.
Richd. Robins	1	.	.	1	.
Chs. Brigs	1	.	.	.	.
Jno. Taylor	1	.	3	.	.
Willm. Hosea	1	3	3	.	.
Nathl. Welch	1	.	2	.	.
Richd. Welch	1	.	2	.	.
Jno. Morris	1	.	1	.	.
Willm. Knowls	1	1	3	.	1
Saml. Jackson	1	3	4	3	.
Nathl. Gorden	1	1	5	.	.
Thos. Weeks	1	2	3	1	.
Pg. 4					
Laml. Weeks	1	.	1	.	.
Willm. Barclift	1	3	3	.	.
Jno. Hopkins	1	1	2	.	.
Willm. Arnold	1	2	1	1	1
Jno. Raper	1	1	4	2	1
Robert Raper	1	.	3	.	.
Jos. Raper	1	1	4	.	1
Jno. Cartee(?)	1	3	2	1	2
Jno. Bateman	1	1	7	2	.
Robinson Raper	1	.	.	.	.
Henry Raper Jr.	1	2	6	.	.
Jos. Sitterson	1	1	5	1	.
Jno. Davis	1	1	3	3	1
Jno. Stanton Jr.	1	.	3	1	1
Pg. 5					
Benja. Roberts	1	.	1	.	.
Hannah Holloway	.	1	3	4	6
David Butt	1	.	2	.	.
Abel Elliott	1	1	4	.	.
Thos. Wright	1	3	3	.	.
Josiah Albertson	1	3	3	.	1
Elihu Albertson	.	2	4	3	1
Jno. Horton	1	.	.	.	.
Willm. Robins	1	5	4	2	.
Geo. Sutton	1	1	4	4	8
Elisa. Jaycocks	.	.	3	4	5
Ashy. Sutton	1	1	3	12	14
Pg. 6					
Benja. Reed	1	1	2	7	8
Jos. McAdam	1	1	3	.	1
Zadoc Mullen	1	2	4	.	.
Thos. Bateman	1	1	1	2	.
Jno. Wright	1	.	.	.	.
Jos. Turner Sr.	1	2	2	1	.
Eliza. Stokes	.	7	3	.	.
Jno. Fiveash	1	.	1	.	.
Duke Kinyon	1	.	.	.	.
Willm. Whedbee	1	.	2	.	.
Zebulon Snowden	1	3	2	.	.
Moses Jackson Sr.	.	1	2	.	.
Pg. 7					
Willm. Jackson Sr.	1	1	1	.	.
Jno. Toms	1	3	5	4	4
Willm. Humphrass	1	3	3	3	2
Thos. Whedbee	1	8	3	13	11
Thos. Whedbee for Grenbury Sutton	.	.	.	1	2
Thos. Whedbee for Laml. Whedbee	.	.	.	4	1
Willm. Chalk	1	.	2	2	.
Jno. Barclift	1	1	1	2	.
Marwood Barclift	.	.	1	1	3
Eliza. Barclift	.	.	1	1	1

Head of Household	WM 21-60 yrs.	WM under 21 & above 60	WF all ages	Blacks 12-50	Blacks under 12 & above 50
Thos. Holloway	1	3	1	1	.
Jno. Clayton	1	3	4	5	5
Samll. Sutton	1	3	2	5	5
Leah Clayton	.	.	1	2	1
Lockl. Williams	1	.	1	3	2
Franses Layden	1	1	3	6	1
Jno. Tucker	1	1	1	.	.
Jno. Clark	1	.	.	.	.
Willm. Reed	1	4	2	10	12
Susannah Pitts	.	.	2	.	.
Lamll. Overton	1	.	.	.	.
Jas. Sumner	1	.	3	.	.
Wilson Weeks	1	.	.	.	.
Jos. Jones	1	.	.	.	.
Pg. 9					
Gosby Toms	1	1	.	5	.
Jno. Wheedbee	.	1	1	6	.
Martha Toms	.	.	2	2	7
Foster Toms	1	1	1	3	5
Lazs. Linton	1	.	.	6	1
Wilson Weeks	.	.	1	5	6
Caleb Burnham	1	1	3	1	.
Abner Knowls	1	.	1	3	.
Henry Butt	1	2	2	.	.
Moses Jackson	1	1	1	1	.
Jno. Saunders	1	2	2	3	5
Jos. Turner Jr.	1	2	4	4	5
Pg. 10					
James Whedbee	.	2	2	5	4
Richd. Whedbee	.	3	2	4	2
Jno. Whedbee	1	3	2	1	3
Joseph Sutton	1	1	.	11	11
Joseph Lasey	1	2	4	.	.
Aaron Barber	1	2	3	.	.
Jos. Outlan	1	.	2	3	2
Joab Kinyan	1	2	2	.	1
Benja. Forehan	1	1	1	.	.
Jos. Godfree	1	3	3	2	1
Mary Foster	.	1	2	2	1
Cornelius Forhand	1	1	1	.	.
Thos. Stafford Jr.	1	2	5	.	1
Thos. Stafford Sr.	.	1	1	.	.
Pg. 11					
Willm. Stafford	1	.	1	.	.
Willm. Clayton	1	1	2	2	3
Jno. Roberts	1	.	.	.	.
Benjan. Bedgood	1	1	1	.	.
Frans. Foster	1	.	.	.	.

Head of Household	WM 21-60 yrs.	WM under 21 & above 60	WF all ages	Blacks 12-50	Blacks under 12 & above 50
Thos. Layden	1	2	1	1	1
Jos. Clayton	1	4	1	.	.
Thos. Reed	1	2	1	.	.
Francis Potter	1	4	5	2	3

"About Ten Small Familys not Given in"

List taken by Francis Newby, Octr. 12th, 1786.

Pg. 1; column 1					
Joshua Bozwell	1	.	2	.	1
Samuel Anderson	1	.	3	1	.
Thos. Tarton(?)	1	.	1	.	.
Thos. Modlin	1	1	2	.	.
John Hasket	1	4	5	1	1
Siles(?) Hasket	1	4	2	2	.
Josiah Stafford	1	1	2	.	.
Jessee Hasket	1	1	1	2	3
Jobe Hendrix	.	2	.	.	.
Solomon Hendricks	2	1	2	.	.
John Hendrix	1	1	2	.	.
Elizabeth Hendrix	.	1	2	.	.
Thos. Haskel	1	2	1	3	6
Florella Modlin	.	1	2	.	.
Izbell Bozwell	.	4	5	.	.
Betty Wilson	.	1	2	.	.
Thos. Ray	1	2	1	.	.
Wm. Roberts	1	2	3	.	1
Wm. Lacey	1	1	4	.	.
Pennina Nixon	.	4	3	.	.
Pg. 1; column 2					
Nathanl. Pierce	1	1	2	.	1
Benjn. Albertson	1	3	4	.	.
Wm. Small	1	1	4	.	1
Abner Pierce	1	.	3	.	1
Rd. Sanders	1	5	2	.	1
Joshua Fletcher	.	3	2	6	9
Thos. Newby	1	3	3	4	1
Thos. Weir(?)	1	.	.	.	.
Robert Newby	1	.	.	.	.
Josiah Bundy	1	2	7	.	.
George Metcalfe	3	3	1	3	1
Sarah Nicholson	.	1	2	2	.
Nicholas Nicholson	1	4	4	1	.
Joseph Bailey	1	1	1	1	2
Daniel Saint	1	.	.	.	.

Head of Household	WM 21-60 yrs.	WM under 21 & above 60	WF all ages	Blacks 12-50	Blacks under 12 & above 50
Zachariah Nixon	1	5	2	.	10
Joshua Iver	1	7	3	2	.
George Boswell	1	.	.	.	.
Pg. 2; column1					
Nathan Modlin	1	2	2	.	.
Thos. Henley	1	5	3	.	.
Marthy Modlin	.	.	2	.	.
Joseph Wells	1	.	5	2	6
Antony Bartee(?)	1	4	3	1	.
John Baxter	1	.	.	1	.
John Bartee(?)	1	6	3	.	.
Joshua Albertson	1	4	3	1	.
Henry White	1	3	2	1	.
Thos. Ward	1	.	.	.	.
Charles Overman	1	.	.	.	.
Thos. Saint	1	2	2	.	.
Ephraim Winget	1	.	3	.	.
Isac(?) Stone	1	1	3	.	.
Phinehas Nixon	1	.	2	2	.
Benjn. Albertson	1	7	3	1	1
Chalkley Albertson	1	4	3	1	1
Joshua Guyer	1	2	1	.	.

Head of Household	WM 21-60 yrs.	WM under 21 & above 60	WF all ages	Blacks 12-50	Blacks under 12 & above 50
Pg. 2; column 2					
John Newby	1	1	1	2	1
Saml. Smith	1	.	2	1	.
Zach. Newby	1	4	.	3	1
Joshua Moore	1	3	3	4	4
Seth Sumner	1	1	1	18	17
David Peirce	1	.	4	.	.
Joseph Ratliff	1	.	5	2	2
Francis Newby	1	.	4	13	10
John Anderson	1	.	4	2	2
Joseph Modlin	1	3	2	.	.
Moses Barber	1	.	1	.	.
Keziah Pretlow	.	3	3	8	8
David Whithead	1	1	1	.	.
Jessee Perry	1	5	4	2	1
Wm. Boswell	1	1	1	.	.
Wm. Burk	1	.	3	10	4
Oney Damron	.	.	.	3	1
Joshua Talton	1	2	1	.	.
Aaron Cosand	1	1	1	1	.
Charles White	1	.	.	.	.
Joseph Newby	1	5	2	4	3

Head of Household	WM 21-60 yrs.	WM under 21 & above 60	WF all ages	Blacks 12-50	Blacks under 12 & above 50	White Poles	Black Poles	No. Acres Land	No. Town lots

A List of the Taxable Property in Hertford District of Perquimons. Taken by Charles Moore for the Year 1786.

Pg. 1

Head of Household	WM 21-60	WM u21/a60	WF	Bl 12-50	Bl u12/a50	Wh Poles	Bl Poles	Acres	Lots
Nath¹. Williams, Sr	1	.	.	2	.	1	2	550	.
Jessee Bogue	1	7	4	.	.	1	.	100	.
Mary Wilson	.	1	3	.	.	.	.	50	.
Samˡ. Elliot	1	.	.	.	.	1	.	.	.
Jessee Chapple	1	.	3	1	.	1	.	.	.
Joshua Bagley	1	1	2	2	.	1	2	50	.
Robert Nicholson	.	1	.	.	1	1	.	.	1
Wm. Coppage	1	.	2	.	1	1	.	.	.
Thoˢ. Bagley	1	5	2	.	.	1	.	50	.
Eleazar Creecy	2	.	2	2	4	2	2	150	.
Elizabeth Townsend	.	3	2	1	3	.	1	340	1/2
Wm. Richards	1	4	3	.	.	1	.	400	.
Sarah Saint	.	.	2	.	.	.	.	170	.
Richᵈ. Hatfield	2	3	3	.	1	2	.	.	.
Hezekiah Rogerson Sen	1	6	3	1	5	1	1	125	.
Sarah Phelps	.	.	4	2	3	.	2	200	.
Wm. Newbould	2	.	4	3	3	2	3	700	6
Thoˢ. Newby	2	1	4	.	1	2	.	150	.

Pg. 2

Head of Household	WM 21-60	WM u21/a60	WF	Bl 12-50	Bl u12/a50	Wh Poles	Bl Poles	Acres	Lots
Jno. Rogerson	1	.	3	.	.	1	.	25	.
Richᵈ. Goodwin	1	2	2	.	.	1	.	50	.
Jacob Wilson	2	.	1	2	2	2	2	200	.
Thoˢ. Portlock	1	1	3	1	.	1	.	.	.
Robᵗ. Avery	1	.	.	.	.	1	.	.	1
Phenehas Lamb	1	3	3	1	.	1	1	175	?
Miles Small	1	.	.	.	.	1	.	.	.
Abraham Small	1	.	.	.	.	1	.	.	.
Humphy Parks	3	1	3	5	2	3	5	400	.
Isaac Elliot	2	4	6	1	.	2	1	150	.
Samˡ. Smith	1	1	2	4	4	1	5	190	.
Job Smith	1	3	2	.	1	1	.	.	.
Caleb White	2	6	4	2	.	2	2	212 1/2	.
Joseph Newby Sen.	2	4	5	1	6	2	1	200	.
Benorie Park	1	.	1	.	.	1	.	.	.
Joseph Newby	1	.	.	.	.	1	.	152 1/2	.
William Colson	1	.	4	.	.	.	.	.	.
Josiah Sanders	1	.	1	.	.	1	.	.	.
Joseph Smith	2	4	2	2	1	2	2	190	.
Samˡ. Williams	1	3	5	.	.	1	.	225	.
Demcey Elliot	1	1	3	.	1	1	.	.	.
Thoˢ. Elliot	1	2	2	.	.	1	.	.	.
Joseph Sanders	1	.	.	.	.	.	.	.	.
						46	32	5765	

Pg. 3

Head of Household	WM 21-60	WM u21/a60	WF	Bl 12-50	Bl u12/a50	Wh Poles	Bl Poles	Acres	Lots
---- ----	1	3	4	.	.	1	.	197	.
---- --why	1	2	.	1	1	1	.	231	.

Head of Household	WM 21-60 yrs.	WM under 21 & above 60	WF all ages	Blacks 12-50	Blacks under 12 & above 50	White Poles	Black Poles	No. Acres Land	No. Town lots
--- --by	.	.	3	3	4	.	3	200	.
--- ---	1	.	3	.	.	.	.	.	.
--- ---	1	3	1	1	8	1	1	.	.
--- ---	1	.	1	.	.	.	.	.	.
--- ---	1	6	2	1	.	1	1	85	.
--- ---	1	.	1	.	.	1	.	50	.
--- ---	1	3	1	.	.	1	.	.	.
--- --odwon(?)	1	2	1	.	.	1	.	100	.
--- ---	1	1	1	1	.	1	1	.	.
--- ---	.	2	1	.	.	.	.	.	.
--- --er	1	.	.	4	3	1	4	190	.
--- Harrel	1	3	4	.	.	1	.	15	.
--- --llock	1	1	2	.	1	1	.	125	.
--- Lamb	1	2	2	.	.	1	.	331	.
--- Williams Junr.	1	.	.	2	1	1	2	.	2
--- ---el	2	.	4	.	1	2	.	100	.
--- --by	1	.	.	.	.	1	.	.	.
--- ---	1	3	2	1	.	?	?	?	?
Pg. 4									
--- ---	1	.	.	.	.	1	.	100	.
--- --- Senr.	.	2	3	.	.	.	.	100	.
--- Elliot	1	.	.	.	.	.	.	.	.
--- Gregory	1	.	1	3	.	1	3	.	1
---s Sitterson	1	3	2	.	.	1	.	.	.
--- Làttimore	1	2	4	.	.	1	.	.	.
---iah Wilson	1	.	.	1	3	1	1	100	.
--- Nasa(?)	.	.	1	.	.	.	.	.	.
--- Goodwin	2	.	5	2	3	2	2	300	.
--- Sanders	1	.	2	.	.	1	.	50	.
--- --why	.	2	2	6	12	1	6	320	.
--- --ale	1	2	4	.	.	1	.	25	.
--- --lliam(?)	2	3	2	4	4	2	4	50	2
--- Long	1	2	4	.	.	1	.	.	.
--- Newby	.	4	3	6	5	.	6	1900	.
--- --dwin	1	3	6	2	4	1	2	350	.
---am Wilson	1	.	1	.	1	.	.	383	.
--- Laine	1	4	1	.	.	1	1	50	.
---m. (?) Arrington	2	1	5	2	2	2	2	576	.
---hos. Sitterson	1	2	2	.	.	1	.	.	.
---aml. Sitterson	1	.	1	.	.	1	.	.	.
---ter Salter	1	.	.	.	.	1	.	.	1
						36	4?	6023	6

Head of Household	WM 21-60 yrs.	WM under 21 & above 60	WF all ages	Blacks 12-50	Blacks under 12 & above 50	Total

PITT COUNTY

A List of the number of souls in
Pitt County for the year 1786.

	WM 21-60 yrs.	WM under 21 & above 60	WF all ages	Blacks 12-50	Blacks under 12 & above 50	Total	
Capt. Barrow's Co.	106	193	254	72	75	100	
Bucks	104	192	307	154	184	931	(sic)
Stancills	195	*	175	57	40	460	(sic)
Ringold	75	135	217	31	18	476	
Moyes	61	127	180	53	49	470	
Rieves	135	*	185	75	*	335	
Cannon's	64	148	215	47	49	523	
Moore's	181	*	167	32	28	408	
Forbes	86	111	202	79	85	563	
Hodges	47	85	114	65	63	374	
Dupree	65	35	190	83	80	453	
	1119	1026	2206	748	671	5753	

A True Return agreeable to Return of the Justices
Lists Returned in October Term 1786.
Henry Ellis, C. C. C.

* Figures combined with previous column.

The only district for which names are given
is that of Capt. Robert Hodges. He has not
conformed to the usual breakdown, therefore
his is shown to the right.

	White males above 60 yrs.	White males 16-60	White males under 16	White females above 16	White females under 16	Male slaves above 16	Male slaves under 16	Female slaves above 16	Female slaves under 16	Total sum
Pg. 1										
Robt. Hodges	.	4	3	1	2	4	2	2	4	22
Jno. Knowis	1	1	2	2	1	4	4	2	3	20
Solo. Sheppard	.	3	6	5	1	16	14	6	10	56
Jno. Ball	.	3	1	4	4	.	.	.	.	12
Joseph Tettarton	.	1	1	1	.	.	.	.	.	3
Wm. Tettarton	.	1	2	1	1	.	.	.	.	5
Geo. Jackson	1	1	3	1	3	.	.	.	.	9
Lemu¹. Morris	.	2	2	1	3	.	1	1	2	12
Michael Ellis	.	1	2	1	1	.	.	.	.	5
Andrew Brown	1	1	1	3	2	.	.	.	.	8
Ephraim Brown	.	1	3	1	1	.	.	.	.	6
Jacob Brown	.	1	1	3	1	.	.	.	.	6
Levi Branton	.	1	.	1	1	.	.	.	.	3
Jno. Wells	.	2	3	1	3	.	.	.	.	9

STATE CENSUS OF NORTH CAROLINA 1784-1787

Head of Household	WM above 60 yrs.	WM between 16-60	WM under 16 yrs.	WF above 60 yrs.	WF under 16 yrs.	M sl. above 16	M sl. under 16	F sl. above 16	F sl. under 16	Total sum	
Ann Littel	.	2	2	1	3	1	.	.	.	9	
Thos. Williams	.	1	4	1	3	.	.	.	.	9	
Jno. Floyd	.	2	2	2	.	2	3	2	2	15	
Griffin Floyd	.	1	1	3	3	.	2	.	.	10	
Luke Mount	1	3	.	2	2	.	1	.	.	9	
Simon Taylor	.	1	1	1	.	.	.	.	.	3	
Thos. Bedford	.	1	3	1	2	.	.	.	.	7	
Thos. Hodges Sr.	1	1	1	1	.	.	.	.	.	4	
Phillip Holland	.	2	1	1	1	.	.	.	.	5	
Thos. Hodges Jr.	.	1	2	3	.	.	.	.	.	4	(sic)
Jno. Doudna	.	1	4	1	.	.	1	1	.	8	
Jno. White	1	1	4	2	2	.	.	.	.	10	
Eliza Littel	.	2	.	3	.	1	2	1	.	9	
Jas. Littel	.	2	.	1	.	.	1	.	.	4	
Jas. Cremean	.	1	.	2	1	.	1	1	.	6	
Mathias Crandell	.	2	.	3	.	.	.	.	.	5	
Jno. Brinkley	.	1	2	1	3	.	.	.	.	7	
Jno. Hines	.	1	.	1	2	.	.	.	.	4	
Wm. Smith	.	1	2	1	1	.	.	.	.	5	
Jno. Smith	.	2	.	3	.	.	.	.	.	5	
Math. Hodges	.	2	2	2	4	2	2	1	.	15	
Mary Hodges	.	1	.	1	.	1	1	4	5	13	
Jno. Wallace	.	1	2	2	2	1	.	.	1	9	
Howell Hodges	.	1	1	1	4	2	.	.	1	10	
Henry Hodges	.	4	3	1	5	.	1	2	2	18	
										379	
Pg. 2											
William Speir	1	1	1	1	.	7	8	8	10	37	
Jas. Gorham	.	2	2	2	.	3	11	9	8	31	(sic)
Geo. Fowlars	.	1	1	1	3	.	.	.	.	6	
Amos Pinkett	.	.	4	.	.	.	3	1	.	11	
Isaac Carrel	.	2	2	1	2	.	.	.	1	8	
Anthy. Whichard	.	1	2	1	.	.	.	.	.	4	
Jno. Hodges	.	2	2	2	4	1	.	.	3	14	
Charles Cason	.	1	1	1	.	.	.	.	.	3	
Abia Consaul	.	2	1	1	1	.	.	.	.	5	
Thos. Langley	.	2	1	1	3	.	.	.	.	7	
Jno. Jones	.	2	3	1	1	.	.	.	.	7	
Solo. Whichard	.	1	2	1	4	1	.	.	.	9	
Nathn. Cherry	.	1	2	1	2	.	.	.	.	6	
Caleb Oterson	.	1	2	1	5	2	.	.	.	11	
Jas. Ute(?)	.	1	.	1	1	.	.	.	1	4	
Hillery Cason	.	1	5	2	.	1	.	.	2	11	
Jas. Wainright	.	1	1	1	.	.	.	.	.	3	
Lazarus Cherry	1	1	.	3	.	.	.	.	.	5	

STATE CENSUS OF NORTH CAROLINA 1784–1787

Head of Household	WM above 60 yrs.	WM between 16–60	WM under 16yrs.	WF above 60yrs.	WF under 16yrs.	M sl. above 16	M sl. under 16	F sl. above 16	F sl. under 16	Total sum
Jos[h]. Littel	.	1	.	1	1	.	.	.	1	4
David Vance	.	2	3	2	3	.	.	.	.	10
Jas. Dudley	.	4	.	2	2	.	.	.	.	8
Jno. Griffin	1	2	.	1	1	1	.	1	.	7
Hardy Keel	.	1	3	1	2	.	.	.	.	7
Benj[n]. Loyd	.	1	.	1	1	.	.	.	.	3
Wm. Persey	.	1	.	1	.	.	.	.	.	2
Jno. Persey	.	1	3	2	.	.	.	.	.	6
Ezekiel Keel	.	1	.	1	.	.	.	.	.	2
Wm. Beaman	.	1	.	1	.	.	.	.	.	2
Joseph Gainer	.	1	1	1	6	1	1	2	.	13
Harbert Deal	.	1	2	1	1	.	.	.	.	5
Jas. Crauford	.	3	.	2	.	1	.	1	.	7
Moses Dean	.	2	5	3	1	.	.	.	.	11
Jas. Keel	.	1	3	1	1	.	.	.	.	6
Jas. Williams	.	1	1	2	3	.	.	.	.	7
Wm. Hays	.	1	5	1	2	1	.	.	.	10
Eliza Tettarton	.	2	.	.	.	.	.	.	.	2
Jno. Whitacre	.	5	3	2	1	.	.	.	.	11
Seth Lanier	.	1	1	1	1	.	.	.	1	5
										310
Pg. 3										
Thos. Williams	.	1	.	1	1	.	.	.	.	3
Wm. Lanier	1	1	2	2	2	6	7	6	3	30
Jn[o]. Lanier	.	1	1	1	.	.	.	.	2	5
Ran[l]. McDonald	.	2	3	1	.	.	.	.	1	7
Wm. Davis	.	1	2	1	.	.	.	.	1	5
Mary Powell	.	1	2	1	.	.	.	.	.	4
Jas. Latham	.	2	5	1	2	6	2	3	3	24
										78
										310
										379
										767

137

RICHMOND COUNTY

Head of Household	WM 21-60 yrs.	WM under 21 & above 60	WF all ages	Blacks 12-50	Blacks under 12 & above 50
Pg. 1					
Coln. Charles Medlock	3	2	2	6	6
James James	1	2	4	.	.
Isreal Snead	1	1	2	6	10
Robert Webb	1	6	3	2	1
David Sneed	1	1	2	.	.
Randolph Haley	1	.	.	.	.
Daniel Sneed	1	2	4	1	1
Zach. Martin	1	2	4	.	.
David Sneed Jr.	2	1	2	.	1
Isreal Sneed Jr.	1	4	2	.	1
Solomon Rye	1	2	3	.	.
Lott Stricklin	1	1	1	.	.
Gilbert McNear	1	1	6	1	.
Allen McKaskill	2	3	2	.	.
Robert Melson	1	3	6	.	.
Swine McIntosh	2	4	3	.	.
Benj. Skipper	1	1	3	.	.
John Bone	1	2	5	.	.
Dun Rye	1	1	3	.	.
John Watkins	1	4	4	.	.
Barnaby Skipper	.	6	4	.	.
John Wallace	1	1	1	.	.
Wm. Haley	1	1	3	.	1
John Campble	1	.	3	.	.
Ann Hill	1	1	6	.	.
Benj. Moreman	2	1	1	.	.
Andrew Moreman	1	.	4	.	.
Henry Wm. Herrington	2	2	3	22	22
Shadrack Bagget	1	2	7	.	.
Richd. Griffin	1	2	6	.	.
John Moreman	1	1	4	.	.
James Bagget	1	.	4	.	.
James Bagget Jr.	1	2	2	.	.
Martha Matthew	.	2	2	.	.
James Powers	1	.	1	.	.
Absolum Rye	1	2	5	.	.
Silas Haley	2	1	1	.	1
John Speed Esq.	2	3	1	8	5
John Newbery	1	.	2	.	.
Wm. Newberry	1	1	3	.	.
Christian McKaskill	.	2	8	.	.
Catherine McLeoud	.	3	2	.	.
Ann Morrisson	.	2	3	.	.
Malcom McKaskill	1	1	1	.	.
Daniel Hicks	4	7	9	6	3
Wm. Hicks	1	2	5	4	3
Samuel Curtis	1	3	3	.	.

Head of Household	WM 21-60 yrs.	WM under 21 & above 60	WF all ages	Blacks 12-50	Blacks under 12 & above 50
Thos. Curtis	1	6	2	.	.
	55	97	157	56	55
Pg. 2					
James Smith	1	3	3	1	3
James Smith Jr.	1	.	2	2	4
Walter Leak Esq.	2	.	2	7	6
John Hany	1	1	4	.	.
John McCray	1	2	1	.	.
Anguish Steward	1	2	5	.	.
John McDuffee	1	3	5	.	.
Duncan McCray	1	3	2	.	.
Daniel McCaul	1	1	1	.	.
Farquar McCray	1	.	.	.	.
Alexr. McCray	1	4	4	.	.
Christopher McCray	1	2	2	.	.
Zpher. McCray	1	3	2	.	.
Alexr. McCray	1	4	3	.	.
John Keachey	1	1	1	.	.
Margaret Keachey	.	1	2	.	1
Reubin Thompson	1	1	2	.	.
Duncan McInnise	.	2	2	.	.
Farquar McCray	1	2	2	.	.
Farquar McCray	.	3	3	.	.
Farquar McCray	1	1	1	.	.
James Keachey	1	3	3	.	.
Christopher McCray	1	2	2	.	.
Martha Henry	.	1	1	.	.
Anthony Mathews	1	4	5	.	.

[next name and figures covered over as pages pasted together]

Head of Household	WM 21-60 yrs.	WM under 21 & above 60	WF all ages	Blacks 12-50	Blacks under 12 & above 50
Thos. Adams	1	2	5	.	.
Alexr. McCray	1	.	1	.	.
Malcom McCray	1	5	2	.	.
Alexr. McCray	1	1	2	.	.
Paul McCaul	1	2	1	.	.
John Morison	.	1	1	.	.
John McCaul	1	2	1	.	.
Wm. Newbery	1	2	1	.	.
Alexr. McCray	1	1	3	.	.
James Smith	1	1	2	.	.
Wm. Johnson	1	5	2	.	.
Jean Shepherd	.	1	3	.	.
John McCaul	.	3	2	.	.
Daniel Smith	1	4	5	.	.
Thos. Blewitt	1	1	2	4	3
Stephen Thomas	1	1	2	.	.

Head of Household	WM 21-60 yrs.	WM under 21 & above 60	WF all ages	Blacks 12-50	Blacks under 12 & above 50	Head of Household	WM 21-60 yrs.	WM under 21 & above 60	WF all ages	Blacks 12-50	Blacks under 12 & above 50
Wm. Blewitt	.	6	4	.	.	George Slaughter	1	1	3	.	.
Simon Thomas	1	.	2	.	.	Christopher McCray	2	5	2	.	.
Jacob Cockraham	.	1	1	.	.	Wm. Mask	1	.	5	2	1
Rich^d. Adams	1	7	4	1	2	Drury Colliers(?)	1	3	3	4	5
Daniel McCaul	1	1	3	.	.	Daniel Kermical	1	1	3	.	.
Wm. Love, Esq.	1	3	3	4	3	Duncan McFarland	1	2	2	3	.
Thos. Thompson	1	.	2	.	.	Edward McPherson	1	2	5	.	.
Micajah Shelton	1	.	3	.	.	Wm. Campble	1	3	1	.	.
Wm. Thomas	2	3	3	3	2	Duncan McFarland	1	2	3	.	.
Jeremiah Mennasco	1	2	5	.	.	Daniel McFerson	.	1	2	.	.
John Pemberton Esq.	1	.	1	3	1	David McColle	1	2	3	.	.
Daniel McDuffe	1	3	2	.	.	Duncan McBridge	1	1	4	.	.
John Gillis	1	3	1	.	.	Anguish Curry	1	2	4	.	.
	102	207	285	81	80	Malcon Furguson	1	1	3	.	.
Pg. 3						Daniel Shaw	1	3	4	.	.
Sampson Sellers	1	2	4	.	.	James Dees	2	4	3	.	.
John McFarland	1	2	6	.	.	Alex^r. Watson	1	1	4	.	.
Edward McNear	1	1	3	.	.	Malcom McMillon	1	5	3	.	.
John Robertson	1	2	2	.	.	John Buie	1	2	1	.	.
Josiah Lyon	4	5	3	5	6	Robert Buie	1	3	4	.	.
Owen Slaughter Jr.	1	2	2	.	.	Wm. Dees	1	3	1	.	.
Joseph Hines Esq.	2	.	3	3	1		163	330	457	110	100
Wm. McDaniel	1	1	7	2	1	Pg. 4					
Jonathan Hany/Harry?	1	2	.	.	.	Daniel McKaskill	1	4	5	.	.
Stephen Pitcocck(?)	.	3	4	.	.	Moses Hodges	1	1	4	.	.
James McDaniel	1	2	1	.	.	Daniel Duglas	1	.	5	.	.
John McDaniel	1	2	1	.	.	Hugh Carmical	1	.	2	.	.
John Spurlin	1	7	4	.	.	James Smiley	1	3	5	.	.
John Ewen	3	3	4	.	.	Dugal Blue	1	1	3	.	.
Solomon Alred	1	4	3	.	.	Malcom Blue	1	.	.	.	.
Randolph McDaniel	1	3	1	.	.	James Duncan	1	1	4	.	.
Wm. Bolton	1	1	4	.	.	Neil McNear	.	2	4	.	.
John Coleman	1	3	1	8	4	John McDaniel	1	1	2	.	.
Solomon Phillips	1	1	2	.	.	Norman McLeoud	.	3	3	.	.
Jonathon Newbery	1	2	3	.	.	Alex^r. McLeoud	1	5	1	.	.
Charles Robertson	1	.	3	.	.	Zebilley McDonald	.	1	4	.	.
John Jinkins	1	3	5	.	.	Duncan McRae	1	.	5	.	.
John Bennet	2	3	2	.	.	Malcom McCarskill	1	2	4	.	.
John Hadley	1	1	5	.	.	Dugal McFarland	1	.	.	1	4
Wm. Ussery	1	2	6	.	.	Alex^r. Farley	1	.	.	.	.
Solomon Sprawles	1	5	4	.	1	Archabald McMillon	1	3	7	.	.
John Smith	1	4	7	.	.	Wm. Betty	1	2	2	.	.
Brid Shepherd	1	2	3	.	.	Malcom McCuagge	1	3	3	.	.
Owen Slaughter	1	1	5	.	.	Laughlin McKinon	2	.	5	.	.
Thos. Andrewson	1	3	2	.	.	Thos. Turner	1	3	4	1	.
John Hilyard	1	2	2	.	.	Archabald Campbel	1	1	6	.	.
Alex^r. McCoy	1	2	3	.	.	Kathrine McIntire	.	3	3	.	.
Wm. Ezel	1	.	5	2	1	John Murphy	1	.	2	.	.

Head of Household	WM 21-60 yrs.	WM under 21 & above 60	WF all ages	Blacks 12-50	Blacks under 12 & above 50
Dugal Carmical	1	.	6	.	.
Daniel Smith	1	4	5	.	.
Alexr.Watson Jr.	1	4	2	.	.
Neil McFarland	1	1	2	.	.
Daniel McCoy	1	1	4	.	.
Aron Stricklen	1	5	2	.	.
John Martin	1	1	.	.	.
Silas Overstreet	1	1	3	.	.
Wm. Husbands	1	.	.	.	.
John Watson	1	.	3	.	.
Alexr. Gordon	1	3	4	.	.
John Dove	1	4	4	.	.
John Dunbarr	2	2	3	.	.
Moses Turner	1	4	3	.	.
Duncan Finlah	1	3	3	.	.
John McNear	2	.	2	.	.
Norman McLeoud	1	2	3	.	.
Charles McLain	1	1	2	.	.
Archd. Carmical	1	2	4	.	.
John McRae Sr.	.	3	4	.	.
Alexr. McDonald	1	1	1	.	.
Isaac Stricklin	1	3	2	.	.
Elisabeth Stricklin	.	4	4	.	.
Joseph Stricklin	.	1	1	.	.
Finlay McInnise	1	1	3	.	.
John Dearman	1	2	5	.	.
	211	425	616	112	104
Pg. 5					
Dugal Carmical	.	2	4	.	.
Peter McCuagge	1	.	1	.	.
Daniel McCarny	1	3	6	.	.
Mary Blue	.	1	6	.	.
Archd. Henderson	1	5	3	.	.
John Munroe	1	1	1	.	1
Margaret McNear	.	1	1	.	.
James Lewis	1	.	10	.	.
Jeremiah Jadwin	1	3	3	.	.
William Williams	1	2	1	.	.
Murdock Shaw	1	3	3	.	.
Normon McLeoud	1	4	4	.	.
Anguish McGill	1	3	4	.	.
Allen McGill	1	4	.	.	.
John Farley	1	2	1	.	.
Archd. Farley	1	3	2	.	.
Roger McNear	.	4	4	.	.
Niel Wilkerson	1	1	4	.	.
Hugh Tompson	1	5	2	.	.
Edward Curry	1	2	2	.	.

Head of Household	WM 21-60 yrs.	WM under 21 & above 60	WF all ages	Blacks 12-50	Blacks under 12 & above 50
Thos. Johnson	1	2	4	.	.
Joel Coward	1	2	1	.	.
Archabald McQueen	1	1	4	.	.
Matthew Watson	1	.	2	.	.
Duncan McCallum	1	1	3	.	.
Hector McNiel	2	1	2	.	.
Anguish McAlister	1	2	1	.	.
Allen Smith	1	2	1	.	.
Archabald McRay	1	1	1	.	.
Daniel McCaskill	1	3	3	.	.
Duncan McLaurance	1	.	4	.	.
Alexr. Martin	1	3	3	.	.
Alexr. McMillan	1	.	1	.	.
Daniel McLaughlin	1	2	2	.	.
Alexr. McInnise	1	5	2	.	.
John McNear	1	.	1	.	.
Daniel Campble	1	.	.	.	.
Daniel Dearman	1	.	.	.	.
Daniel McLendon	1	1	4	.	.
Rebeckah Overstreet	.	.	4	.	.
Norman Shaw	1	1	2	.	.
John Ray	1	.	.	.	.
Dugal Graham	1	1	1	1	.
John McCalmon	1	2	5	.	.
Benj. Dees	1	5	3	.	.
Anguish McMillan	1	1	.	.	.
Langhlin McLain	2	.	4	.	.
Dudley Mask Esq.	1	1	2	7	6
John Mask	1	4	5	1	1
Thomas Walker	1	2	2	.	1
John Bostick	1	1	3	.	.
Dorcas Price	.	2	5	.	.
	259	520	753	121	113
Pg. 6					
James Bostick	1	6	4	1	1
Isaac Brown	1	4	6	.	.
Joseph Gadd Sr.	1	2	4	.	.
James Pickett	2	1	2	3	3
Thos. George	1	2	6	.	.
Thos. Stanback	1	5	3	2	2
John Crouch	1	2	1	.	.
Thos. Phillips	1	2	2	.	.
Thos. Jowers	2	3	1	.	.
Zach. McDaniel	1	3	4	.	.
James Patterson	1	.	.	4	1
James Crouch	1	1	4	.	.
Benj. Dumas Sr.	1	7	3	10	11
Phenias Alred	1	3	2	.	.

Head of Household	WM 21-60 yrs.	WM under 21 & above 60	WF all ages	Blacks 12-50	Blacks under 12 & above 50
Wm. More	2	3	3	.	.
Wm. Frazer	1	4	2	.	.
Peter Watts Jr.	1	1	1	.	.
Rich^d. Powel	2	2	4	.	.
Joshua Long	1	.	1	.	.
Andrew Squire	1	.	4	.	.
Rachel Balddin	5	.	3	.	.
Benj. Dumas Jr.	2	2	1	.	1
Samuel Usher	1	.	2	.	.
Joseph Gadd Jr.	1	3	5	.	.
Nathl. Powel	.	3	5	.	.
John Burt	1	1	1	.	.
Thos. Usher	2	.	1	.	.
Jonathan Alred	1	.	4	.	.
Charles Robertson Sr.	1	2	2	6	6
Joseph Tarbutton Jr.	1	3	4	.	.
Benj. Powel	1	2	3	1	.
Joseph Tarbutton Sr.	.	1	2	.	.
George Tarbutton	1	1	1	.	.
Samuel Lipscomb	.	1	.	5	5
Wm. McGuire	.	4	3	.	.
Susannah Roe	.	4	2	.	.
Wm. Hendley	1	3	3	.	.
Samuel Wilkerson	1	1	3	.	.
Hardy Stephens	1	.	2	.	.
Daniel McDaniel	1	2	3	.	.
Silvanus Chun	1	1	4	1	.
Samuel Scott	1	2	1	.	.
Nathl. Chears Esqr.	1	4	5	.	.
Andrew Dumas	1	.	6	.	1
Simons Harvil	1	1	5	.	.
John Tanner	1	3	2	.	.
Peter Ussery	1	3	3	.	.
Andrewson Ranels	1	3	2	.	.
John Howard	1	2	1	4	.
Edward Williams	1	3	3	4	4
	314	626	890	162	148
Pg. 7					
Wm. Arnold	1	1	2	.	.
Wm. Cottengame	1	2	2	.	.
John Graham	1	.	3	.	.
George Graham	.	3	4	.	.
George Graham Jr.	1	3	2	.	.
Wm. Graham	1	4	6	.	.
George Green	1	1	4	.	.
Jacob Perkins	1	4	3	.	.
Isaac Williamson	1	2	3	.	.
Solomon Sneed	1	2	2	1	.
Solomon Dearman	1	3	4	.	.

Head of Household	WM 21-60 yrs.	WM under 21 & above 60	WF all ages	Blacks 12-50	Blacks under 12 & above 50
Shadrach Williamson	1	3	2	.	.
Elisha Cottengame	1	.	.	.	.
John Matthews	1	3	3	.	.
Mary Goodman	.	1	4	.	.
John Peck or Peek	1	1	2	.	.
John Turnage	1	.	1	.	.
Luke Williams	1	4	3	.	.
John McGill	1	1	2	.	.
John Walters	1	2	5	.	.
Rich^d. Hill	1	1	5	.	.
Saml. Cottengame	1	.	4	.	.
Wm. Woodle	1	4	3	.	.
James Bounds	1	2	3	.	.
Sterling Williamson	1	4	3	.	.
Charles Longe/Louge ?	1	.	2	.	.
Wm. Hall	1	1	4	.	.
John Graham	1	1	2	.	.
Wm. Hathcock	1	1	2	.	.
Thos. Dearman	1	2	5	.	.
Zach^r. Johnson	1	4	3	.	.
Wm. Brown	1	1	3	.	.
Charles Cottengame	1	.	1	.	.
Easter Hathcock	.	2	4	.	.
Benj. Arnold	1	2	2	.	.
Jacob Mangrum	1	3	4	.	.
Thos. Slay	1	.	3	.	.
Wm. Cottengame	1	2	5	.	.
James Patterson	2	.	5	.	.
John Jones	3	3	4	.	.
Isaiah Steely	.	1	2	.	1
Hendley Sneed	1	1	6	.	1
James Allen	1	.	.	.	.
John Brown	1	1	4	.	.
Valentine Morris	2	2	5	.	.
George McDaniel	1	1	3	.	.
Joel Hall	1	.	1	.	.
James Bennit	1	3	4	.	.
Joseph Hall	1	.	2	.	.
Wm. Thomas	1	3	3	.	.
John Hall	1	5	3	.	.
Darby Hanagan	1	1	3	4	2
	366	720	1050	167	152
Pg. 8					
John More or Man(?)	1	1	6	.	.
Margaret Harris	.	.	2	.	.
Rebackah Pearce	.	1	5	.	.
Easter Smith	.	2	1	.	1
Asha Brigman	.	2	5	.	.
John Thornton	1	.	6	.	.

Head of Household	WM 21-60 yrs.	WM below 21 & above 60	WF all ages	Blacks 12-50	Blacks under 12 & above 50
Samuel Pate	1	2	2	.	.
Wm. Walsh	1	2	1	.	.
Elizabeth Dees	1	3	7	.	.
Wm. Vines	.	3	4	.	.
Darrious Barns or Burns	1	1	5	.	.
Mary Adkins	.	2	3	.	.
Thos. Clerk	1	.	1	.	.
Lewis Clerk	1	2	1	.	*
Lott Watson	1	1	5	.	*
John Cook	1	2	4	.	.
Thoroughgood Pate	1	2	4	.	*
George Gullet	1	1	4	.	.
Rich^d. Odum	.	2	1	1	.
Edward Graham	1	4	4	.	.
Benj. Covington	1	4	5	.	.
	380	757	1126	168	154

Total 2585

A true copy from the several returns.

Test.   Wm. Love

SULLIVAN COUNTY

Sullivan, July 4th, 1787.

The number of people of every age and colour as has been ascertained in this county is one thousand and thirty eight white males; nine hundred and twenty females; twenty three Black male slaves and eighty females.

I have the Honor to be mo(illegible) (illegible) Your Excellency's very humble svt.
                                John Rhea

His Excellency
Richard Casswell, Esq.

Head of Household	WM 21-60 yrs.	WM under 21 & above 60	WF all ages	Blacks 12-50	Blacks under 12 & above 50

SURRY COUNTY

A list of souls for the District of Capt. Lovel, taken by Robert Walker - 591.

Column 1

Head of Household	WM 21-60 yrs.	WM under 21 & above 60	WF all ages	Blacks 12-50	Blacks under 12 & above 50
Robert Walker	1	2	4	3	2
Joseph Eist(?)	1	2	4	.	.
Robt. Castisoun	1	.	3	.	.
Adoniga Harbourt	1	2	2	4	2
Thomus Gordoun	1	4	2	.	.
Arthour Jett	1	1	1	.	.
John Frankland	1	1	3	.	.
Mallachey Frankland	1	.	1	.	.
Lott Ivey	2	3	3	.	.
John Dunigan ?	1	4	2	.	.
Abraham Coully	2	2	4	.	.
Rubin Pennioun	1	.	3	.	.
John Stephen	1	3	3	.	.
Ezaghazh Gaymount	1	2	6	.	.
William Still	1	3	2	.	.
Humphres Dourram	1	2	2	.	.
William Vannabl Jr.	1	1	1	.	.
William Vannabl Sr.	1	.	1	.	.
John Vanable	1	1	1	.	.
Shousanah Prether	.	1	2	.	.
Eduart Eduarts	1	1	2	.	.
Danil Cockeroum	1	.	4	.	.
Joseph Darnel	1	1	3	.	.
Hendry Arnald	1	2	4	.	.
Mathou Davis (?)	1	2	4	2	.
William Lenn	1	2	5	.	.
John Stoun	1	4	3	.	.
Emick Stoun	1	2	1	.	.
Thomas Evans	3	3	3	.	.
Gorge Sprinkel	1	4	3	1	.
John Meltoun	1	1	1	.	.
Sarrah Davis	.	4	3	.	.
Adam Fiskus	1	2	2	.	.
Jessy Horn	1	1	3	.	.
Hendry Spin hour	1	1	1	.	.
Thomas Pinnioun	1	2	4	.	.
Basell Riddel	1	3	3	.	.
Thomas Eist	2	2	5	.	.
Sarrah Wright	1	1	3	.	.
Eiseabel Flinn	1	1	1	.	.
Abraham Childrs	1	2	3	.	.
Jacob Sheppard Sr.	1	2	5	.	.
Eduart Lovell	2	1	3	.	.
William Londoun	1	4	3	.	.

Head of Household	WM 21-60 yrs.	WM under 21 & above 60	WF all ages	Blacks 12-50	Blacks under 12 & above 50
William Counning	1	3	4	.	.
John Wattrs	1	.	2	5	.
Elisabeth Karr	.	3	1	.	.
Rannal Broun	.	2	5	5	.
Thomas Loyd	.	2	3	2	.
Petter Simiaens	2	1	2	4	.
Petter Simiaens Jr.	1	.	.	1	5
Royal Simiaens	1	1	2	.	.
	59	94	145	27	9

Column 2

Head of Household	WM 21-60 yrs.	WM under 21 & above 60	WF all ages	Blacks 12-50	Blacks under 12 & above 50
Samul Coumins or Coumns(?)	1	4	1	3	2
Handry Arnald	1	4	4	.	.
Malkum Courry	2	.	5	.	.
Hendry Kerby	3	1	1	2	.
John Ways	1	2	1	.	.
William Herris	1	1	3	.	.
James Short	2	2	3	.	.
William Pretter(?)	1	1	2	.	.
John Connal	1	.	3	.	.
Roger Jediouns	1	2	4	.	.
Samuel Humphres	1	4	3	.	.
Thomas Ways	1	.	3	.	.
Michal Colluns	1	1	1	.	.
Ellinar Broun	.	.	2	.	.
Laflin Flinn	1	2	3	.	.
Robert Briggs	1	2	2	.	.
Thomas Carral	1	.	2	1	.
John Rann(u?)man	1	.	1	.	.
William Hallet	1	1	1	1	.
Charls Vastt [West]	1	1	1	.	.
Jacob Hatth	1	1	1	.	.
Houl Hartgra	1	.	1	.	.
Thomas Haus	2	1	4	.	.
Martin Armstrang	1	3	2	3	3
William Eist	1	1	6	.	.
John Fitch Patrik	1	3	4	.	.
J. Isoun 1st	1	2	1	.	.
John Armstroung	2	2	4	1	8
Edmun Kerby	2	8	1	.	.
Thomas Briggs	2	6	4	.	.
John Shepeerd	1	.	.	1	.
William Freman	1	1	4	1	2
Sarrah Hubb	.	4	2	.	.
Ahagay Alifer	2	4	5	.	.
John Horn	1	3	.	.	.
Jacob Shepard	1	2	4	2	3

Head of Household	WM 21-60 yrs.	WM under 21 & above 60	WF all ages	Blacks 12-50	Blacks under 12 & above 50
Jessi Bumps	1	.	3	.	.
Charls Doudly	2	3	1	.	.
John Dounigan Jr.	1	1	2	.	.
Ezophar Genn	1	3	2	.	.
Joseph Eisly	3	6	4	.	.
John Scritchfild	1	.	.	.	.
Thos. Dounigan	1	2	2	.	.
Pettr Colman	1	3	3	.	.
Mark Keddel	2	3	3	.	.
Henry Boush/Beush ?	1	3	3	.	.
Nathanil Williams	1	1	1	.	.
	56	89	113	15	18
	43	44	145	23	9
	99	183	254	38	27

"A List of the Number of Souls taken in Willeses District.

John Taliaferro."

Pg. 1

Head of Household	WM 21-60 yrs.	WM under 21 & above 60	WF all ages	Blacks 12-50	Blacks under 12 & above 50
Samuel Riggs	2	1	3	.	.
Zadock Riggs	1	3	3	.	.
David Riggs	1	5	5	.	.
Iram Riggs	1	2	1	.	.
Joseph Lasswell	1	1	5	.	.
Benja. Scott	1	1	2	.	.
Moses Baker	1	1	5	.	.
Charles Waddle	1	1	2	.	.
William Stewart	1	3	3	.	.
Leonard Davis	1	2	4	1	.
James Tucker	1	2	3	1	1
[1 wm under 21; 1 above 60]					
Gardner Tucker	1	1	4	1	.
[1 wm under 21]					
William Tucker	2	1	2	.	.
Edmond Wood	1	3	3	.	.
Charles Sowel	1	1	4	.	.
William Bledsoe	1	2	3	.	.
Philip Pritchard	1	2	2	.	.
Joseph Porter	1	3	3	.	.
William Muncas	1	3	3	.	.
Thomas Norman	1	*	2	.	.
[* 1 above; 1 under]					
Silraner Raburn	1	.	1	.	.
Thomas Raburn	1	1	2	.	.
Charles Ross	1	1	2	.	.
Jobe Ross	1	1	1	.	.
Henry Norman	1	2	4	.	.
Richard Murphy	1	1	2	1	1
William McFee	1	4	5	.	.
Thomas Cody	1	3	5	.	.

Head of Household	WM 21-60 yrs.	WM under 21 & above 60	WF all ages	Blacks 12-50	Blacks under 12 & above 50
Mark Roberts	1	.	3	.	.
Abraham James	2	3	6	.	.
Gideon Edwards	1	2	2	6	4
Samuel Davis	1	1	2	.	.
William McCloud	1	3	4	.	.
Samuel Hails	1	2	1	.	.
Edward Taylor	1	.	2	.	.
Moses Endicot	1	2	1	.	.
Edmond Hodges	1	7	1	.	.
Elipholet Jarvis	1	3	3	.	.
Bartholemus Hodges	1	.	3	.	.
Michel Lawless	1	1	1	.	.
Larkin Straun	1	1	3	.	.
John Cartey	1	3	3	.	.
John Jarvis	1	4	4	.	.
Reziah Jarvis	1	2	4	.	.
Jabes Jarvis	.	1	1	.	.
Abner Rose	1	1	1	.	.
Sarah Rose	.	3	4	.	.
	48	96	133	10	5

Pg. 2

Head of Household	WM 21-60 yrs.	WM under 21 & above 60	WF all ages	Blacks 12-50	Blacks under 12 & above 50
West Mosley	1	3	3	.	.
John Inglish	1	1	2	.	.
Stephen Crowder	2	3	3	.	.
Robert Willes	1	3	3	.	1
[1 in last col. "above 50"]					
George Avery	1	1	2	.	.
Abner Hodges	1	2	1	.	.
John Lantrip	1	.	1	.	.
Charles Guin	1	.	1	.	.
Cornelous Guin	1	1	1	.	.
Darby Ryon	1	5	2	.	.
David Bray	1	5	5	.	.
Thos. Stanfield	1	.	3	.	.
Thos. Stanfield Jr.	1	1	2	.	.
John Marsh	1	6	3	.	.
Benja. Bledsoe	1	4	5	.	.
Wm. Thompson (Above 60)					
Nathl. Chamblis	1	1	2	.	.
John Stots	1	.	2	.	.
Joseph Haman	1	1	2	.	.
John Shoars	1	.	3	2	2
[2 in last column "under 12"]					
John Burch	2	1	3	1	1
Edward Welburn	1	3	3	2	1
Abner Philips	1	4	5	.	.
Wm. Burc(h)	1	.	3	.	.
Bya(?) Buck	1	4	6	2	1
David Burk	1	2	3	.	.

Head of Household	WM 21-60 yrs.	WM under 21 & above 60	WF all ages	Blacks 12-50	Blacks under 12 & above 50
Thos. Woodrough	1	4	3	.	.
Sarah Howard Jr.	1	5	6	.	.
Jess Mobs	1	.	2	.	.
Thos. Ross Jr.	1	1	2	.	.
John Ross	1	.	1	.	.
Elijah Glaspy	1	1	4	.	.
Hall Hudson	1	3	2	.	.
John Pearce	1	3	2	.	.
Thos. Ross	1	1	1	.	.
[1 wm above 60]					
Margret Nelson	1	.	1	.	.
Mary Nowlen	.	1	1	.	.
Bya. Sneed	1	1	5	.	.
Stepen(?) M(?)odlin	1	4	1	.	.
James Ranewater	1	1	5	1	.
John Taliaferro	1	2	7	2	.
Dorcas Teliaferro	.	.	4	.	.
Wm. Mash	1	4	2	.	.
	42	83	125	10	6

A List of the inhabitants in Capt.
Humphre's District"
Pg. 1

Head of Household	WM 21-60 yrs.	WM under 21 & above 60	WF all ages	Blacks 12-50	Blacks under 12 & above 50
Hugh Armstrong	1	3	4	2	7
John Fleming	1	3	4	7	2
James Mathewes	1	6	4	.	.
William Armstrong	1	1	.	1	.
Ratliff Boon Sr.	1	2	3	4	6
Ratliff Boon Jr.	1	1	2	.	.
Thoms. Boone	1	4	4	.	.
Jonathan Harriss	1	1	2	.	.
Mathew Cox	1	2	3	.	.
Joel McKey	1	2	5	1	2
John Harriss	2	2	4	1	4
John McCarver	.	2	6	.	.
Benja. Benson	1	1	6	.	.
Joel Applin	1	3	4	.	.
Levy Jones	1	3	5	.	.
Joel Blantchet	1	.	1	.	.
William Chandler	1	3	3	.	.
Richard Gittons	.	2	2	1	4
David Coller	2	2	3	.	.
Shadrick Collyer	1	2	2	.	.
Elizebeth Griffe	1	2	3	.	.
William Hammons	2	.	1	.	.
John Burck	1	1	5	.	.
Robert Harriss	1	4	4	5	3
David Blackwell	1	1	2	1	.
Joseph Waldram	1	1	3	.	.
James Doake	1	2	6	4	3

Head of Household	WM 21-60 yrs.	WM under 21 & above 60	WF all ages	Blacks 12-50	Blacks under 12 & above 50
James Boyd	1	1	1	.	.
Peter Crawford	1	1	3	.	.
Obed Baker	1	2	4	.	.
Patrick Molton	1	3	5	.	.
Roger Gittens	2	3	4	.	.
Benja. Cadle	.	1	2	.	.
Zack Cadle	1	2	2	.	.
John Davis	1	5	5	.	.
Bennet Creedle	1	4	3	.	.
	37	78	120	27	31
Pg. 2					
Richard Hill	1	4	3	.	.
John McCinne Sr.	2	3	4	.	.
John Cox	1	3	1	.	.
Richard Laurance	1	7	5	5	5
Claborn Laurance	1	.	2	.	1
James Laurance	1	2	4	1	.
Joseph Laurance	1	.	4	.	.
Curnelius Ceeth Jr.	1	5	1	.	.
William Steward	1	1	1	.	.
James Steward	1	1	4	.	.
John Fletcher	1	.	2	.	.
Mathew Creed	2	2	3	.	.
Henry Herring	1	.	6	.	.
Daniel Humphress	5	1	2	1	.
John Haborn	1	4	4	.	.
Joseph Boyd	1	2	4	.	.
Joseph Boyd	1	2	4	.	.
James Lintch	1	1	1	.	.
Mosses Harriss	1	.	3	.	.
James Evins	1	.	2	.	.
Richd. Haselwood	1	3	2	.	.
Mathew Davis	1	4	3	1	.
Robert Bryant	1	3	3	.	.
John Hanna	1	3	5	.	.
Samiel Hanna	1	4	4	4	.
James Roberts	1	1	1	.	.
John Bledso	.	1	.	.	.
Nathaniel Steward	1	5	2	.	.
Charles Steward	1	1	3	.	.
Mosses Bledso	1	1	6	.	.
Edward Steward	1	.	2	.	.
Denes Laffoon	1	1	1	.	.
William Laffoon	1	2	3	.	.
John Steward	1	.	1	.	.
Edward Noarth	1	1	1	.	.
Thomas Burriss	.	.	4	3	5
	39	73	98	15	21

145

STATE CENSUS OF NORTH CAROLINA 1784-1787

Head of Household	WM 21-60 yrs.	WM under 21 & above 60	WF all ages	Blacks 12-50	Blacks under 12 & above 50
Pg. 3					
William Goldan	.	2	1	.	1
Stephen Smith	1	2	4	.	1
Charles Smith	1	2	5	3	.
Christopher Rowles	1	1	4	.	1
John Bryson Sr.	.	1	6	.	.
William Smith	1	5	5	.	.
John Bryson Jr.	1	2	2	1	1
Robt. Hammack	1	1	3	.	.
Samil Wood	2	.	5	.	.
Joseph Harvey	1	2	2	.	.
Thomas Ballard	1	2	3	.	.
Collins Hampton	1	3	6	.	.
William Burress	1	4	8	1	2
John Litten Jones	1	1	2	5	5
Ellet Bohannan	1	5	4	.	.
William Cook	1	3	5	.	.
Silvanus Raburn	1	1	3	.	.
Thomas Normon	1	2	2	.	.
Thomas Raburn	1	1	2	.	.
John Hocks	1	4	7	.	.
Abr^a. Hocks	1	1	1	.	.
John Holder	1	1	2	.	.
Lewis Holder	1	.	4	.	.
Joseph Holder	1	5	3	.	.
Hamilton Steward	1	.	2	.	.
Jean Morgan	.	1	3	.	.
Duncan Keith	1	2	1	.	.
Samil Stidham	1	4	2	.	.
John Douglass	2	2	3	2	4
John Steward	.	1	3	.	.
Mosses Cockram	1	4	6	1	.
Thomas Aplin	1	.	2	1	1
William Forkner	1	5	4	1	4
George Read	1	1	5	.	.
John Jineans	3	2	3	1	2
David Aplin	1	3	2	.	.
John Roberts	2	5	6	1	2
James Bryson	1	6	3	.	.
William McCraw	2	2	5	3	1
John Hammons	2	3	5	5	2
Rich^d. Hooper	2	3	5	5	2
	49	99	149	27	32
Pg. 4					
Jacob McCraw	1	3	2	3	1
Chichoster Benson	1	.	1	.	.
James McGee	1	2	2	.	.
	3	5	5	3	1

Feb. 13, 1786. By Hugh Armstrong,
Total 909

Head of Household	WM 21-60 yrs.	WM under 21 & above 60	WF all ages	Blacks 12-50	Blacks under 12 & above 50
"A List of the inhabitance in Capt. Hickman's district."					
Pg. 1					
John Childress	1	6	2	2	3
John Faulkner	1	5	4	.	.
Mary Childres	.	.	2	1	.
John Farmer	1	3	3	2	2
Charles Beaseley	1	2	2	.	.
David Childres	1	.	.	.	.
Milley Cox	.	2	6	2	6
James Meredith Sr.	.	1	2	.	.
William Martin	1	2	5	3	4
John Meredith	1	2	6	.	.
Andrew Moore	1	4	4	.	.
Thomas Jones	1	2	2	.	.
James Dillard	.	1	3	.	.
Arthur Johns	1	2	2	.	.
Philemon Manuel	1	5	3	.	.
Jno. Robertson	1	1	7	.	.
Joseph Read Jr.	1	3	6	.	.
James McComack	1	.	2	.	.
James Duncan	1	3	7	.	.
John Vauters	1	3	3	1	.
John Newman	1	9	2	.	.
James Meredith	1	4	3	.	.
Samuel Meredith	1	1	1	.	.
Betty Nixon	.	4	1	.	.
Wm. Hutcherson	1	6	2	.	.
Rich^d. Hutcherson	1	4	7	.	.
Daniel Hutcherson	1	.	1	2	.
Thos. Gill	1	.	1	.	.
Wm. Gill	.	4	3	.	.
Young Gill	1	.	.	.	.
	25	79	93	14	15
Pg. 2					
John Gibson	.	1	1	.	.
James Jacson	.	2	4	.	.
James Walker	1	.	3	.	.
Moses Walker	1	.	.	.	.
Jesse Walker	1	.	.	.	.
William Webb	1	2	5	.	1
John Hart	1	3	4	1	1
Wm. Chandler	1	1	6	2	.
Ben Tilley	1	2	1	.	.
Elexous Musick	1	2	5	.	.
Paterson Childres	1	1	1	.	.
Martha Smith	.	3	6	.	.
John Hughes	1	1	2	4	3
John Riddle	1	2	2	.	.
William Nelson	1	4	5	.	.

146

Head of Household	WM 21-60 yrs.	WM under 21 & above 60	WF all ages	Blacks 12-50	Blacks under 12 & above 50
James Milwood	1	4	6	.	.
William Kearns	2	2	2	.	.
Samuel Crawley	1	.	.	.	.
James Duncan	1	2	5	.	.
John Nelson	.	.	2	.	.
Charles Whitlock	1	4	3	.	.
Jacob Nelson	1	3	2	.	.
John Shelton	1	3	4	.	.
Joseph Shelton	1	1	3	.	.
Wm. Shelton	1	1	1	.	.
Samuel Parker	1	4	5	.	.
Shadrick Prewitt	1	1	3	.	.
John Easeley	1	2	6	.	.
Charles Elliott	1	3	5	.	.
Richard Wood	1	2	3	.	.
John Serjant	.	4	1	.	.
George Musick	.	1	3	.	.
Jonas Lawson	1	3	2	.	.
Benjamin Smith	1	.	4	.	.
Nathaniel Shelton	1	2	5	.	.
Joseph Januway	1	6	5	.	.
Rebeckah Wood	.	2	5	.	.
	35	73	118	7	5

Pg. 3

Head of Household	WM 21-60 yrs.	WM under 21 & above 60	WF all ages	Blacks 12-50	Blacks under 12 & above 50
Elizabeth Morriss	.	2	3	.	.
Wm. Hickman	1	2	7	1	.
Henry Nixon	1	2	3	.	.
Alexander Joyce	1	3	4	1	.
Wm. Bingham	1	5	1	.	.
Randol Riddle	1	1	2	.	.
John Riddle	1	1	2	.	.
John Phail	1	2	2	.	.
Absalum Nixon	1	2	1	.	.
Isaac Joyce	1	1	1	2	.
Ambross Gains	1	.	.	.	.
James Young	1	5	5	.	.
John Hilton	1	5	8	.	.
Daniel Chandler	1	2	4	.	.
John Tilley	1	3	1	.	.
Henry Tilley Sr.	1	1	.	1	2
Henry Tilley Jr.	1	4	3	.	.
Henry Baker	1	1	2	.	.
John Nichals	1	5	2	.	.
Timothy Sisk	1	1	1	.	.
John Wilkins	1	2	4	.	.
Thomas Neal	1	6	3	.	.
William Radford	1	1	3	.	.
William Holt	1	4	7	.	.
William Southern	1	.	1	.	1
Jeremiah M'daniel	1	1	1	.	.

Head of Household	WM 21 to 60 yrs.	WM under 21 and above 60	WF all ages	Blacks 12-50	Blacks under 12 & above 50
Henry Baker Sr.	.	2	3	1	1
William Whitlock	1	.	.	.	.
Robert Gains	1	1	4	1	2
Robert Gains	1	1	4	1	2
Edmond Graves	1	.	1	.	.
Joseph Welch	1	.	.	.	.
Moses Pagett	1	.	3	.	.
Joel Goodman	1	3	4	.	.
Margret Gillington	.	2	3	.	.
Nat. Austin	.	1	.	.	.
Wm. Meredith	3	5	7	.	.
Thos. Loving	1	4	4	.	.
Reubin George	1	6	4	.	.
Ambross Holt	2	3	2	.	.
Ben Hawkins Jr.	1	.	4	.	.
Ben Hawkins	1	1	2	.	.
Wm. Hawkins	1	1	1	1	.
	41	90	114	8	6
James Martin	2	3	6	6	7

Total 735

List taken by John Childres

"Return of the Inhabitanc of my District of Every sex age and Demonination by me Agreable to order of Cort. Absalom Bostick"

Pg. 1

Head of Household	WM 21 to 60 yrs.	WM under 21 and above 60	WF all ages	Blacks 12-50	Blacks under 12 & above 50
Absalom Bostick	1	4	3	6	7
Mathew Warnock	1	.	.	.	.
Seblellar Angill	.	1	2	.	.
Edward Taylor	1	3	4	.	.
Noble Ladd	2	.	2	3	1
Moses Haslit	1	2	4	.	.
John Bradley	1	1	3	2	2
Elijah Oliver	1	3	7	.	.
Edward Bradley	1	.	.	.	.
William Lewis	1	4	5	6	7
Elijah Simmons	1	3	1	.	.
Noble Ladd	1	3	2	1	.
Edmon Peters	1	2	6	1	4
Almon Gwin	1	1	4	5	4
William Sothern	4	3	.	.	.
William Brooks	1	3	1	.	.
Robin Haslet	1	3	2	.	.
Amos Ladd	1	3	3	1	.
William Asher	1	1	2	.	.
John Daniel	2	3	6	.	.
Major Childriss	1	3	4	.	.
Charles Ross	2	.	2	.	.
Jesse Georg	1	4	4	.	.

STATE CENSUS OF NORTH CAROLINA 1784–1787

Head of Household	WM 21-60 yrs.	WM under 21 & above 60	WF all ages	Blacks 12-50	Blacks under 12 & above 50
Valintine Morgin	1	.	3	.	.
Samuel McChesney	.	1	2	.	.
Anthoney Dearing	1	3	3	3	2
Nimrod Siras	.	2	3	.	.
John Golahorn	1	4	4	.	.
Rubin Morgin	1	.	.	.	.
John Webstor	1	1	4	.	.
Jonathin Varnom Sr.	1	1	2	.	.
James Dunlap	2	1	6	.	.
Drury Williams	1	1	2	3	2
Major Wilkerson	1	4	4	.	.
Thomas Stamps	1	3	4	.	.
Jonathin Jarmon Sr.	.	2	3	.	.
Gibson Sothern	1	.	2	.	.
Michal Gilbert	1	1	9	.	.
Edward Thompson	1	1	2	.	.
Elisha Parker	1	1	3	.	.
Thomas Creel	1	.	4	.	.
Richard Taylor	2	2	4	.	.
	46	78	116	31	25

Pg. 2

Head of Household	WM 21-60 yrs.	WM under 21 & above 60	WF all ages	Blacks 12-50	Blacks under 12 & above 50
Samuel Warnock	.	2	.	.	.
Richard Webstor	.	1	5	.	.
Jacob Camplin	1	1	3	.	.
Joseph Read	1	4	2	.	.
Joshua Dodson	2	2	3	.	.
Adam Craford	1	.	2	.	.
Charles Dodson	1	2	4	.	.
Joseph Vaughn	1	2	4	.	.
Rubin Sothern	1	2	3	.	.
Joshua Dodson Jr.	1	1	1	.	.
Charles Angill	1	2	4	.	.
John Dunlap	2	1	1	.	.
William Kinmon	1	2	3	.	.
John Davis	1	2	2	.	.
George Ray	1	1	3	.	.
Joseph King	1	.	1	.	.
John Thompson	1	2	3	.	.
Partrick Bair	1	2	1	.	.
Thomas Gunn	1	3	6	.	.
John Morgin	1	4	3	.	.
John Bair	1	.	.	.	.
Ann Ladd for Wm. Ladd	.	1	.	2	.
Ambros May	1	4	2	.	.
Thomas Eason	1	.	1	.	.
Mary Eason	1	.	2	.	.
Robin Majors	1	.	2	.	.
James Eason	1	.	2	.	.
John Majors	1	2	4	.	.
Harry Terril	3	5	9	6	10

Head of Household	WM 21-60 yrs.	WM under 21 & above 60	WF all ages	Blacks 12-50	Blacks under 12 & above 50
Judah Ladd	.	.	2	1	2
Martin Burrus	1	2	4	7	5
Mary Grinder	.	1	5	.	.
Peter Harston	1	1	2	6	13
Meridith Smith	1	.	2	.	.
James Bools	1	3	2	.	.
Peter Eason	1	.	.	.	.
Jesse Standley	1	1	4	.	.
Benjamin Bennit	1	4	3	.	.
Elias Smith	1	.	3	.	.
John Wood or Ward	1	1	4	.	.
Joseph Ladd	1	.	2	2	.
Robin Crump	1	6	4	1	.
	41	66	113	25	30

By: Absalom Bostick

Pg. 1

Head of Household	WM 21-60 yrs.	WM under 21 & above 60	WF all ages	Blacks 12-50	Blacks under 12 & above 50	
Henry Banner	.	1	2	7	8	18
Henry Fry	1	3	2	.	.	6
Abel Wakefield	1	1	2	.	.	4
Hammon Morriss	1	4	1	1	.	7
William Morriss	1	.	4	.	.	5
Traviss Morriss	1	.	5	.	.	6
Thos. Morriss	1	.	1	.	.	2
John Appleton	1	2	6	1	.	10
John Cooley	1	6	3	.	.	10
Isaac Garrison	1	4	7	.	.	12
John Goode	1	1	2	.	.	4
John Scott	1	6	5	.	.	12
Delany ? Hearin	1	3	3	.	.	7
Thos. Bolkum	1	.	1	.	.	2
Gabriel Waggoner	1	.	5	.	.	6
Thos. Flynt	1	4	2	2	3	12
Saml. Waggoner	.	1	4	.	1	6
Joseph Waggoner	1	1	4	.	.	6
John Clayton	1	1	3	1	.	6
Thos. Smithermon	1	2	4	.	.	7
Jas. Day	1	2	2	.	.	5
Thos. Day	1	2	2	.	.	5
John Snow	1	.	1	.	.	2
Usly Ray	.	2	1	.	1	4
Thos. Ring	.	2	1	.	.	3
Thos. Wilson	1	1	3	.	.	5
John Wells	.	7	3	.	.	10
William Wells	1	.	2	.	.	3
Mary Wakefield	.	7	2	.	.	9
John Martin	1	2	2	.	.	5
Johnson Heath	1	1	4	.	.	6
	25	64	103	12	14	218

STATE CENSUS OF NORTH CAROLINA 1784-1787

Head of Household	WM 21-60 yrs.	WM under 21 & above 60	WF all ages	Blacks 12-50	Blacks under 12 & above 50	Total
Pg. 2						
James Hampton	.	1	1	2	1	5
Wm. James Sr.	1	3	3	3	1	11
John Angle	1	3	1	.	.	5
Thos. Wilson	1	.	2	.	.	3
James Wilson	1	1	4	.	.	6
John Wilson	1	1	2	.	.	4
Valentine Fry	1	7	2	.	.	10
Jacob Petree	1	2	5	.	.	8
John Petree	1	2	3	.	.	6
Charles Davis	1	1	4	.	.	6
Jesse Hill	1	1	3	1	2	8
Moses Martin Jr.	1	2	2	.	.	5
James Merritt	1	2	1	.	.	4
Abraham Vanderpool	1	3	3	.	.	7
Joseph Brown	1	2	1	.	.	4
Edward Merritt	1	3	1	.	.	5
Philip Southerland	1	5	1	.	.	7
John Blackburn	1	4	2	1	.	8
Elizabeth Blackburn	.	1	1	1	1	4
William Heath	1	1	2	.	.	4
Benjn. Jones	1	.	1	.	.	2
Dann Hill	1	.	4	1	.	6
Thos. Heath	.	3	4	.	.	7
William Waggoner	1	3	5	.	.	9
John Tittle	1	2	1	.	.	4
Michael Fry	2	2	5	.	.	9
Henry King	1	2	5	.	.	8
James Foster	1	3	4	.	.	8
Joel Hill	1	.	.	.	1	2
John Adams Sr.	.	2	3	.	.	5
William Adams	1	1	3	.	.	5
John Adams	2	.	3	.	.	5
Patrick Adams	1	1	3	.	.	5
Stephen Fountain	1	1	4	.	.	6
John Winston	1	.	.	1	2	4
	35	**66**	**88**	**10**	**8**	**415**
Pg. 3						
Maj. Richd. Goode	1	3	7	3	2	16
Thos. Goode Jr.	1	3	4	.	.	8
William Gibson	1	3	5	1	.	10
Joseph Hamm	1	3	2	.	.	6
Joseph Johnson	1	.	1	.	.	2
John Holebrook	2	4	2	1	.	9
James LaFoy	1	1	3	.	.	5
Mordica Hamm	1	.	3	.	.	4
John Hamm	1	.	4	.	.	5
William Merritt	1	2	1	.	.	4
William Brown	1	5	2	.	.	8
Lutisha Daviss	.	3	2	.	.	5

Head of Household	WM 21-60 yrs.	WM under 21 & above 60	WF all ages	Blacks 12-50	Blacks under 12 & above 50	Total
Thos. Ring	1	1	3	.	.	5
John Ring	1	4	3	.	.	8
William Brown Jr.	1	.	2	.	.	3
Edward Evins	1	.	4	.	.	5
Thos. Evins	1	1	3	.	.	5
Philip Evins	1	1	2	.	.	4
Joseph Baner	1	2	4	.	.	9
Ephraim Baner	1	4	2	.	.	7
Paris Sims	1	1	2	.	.	4
Benjn. Baner	1	3	3	.	.	7
Robert Chapman	1	.	.	.	.	1
Abraham Martin	1	2	2	5	3	13
William Wilson Sr.	1	2	5	.	.	8
Sarah Charles	.	3	4	2	1	10
Augustin Samuel	2	2	4	.	.	8
John Hall	1	1	3	.	.	5
William Brook	1	3	5	.	.	9
Yong Bynum	1	4	4	3	1	13
Thos. Walker	1	.	.	.	.	1
Thos. Raper	1	.	1	.	.	2
Edward Cooley	1	.	1	.	.	2
James McKnown	1	.	4	.	.	5
	34	**61**	**97**	**15**	**8**	**629**
Pg. 4						
Robert Hill	1	4	5	2	2	14
William Martin	1	2	2	1	1	7
John Halbert	1	4	3	1	.	9
William Daviss	1	1	4	.	.	6
Joseph Cummins	1	2	7	.	.	10
Thomas Tuttle	2	3	2	.	.	7
Thomas Hall	1	1	2	.	.	4
Joel Halbert	1	3	3	1	.	8
Benjn. Young Sr.	1	4	3	.	.	8
William Young	1	.	3	.	.	4
Saml. Young	1	1	1	.	.	3
Benjamin Young Jr.	1	1	1	.	1	4
Thos. Goode Sr.	2	3	3	3	4	15
Saml. Clark	1	3	2	.	.	6
Robert Hammitt	1	.	2	.	.	3
Thos. Es(?) (---)	1	5	3	.	.	9
Jack Fargerson	1	.	.	.	.	1
Jo. Winston	1	5	3	9	5	23
Henry Hampton	1	5	5	.	.	11
Ruben Knight	1	1	4	.	.	6
	22	**48**	**68**	**17**	**13**	**760**

By Jo. Winston. "Errors, omissions & bad writeing &c Excepted."

Capt. Gaines' District, Taken pr Mattw.
Moore, J. P.

Pg. 1

Head of Household	WM 21-60 yrs.	WM under 21 & above 60	WF all ages	Blacks 12-50	Blacks under 12 & above 50
Math Moore	2	7	4	6	8
Jacob Haines	2	.	3	.	.
Archbd. Lister	1	2	8	.	.
William Lankford	1	1	3	.	.
Joshua Nelson	1	5	6	.	.
Edmd. Tilley	1	6	2	.	.
Joseph Lewis	1	.	3	.	.
Richd. Nunn	1	1	4	.	.
Thos. Cooper	1	1	2	.	.
John Nunn	1	3	3	.	.
William Sherrey	1	2	4	.	.
Watson Collins	1	2	2	.	.
Lanceford Field	1	1	7	.	.
Charles Pruitt	1	3	4	.	.
Stevin Field	1	4	3	.	.
Davd. Davidson	1	2	4	.	.
Shaderick Pruitt	1	1	2	.	.
David Field Jr.	1	.	3	.	.
James Gibson	1	2	3	.	.
John Henderson	1	4	5	.	.
Samuel Bond	1	2	4	.	.
John Lawson	1	4	1	.	.
Joseph Young	1	.	2	.	.
Patman Lawson	1	1	1	.	.
Peter Pruitt	1	1	2	.	.
Randol Hall	1	2	3	.	.
William White	1	3	2	.	.
Sarah Royall	.	.	3	.	.
Samuel Edgeman	1	.	1	.	.
Alexdr. Byrge	1	3	5	1	.
Thos. Cardwell	1	2	3	2	3
Edwin Hickman Jr.	1	2	1	.	.
Joseph Shipp	.	3	2	1	.
John Wilson	1	.	3	.	.
Thomas Shipp	1	.	2	1	1
Edwin Hickman Sr.	1	3	4	.	.
John Williams	1	2	3	.	.
Isaiah Madkiff	1	1	2	.	.
John Wilson Jr.	1	.	1	.	.
	37	76	129	11	12

Pg. 2

Head of Household	WM 21-60 yrs.	WM under 21 & above 60	WF all ages	Blacks 12-50	Blacks under 12 & above 50
John Cantwell	1	2	2	.	.
Thomas Lankford	1	2	3	.	.
William Edgeman	1	.	1	.	.
John Owens	1	.	1	.	.
John Deatherage	2	3	2	3	1
George Deatherage	1	4	2	3	1

Head of Household	WM 21-60 yrs.	WM under 21 & above 60	WF all ages	Blacks 12-50	Blacks under 12 & above 50
Ben Isbell	1	1	4	.	.
Thomas Madkiff	1	3	5	.	.
Voll. Gibson	1	2	4	.	.
Archls. Mahoan	1	3	2	.	.
John Lankford	1	2	4	.	.
Joseph Goine	1	2	2	1	.
William Lankford	1	.	1	.	.
John Bristowe	1	2	1	.	.
John Sherry Sr.	.	2	1	.	.
John Shelton	2	3	7	.	.
Abrahm. McMillian	1	6	3	.	.
John Harper	1	1	2	.	.
Boeter Bailes	1	.	2	.	.
Margrett Gillinton	.	2	3	.	.
Danl. Bailes	1	3	3	.	.
Wm. Edgeman Sr.	1	2	2	.	.
Garrott Gibson	1	1	2	.	.
Jason Isbell	1	1	3	2	1
Richard Cox	1	.	8	.	3
Akilliss Deatherage	1	5	5	.	.
Benjamen Carr	1	1	1	.	.
Thomas Johnson	1	2	4	.	.
William Hiett	2	5	3	.	.
James Findly	1	4	4	.	.
Ben. Wheeler	1	.	6	.	.
Joseph Harte	1	1	5	.	.
Lazarus Tilley	2	3	7	1	1
James McKenney	1	5	3	.	.
Peter Miers	1	1	2	.	.
William Boyles Jr.	1	4	2	.	.
Christian Eaton	1	1	1	.	.
James Cooke	1	1	2	.	.
Aron Lisby	1	3	4	.	.
	41	83	109	10	7

Pg. 3

Head of Household	WM 21-60 yrs.	WM under 21 & above 60	WF all ages	Blacks 12-50	Blacks under 12 & above 50
John Bullock	1	2	3	.	.
Mattw. Harriss	1	5	6	.	.
Isaac Jones	1	2	4	.	.
Peter Bellose	1	5	4	.	.
Richd. Beasley	1	5	5	.	.
William Beasley	1	1	1	.	.
Jessee Nighting	1	1	3	2	.
Thomas Ballard	1	5	5	.	.
John Jackson Sr.	1	3	5	.	.
John Bailey	1	1	3	.	.
Edwd. Bailey	.	2	1	.	.
Phebe Sumner	.	1	3	.	.
Sarah Bailes	.	2	3	.	.
Caleb Sumner	1	4	3	.	.
Thos. Sumner	1	2	2	.	.

Head of Household	WM 21-60 yrs.	WM under 21	& above 60	WF all ages	Blacks 12-50	Blacks under 12 & above 50
Sam. Jackson Sr.	1	4	4	.	.
Henry Worldley	1	3	6	.	.
Wm. Sceife	1	1	6	.	.
Peter King	1	4	4	.	.
Saml. Jackson Jr.	1	1	1	.	'.
Steven Jean	1	2	2	.	.
Thomas Hall	1	1	3	.	.
Joseph Easley	1	.	.	.	.
Wm. Deatherage	1	2	1	.	.
John Holt	1	1	3	.	.
Joseph Jessepp	2	7	5	.	.
Thos. Jessepp	1	4	4	.	.
Richd. Pruitt	1	3	2	.	.
Joshua Cox	1	4	4	2	4
Wm. Lawson	1	1	3	.	.
John Gibson	1	1	3	.	.
Elock Condry	1	1	4	.	.
Jacob Jackson	1	1	5	.	.
Steven Bond	1	1	7	.	.
Thos. Wiles	1	4	3	1	.
Daviss Field	1	4	4	.	.
Rachel Green	.	.	3	.	.
Moses Grigg	1	4	4	.	.
Timothy Jessepp	1	2	6	.	.
John Burrows	2	5	2	.	.
	30	102		5	4
Pg. 4					
James Clark	1	1	5	.	.
Welcom Garrott	1	4	4	.	.
Jas. Freeman	1	4	2	.	.
James Ritter	1	.	1	.	.
John Jackson	1	1	3	.	.
Geo. Martin	1	.	4	.	.
Curtis Jackson	1	2	4	.	.
Wm. Oaks	1	2	3	.	.
Micaj. Clark	1	4	1	2	.
Jonathen Harreld	2	3	6	.	.
Thos. Beason	1	1	3	.	.
Jno. Horton	1	2	3	.	.
Saml. Bond	1	2	4	.	.
Jno. Byrcham Jr.	1	1	1	.	.
Joseph Hiett	3	5	5	.	.
Boeter Sumner	1	1	4	.	.
Richd. Harreld	1	7	1	.	.
Wm. Bailes	1	4	4	.	.
Isaac Cloud	1	3	2	.	.
Masey Beason	1	1	1	.	.
Barn. Rowark	.	1	2	.	.
Timo. Rowark	1	.	2	.	.
Joseph Cloud	1	3	5	.	.

Head of Household	WM 21-60 yrs.	WM under 21	& above 50	WF all ages	Blacks 12-50	Blacks under 12 & above 50
Benaj. King	.	4	5	.	.
Margart. Lisby	.	2	3	.	.
Jno. Garrott	.	5	3	.	.
Wm. Nunn	1	1	2	.	.
Caleb Floyd	1	3	4	1	.
Davd. Chandler	1	2	4	.	.
Wm. Tansey	1	.	5	.	.
Wm. Davidson	.	1	2	.	.
Wm. Runnalds	1	5	1	.	.
John Martin	2	.	2	1	.
Thos. Isbell	1	1	1	.	.
Elisha Pierce	1	2	8	.	.
James Gaines	1	5	7	1	,
Morm Ballard	1	4	3	.	.
John Byrcham	1	3	5	.	.
	37	90	135	5	.

"List of Capt. Wright's Distr. Number of Inhabitants Taken by William Cook, Feby. 1786."

Pg. 1; column 1

Head of Household	WM 21-60 yrs.	WM under 21	& above 50	WF all ages	Blacks 12-50	Blacks under 12 & above 50	Total
Ayres Hudspeth	1	4	7	.	.	12
Noel Waddel	1	1	2	.	.	4
Henry Hambrick	1	2	1	.	.	4
Thomas Wright	1	2	2	.	.	5
Ephraim Mclemore	1	4	5	.	.	10
James Elliott	1	2	5	.	.	8
John Moor	1	4	5	.	.	10
George Moor	1	1	1	.	.	3
Benjan. Kettle	1	.	2	.	.	3
William Elles	1	2	3	.	.	6
James Shaw	1	2	3	.	.	6
John Whalen	1	1	1	.	.	3
Carter Hudspeth	1	.	.	.	.	1
John Hudspeth	1	1	4	.	.	6
Sterlin Mclemore	1	2	3	.	.	6
Jacob Jones	1	2	1	.	.	4
Benjan. Shaw	1	.	1	.	.	2
Mary Hudspeth	.	3	3	.	.	6
Jacob Iden	1	.	1	.	.	2
Buckner Russel	1	2	3	.	.	6
William Pettey	1	5	3	1	.	10
John Copelin	1	4	2	.	.	7
William Masters	.	2	2	.	.	4
John Stephens	1	1	3	.	.	5
Zachariah Pettey	1	.	4	.	.	5
Daniel Hoppus	1	.	.	.	.	1
George Hoppus	.	1	1	.	.	2
John Blackman	1	.	4	.	.	5
James Burnside	1	1	5	.	.	7

151

Head of Household	WM 21-60 yrs.	WM under 21 & above 60	WF all ages	Blacks 12-50	Blacks under 12 & above 50	Total
Loclan Muckleyea	.	5	2	.	.	7
Pg.1; column2						
William Woldridge	1	1	1	3	4	10
Jeremiah Riley	1	2	2	4	4	13
Robert Frazier	1	2	3	2	.	8
Edward Riley	1	.	.	.	.	1
Ninian Riley	2	2	2	.	.	6
Isaac Windsor	1	.	3	.	.	4
William Alnutt	1	1	4	.	.	6
Jarrott Riley	1	.	1	.	.	2
Isaac Johnson	1	2	4	1	1	9
William Frazier	1	1	3	.	J	5
John Johnson	1	3	4	3	4	15
Stephen Wood	1	2	6	.	.	9
John Wright	1	4	7	2	.	14
Benjamin Johnson	1	.	5	.	.	6
Nancy Chapel	.	3	3	.	.	6
Samuel Arnold	1	4	2	1	.	8
Jonathan Parker	2	6	5	.	.	13
Briaset(?) Obanyan	1	3	4	.	.	8
John Ward	1	1	4	.	.	6
Richd. Jacks	1	4	4	.	.	9
Edward Clanton	1	2	3	.	.	6
Thomas Jacks	1	.	1	.	.	2
Thomas Clanton	.	2	3	3	2	10
William Pettey Jr.	1	.	2	.	.	3
Joseph Hill	1	3	7	.	.	11
Allen Gentry	1	2	4	.	.	7
John Crawford	1	1	1	.	.	3
Nicholas Gentry	1	1	3	.	.	5
John Elsberry	1	.	4	.	.	5
Isaac Elsberry	1	4	2	.	.	7
Pg.1; column 3						
John Parsons	1	4	8	.	.	13
James Parsons	1	2	1	.	.	4
Jeremiah Blackman	1	1	1	.	.	3
Henry Wagoner	1	3	5	.	.	9
John Keen	1	.	1	.	.	2
Mathew Sparks	1	1	3	.	.	5
Matthias Carpeter	1	1	3	.	.	5
Charles Johnson	1	3	6	.	.	10
William Ray	1	1	4	.	.	6
Richd. Wootan	1	4	5	.	.	10
George Nelson	1	2	1	.	.	4
William Coxsey	1	.	6	.	.	7
George Philips	1	3	4	.	.	8
Christian Weatherman	1	4	4	.	.	9
John Wright (crossed out)	1	4	7	2	.	
Joseph Barratt	1	2	3	.	.	6

Head of Household	WM 21-60 yrs.	WM under 21 & above 60	WF all ages	Blacks 12-50	Blacks under 12 & above 50	Total
James Murprey	1	4	5	.	.	10
John Rector	1	4	3	.	.	8
Joseph Miers	1	3	5	.	.	9
Richd. Blalock	1	1	3	.	.	5
William Karr	1	2	2	.	.	5
Lewis Elliott	1	3	2	1	4	11
Christian Fender	1	4	4	.	.	9
John Blalock	1	4	5	1	1	12
Cade Blalock	.	1	2	.	.	3
William Elliott	1	4	5	1	1	12
Jacob Miller	1	3	4	.	.	8
Christian Miller	1	1	1	.	.	3
James Sanders	2	4	3	6	6	21
George Long	1	5	6	.	.	12
Henry Ward	1	1	5	.	1	8
John Anderson	1	2	2	.	.	5
Isaac Mois	1	3	3	.	.	7
Joseph Wabbleton	1	.	1	.	.	2
Pg.2; column 1						
Micajah Harmon	1	3	2	.	.	6
John Brown	2	2	2	.	.	6
Daniel Bills	1	5	6	.	.	12
Wm. Davies	1	3	5	.	.	9
Jacob Miller	1	3	4	.	.	8
Peter Myers	.	2	4	.	.	6
Thomas Gallion	1	2	1	.	.	4
Charles Russel	1	2	3	.	.	6
John Williams	1	.	3	3	1	8
Ambrose Bramlet	1	4	4	2	.	11
George Holcomb	1	4	4	.	.	9
Philemon Holcomb	1	2	5	.	.	8
Greenberry Patterson	1	5	4	.	.	10
John Bohannum	1	2	4	.	1	8
David Crawford	.	2	1	.	.	3
William Walden	1	2	5	.	.	8
Alexr. Thompson	1	4	3	.	.	8
Frederick Long	1	4	7	.	.	12
George Long	1	3	7	.	.	11
Joseph Hinshaw	1	1	2	.	.	4
Thomas Hinshaw	1	4	5	.	.	10
Youngs Coleman	1	4	2	.	.	7
Thomas Hadley	1	1	5	.	.	7
Simon Hadley	1	4	4	.	.	9
Robert Mathews	1	2	6	.	.	9
Elisha Johnson	2	.	1	.	.	3
William Pilgrim	1	4	6	.	.	11
Peter Sprinkle	1	5	4	.	.	10
John Johnson	1	4	4	1	.	10
Henry Burcham	1	2	6	.	.	9
Job Felton	1	1	2	1	2	7

STATE CENSUS OF NORTH CAROLINA 1784-1787

Head of Household	WM 21-60 yrs.	WM under 21 & above 60	WF all ages	Blacks 12-50	Blacks under 12 & above 50	Total
Abra^m. Stor(?)	1	1	1	.	.	3
	58	150	196		4	
Pg. 2; column 2						
Strangeman Hutchens	1	.	2	1	.	4
Valentin Rees	1	4	5	.	.	10
Benjamin Clanton	1	2	3	.	.	6
John Currey	1	2	3	.	.	6
Charles Pearson	1	2	5	.	.	8
Benjamin Hutchens	1	4	2	2	.	9
James Jones Sr.	1	3	3	.	.	7
Thomas Burch	1	.	1	.	.	2
James Jones Jr.	1	.	.	.	.	1
Palmer Critchfield	1	.	6	.	.	7
Samuel Shinn	2	2	7	.	.	11
Anne Whitehead	.	5	2	.	.	7
Daniel Huff	1	3	7	.	.	11
Abijah Elmore	1	4	4	.	.	
[crossed out]						
John Hoppus	1	1	3	.	.	5
George Hoppus	1	2	2	.	.	5
William Rutledge	1	4	3	.	.	8
Amos Pilgrim	1	3	5	.	.	9
Joseph Bradley	2	2	6	.	.	10
John Dyal	1	2	3	.	.	6
Thomas Clark	1	4	2	.	.	7
Job Pettejohn	1	1	2	.	.	5
Jane Mckinne	.	3	2	.	.	5
George Bates	1	.	.	.	.	1
Thomas Holecomb	1	5	1	.	.	7
Jones Reynolds	1	2	2	.	.	5
Silas Murphy	1	3	2	.	.	6
Grimes Holcomb	1	4	2	.	.	7
Gideon Brown	1	9	2	.	.	12
Archur Jentry	1	1	3	.	.	5
Pg. 2; column 3						
Elizabeth Lakey	1	1	2	.	.	4
Thomas Stone	1	.	4	.	.	5
Wm. Huff	1	3	4	.	.	8
Isaac Wilkins	1	1	4	.	.	6
Nathl. Woodruff	1	6	3	.	.	10
Walter Ashmore	1	4	4	.	.	9
John Calton	1	6	4	.	.	11
Lindsey Calton	1	.	1	.	.	2
Abrahm Rees	1	5	3	.	.	9
Lawrence Holcomb	1	3	3	.	.	7
John Durham	1	3	5	.	.	9
Peter Shearmer	2	.	2	.	.	4
Frederick Tanner	1	2	2	.	.	5
Daniel Liberton	1	.	3	.	.	4

Head of Household	WM 21-60 yrs.	WM under 21 & above 60	WF all ages	Blacks 12-50	Blacks under 12 & above 50	Total
Deborah Gwin	1	1	2	.	.	4
Wm. Zackary	1	3	2	.	.	6
James Wells	1	2	3	.	.	6
Thomas Hutchens	1	1	2	1	.	5
John Marten	1	.	3	.	.	4
James McCollum	1	3	4	.	.	8
Jacob Brown	1	3	2	.	.	6
Patrick Brown	1	4	6	.	.	11
Jestias Reynolds	1	2	2	.	.	5
John Allen	1	3	3	.	.	7
John Hammons	1	3	3	.	.	7
Martha Mackhan	.	2	4	1	.	7
John Reaves	1	1	2	.	.	4
John Mackee	1	2	2	.	.	5
Jas. Badgett	1	2	4	4	5	16
Blunt Garriott	1	3	4	.	.	8
Amariah Felton	1	.	4	.	.	5
	64	152	210	17	18	
	182	424	595	58	37	

Total 1292

"List of Inhabitants of Blackburn's District. Taken by Chas. McAnally.

Column 1

Head of Household	WM 21-60 yrs.	WM under 21 & above 60	WF all ages	Blacks 12-50	Blacks under 12 & above 50
Chas. McAnally	2	3	6	1	.
John McAnally	1	3	3	.	.
Jesse McAnally	1	1	2	.	.
Elisha Dodson	1	1	2	.	.
Drurias Ward	1	.	2	.	.
Betty Ward	.	2	6	.	.
James Moore	1	2	4	.	.
Abner Barns	1	1	3	.	.
John Spray	1	.	.	.	.
William Davis	1	2	5	.	.
James Davis	2	1	5	.	2
John Davis	1	2	3	.	.
John Dunlap	2	1	1	.	.
John Parford	1	.	2	.	.
Patrick Kenney	1	.	2	.	.
Nancy Dunlap	.	1	2	.	.
Stephen Cleaton	1	4	4	.	2
William Cleaton	1	.	1	.	.
Joseph Wadkins	1	3	3	.	1
Henry Childs	1	3	7	.	.
Hugh Denum	.	1	1	1	.
Henry Wadkins	1	3	7	.	.
James Coffey	1	2	4	.	.
Jehu Brown	1	5	4	.	.
Adam Mitchel	1	5	5	1	.
Joseph Hann	1	.	.	.	.

STATE CENSUS OF NORTH CAROLINA 1784-1787

Head of Household	WM 21-60 yrs.	WM under 21 & above 60	WF all ages	Blacks 12-50	Blacks under 12 & above 50
Daniel Davis	1	1	6	.	.
James Thomson	1	6	6	.	.
Rich^d. Baize	1	.	1	.	.
Hardy Redick	1	2	6	.	.
Nathl. Baize	1	2	4	.	.
James Baize	1	.	.	.	.
Alexd^r. Moore	1	4	4	.	.
James Moore	1	2	2	.	.
John Merit	1	1	3	.	.
Wm. Rutlage	1	2	3	.	.
Benjⁿ. Branum	1	3	6	.	.
Column 2					
John Kyser	1	3	1	.	.
John Moore	1	3	3	.	.
Christian Messor	1	2	4	.	.
John Boles	1	3	5	1	.
James Ross	1	3	4	1	.
Younger Blackburn	1	3	3	1	.
William Moore	1	2	8	.	.
Wm. Winkfield	1	3	4	.	.
Johnson Rutlage	1	1	1	.	.
Ant^o. Collins	1	3	1	.	.
Roger Collins	1	2	5	.	.
Moses Mott	1	2	4	.	.
William Cook	1	.	3	.	.
Rebecka Furguson	.	3	5	.	.
Sam Fitzpatrick	1	3	5	.	.
Wm. Rutlage Sr.	1	2	2	3	5
Thos. Fitzpatrick	1	2	4	.	.
Wm. Boles	1	1	1	.	.
Wm. Campble	1	2	5	1	2
Wm. Johnson	1	.	.	.	.
Thomas Cook	3	.	5	.	.
Alexd^r. Boles	1	1	2	.	.

Head of Household	WM 21-60 yrs.	WM under 21 & above 60	WF all ages	Blacks 12-50	Blacks under 12 & above 50
Richard Fanshear	1	1	1	.	.
Morgan Davis	2	4	5	.	.
Matt^w. Hill	1	4	4	.	.
Robert Meab(?)	1	4	4	.	.
David Moore	1	1	1	.	.
John Smith	2	6	3	.	.
Philip Wilson	2	3	4	.	.
Robt. Brasheer	1	2	1	.	.
Wm. Mullen	1	2	4	.	.
Daniel Horton	1	1	1	.	.
Major Slatton	1	.	1	.	.
John Meab	2	3	5	.	.
John Slatton	1	4	5	.	.
George Slatton	1	5	4	.	.
Thos. Hampton	1	3	5	.	.
* Samuel Davis	1	2	2	.	.
* George Davis	1	1	1	.	.
* Thos. Ham	1	.	1	.	.

* Designated as being in "In Hill's Dist."

Total 463

No. 10 - 2,088

Capt. Krouses District, taken by
Jacob Bloom, J. P.

The Number of all white & Black Inhabitants
in Capt. Krouses Dist. Feb. 1786.

333 686 952 58 55

Head of Household	WM 21-60 yrs.	WM under 21 & above 60	WF all ages	Blacks 12-50	Blacks under 12 & above 50	Head of Household	WM 21-60 yrs.	WM under 21 & above 60	WF all ages	Blacks 12-50	Blacks under 12 & above 50
						TYRRELL COUNTY					

"A List of The in Habetes maid by Thos. Garrett". from the Old Court House Bridge to the upper End of the County in the Year 1786. "

Head of Household	WM 21-60 yrs.	WM under 21 & above 60	WF all ages	Blacks 12-50	Blacks under 12 & above 50
Pg. 1					
Jonathan Corprew	.	3	1	5	1
Thos. Harrisson	.	2	2	.	.
Luke Leggett	1	.	1	.	.
Joshua Corprew	1	2	2	1	.
Will. Dwight	1	.	1	1	.
Josiah Harrisson	1	3	4	.	.
Jno. Corprew	1	1	2	.	.
Will. Adams	1	1	3	.	.
James Harrisson	2	2	3	.	.
Wm. Fagins	1	.	.	.	.
Mat. Corpw(?)	.	1	2	.	2
James Garrett	.	2	1	3	.
Thos. Rogers	1	1	3	.	.
Thos. Adamas	1	.	1	.	.
Joes. Evritt	1	4	3	.	1
Thos. Garett	1	1	3	.	1
Joes Jones	1	1	3	.	.
Marget Jones	.	.	2	.	.
Sturd Hamptton(?)	.	1	1	.	.
Henery Allen	1	2	1	.	.
Nat. Everitt	1	1	1	.	.
Armet Hollies	1	3	5	.	.
James Hollies	1	2	3	.	.
John Paget	1	1	3	.	.
Will[m]. Harson	1	1	4	3	.
Elies Adamas	.	1	5	1	.
	20	38	62	14	5
Pg. 2					
Thos. Stewart	2	.	1	5	3
Benj[n]. Blount Jr.	1	1	2	3	2
Jereysiah Everitt son of John	1	1	6	1	2
Thos. Harson	1	3	3	3	2
Airs Rogers	1	1	.	.	.
Levey Stubbs	1	.	3	.	1
Joseph Vandikes	1	.	1	.	.
Stephen Roads	1	1	2	3	.
William White	1	.	1	.	.
Daniel Garrett	1	2	1	.	.
Mary Bryant	.	.	1	.	.
Benjn. Blount Sr.	.	3	3	10	18
Timithy Cunningham	1	4	1	.	.
Jonithan Adams	1	3	3	.	.

Head of Household	WM 21-60 yrs.	WM under 21 & above 60	WF all ages	Blacks 12-50	Blacks under 12 & above 50
Cutbert Phelps	1	.	1	.	.
Harman Webb	1	1	3	3	5
Nathan Rogers	.	2	2	.	.
John Garrett	1	3	3	6	4
George Mathews	1	2	1	3	.
David Airs	1	4	3	.	.
Els. Everitt	.	1	4	.	.
Bilah Jones	.	.	1	5	.
Thos. Everitt	1	2	3	2	2
Daniel Legget	1	1	5	.	.
Charles Clifton	1	1	5	.	.
Elizabeth Hassell	.	1	3	.	.
Anna Jones	.	2	3	.	1
Mary Hassell	.	.	3	.	.
	21	37	70	44	38
Pg. 3					
Isaac Airs	1	4	3	.	.
Tho. Midelton(?)	1	1	1	.	1
Tho. Airs	1	.	.	.	.
Thomas Buncombe	.	.	.	21	22
Richard Swinson	1	3	4	1	.
John Swinson	.	.	2	.	3
Steward Walker	1	3	.	1	.
James Jones Jr.	1	.	3	.	1
Caleb Bembridge	1	4	3	1	4
James Jones	1	2	3	.	1
Jesse Stubbs	1	1	2	.	.
Thos. Stalley(?)	1	1	1	1	3
Mcajah Stubbs	1	1	3	.	.
Richard Stubbs	1	.	1	.	1
Everald Stubbs	1	2	4	5	1
William Ward	1	1	.	.	1
Ben Howrd(?)	1	.	1	.	.
William Earl(?)	1	.	1	4	5
Jasper Hardison	1	2	5	.	.
Harmon Webb(?)	1	.	.	.	.
Henery Gared	1	1	1	.	.
Burd Land	1	3	2	4	4
Ed Blunt	1	1	4	1	.
	21	34	44	43	47
Pg. 4					
John Jordan	1	1	3	.	2
Arthur Rhoads	1	.	.	.	.
Richard Huff	1	1	3	.	1
John Aries(?)	1	.	1	.	.
John Airs	1	1	.	.	.
	5	3	7	2	4

155

Head of Household	WM 21-60 yrs.	WM under 21 & above 60	WF all ages	Blacks 12-50	Blacks under 12 & above 50
Pg. 5					
Jonathan(?) Davies(?)	.	4	2	.	1
Demcey Sexton	1	.	.	.	.
Thos. Harson	1	3	2	1	.
Ben(?) Harson	1	2	2	.	.
Thos. Garrett Sr.	.	1	2	.	.
Thos. Garrett Jr.	1	1	3	.	.
C. (?) Blount Jr.	1	1	3	5	6
Richard Draper	.	2	2	.	1
H. (?) Blount	1	4	2	.	.
Ed. Walker	1	2	4	.	.
Thos. Lee	1	.	3	8	5
Jos. Adames	2	.	3	1	.
Vooleo(?) Roades	1	.	.	.	.
Steven Fagins	1	.	2	.	1
Marey Lee	.	.	2	5	5
Shadrack Fagan	1	1	1	.	1
Stephen Williams	1	.	4	.	.
Thos. Walker	1	2	3	5	3
Marey Fagenes	.	3	2	.	1
Thos. Stubbs Jr.	1	2	4	.	1
Ephram Ethridge	1	3	4	1	.
Thos. Williams	1	2	4	.	.
Friley Jones	1	1	3	5	5
John Walker	1	1	4	1	.
Fredrick Swinson	.	1	.	.	.
Ann Burns	.	.	1	.	.
John Stubbs	1	.	2	4	3
Thos. White	1	1	1	.	.
Charles Martin	1	.	.	.	.
	23	37	72	38	33
Pg. 6					
George Matthews	1	2	2	2	1
Thomas Mackey	1	1	1	13	10
	2	3	3	15	11

Total 784

"A list of the number of inhabitants taken by Stephen Swain from this Marked Poplar Swamp to Scuppernong River this day 1786.

Head of Household	WM 21-60 yrs.	WM under 21 & above 60	WF all ages	Blacks 12-50	Blacks under 12 & above 50
Pg. 1					
James Devonport	1	2	1	2	.
David Devonport	1	1	1	1	.
Saml. Carswell	1	3	5	.	.
Benony Hassell	1	.	3	.	.
Joel Norman	1	.	.	.	.
Thos. FPatrick (Fitzpatrick?)	1	4	2	.	.
John Oliver	1	.	.	.	.

Head of Household	WM 21-60 yrs.	WM under 21 & above 60	WF all ages	Blacks 12-50	Blacks under 12 & above 50
Jonathan Bateman Jr	1	.	5	1	.
Jesse Bateman	1	1	3	.	.
John Carswell	1	.	2	.	.
Enock Phelps	1	.	5	.	.
John Tarkington	.	1	2	1	1
Edwd. Hassell	1	.	4	.	.
Tabitha Marriner	.	2	4	.	.
James Devonport	.	2	5	2	.
Timothy Pearce	1	.	3	.	.
Robert Wynne	1	1	1	.	2
Sarah Snell	.	3	7	.	.
Ezekiel Hill	2	.	4	.	.
James Phelps Jr.	1	3	2	1	.
John Alexander Sr.	1	3	1	.	.
Anthony Alexander	1	1	3	.	1
Jesse Phelps	1	2	1	.	.
Isaac Patrick	1	2	2	.	.
Robert Daves(?)	.	2	3	2	1
Michael Smith	1	.	2	.	1
Absolam Clifton	1	.	.	.	.
	23	33	71	10	6
Pg. 2					
Joseph Ansley	1	2	3	.	.
Joseph Tarkington	1	2	2	5	.
James Ambrose	1	1	2	.	.
Keziah McClary	.	.	3	.	.
John Ansley	1	2	5	6	1
Sarah Melton	.	.	5	.	.
Joanna Padget	.	1	1	.	.
John Alexander Jr.	1	.	.	.	.
Asa Phelps	1	.	.	.	.
Benjn. Tarkington	1	3	3	.	.
Mathew Mashaw	1	.	1	1	2
John FitsPatrick	1	3	4	1	.
Evan Spruil	1	3	3	.	.
John Davis	1	1	4	2	.
James Long Jr.	1	2	1	.	.
EdW. Alexr.	1	.	3	.	.
John Devonport	1	3	2	.	.
John Farlaw	1	6	2	.	.
Jacob Devenport	1	.	2	.	.
Joseph Norman	1	2	3	.	.
Andrew Bateman	1	3	2	1	1
Joshua Phelps	1	3	4	.	.
Elisha Timmons	1	2	2	.	.
James Hase(?)	1	3	2	.	.
Nath. Hooker	1	.	2	3	2
Nehh. Spruel	1	4	3	2	4
Levi Hassell	1	2	7	.	1

Head of Household	WM 21-60 yrs.	WM under 21 & above 60	WF all ages	Blacks 12-50	Blacks under 12 & above 50
Hezk^h. Normans	1	1	1	.	.
Jesse Hill	1	.	2	.	1
	26	48	7	21	12
Pg. 3					
Mary Norman	.	2	3	.	.
Edm^d. Harrison	1	6	1	.	.
Zebulum Tarkington	1	3	7	.	.
Moses Devonport	1	1	1	.	.
Joseph Phelps	1	.	.	.	.
Benjn. Tarkington	1	4	4	.	.
Joseph Tarkington	1	.	2	.	.
Sarah Woodland	.	3	1	.	.
Thos. Davis Sr.	1	3	2	.	.
Joseph Wyat Esq.	1	2	1	2	3
Sarah Spruel	1	.	2	.	.
Levi Roew or Row/Rowe	1	2	3	2	2
Jacob Devonport	1	.	.	.	.
Miles Spruel	1	1	.	.	.
Isaac Cullifor	1	2	3	.	.
Nehem^h. Hadder(?)	1	.	.	.	.
Joana Phelps	.	1	2	.	.
James Dilling	1	2	4	.	.
Willm. Chesson	1	4	3	.	4
Isaac Norman	1	1	2	.	.
Joshua Alex^r.	1	1	7	.	.
James Phelps	1	1	4	.	.
Thomas Spruel	1	1	8	.	.
Joseph Phelps Jr.	1	3	6	.	.
	21	43	66	4	11
Pg. 4					
John Spruel	1	2	4	.	.
John Clifton	1	1	1	.	.
Elijah Phelps	1	.	.	.	.
Willm. Spruel	1	.	1	1	.
Joseph Oliver	1	.	2	.	.
John Bateman) Isaac Bateman)	1	1	6	.	.
Wm. Barnes	1	4	4	.	.
John Dilling	1	3	1	.	.
Alex^r. Oliver	1	.	3	.	.
John Phelps Jr.	1	.	.	.	.
Wm. Spruel	1	2	4	.	.
Wrixom Marriner	1	2	4	.	.
Joseph Spruel	.	3	.	3	1
John Devonport	1	.	2	.	.
James Norman	1	1	2	.	.
Joseph Arnold	1	6	4	.	.
Jesse Ambrose or Ambrose [Ambrus on 1790 census]	1	1	4	.	.
Stephen Bateman Jr.	3	4	6	.	.
John Bateman Sr.	1	1	2	.	.
Nathan Bateman Jr.	1	3	1	.	.
Dreadful Simpson	1	.	.	.	.
Saml. Spruel	1	4	2	.	.
Isaac Alexander [son of Mocson. (?)]	1	.	.	.	.
Joseph Ansley Jr.	1	.	1	.	.
J. Phelps Jr.	1	2	2	.	1
	26	39	56	4	1
Pg. 5					
Abr^m. Smith	1	3	5	.	.
Jerem^h. Bateman	1	2	2	1	1
Edwd. Hassell Sr.	1	1	2	.	.
Jacob Smith	1	3	2	.	.
Solomon Ansley	1	.	.	1	.
Reubin Barns	1	1	3	.	.
John Normans	1	3	4	.	.
Joseph Phelps	1	.	2	.	.
Godfrey Phelps	1	4	5	.	.
Meriam Timble(?)	.	3	1	.	.
Isaac Ram(?)	1	.	1	.	.
John Fanning	1	.	4	.	.
Joshua Powers	1	1	4	.	.
John Davis Jr.	1	2	2	.	.
Joshiah Spruel	1	2	2	.	.
Shimi Ambrose	1	2	1	.	.
Joseph Devonport	1	3	1	.	.
Edwd. Phelps Sr.	1	4	6	.	.
Rich^d. Davis	1	1	1	2	.
James Ambrose Sr.	1	2	3	.	.
Stephen Long	1	4	5	.	.
Thos. Olds	1	.	.	.	.
Benjn. Spruel	3	.	.	3	5
Stephen Bateman	1	1	1	.	.
Willm. Tarkington	1	3	7	2	.
Jemima Burtenshal	.	1	2	.	.
	26	44	66	9	6
Pg. 6					
John Padget	1	.	1	.	.
George Ivah	1	.	.	.	.
James Spruel	1	2	2	.	.
Assa Hill	1	.	2	.	.
Simeon Spruel	1	2	5	4	1
Robert Clifton	1	2	7	.	.
Henry Alex^r. Mockason?	1	.	.	.	.
Andrew Oliver	1	2	1	.	.
Josiah Phelps	1	3	2	2	.
Joseph Alexander	1	4	4	1	.

Head of Household	WM 21-60 yrs.	WM under 21 & above 60	WF all ages	Blacks 12-50	Blacks under 12 & above 50
Marian(?) Alexander	.	1	2	.	.
Joseph Devonport	1	4	1	.	.
Jonathan Bateman	3	4	2	1	1
John Bateman	1	.	.	.	1
John Bateman Sr.	1	4	3	.	.
Ebenezer Spruel	1	.	5	.	.
Mary Normand	.	3	5	.	.
John Todd	1	2	4	.	.
Thos. Hawkins Spruil	1	1	1	.	.
Jose Spruil	1	3	3	.	.
Joseph Chesson	1	2	2	.	.
Joshua Chesson	1	2	1	1	.
John Swain	1	2	3	.	.
Stephen Swain Esq.	1	2	3	.	.
Stephen Long	1	3	.	.	.
	25	46	59	9	3

Total 390

Total No. 16 - 890

List of People in Stephen Swain's District, 1786.

"A List of White and black or Number of Each family for the Year 86 in the District of Little Alligator."

Pg. 1

Head of Household	WM 21-60 yrs.	WM under 21 & above 60	WF all ages	Blacks 12-50	Blacks under 12 & above 50
Assa Trublood	1	2	1	.	.
Frances Cummine	1	2	2	.	1
John Foster	1	1	2	2	4
Obediah Larence	1	.	2	.	.
Jesse Merret	1	2	3	.	.
James Basnight	1	3	3	.	.
John Alexander	1	1	3	.	.
Isaac Alexander	1	2	3	.	.
Jacob Basnight	1	3	4	.	.
Martha Alexander	.	1	2	.	.
Benjamin Mann	1	1	3	.	.
Col. Warrington	1	1	3	2	1
Agness Rowton	1	1	1	1	.
Edward Rowton	1	.	1	1	1
Daniel Rowton	1	.	.	.	.
Richard Rowton	1	1	3	.	.
William Basnight	1	1	1	.	.
John McClean	1	1	3	.	.
Henry Alexander	1	2	.	.	.
Joshua Alexander	1	2	1	.	4
John Godwin	1	2	2	.	.
Armsted Perish/Perisho	1	.	2	.	.
Elikam Swain	1	2	2	.	.
John Alexander	1	2	4	.	2
Levy Crank	1	2	4	.	.

Head of Household	WM 21-60 yrs.	WM under 21 & above 60	WF all ages	Blacks 12-50	Blacks under 12 & above 50
Miles Peirce	1	4	3	.	1
Rebeca Hunning	.	2	3	.	.
Randle Johnson	1	1	2	.	.
Rufus Perisho	1	1	2	.	.
Ann Hassel	.	5	2	2	1
Robert McAlister	1	.	1	3	.
	28	47	68	11	15

Pg. 2

Head of Household	WM 21-60 yrs.	WM under 21 & above 60	WF all ages	Blacks 12-50	Blacks under 12 & above 50
Johnathan Johnson	1	.	1	.	.
James Perisho	1	4	3	.	.
Henry Alexander	1	5	2	.	.
William Flood	1	3	6	.	.
William Phelps	1	3	6	.	.
Antony Alexander	1	.	2	.	.
John Hoskins	1	3	4	5	5
Jacobus Heath	1	.	.	.	.
James Anderson	1	1	6	4	.
Randle Johnson	1	.	2	.	.
Thomas Mann	1	2	2	.	.
Devohon Perisho	1	1	2	.	.
Joseph Pledger	1	3	5	3	5
Mary Alexander	2	2	1	.	4
Joseph McKennry	1	1	2	.	.
Joseph Cooper	1	.	2	.	.
William Mann	1	.	.	.	1
John Deval	1	2	4	.	.
Willis Cooper	1	2	1	.	.
Susanah Hassel	.	.	2	.	.
James Best	1	2	2	.	.
Spier Holland	1	2	1	.	.
Thomas McKemmy	1	.	.	.	.
Elizabeth Hunnings	.	2	2	.	.
Elizabeth Hunnings	.	2	2	.	.
Joseph Crain	1	.	1	.	.
Robert Heath	1	1	4	.	.
Joseph Alexander	1	.	1	.	.
John Alexander	1	.	1	.	.
Thomas Hopkins	1	.	1	3	2
Robert & William Dunlap	2	1	.	2	.
	30	40	66	17	17

Pg. 3

Head of Household	WM 21-60 yrs.	WM under 21 & above 60	WF all ages	Blacks 12-50	Blacks under 12 & above 50
Hez. Spruill (Col.)	1	2	5	2	3
Total 342	59	89	139	20	35

158

Head of Household	WM 21-60 yrs.	WM under 21 & above 60	WF all ages	Blacks 12-50	Blacks under 12 & above 50
"A List of the Families in Meltail the Lake to the Lower End of the County taken by John Hooker." (a one-page list)					
John Caroon	1	5	4	5	8
John Payne	1	5	3	1	.
Joseph Hassell	1	1	2	.	.
Thomas Mann	1	1	2	1	.
John Midgett	1	2	1	1	3
George Poplewell	1	2	2	.	.
Richard Oneal	1	.	4	.	.
Daniel Wrasco	1	2	5	.	.
Stephen Barnett	1	2	5	.	.
Henry Smith	1	1	4	.	.
David Hill	2	3	2	.	.
Zachariah Owens Sr.	1	6	3	.	.
Thomas Owens	1	3	5	1	3
Zachariah Owens Jr.	1	.	3	.	.
Adam Owens	1	4	3	1	1
Isaac Carroon	1	2	2	3	4
William McDaniel	1	2	2	.	.
Henry Homes	1	2	1	.	.
Henry Fountain	1	1	1	.	.
George Battin	1	1	3	.	.
Dorcas Cook	.	4	2	.	.
Dorothy Barnes	1	.	2	.	.
Zachariah Hunnings	1	4	3	4	5
William Cowell	1	1	2	3	5
William Twyford	1	1	4	1	1
Joseph Browne	1	2	5	.	.
John Tweedy	2	2	4	.	.
Joseph Basnight	1	.	5	.	.
John Smith	1	2	3	.	.
Stephen Hooker	1	3	3	.	.
John Hooker Jr.	1	2	2	.	.
William Basnight	1	5	5	.	.
John Hooker Sr. (aged over 60)	1	3	2	.	.
Total 258	34	74	99	21	30

"Number of Inhabitants in Beaverdam District, Taken by John Pope 1786".
Pg. 1

Head of Household	WM 21-60 yrs.	WM under 21 & above 60	WF all ages	Blacks 12-50	Blacks under 12 & above 50
Samuel Mosely	1	.	.	.	.
Henry Harp	1	2	4	.	.
John Mosely	1	.	2	.	.
Sherwood Winningham	1	2	2	.	.
Christopher Harris	1	3	3	.	.
John Prewit	1	4	5	1	.
John Bridgers	1	3	4	.	.
Simon Hancock	1	4	3	.	.

Head of Household	WM 21-60 yrs.	WM under 21 & above 60	WF all ages	Blacks 12-50	Blacks under 12 & above 50
Richd. Bridgers	1	1	2	.	.
John Harriss	1	2	4	.	.
John Rains	1	3	2	.	.
George Cavaner	2	5	4	1	.
James Blackwell	2	1	6	6	7
Willm. Taburn	.	.	.	.	.
Jacob Hawley	1	3	2	.	.
David Phillips	1	2	2	.	.
Fielding Heflin	1	2	3	.	.
Wm. Heflin	1	4	2	.	.
Druery Bridgers	1	.	1	.	.
Wm. Carrel	1	3	1	.	.
Edward Harris	1	2	5	2	2
Wm. McGehee	1	.	5	.	.
Elizabeth Carrel	.	.	3	.	.
Thos. Roberts	1	2	2	.	.
Richd. Bailey	1	2	7	.	.
Jeremiah Bailey	1	3	.	2	2
Jones Fuller	1	7	4	3	6
Pg. 2					
Jas. Weathers	1	2	4	1	5
John Whitfield	1	1	5	2	2
Daniel Knowlin Sr.	.	1	2	.	.
Jesse Carrel	1	.	.	.	.
Wm. Hewit	1	3	4	.	.
Arnold Mann	1	2	2	2	.
Ebernezer Loyd	1	1	3	.	.
Hannah Wright	1	.	7	2	.
Robt. Allen	1	1	2	.	.
Benjn. Morgan	1	1	4	1	.
Jinnings Tanner	1	2	6	.	.
Charles Champion	1	1	6	.	.
John Champion Jr.	1	.	1	.	.
Binn. (?) Clement	1	.	2	3	2
John Champion Sr.	1	1	1	.	.
Laurence Griffin	1	2	1	.	.
John Huscat Sr.	1	3	1	.	.
John Bailey	1	1	5	1	.
David Bradford	1	1	3	3	.
John Hooker	1	4	2	2	.
Richd. Nance	2	3	4	.	.
Wm. Tanner	1	4	2	.	.
Phillh. Bradford	1	2	2	2	1
Booker Bradford	1	.	.	.	.
Joseph Fullar	1	5	2	.	.
Darvin Harris	1	3	2	.	.
Wm. Buckhannon	1	4	2	.	.
George Taylor	1	2	4	.	.
John Thomas	1	1	1	.	.

Head of Household	WM 21-60 yrs.	WM under 21 & above 60	WF all ages	Blacks 12-50	Blacks under 12 & above 50
Pg. 3					
Williamson Cape	1	3	3	.	.
John Hall	1	2	1	.	.
John Heflin	1	5	7	.	.
Jane Mitchel	.	1	3	.	.
John Holt	2	4	5	.	.
John More	1	1	1	.	.
Rich^d. Bradford	1	1	5	.	.
Joseph Hawley	1	3	2	.	.
Phil. Bradford Sr.	1	1	4	.	.
Wm. Wilkerson	1	3	5	.	.
John Hooker Jr.	1	3	3	.	.
Perry Sandy	1	2	3	.	.
David Bradford	1	.	3	2	1
Champion Allen	1	.	2	.	.
John Huskath Jr.	1	2	2	.	.
William Liles	4	2	4	5	.
Gillam Harris	.	2	1	.	.
Charles Holts	2	.	1	.	.
David Fullar	1	5	4	.	.
Joseph Neal	1	1	5	.	.
George Nicholson	1	2	3	2	.
John Pope Jr.	1	2	2	3	2
Wm. Hendley	2	3	5	.	.
John Hendley	1	.	1	.	.
Robert Goodloe	1	4	2	12	16
John Pope Esq.	1	2	1	2	2
Daniel Knowlin Jr.	.	.	3	.	.
James Heflin	.	3	4	.	.

"A True List Taken by John Poole"

"List of the Number of Inhabitance in Great Allegator 400 Whites, 156 Blacks, 556 Souls by John Poole"

[This page has no names; only figures, and the microfilm is marked "very very poor material". It is faded.] The total figures: 79 129 199 25 31 463

"A List of the Number of Inhabitance in Capt. Benjamin Hassels Company in G---(?)"

[This page is also marked "very very poor material".]

WARREN COUNTY

A List of the number of Souls in Capt. White's District.

Pg. 1

Head of Household	WM 21-60 yrs.	WM under 21 & above 60	WF all ages	Blacks 12-50	Blacks under 12 & above 50	Total
Wm. Johnson, Esq.	1	1	2	16	16	36
Phil Johnson	1	3	4	.	.	8
John Haithcock	1	4	5	1	2	13
John Tanner	.	4	1	7	4	16
John Childres	2	.	2	.	.	4
Thos. Davis	1	4	2	.	.	7
Mary Duke	.	4	4	2	2	12
Frances Smith	1	.	1	.	.	2
John Maddrey	1	2	1	.	.	4
Nimrod Williams	1	2	4	5	3	15
Lewis Williams	1	1	3	.	1	6
Benjn. Kelley	1	1	1	.	1	4
John Williams	1	5	2	.	.	8
Thos. Christamas	1	3	5	10	8	27
Wm. Allen	1	2	.	1	1	5
Moses Parks	.	1	4	36	24	65
Obed. Green	1	1	3	4	4	13
Wm. Duke	.	2	1	26	21	50
John Green	1	.	.	1	.	2
	18	39	55	80	67	269

Pg. 2

Head of Household	WM 21-60 yrs.	WM under 21 & above 60	WF all ages	Blacks 12-50	Blacks under 12 & above 50	Total
John Scott	1	1	4	2	3	11
Wm. Cammell	1	.	1	1	1	4
Andrew Armstrong	1	.	.	.	.	1
John Sales	1	2	3	.	.	6
Thos. Sales	.	2	4	.	.	6
John Mary Salley	1	1	1	.	1	4
Joseph Green	1	2	1	1	.	5
John Berey	1	1	.	2	.	4
Wm. Person	2	2	2	8	8	22
	9	11	16	14	13	62
	68	130	176	163	142	683

Pg. 3

Head of Household	WM 21-60 yrs.	WM under 21 & above 60	WF all ages	Blacks 12-50	Blacks under 12 & above 50	Total
Darling Maddrey	1	1	3	.	.	5
Wm. Guin	1	2	2	.	.	5
Theophelus Willofred	1	.	.	.	.	1
Jessey Beckam	1	2	3	1	2	9
Wm. Wortham	1	7	3	9	5	25
Edmund Green	1	.	1	1	5	8
Nickles Powell	1	.	1	.	.	2
Thos. Green	1	4	2	1	.	8
James Pitts	1	1	1	.	.	3
James Stiles	.	1	2	.	.	3

Head of Household	WM 21-60 yrs.	WM under 21 & above 60	WF all ages	Blacks 12-50	Blacks under 12 & above 50	Total
Richard Maddrey	1	.	1	1	1	4
Calep Caps	1	4	4	.	.	9
Mathew Duke	1	4	1	2	2	10
John Duke	1	3	7	4	5	20
Reubin Weathers	2	1	4	.	.	7
James Bennet	1	3	3	.	1	8
Wm. Twittey	1	.	.	.	.	1
Wm. Johnson	1	.	3	9	3	16
MDuke [Marmaduke] Johnson	1	2	2	12	11	28
Benjamin McInvail	1	.	1	.	.	2
James Roberson	1	1	1	.	.	3
William Thomas	1	1	4	.	.	6
	22	37	49	40	35	183

Pg. 4

Head of Household	WM 21-60 yrs.	WM under 21 & above 60	WF all ages	Blacks 12-50	Blacks under 12 & above 50	Total
John Lankford	1	.	.	.	.	1
Thos. Clerk	1	3	3	.	.	7
Richd. Thomas	1	1	1	.	.	3
John Emerson	1	4	5	3	2	15
Lenard Jones	1	3	6	1	.	11
Wm. Roberds	1	5	3	.	.	9
Charles White	1	2	3	.	.	6
Wm. Robins	1	.	3	1	1	6
John Laughter	1	1	5	2	.	9
Wm. Duke Jr.	1	2	3	.	1	7
Archd. Brown	1	1	3	.	.	5
John Kicker	1	1	8	.	.	10
John Davis	1	3	2	.	.	6
Mathew Davis	1	3	2	2	3	11
John Hackney	1	3	6	.	.	10
Wm. Beckam	1	.	1	.	.	2
James Grigory	1	2	1	.	.	4
John Mary Salley	1	1	1	.	.	3
Lewis Bobbitt	1	5	4	1	.	11
Miles Bobbitt	2	2	6	.	.	10
	19	43	56	29	27	174

"A List of inhabitants in Capt. Twilley's District."

Pg. 1

Head of Household	WM 21-60 yrs.	WM under 21 & above 60	WF all ages	Blacks 12-50	Blacks under 12 & above 50	Total
William E. Johnston	2	2	2	17	19	42
Wyatt Hawkins	1	3	2	6	4	16
Joshua Mabry	1	4	2	3	8	18
David Moss	1	6	5	5	8	25
Thos. Wilson	5	1	1	.	.	7
George Twitty	1	1	3	1	1	7
Rawleigh Hammond	1	1	2	1	1	6

Head of Household	WM 21-60 yrs.	WM under 21 & above 60	WF all ages	Blacks 12-50	Blacks under 12 & above 50	Total
Phil Hawkins	1	.	3	4	5	13
Salley Caller	.	1	3	5	5	14
Mary Puckett	.	.	2	.	1	3
Phil Hilliard	1	2	2	2	.	7
Ann Rose	.	2	6	.	.	8
Jno. Cole	1	1	2	.	.	4
Wm. Ellington	1	3	2	.	.	6
Henry Tucker	1	5	2	.	.	8
Jas. Ellington	1	2	2	1	1	7
Edwd. Tanner	1	1	3	.	.	5
Abm. Mayfield	.	2	4	10	12	28
Wm. Fann	1	.	2	.	.	3
Mary Fann	.	.	5	2	1	8
Jno. Long	1	1	6	1	.	9
Wm. Scott	.	.	.	1	.	1
Jno. Mayfield	1	3	4	1	.	9
Pg. 2						
Thos. Mayfield	.	3	3	.	.	6
Jno. Tucker	1	4	4	6	4	19
Wm. Wood	1	4	7	.	.	12
Judy Lankford	1	2	1	.	.	4
Robt. Caller	1	3	5	14	13	36
Wm. Darnold	1	.	.	.	.	1
Jno. Paschal	1	2	1	.	.	4
Robt. Paschal	.	1	.	.	.	1
Rd. Proctor	1	.	2	1	1	5
Jas. Bartlet	1	2	1	.	.	4
B. Hartgrove	1	.	.	.	.	1
Thos. Paschall	1	5	4	2	.	12
Ann Fane	.	3	2	.	.	5
Wm. Cuningham	1	1	2	.	.	4
Jno. Coleman	2	.	3	.	.	5
John Pennix	1	2	6	.	.	9
Edwd. Sims	.	1	1	2	4	8
Elisha Towns	1	.	.	.	.	1
Joshua Rivers	1	2	3	.	.	6
Jno. Corthron	1	.	.	2	8	11
	42	97	102	75	93	
Totals	84	185	232	164		780

By, Dixon Marshal

Next list is by Theod. Webb, J. P. and has no names; only figures

"A List of the number of Inhabitants in Capt. Moses District.

	WM 21-60 yrs.	WM under 21 & above 60	WF all ages	Blacks 12-50	Blacks under 12 & above 50	Total
Pg. 1						
Peter Jones	1	.	.	6	1	7
John Pope	1	2	6	.	.	9

Head of Household	WM 21-60 yrs.	WM under 21 & above 60	WF all ages	Blacks 12-50	Blacks under 12 & above 50	Total
Moses Shearin	1	3	2	1	1	8
Fredrick Talley	1	3	3	2	.	9
William Thompson	1	1	3	.	.	5
William Ellis Jr.	1	1	2	.	.	4
Samuel Keel	1	.	5	.	.	6
Charles Hicks	1	.	4	2	.	7
William Cole	1	3	1	.	1	6
John Hastings	1	3	2	1	2	9
Benjamin Jones	1	3	3	2	3	12
Thomas Adams	1	2	1	2	2	8
Ludson Worsham	1	3	3	6	4	17
George Rayborne	1	2	1	.	.	4
John Shearin Sr.	.	2	.	4	7	13
Randolph Sturdivant	1	.	4	2	2	9
Samuel Walker	2	3	2	.	1	8
[name torn off]			4		5	6 17
Pg. 2						
[name torn off]	2	4	.	.	.	6
Benjamin Ellis	1	4	3	2	.	10
Henry Sturdivant	1	2	5	3	6	17
Matthew Sturdevant	.	1	1	.	.	2
Henry Dickins	1	4	5	.	.	10
John Ellis Sr.	.	1	4	.	.	5
Absalum Bennett	1	1	5	.	.	7
Jonathan Wood	2	.	4	.	1	7
Mary Dent	.	.	4	2	3	9
Elisabeth Mulone	.	.	2	.	2	4
Benjamin Duke	1	5	8	3	2	19
Peter Coleman	2	4	4	2	2	14
Henry Watson	1	6	3	1	.	11
Owen Ballard	.	1	2	.	.	3
John King Rosser	1	2	9	.	.	12
Jesse Fann	1	4	6	.	.	11
John Hicks Jr.	2	4	3	1	.	10
James Hicks	1	1	2	.	.	4
John Hicks Sr.	.	2	3	.	.	5
Daniel Tommas	.	4	4	.	.	8
Ephraim Ellis	1	2	4	1	1	9
William Brintle	1	3	3	.	.	7
Abraham (torn)						7
John Patterso(n)	1	2				
Dudley Ballard	1	.	3	.	.	4
John Fann	1	2	7	2	4	16
John Ellis Jr.	1	3	5	1	3	13
Susannah Ellis	.	.	1	.	.	1
Hailey Talley	1	2	2	.	.	5
William Hansell	.	5	2	.	.	7
Simon Duke	1	3	6	1	.	11
Alexander Nicols	1	2	3	.	.	6

Head of Household	WM 21-60 yrs.	WM under 21 & above 60	WF all ages	Blacks 12-50	Blacks under 12 & above 50	Total
Hicks Ellis	1	1	1	.	.	3
Richard Talley	1	3	4	1	2	11
Isaac Marshall	1	.	1	.	.	2
Margret Shearin	.	1	4	2	5	12
William Foot	.	1	1	1	2	5
Joseph Garriott	1	1	2	.	.	4
Starling Talley	1	.	.	.	.	1
David Tommas	1	.	.	.	.	1
William Duke	1	2	3	.	.	6
Elisabeth Murphe	.	1	2	2	2	7
Jemimah Robbertson	.	1	4	.	.	5
						191
Wilmoth Partrick	1	2	1	1	1	6
Richard Towns	1	4	5	.	.	10
[name torn off]				.	.	5
Pg. 3						
James Towns	2	.	[blur]			
William Russell	1	1	4	2	2	10
William Ellis Sr.	2	3	6	1	.	12
George Allen Sr.	2	1	5	1	.	9
Jesse Wright	1	1	2	.	.	4
Jonathan Solmon	1	1	3	.	.	5
Jesse Ellis	1	2	5	.	.	8
David King Sr.	.	1	4	.	.	5
Wiatt Ballard	1	.	3	.	.	4
William Ballard	1	4	3	.	.	8
Catherine Ballard	.	.	2	.	.	2
Henry Glover	2	4	4	.	.	10
John Towns	1	2	1	.	.	4
John Pettway	2	4	7	7	5	25
						155
Anthony Beard	1	3	5	.	.	9
George Harrison	1	.	4	1	2	8
Abner Powell	1	.	4	.	.	5
Richard Marshall	1	3	4	4	5	17
Hugh Johnston	1	.	.	9	7	17
Wood King	2	2	2	.	1	7
Anthony King	1	1	2	1	.	5
Mournin Ballard	1	.	1	.	.	2
Cudbeth King	1	2	3	.	.	5
Dwelley Darnal	1	2	4	.	.	7
Joseph Renn	1	1	3	.	.	5
Sarah Ballard	.	2	2	.	.	4
David Towns	1	1	6	2	3	13
John Pitts Beasley	2	6	3	5	4	20
James White	1	6	4	6	3	20
Joseph Jeffress	1	4	3	.	.	8
Thomas Ivans	.	5	3	.	.	8
William Cavender	.	1	.	4	3	8
817	**91**	**207**	**313**	**105**	**101**	**168**

Head of Household	WM 21-60 yrs.	WM under 21 & above 60	WF all ages	Blacks 12-50	Blacks under 12 & above 50
Capt. Ward's District.					
Pg. 1					
Edwd. Jones	1	4	4	10	13
Ben. Ward Esq.	1	3	4	3	7
Capt. Ben. Ward	1	.	.	2	1
Hardy Smith	1	1	2	.	.
Sugan Jones	.	2	1	1	.
Abraham Smith	1	2	3	.	.
Roger Cragge	1	1	2	.	.
George Cuningham	1	1	3	.	.
Gemima Crissick	.	.	1	.	.
Jas. Miller or Miles	2	1	5	3	2
James Alston	2	2	2	15	12
John Easter	1	5	3	1	.
George Torrence	1	1	.	1	.
Abigail High	.	.	3	1	1
Thomas Cook	1	3	6	11	12
G. H. Macon	2	3	4	6	5
James Martin	.	1	1	.	.
Hezekiah Massy	1	1	2	.	.
William Elliott	.	5	4	6	.
James Cannon	1	4	8	.	.
Nathl. Mason	1	.	2	8	4
Jesse Beckham	1	2	3	1	2
John Hawkins	2	6	6	25	9
Robt. Childers	1	.	5	.	.
Isaac Hunter	2	2	4	14	14
Wm. Weldon	1	3	2	.	.
John Lanier	1	2	3	3	4
Joshua Perry	1	2	4	11	10
John Sanders	1	3	4	1	1
James Ransom	1	1	4	10	13
Joseph Ward	1	.	4	.	2
Barriman Bilbro	1	.	3	2	2
	33	61	98	138	113
Pg. 2					
Spence Waddey	1	2	6	1	.
Joseph Lonsford	1	2	4	.	.
Sollomon Williams	1	2	2	30	30
William Green	1	3	7	21	22
Daniel Barrow	2	.	.	5	4
Sarah Martin	1	4	5	6	6
Wm. Myrick	2	4	3	15	10
James Johnson	2	3	4	14	13
Nathl. Macon for Henry Lyne	.	.	.	7	16
Wm. Williams	1	.	1	17	11
Phil. Kerney	1	3	6	40	40

STATE CENSUS OF NORTH CAROLINA 1784–1787

Head of Household	WM 21–60 yrs.	WM under 21 & above 60	WF all ages	Blacks 12–50	Blacks under 12 & above 50	Total
Henry Montfortt	2	.	2	42		55
Rubin Smith	1	1	3	.	.	.
Benjn. Johnson	2	3	7	10		16
Benjn. McColloch for the Estate of G. Sumner, dec'd	.	.	.	10		5
William Plummer	2	.	.	6		1
William Walker	1	4	4	.	.	
Richard Ward	1	3	3	3		3
Elizebeth Night	.	.	2	.	.	
Ralph McGee	1	1	4	.	.	
John Smart	1	4	2	.	.	
George Harper	1	2	4	.	.	
Peter Cox	2	2	2	8		9
	27	43	71	241		240
	33	61	98	138		113
Total	60	104	169	379		353

Taken by Edwd. Jones

Capt. Colclough's District
Pg. 1

Head of Household	WM 21–60 yrs.	WM under 21 & above 60	WF all ages	Blacks 12–50	Blacks under 12 & above 50	Total
William Vasser	1	3	3	1	.	8
James Milam	1	2	5	1	.	9
Jere Bush	1	2	6	2	4	15
Geo. Pegram	1	3	5	.	.	9
John Thompson	2	1	3	1	2	9
Jacob Riggan	2	2	3	.	.	7
Wm. N. Norsworthy	1	5	3	2	1	12
Gideon Pegram	1	.	1	.	.	2
Danl. Pegram	1	3	3	1	.	8
John Harton	1	.	2	.	.	3
John Wright	2	4	5	2	.	13
Casabeth (Cajebeth?) White			2	[blurred]		12
Richard Jones	1	2	7	.	.	10
Cader Powell	1	2	1	.	.	4
William Noles	1	4	3	1	2	11
Nathl. Baxter	1	4	3	5	2	15
John Balthrop	1	2	1	1	.	5
Peter Jackson	1	1	1	.	.	3
John Coleman	1	3	4	1	1	10
James Mitchell	1	1	4	.	4	10
Edwd. Coleman	1	.	1	.	.	2
John Riggan	1	3	4	.	.	8
William Smith	.	3	3	.	.	6
John Colclough	1	3	6	2	4	16
Danl. Willson	1	4	3	1	1	10
Thomas Bell	1	.	2	.	.	3
Mary Bell	.	3	4	.	.	7
Joel Riggan	1	.	2	.	.	3
Ross Brewer	1	3	5	2	7	18

[one name lost off bottom prior page]

Pg. 2

Head of Household	WM 21–60 yrs.	WM under 21 & above 60	WF all ages	Blacks 12–50	Blacks under 12 & above 50	Total
Willm. Willson Sr.	.	1	2	5	2	10
Saml. Crutchfield	1	3	3	.	.	7
William Owen	2	1	2	.	.	5
Willm. Balthrop	1	2	6	2	2	13
Patty Short	1	3	5	.	.	9
John Liddle	1	1	1	1	1	5
James Thompson	1	1	1	2	4	9
Isaac Acree Jr.	1	1	1	.	1	4
John Mosely Jr.	1	2	2	1	.	6
William Acree	1	2	7	.	.	10
Mary Miller	.	.	2	6	1	9
Isaac Acree	1	2	3	1	1	8
Lydia Mitchell	.	1	2	.	.	3
Rebh. Merritt	.	.	3	.	.	3
James Paine	1	2	7	9	11	30
Howell Horton	2	2	4	.	.	8
John Rodwell	1	5	2	1	.	9

Pg. 3

Head of Household	WM 21–60 yrs.	WM under 21 & above 60	WF all ages	Blacks 12–50	Blacks under 12 & above 50	Total
Law Noles	1	2	3	.	.	6
Jesse Bell	1	5	5	.	.	11
John Brown	1	5	5	1	6	18
John Renn	1	.	3	.	.	4
Wm. Durham	.	1	.	2	1	4
Wm. Durham Jr.	1	4	5	1	.	11
John Durham	1	1	6	1	.	9
Thomas Dudly	1	.	.	.	.	1
John Baxter	1	5	4	.	1	11
Thos. Read	1	4	5	.	.	10
Mattw. Myrick	1	1	3	3	3	11
James Myrick	1	2	4	3	4	14
John Willson	1	2	4	2	2	11
Judah Radsdale	.	1	5	.	.	6
Adam Milam	1	1	2	3	1	8
Solon. Jackson	1	1	2	.	.	4
						299
John Mosely	1	.	1	5	5	12
John Badget	1	.	.	.	.	1
Jesse Mosely	1	.	2	7	5	15
Mary Colclough	1	1	3	5	10	20
John Jackson	1	.	.	.	.	1
Joseph Hudson	1	1	2	.	.	4
James Hudson	.	3	2	.	.	5
John Milam	1	2	1	.	.	4
Will Shearin	2	5	6	6	7	26
Thos. Hall	1	4	2	3	1	11

Head of Household	WM 21-60 yrs.	WM under 21 & above 60	WF all ages	Blacks 12-50	Blacks under 12 & above 50	Total
Fredk. Hawks	1	5	3	.	.	9
Edwd. Durham	1	2	7	.	.	10
Augt. Balthrop	1	3	7	12	14	37
Robt. Waller	1	.	2	1	2	6
Ann Ray	.	.	3	6	5	15
Thos. Miller	1	5	1	9	13	29
Thos. Harton	.	3	3	1	.	7
Tho. Gardner	1	1	5	4	3	14
Gideon Christian	1	2	3	5	4	15
Will Rainwater	1	2	4	.	.	7
						247
Pg. 4						
Francis Thornton	.					
John Maye	1	2	3	.	.	6
Saml. Carpenter	1	3	9	1	1	15
Lewis Milam	1	.	6	.	.	7
Rowland Milam	1	2	1	.	.	4
Robt. Jones	1	3	5	.	.	9
Amey Bell	.	2	6			
William Price	1	1	3			
	91	80	307	130	150	

By, Thomas Miller

Names of the Master &c of Families in Capt. William St. John's District.

Pg. 1	WM 21-60 yrs.	WM under 21 & above 60	WF all ages	Blacks 12-50	Blacks under 12 & above 50
Coln. Philemon Hawkins	.	1	1	31	24
Daniel Vaulx	1	1	3	7	7
Reubin Huff (O. [overseer] for Gunn)	1	3	1	4	.
Charles Allen Jr. Overseer for Merritt	1	2	1	6	.
Stephen Beckham	1	4	3	.	.
Simon Beckham	1	3	1	.	.
Elizabeth Baskett, widow	.	1	1	1	1
William Neal	1	.	2	.	.
James Beckham	1	2	2	.	.
Robert Williams	1	2	2	.	.
William Pardue	3	2	5	2	.
Patram Pardue	1	2	1	.	.
William Duty	1	3	5	.	.
Phileson Howell	1	.	1	.	.
Naomah(?) Beckham	.	3	4	.	.
Samuel Davis	1	1	2	5	7
William Gray	1	4	3	.	.
William Turner	1	2	2	3	.
Martin Dye	1	4	2	4	6
Thomas Swinny	1	.	6	.	.

Head of Household	WM 21-60 yrs.	WM under 21 & above 60	WF all ages	Blacks 12-50	Blacks under 12 & above 50
William Clerk	.	3	3	.	.
John Dinkins	1	4	5	5	5
Majr. Charles Allen	2	3	6	3	3
Charles Regan	.	2	6	2	2
James Baskett	1	5	4	2	2
Capt. Wm. St. John	1	.	.	5	.
Thomas Midleton (overseer) for Col. Blunt	1	1	3	6	4
Margret Sertain, W.	1	1	2	1	3
Peter Kimbell	1	2	2	.	.
James Bailey	2	.	5	.	.
Pg. 2					
Samuel Smith	1	3	2	.	.
Patrick McBoyd	1	2	2	.	.
Daniel Smith	1	.	2	.	.
Nancy Mitchell	.	3	4	.	.
John Bowdon	2	.	9	4	5
Joseph Darnall	1	1	7	2	5
James Walker	1	5	2	.	.
William Cauthron	1	1	1	.	.
James Cauthron	1	.	3	.	.
Elizabeth Jarrett, W.	.	3	4	.	.
Capt. John White	1	3	3	.	5
Thomas Key	1	4	3	.	.
James Harrison	1	2	3	.	.
John Haynes	1	1	3	.	.
John Wortham	1	3	2	7	8
Tabitha Marshll	.	3	2	11	5
George Smith	1	1	3	1	.
Mrs. Bowden, wid.	.	1	1	.	.
Green Duke	1	2	7	14	14
Jonan. Davis	1	5	2	7	9
	46	106	150	138	117

A List of the Inhabitants in Capt. Aaron Fussell's District.

Pg. 1	WM 21-60 yrs.	WM under 21 & above 60	WF all ages	Blacks 12-50	Blacks under 12 & above 50
Young McLemore	1	.	2	7	9
Elizabeth Ballard	1	4	2	.	2
Philip Beckham	1	1	4	1	.
Luck Kee	1	3	5	.	.
Mary Morrice	1	3	5	3	6
Reuben Bennett	2	2	2	.	.
Solomon Arnold	1	2	2	.	.
John Clark	1	4	3	.	.
Christopher Robertson	.	1	1	6	9
Charles Drury	1	3	2	.	.
Alexander Fowler	1	2	1	.	.

STATE CENSUS OF NORTH CAROLINA 1784–1787

Head of Household	WM 21-60 yrs.	WM under 21 & above 60	WF all ages	Blacks 12-50	Blacks under 12 & above 50
Daniel Ball Sr.	3	1	1	.	1
Benjamin Beckham	1	1	.	.	.
David Kimball	1	2	1	.	1
John Nicholson	1	3	8	3	1
Benjamin Jackson	1	1	2	.	2
Joseph Pardue	1	4	5	.	1
Thomas Thorn	1	1	7	1	1
William Clements	1	.	1	7	4
Isham Robertson	1	1	3	3	4
Daniel Ball Jr.	1	1	2	3	2
Pg. 2					
Seth Williams	1	.	4	3	2
James House	3	4	3	3	4
Emanuel Forkner	1	3	3	.	.
William Bagley	1	2	2	5	10
Wm. House, Gent.	1	4	4	6	7
Thomas Norman	1	2	3	.	1
Isrom Cogwell	1	3	4	.	.
James Cogwell	1	.	2	.	.
Amelia Peebles	.	2	1	2	2
Marcellas Jordan	2	3	3	8	8
John Allen	1	2	4	2	2
Thomas Jenkins	1	3	3	2	2
William Beckham	1	2	5	.	.
William Clark	1	1	5	.	.
John Forkner	1	3	3	.	.
James Ball	1	1	3	.	.
Joseph Merritt	.	3	5	.	.
James Merritt	1	3	5	.	.
Britain Duke	2	2	4	4	3
James Arnold	1	1	7	.	.
Samuel Duke	8	.	2	.	.
Burwell Duke	1	5	6	2	.
Pg. 3					
Harrell Duke	1	1	3	.	.
Benjamin Kimball	2	2	3	4	7
James Kimball	1	2	1	2	1
William Garritt	1	4	2	.	.
Jesse Jenkins	1	2	6	3	5
William Howell	1	5	4	.	.
Moses Forkner	1	1	2	.	.
Aaron Fussell	1	2	2	3	4
Atkins McLemore	1	3	3	13	9
Thomas Garritt	1	4	6	.	.
James Gray	1	1	4	17	11
Sterling Duke	1	3	3	.	.
William Cowper	1	5	3	.	.
James Gray (for Sumner Estate)	.	.	.	6	6

Head of Household	WM 21-60 yrs.	WM under 21 & above 60	WF all ages	Blacks 12-50	Blacks under 12 & above 50
Matthew Garritt	1	2	7	.	.
Brewer Rieves	1	.	3	.	.
Joseph Mangum	1	5	4	.	.
Griffin Dickerson	1	4	6	.	.
	45	136	205	127	136
	28	41	60	44	53
	73	177	265	171	189

March 15, 1786

p[per] J. Gray, Secy.

List of Capt. Clanton's District Taken by Jo. Moseley

Pg. 1	WM 21-60 yrs.	WM under 21 & above 60	WF all ages	Blacks 12-50	Blacks under 12 & above 50
Joseph Shearin	.	7	3	8	10
Federick Shearin	1	.	1	.	.
Austin Pattillo	2	2	4	4	4
Burwell Robinson	2	2	5	7	10
Howel Tayler	1	.	1	4	5
Thos. Carrell	1	3	5	3	4
Nancey Shadburn	.	1	1	.	.
James Moseley	1	1	1	.	1
Stephen Shell	1	3	5	6	5
Thos. Eaton Esqr. p[per] G. Carter	.	3	3	9	5
Hannah Hall	.	2	2	.	.
John Mabrey	1	2	4	5	7
Thos. Meadows	1	2	4	.	.
William Wilson Jr.	1	4	5	5	4
Robt. Wall	1	3	2	.	.
George Webb	1	3	6	.	4
James Nichols	1	2	.	5	9
Nathaniel Nichols	1	3	3	4	6
Urbana Nichols	1	1	2	1	2
Benja. Mabrey	1	1	4	.	.
Sarah Pickrell	2	.	4	.	.
James Walker	1	1	2	.	.
Archabell Nichols	1	.	5	.	1
John Williams	1	1	2	.	.
Allen Williams	1	.	3	1	4
Samuel Willeford	1	3	6	.	.
Newet Harris	1	3	5	.	.
Lewis Shearin	1	.	.	.	1
Delk Mabrey	1	1	5	1	.
William Myrick	1	3	4	1	.
Sterling Shearin	1	.	.	.	.
John White	1	5	2	6	6
John Crenshaw	.	4	2	2	2
Thos. Merritt	2	.	2	.	.
John Merritt	.	1	2	.	.
William Tolson	1	2	5	.	.

STATE CENSUS OF NORTH CAROLINA 1784-1787

Head of Household	WM 21-60 yrs.	WM under 21 & above 60	WF all ages	Blacks 12-50	Blacks under 12 & above 50	Total
Stephen Shell Jr.	1	3	3	1	2	
Wm. Collensworth	1	1	4	.	.	
Mathew Myrick	.	.	.	11	12	
Mark Moor	2	.	.	2	3	
	38	70	114	71	94	
Pg. 2						
George Wray	1	4	3	.	.	
William Wray	.	1	.	.	.	
Baker Wray	.	1	.	.	.	
William Storey	1	.	2	.	.	
William Price	1	1	1	.	.	
Ezekial Blanch	1	1	1	.	.	
Benjª. Bradley	1	1	3	6	2	
Dinatious Sherry	.	.	1	.	.	
Hannah Little	.	3	3	.	.	
Moses Myrick	1	3	2	12	12	
Isam Sledge	1	2	1	3	2	
William Clanton	1	4	2	13	7	
Mary Jones	.	1	3	.	.	
Isam Shearin	1	1	1	.	.	
James Cheatom	1	3	1	3	4	
Thomas Eaton	1	2	3	38	40	
Herbert Haynes in Halifax & Warren	10	6	14	48	32	
	22	35	46	123	99	
	38	70	114	71	94	
Total	60	105	160	194	193	

A List of Souls in Capt. John Weather's District, taken by James Kearny.

Head of Household	WM 21-60 yrs.	WM under 21 & above 60	WF all ages	Blacks 12-50	Blacks under 12 & above 50	Total
Pg. 1						
Thos. Blanchett Sr.	.	5	5	.	.	10
Thos. Blanchett Jr.	1	1	1	4	3	10
William Alston	1	8	1	45	32	87
Wm. Alston for Samˡ. Alston	1	.	.	9	14	24
Sherod Walker	1	2	3	.	.	6
Henry Alston	1	2	2	17	14	36
Isham Hawkins	1	3	3	1	3	11
Hezeciah Brewer	1	1	5	.	.	7
William Powell	1	3	4	13	8	29
Wm. Sanders	1	3	4	.	.	8
Charles Marshel	1	6	1	.	.	8
Mat. Goodrich	1	1	3	.	.	5
John Tucker	1	2	4	.	.	7
Gilbert Ward	1	.	1	.	.	2
Dev. Ballord	1	1	2	3	5	12
Jas. Arrington	1	4	4	2	4	15
Samˡ. Marshel	1	5	6	.	.	12

Head of Household	WM 21-60 yrs.	WM under 21 & above 60	WF all ages	Blacks 12-50	Blacks under 12 & above 50	Total
Stephen Marshel	1	2	5	3	.	11
Joel Harriss	1	5	2	2	.	10
John Hulm	1	5	1	.	.	7
Amos Harriss	1	3	5	.	.	9
Moses Harriss	2	3	5	4	.	14
James Evans	1	3	3	.	.	7
Joseph Cooke	1	1	1	8	3	14
	25	69	72	121	86	368
Pg. 2						
Ann Prson (Person)	1	2	2	1	.	6
Samuel Person	1	.	.	1	2	
John Tomson	1	1	1	2	.	4
Wm. Yarbough	.	4	5	5	4	18
Isham Bennet	1	1	3	.	.	5
Phillemon Wood	1	.	5	1	1	8
Thos. Turner	3	1	1	19	26	50
John Radford	1	3	2	.	.	6
Mysel Wood	1	1	1	.	1	4
Lewis Warlhite(?)						
Isack James	1	2	3	3	.	9
Wm. Brinkley Counted (sic)			1	1	2	
Jerremyah Brown	.	2	2	.	.	4
Samuel Williams	1	.	.	13	5	19
Abigail Brown	1	2	4	12	6	25
Thomas Walston	1	.	.	18	2	21
Wm. Dannel	1	5	2	.	.	8
Philip Gallston	1	1	1	12	12	27
Francis Wilks	1	.	.	.	.	1
Joel Rivers	2	2	4	4	6	18
Elias Blackbun	1	.	1	6	6	14
	21	28	37	99	74	257
Pg. 3						
William Cooper	.	2	1	.	.	4
David Sares for Jos. John William	.	.	.	5	15	20
David Sares	1	1	4	2	.	8
Patty Bentt	.	1	2	1	.	4
James Kearny	1	.	.	4	.	5
Edmund Keary	1	.	1	7	8	17
Frances Capps	.	2	1	1	.	4
Joseph Foog (Fogg)	1	.	.	1	2	4
Henry Hudson	2	1	6	4	2	13
Wm. Cheek	.	2	2	7	11	22
James Ellums	1	.	1	.	1	3
John Cooper	1	3	3	.	.	7
Jacob Cooper	1	2	2	1	1	7
Samˡ. Morriss	1	1	5	1	1	9
Moses Neall	1	.	1	.	.	2

Head of Household	WM 21-60 yrs.	WM under 21 & above 60	WF all ages	Blacks 12-50	Blacks under 12 & above 50	Total
Jeremiah Neall	.	1	1	.	.	2
Aaron Neall	1	1	2	.	.	4
Serling Harvill	1	1	5	6	4	17
Buckner Abernatha	1	.	1	.	1	3
James Sledge	2	4	2	5	3	16
Daniel Sledge	2	1	4	8	9	24
John Smith	1	3	4	2	1	11
Jesse Person	1	4	3	5	3	16
Wm. Hogwood	1	.	1	.	.	2
Richard Bennitt	1	4	6	.	.	11
James Duling	1	2	8	.	.	11
Joshua Caps	1	2	3	.	.	6
John Capps	1	4	4	1	1	11
Orasha Caps	1	4	4	.	.	9
	26	46	77	61	64	274
Pg. 4						
James Upcurch	1	1	2	.	1	5
James Merrett	1	5	6	.	.	12
George Betty	1	6	1	.	.	8
Henry Jackson	1	6	4	1	2	14
John Sensing	1	.	1	.	.	2
Richard Acok	1	2	2	.	.	5
Mary Gardner	.	3	2	.	.	5
Peter Randolph	2	3	7	2	2	16
Henry Blanchett	1	.	.	.	.	1
Josiah Green	1	2	2	3	2	10
Hon^s. Powell	1	2	1	1	2	7
Lucy Goodrik	.	.	2	.	.	2
Abner Acock	1	2	3	1	.	7
John Acock	1	4	3	1	.	9
Randolph Cheek	1	.	1	1	1	4
Peter Davis	2	4	4	3	.	13
Peter Sensing	1	4	4	.	.	9
Fedrick Threet	1	.	3	.	.	4
Henry Capps	1	1	3	.	.	5
CP. John Weathers	1	.	.	2	1	4
Charles Pricheet	1	.	2	.	.	3
John Cheek	1	1	3	3	.	8
James Sensing	1	.	2	.	.	3
Charles Sensing	1	3	5	.	.	9
Wm. Maddrey	1	5	1	1	2	10
Jos. Mayfield	1	1	5	5	1	13
	26	57	69	25	14	109

Head of Household	WM 21-60 yrs.	WM under 21 & above 60	WF all ages	Blacks 12-50	Blacks under 12 & above 50	Total
Billy Williams	1	.	2	.	.	3
Thomas Judkins	1	.	.	2	.	3
Lawrance Lancaster Sr.	.	1	.	4	6	11
Lawrence Lancaster Jr	1	1	2	.	.	4
John Lancaster	1	2	2	.	.	5
Spell Kimball	1	3	1	2	.	7
Leon^d. Kimball	4	3	2	.	1	7
Simon Harris	1	.	.	.	.	1
John Faulcon	1	2	2	22	43	70
Warwick Haselwood	1	.	1	.	.	2
John Lancaster	.	2	5	1	.	8
Mathew Harris	2	1	3	5	3	14
Joel Lancaster	1	4	4	.	.	9
Robert Crocker	1	.	1	.	.	2
Eden Coleman	1	.	.	.	.	1
Edwin Harris	1	2	3	.	.	6
Michall Harris	.	3	3	1	.	7
Isham Meadows	1	10	5	.	.	16
Unity Coleman	.	2	3	4	6	15
Claborn Harris	1	1	2	2	1	7
John Coleman	1	.	1	1	.	3
Moses Lancaster	1	1	4	.	.	6
Jordan Harris	1	1	6	1	2	11
Robert Harris	1	.	.	.	.	1
Joseph Harris	.	2	6	1	.	9
Howard Harris	1	.	2	.	.	3
Edmond Harris	1	3	5	.	.	9
	25	47	72	42	73	188
Pg. 2						
Edward Ellis	1	2	5	.	.	8
William Roberson	1	5	1	3	.	10
William Dent	1	1	2	.	.	4
Bedford Harris	1	.	.	.	.	1
Rachell Harriss	.	1	4	4	4	13
Benjamin Williams	1	2	1	.	1	5
Federick Harris	1	.	.	.	.	1
Rowland Felts	1	1	2	1	.	5
Steven Bobbit	1	4	2	3	1	11
Isham Felts	1	.	1	.	.	2
James Mealer	1	1	1	1	1	5
Nathl. Felts	1	3	2	.	.	6
Randolph Felts	1	1	3	.	.	5
James Harris Sr.	1	.	1	5	7	14
James Harris Jr.	1	.	1	2	2	6
Henry Clarke	1	1	5	.	.	7
Josiah Womble	1	.	3	.	.	4
Wilmot Egerton	1	4	3	1	.	9
Martha Egerton	1	4	4	1	1	11
Saml. Taylor	1	1	4	.	.	6

"A List of the Number of Souls in Capt. Jordan Harris's District, taken by Nathl. Harris, Feb. 1786.

Pg. 1						
Nathl. Harris	1	2	4	5	5	17
Sterling Harris	1	1	3	1	3	9

Head of Household	WM 21–60 yrs.	WM under 21 & above 60	WF all ages	Blacks 12–50	Blacks under 12 & above 50	Total
Saml. Coleman	.	2	1	3	1	7
James Darden	1	5	3	5	4	18
Randolph Hazelwood	.	1	1	6	6	14
John Bartholomew	1	2	2	.	.	5
James Harris	1	1	2	.	.	4
George Hazelwood	1	2	2	.	.	5
Charles Bartholomew	.	3	5	.	.	8
Peter Roberson	1	1	3	1	2	8
Richard Moss	1	3	3	2	.	9
Wilkim Moss	1	2	2	.	.	5
William Nowell	1	.	.	.	.	1
	29	52	63	38	30	405
Pg. 3						
James Paterson(?)	1	.	.	.	.	1
William Burrow	1	5	4	7	1	17
John Davis	1	4	1	1	.	6
John Felts	1	1	2	.	.	4
Jordan Felts	1	.	.	.	.	1
William Redden	1	3	2	.	.	6
Francis Felts	1	5	3	.	.	9
George Paterson	1	4	3	.	.	8
Edward Pegrom	1	3	2	.	1	7
Abigal Dunisson	.	1	4	.	.	5
Nathan Holloman	1	.	.	.	1	2
Elisabeth Harris	.	2	3	.	.	5
Robert Harris	.	1	.	.	.	1
Saml. Harper	1	5	5	5	5	21
John Harper	1	1	1	.	.	3
William Rowland	1	5	3	2	.	11
John Burch	.	1	1	.	.	2
Isham Paterson	.	1	1	.	.	2
Wm. Coggin	1	.	4	.	.	5
Archur Harris	1	2	3	2	.	8
Isham Lucy	1	5	5	1	4	16
Thos. Dent	1	1	2	.	.	4
Lewis Paterson	1	4	2	.	.	7
Jno. Coggin	1	1	6	.	.	8
Wm. Holoman	1	3	1	1	1	7
Silvanius Merret	1	1	5	.	.	7
Wm. Felts	1	.	.	.	.	1
Jno. Bobbit	1	.	.	.	.	1
Lot Horne	1	.	.	.	.	1
Howard Hollamon	2	.	3	1	1	7
	27	47	62	19	14	509
Pg. 4						
John Jones	1	.	1	9	6	17
Drury Bobbit	2	2	7	3	4	18
John Newell	2	3	4	8	2	19
James Nicholson	1	3	3	2	4	13

Head of Household	WM 21–60 yrs.	WM under 21 & above 60	WF all ages	Blacks 12–50	Blacks under 12 & above 50	Total
Saml. Williams	1	.	2	1	1	5
Dudley Hail	1	.	2	1	3	7
William Pryer	1	2	1	.	.	4
Lewis More	1	3	3	3	1	11
Spencer Snow	1	4	1	2	1	9
Benjamin Kimball	1	1	1	1	1	5
Charles James	2	.	4	3	1	11
John Bobbit	.	2	1	4	3	10
Wm. Bobbit	1	1	1	1	1	5
	15	25	31	32	28	792
An unidentified district						
Pg. 1						
Thos. Buttrell	1	.	1	3	1	6
Jas. Paschal	1	5	5	.	.	11
Rot. Melone	1	.	.	.	.	1
Go. Lankford	1	.	2	.	.	3
B. Raimey	1	4	4	1	1	11
Isham Kendrick	1	2	3	1	.	7
Michal Wood	1	3	3	.	.	7
Henry Wood	1	1	4	.	.	6
L. Richerson	1	1	2	2	.	6
C. Nuckols	1	3	5	.	.	9
Thos. Newman	2	3	4	1	.	10
Phil Burford	1	2	5	12	10	30
Phil Burford Jr.	1	1	2	.	1	5
Saml. Paschal	1	2	3	3	4	13
Drury Jackson	1	5	3	1	1	11
Mary Bell	.	3	6	2	1	12
Chs. Megee	1	1	.	.	.	2
Mary Pinnex or Pennix	.	.	2	1	.	3
Jno. Smith	1	1	3	.	.	5
Thos. Corthron	1	2	5	.	.	8
Dixon Marshal	1	.	3	2	2	8
	42	88	130	89	8-	22-
Pg. 2						
Danl. Burford	1	3	2	3	4	13
Bennett Wood	1	7	1	2	.	11
Reps Mabry	1	1	2	1	3	8
Lewis Patrick	4	3	3	.	.	10
Wm. Mustian	1	4	1	.	.	6
Wm. Sprunt	1	1	3	.	.	5
Jno. Williams	.	1	1	.	.	2
Jno. Watson	1	2	4	.	.	7
D. Vandlandingham	1	5	5	.	.	11
Jas. Corthron	1	.	.	2	8	11
Phil. Kinneman	1	2	3	.	.	6
Lucy Jones	.	.	2	.	.	2
Dancy Standly	1	2	3	1	.	7

STATE CENSUS OF NORTH CAROLINA 1784–1787

Head of Household	WM 21–60 yrs.	WM under 21 & above 60	WF all ages	Blacks 12–50	Blacks under 12 & above 50	Total
Peter Twitty	1	3	3	2	3	12
Joshua Davis	.	.	.	3	2	5
Simon Wright	1	3	4	.	.	8
Wm. Marks	1	5	4	.	1	11
Jno. Power	1	4	4	24	34	67
Twitty Russul	1	4	1	7	4	17
Rd. Wilson	1	2	1	.	.	4

Head of Household	WM 21–60 yrs.	WM under 21 & above 60	WF all ages	Blacks 12–50	Blacks under 12 & above 50	Total
Jno. Primm	1	4	3	.	.	8
Jno. Ellinton	2	3	6	2	4	17
L. (?) Linsey	1	1	1	1	.	4

1785 Census of Warren (County

No. 7   8293
       703
       8996

STATE CENSUS OF NORTH CAROLINA 1784-1787

WILKES COUNTY

Head of Household	WM 21-60 yrs.	WM under 21 & above 60	WF all ages	Blacks 12-50	Blacks under 12 & above 50
Capt. Nathaniel Vannoy's District.					
Taken by Rowland Judd, 1787.					
Pg. 1					
David Birkit	1	2	3	.	.
Fredrick Black	1	2	4	.	.
John Sparcks	1	3	3	.	.
John Anderson	1	3	7	.	.
William Jones	1	1	2	.	.
Vincen Holinsworth	1	4	2	.	.
Isack Weaver	1	3	3	.	.
Mark Foster	1	1	3	.	.
William Davis	1	3	4	.	.
William McClain	1	1	3	.	.
Stephen Reed	1	3	5	.	.
Moses Smith	1	2	3	.	.
John Reed	1	3	4	.	.
Athani Dorerty	1	.	1	.	.
Esra Cameron	1	2	3	.	.
John Sparks, Smith	1	3	2	.	.
Thomas Smith	1	3	4	.	.
Charles Sweetin	1	.	3	.	.
John Henson	1	1	6	.	.
Paul Henson	1	2	1	.	.
Paul Henson Sr.	.	2	2	.	.
James King	2	4	5	.	.
James Lewis	1	.	1	.	.
Joshua Peninton	1	?	?	.	.
Edward Cross	1	2	5	2	1
Thomas McClain	1	.	1	.	.
Vincen Jones	1	1	2	.	.
William Henson	1	1	2	.	.
George Tirey	1	2	3	.	.
Christian Shearer	1	3	2	.	.
Christian Shearer Sr.	1	4	3	.	.
Christian Birkit	1	2	3	.	.
Aaron Mash	1	3	6	.	.
Justice Boland	1	1	1	.	.
Young Coleman	1	2	6	.	.
Thomas Calloway	1	3	3	.	.
Henry Chambers	1	3	2	.	.
Thomas Wade	1	2	2	.	.
Benjamin Cutbirth	1	2	4	.	.
Samuel McQueen	1	1	4	.	.
Richard Estice	1	2	2	.	.
Daniel Cutbirth	1	2	1	.	.
Thomas Hamton	1	2	3	.	.
Robert Walters	3	4	2	.	.
Benjamin Grear	1	4	2	.	1
Joseph Airs	1	1	2	.	.
Jesse Counsel	1	4	5	.	.
Andrew Wood	1	4	2	.	.
Amos Church	1	2	2	.	.
Pg. 2					
William Copeland	1	7	3	.	.
Joel Copeland	1	6	2	.	.
Joshua Story	1	6	2	.	.
John Andrew	1	2	3	.	.
Henry Mulins	1	3	3	.	.
Joseph Calloway	1	1	2	.	.
William Calloway	1	2	4	.	.
Thomas Calloway Sr.	1	3	3	.	.
John Church	1	1	2	.	.
Barnit Owen	1	3	6	.	.
Robert Reed	1	1	3	.	.
John Jones	1	2	2	.	.
Edward King	1	2	4	.	.
Giles Parmily	1	3	4	.	.
John Parmily	1	.	1	.	.
William Sparks	1	1	3	.	.
Daniel Bomgarner	1	2	2	.	.
John Cane	1	3	1	.	.
Joseph Birket	1	2	2	.	.
William Sturdy	1	.	3	.	.
Andrew Baker	1	4	3	.	.
John Fouts	1	4	4	.	.
James Bunyard	1	4	3	.	.
David Fouts	1	3	6	.	.
	76	171	215	3	2

A List of the Inhabitants in Capt. Thomas Farguson's Dist. 1787, Taken by William Lenoir.

Head of Household	WM 21-60 yrs.	WM under 21 & above 60	WF all ages	Blacks 12-50	Blacks under 12 & above 50
Pg. 1; column 1					
Nehemiah Farguson	.	1	1	.	.
Zebulon Baird	2	7	5	.	.
Francis Bishop	1	1	2	1	.
Joshua Curtis	1	3	7	.	.
Elizabeth Denman	1	.	2	.	.
Elizabeth Hulme	.	1	2	2	2
Edward Grayham	1	4	7	.	.
Thomas Cottral	1	3	5	.	.
Thomas Hodges	1	4	6	.	.
Laurance Bradley	1	1	4	.	.
James Edmunson	.	2	1	.	.
Robert Epperson	1	3	5	.	.

Head of Household	WM 21-60 yrs.	WM under 21 & above 60	WF all ages	Blacks 12-50	Blacks under 12 & above 50
George Stacey	1	.	3	.	.
William Lay	1	1	2	.	.
Elias Wood	.	3	3	.	.
Thomas Fields	2	3	8	.	.
John Coffey	1	2	3	.	.
Joseph Hull	1	4	4	.	.
Thomas Coffee	1	6	4	.	.
Thompson Epperson	1	2	3	.	.
William Hulme	1	.	1	.	.
Reubin Coffey	1	.	3	.	.
Elizabeth Coffey	.	2	1	1	2
Hardy Mills	1	1	1	.	.
Forrest Hutson	1	2	2	.	.
James Farguson	1	2	3	.	.
George Hulme	1	3	1	.	.
Andrew Baird	2	2	1	.	.
Stephen Carpenter	1	4	3	.	.
William Witt	1	1	2	.	.
John Farguson	1	2	5	.	.
Tandy Holeman	1	.	1	.	.
Samuel Forbush	.	1	3	.	.
George Miller	.	1	1	.	.
Dickson Nailer	.	1	2	.	.
William Blackborn	2	.	2	.	.
James Richardson	1	.	2	.	.
Thomas Farguson	2	2	3	.	.
Benjamin Coffey	1	5	4	1	.
John Childris	1	3	2	.	.
Michael Israel	3	6	5	1	3

Pg. 1; column 2

Head of Household	WM 21-60 yrs.	WM under 21 & above 60	WF all ages	Blacks 12-50	Blacks under 12 & above 50
Samuel Bishop	1	3	2	.	.
Wm. Landsdown	1	4	6	.	.
Thomas Lay Jr.	1	1	2	.	.
Agnis Nickols	.	2	1	.	.
Elizabeth Laurance	.	1	4	.	.
Samuel Long	1	4	3	.	.
Robert Long	1	1	6	.	.
Joseph Farguson	2	2	3	.	.
Robert Whiteside	1	4	2	.	.
Moses Denman	2	2	3	.	.
John Moore	1	5	6	.	.
Jane Coffey	.	.	1	2	5
Edmund Northern	1	3	5	.	.
Andrew Tate	1	4	5	.	.
George Grayham	1	3	5	1	.
Jesse Lay	2	3	10	.	.
Elizabeth Diars(?)	?	?	?		
Thomas Lay	1	3	3	.	.
Isaac Preston	1	3	5	.	.

Head of Household	WM 21-60 yrs.	WM under 21 & above 60	WF all ages	Blacks 12-50	Blacks under 12 & above 50
Samuel Sloan	1	.	3	1	1
Daniel Eggers	1	2	3	.	.
James Ross	1	2	4	.	.
Samuel Richardson	.	1	2	.	.
James Lawless	.	1	1	.	.
John Pearce	1	4	3	.	.
Joseph Yarnall	1	1	1	.	.
Daniel Yarnall	1	4	1	.	.
Enoch Williams	1	3	1	.	.
Jeremiah Farguson Jr.	1	1	.	.	.
Joshua Jones	1	5	3	.	.
Moses Hull	2	.	5	.	.
William Lenoir	2	4	4	3	6
Lewis Demoss	1	4	2	3	1
James Demoss	1	1	3	.	1
	73	170	238	17	21

Capt. Hardin's District. Taken by Jesse Franklin.

Pg. 1

Head of Household	WM 21-60 yrs.	WM under 21 & above 60	WF all ages	Blacks 12-50	Blacks under 12 & above 50
James Tackwell	1	2	5	.	.
Partrick Adams	1	1	5	.	.
Edward Crage	1	1	1	.	.
James Williams	1	3	3	.	.
John Hammer	1	.	1	.	.
Henry Kerby	1	.	5	.	.
Joseph Raymey	1	3	6	.	.
William Hardin	1	4	4	2	4
Nathaniel Stewart	1	5	2	.	.
John Conley	1	4	6	.	.
Mark Kanaday	1	.	2	.	.
Jesse Franklin	1	.	.	2	1
	51	121	173	11	23

Not given in:
Charles Cate, John Cate, Jesse Manard

Pg. 2

Head of Household	WM 21-60 yrs.	WM under 21 & above 60	WF all ages	Blacks 12-50	Blacks under 12 & above 50
Henry Snow	1	5	4	.	.
Edward Douglass	1	1	2	.	.
James Pearson	1	4	1	.	.
Jacob Gallion	1	1	1	.	.
Mary Pearson	.	3	1	.	.
William Harmon	1	2	7	.	.
Bershaba Slobridge	.	5	5	.	.
James Ezell	1	1	5	.	.
Bennet Smith	1	1	1	.	.
John Douglass	1	1	1	.	.
Henry Conley	1	4	3	.	.
David Austin	1	4	1	.	.

Head of Household	WM 21-60 yrs.	WM under 21 & above 60	WF all ages	Blacks 12-50	Blacks under 12 & above 50
Dabney Harris	1	3	6	.	.
Daniel Bench	1	2	2	.	.
Jacob Snow	1	1	1	.	.
Oba Snow	1	1	2	.	.
Moses Snow	1	.	3	.	.
John Robinson	1	2	2	.	.
Benjamin Pearson	1	.	2	.	.
Zekiel Wilmoth	1	.	3	.	.
Samuel Sorrel	1	2	4	.	.
Joseph Thomson	1	4	7	2	3
Gibson Maynard	1	3	4	.	.
James Franklin	1	2	2	.	.
John Scott	1	1	3	.	.
William Watts	1	1	7	.	.
John Jinnings	.	3	3	.	.
Thomas Ross	1	1	2	.	.
John Ross	1	2	1	.	.
Samuel Kanaday	1	2	7	.	.
Rachel Isaac	.	5	2	.	.
Caleb Winfree	1	.	.	.	.
Isaac Winfree	2	2	4	1	7
Nathaniel Scritchfield	1	1	2	.	.
George Franklin	1	1	5	.	.
Fredrick Alberty	1	4	3	.	.
Barnard Franklin	1	3	5	4	7
William Raymey	1	4	5	.	.
William Underwood	1	2	1	.	1
Timothy Ezell	1	1	5	.	.
John Underwood	1	4	1	.	.
William Cunningham	1	3	2	.	.
Christopher Kerby	1	1	2	.	.
Andrew Douglass	.	4	5	.	.

This list taken by Ambrose Hamon July 12th, 1787. A List of the number of Sols in Capt. Nall's Dist.

Pg. 1

Head of Household	WM 21-60 yrs.	WM under 21 & above 60	WF all ages	Blacks 12-50	Blacks under 12 & above 50
William Nall	1	3	3	3	2
Martin Gambell	1	2	1	.	.
William Boyd	1	3	1	.	.
Morris Baker	1	4	4	.	.
Charles Rolin	1	2	3	.	.
Daniel Richardson	2	3	3	.	.
John Fips	2	1	4	.	.
Ambrous Collins	1	2	2	.	.
Thomas Gipson	1	5	4	.	.
Alex r. Smith	1	.	2	.	1
David Smith	1	.	.	.	.
William Morris	1	.	2	.	.
Thomas Dixson	.	6	2	.	.

Head of Household	WM 21-60 yrs.	WM under 21 & above 60	WF all ages	Blacks 12-50	Blacks under 12 & above 50
Zachariah Wells	1	4	5	.	.
William Weaver	1	3	2	.	.
Alex r. Johnson	1	.	.	.	.
James Williams	1	5	6	.	.
McCajah Penington	1	.	2	.	.
William Penington	1	.	2	.	.
Johathon Smith	1	4	4	.	.
Moses McDaniel	1	1	3	.	.
John Summons(?)	1	3	2	.	.
Peter Goodman	1	.	2	.	.
Joshua Weaver	.	2	2	.	.
William Penington	1	1	5	.	.
James Boggs [no figures]					
James Lewis	1	3	5	.	.
John Richardson	1	.	.	.	.

Pg. 2

Head of Household	WM 21-60 yrs.	WM under 21 & above 60	WF all ages	Blacks 12-50	Blacks under 12 & above 50
Randol Fugit	1	1	1	1	1
James Baker	1	4	1	1	.
Jurdin Gipson	1	1	1	.	.
James Lewis	.	2	1	.	.
Andrew Gipson	1	3	5	.	.
William Huff	1	3	2	.	.
John Nall	1	1	1	2	.
William Scoot	1	4	6	.	.
Leven Cole	1	.	3	.	.
Gedion Lewis	1	2	4	.	.
James Wooddy	1	2	2	.	.
George Collins	1	3	3	.	.
Isaac Little	1	1	3	.	.
Taulton Wooddy	1	4	3	.	.
Moses Tolliafaro	1	3	3	.	.
John Long	1	4	4	.	.
George Couch	1	3	2	.	.
Samuel Collins	1	.	1	.	.
Samuel Phips	1	2	1	.	.
Joseph Macey	1	3	2	.	.
Mary Gibson	.	2	3	.	.
Julien Bunch	1	2	3	.	.
Jesse Tollafaro	1	.	4	.	.
	48	112	138	6	3

The Names of the Heads of Families in Brown's District.

Pg. 1

Head of Household	WM 21-60 yrs.	WM under 21 & above 60	WF all ages	Blacks 12-50	Blacks under 12 & above 50
James Thompkins	1	5	3	.	.
William Brown	1	3	6	.	.
Garret Hendrix	1	4	4	.	.
John Herman	1	2	3	.	.
William Jackson	1	4	6	.	.

Head of Household	WM 21-60 yrs.	WM under 21 & above 60	WF all ages	Blacks 12-50	Blacks under 12 & above 50
Joseph Stonesiffer	1	3	2	.	.
John Henry Stonesiffer	1	2	3	.	.
Ebenezer Fairchild	1	1	2	.	.
Gilbart Cottral	1	2	6	.	.
Moses Walters	1	3	2	.	.
Abijah Fairchild	1	1	3	.	.
James Robarts	.	2	4	.	.
John Leaps	1	2	2	.	.
Jonas Wiggans	1	.	4	.	.
John Sherran	1	.	1	.	.
Dawson Sewel	1	.	3	.	.
Perrin Cardwell	1	1	5	.	.
Francis Hamby	1	.	3	.	.
John Hamby	1	2	3	.	.
Daniel Gullett	1	4	6	.	.
Thomas Holeman Jr.	1	3	4	.	.
James Jackson Sr.	1	4	2	.	.
Silvester Proffet	1	.	3	.	.
Nathaniel Vannoy	1	4	4	.	.
William Adams Jr.	1	1	6	.	.
Joseph Sewel	1	3	2	.	.
Robert Bingham	1	.	1	.	.
James Brown	1	6	4	.	.
Margret Hawkins	.	1	5	.	.
William Floyd	1	2	7	.	.
John Laws Sr.	.	1	2	.	.
Chesley Cockrham	1	.	3	.	.
William Adams Sr.	.	1	1	.	.
Mathew Francis	1	1	1	.	.
John Adams	1	2	6	.	.
Pg. 2					
John Yates	1	4	2	.	.
Mathew Hawkins	1	1	1	.	.
William Mullens	1	1	3	.	.
Paul Prock	1	1	2	.	.
Benjamin Hendrix	1	4	5	.	.
James Jackson	1	.	.	.	.
Edward Stocksdale	1	.	3	.	.
Nicholas Angel	1	3	2	.	.
John Ferguson	1	4	4	.	.
James Tugman	1	3	2	.	.
Thomas Elmore	1	.	8	.	.
Robert Husband	1	3	6	.	.
Mitchel Childers	1	2	6	.	.
Jane Adams	.	3	3	.	.
Jonathan Hendrix	.	1	1	.	.
William Mitchell	1	3	3	.	.
Thomas Ferguson	1	1	1	.	1
John Brown	1	1	3	.	.
Thomas Perkins	1	5	1	.	.
David McGee	1	5	7	.	.
Darbey Hendrix	1	1	2	.	.
Martin Hall	1	1	2	.	.
George Forster	1	2	4	2	1
Charles Sawyer	1	3	3	.	.
William Proffet	1	.	.	.	.
John Webb	1	.	3	.	.
Ephriam Norris	1	.	.	.	.
Rodger Bishop	1	3	2	1	.
William Triplet	1	2	1	.	.
Daniel Stonesiffer	1	.	2	.	.
Samuel Castle	1	2	4	.	.
Jonathan Hews	1	1	1	.	.
Charles Adams	1	.	1	.	.
John Proffit	1	.	1	.	.
Jesse Adams	1	.	1	.	.
Pg. 3					
Robert Rysedon	1	2	3	.	.
Peter Stonesiffer	1	.	.	.	.
Abraham Sewel	1	2	4	.	.
John Norris	1	3	3	.	.
Henry Joans	1	2	3	.	.
David Laws	1	2	2	.	.
Aaron Case	.	1	2	.	.
Ann Sanders	.	4	3	.	.
Daniel Sutherland	1	3	2	.	.
George Elmore	1	2	4	.	.
William Hamby	1	5	2	.	.
Tomas Holeman Sr.	.	4	3	.	.
George Adams	1	.	1	.	.
William Bruer	1	2	2	.	.
Meradith Minten	1	5	2	.	.
John Lemmons	1	.	3	.	.
Elias Dehart	1	5	2	.	.
William Elliott	1	3	5	1	1
Menoah Dyer	1	2	3	.	.
Elenoer Bunten	.	4	2	.	.
Culbreath Webb	1	1	2	.	.
Elihu Burk	1	1	1	.	.
Joseph Hendrix	1	3	5	.	.
Isaiah Case	1	.	1	.	.
Moses Thompkins	.	1	1	.	.
Aaron Crane	1	1	2	.	.
Elish Stephens	1	2	1	.	.
William Laws	1	2	4	.	.
Francis Webb	1	1	1	.	.
Elenor Triplet	.	2	5	2	.
John Brown	1	.	2	.	.

Head of Household	WM 21-60 yrs.	WM under 21 & above 60	WF all ages	Blacks 12-50	Blacks under 12 & above 50
John Flanagin	.	1	1	.	.
James Sanders	1	.	1	.	.
John Banks	1	.	.	.	.
Leonard Brown	1	2	3	.	.
Benjamin Joans	1	2	6	1	2
James Cottral	1	2	5	.	.
Joseph Carter	1	4	3	.	.
Robert Cleveland	1	7	3	4	4
Pg. 4					
Thomas Ellison	1	.	.	.	.
William Banks	1	.	1	.	.
Nathaniel Banks	1	2	2	.	.
William Ellison	1	7	5	.	1
Andrew Walsh	1	.	2	.	.
Jonathan Thompkins	1	1	2	.	.
John Daws	1	2	2	.	.
John McClane	1	2	6	.	.
John Lovelace	1	3	5	.	.
Jacob Nickolds	1	2	7	1	.
Mason Triplett	1	1	1	.	.
George McNeal	1	3	.	.	.
John Brown	1	7	6	7	14
Jesse Hall	1	.	1	.	.
Pierce Nowland	1	5	3	.	.
William Hendman	1	4	4	.	.
	112	254	357	19	24

A List of the Number of Persons' families in Capt. Isbel's District.

Pg. 1; column 1

Head of Household	WM 21-60 yrs.	WM under 21 & above 60	WF all ages	Blacks 12-50	Blacks under 12 & above 50
John Stapp	1	5	4	1	.
Joel Coffee	1	4	4	4	10
Jno. Shearer	1	2	1	.	.
Benj. Dugger	1	4	6	.	.
Wm. Burns	1	2	3	.	.
Anthony Foster	1	4	2	1	1
Jno. Huddleston	.	3	4	.	.
Jno. Kearby	1	1	2	.	.
Mastain Durram	1	2	6	.	.
John Durrham	1	.	3	.	.
Wm. Kerbey	1	4	4	.	.
Jno. Levingston	1	2	6	.	.
Thos. Isbel	1	1	1	1	2
Jas. Isabel	1	3	2	1	1
Jacob Haglar	1	1	1	.	.
Nancy Isabel	.	.	5	5	4
Thos. Nicoles	1	3	5	.	.
Reubin Stanley	1	1	6	.	.
Abraham Haglar	1	.	1	.	.

Head of Household	WM 21-60 yrs.	WM under 21 & above 60	WF all ages	Blacks 12-50	Blacks under 12 & above 50
Thos. Land Sr.	.	2	3	.	.
Robert Eirs	1	1	2	.	.
Edmond Tilley	2	5	3	2	.
Samuel Tucker	3	3	4	.	.
Jno. Northern	1	5	3	.	.
Isaiah Coffee	1	4	3	.	1
Nathan Stanbury	1	2	2	.	.
Thos. Farmer	1	8	2	.	.
Benj. Tilley	1	.	1	.	.
Philip Davis	2	3	4	.	.
Jno. Land	1	3	2	.	.
Jonathan Land	1	2	4	.	1
Daniel Isbel	1	.	1	.	.
Pg. 1; column 2					
John Haglar	1	1	3	.	.
Thos. Calton	1	3	2	.	.
Isaac Bowin	1	3	3	.	.
Thos. Hall	1	.	4	.	.
Robert Nathary	1	3	2	.	.
Robert Sweton	1	1	2	.	.
Jas. Pagett	1	1	6	.	.
Jno. Vandapool	1	1	3	.	.
Thos. Steed	1	3	1	.	.
Wm. Jacks	1	1	2	.	6
Wm. Baaley	1	.	2	.	.
David Witherspoon	1	.	2	2	.
Wm. Kirby Jr.	1	.	3	.	.
Peter Nowland	.	2	3	1	1
Jno. Bradley	1	3	9	.	.
Jas. Witherspoon	2	1	3	1	1
Jas. Forguson	1	4	5	.	.
Edward Baaley	2	2	4	.	.
Francis Pierce	1	.	3	.	.
Daniel Triplit	1	3	2	.	.
Laewis Calton	2	1	3	1	.
Coleby Rucker	1	.	2	.	.
Joseph Rash	1	4	4	.	.
Levi Laxton	1	.	3	.	.
Samuel Walker	1	3	3	.	.
Jno. Barlow	1	3	4	.	.
Wm. Ferguson	1	.	1	.	.
Jas. Elmore	1	.	3	.	.
Wm. Swonson	1	.	5	.	.
Anne Wisdom	.	.	2	1	3
Thos. Witherspoon	1	5	2	.	1
Dutton Sweton	1	1	5	.	.
Pg. 1; column 3					
Jno. Haglar Sr.	1	3	4	1	1
David Forbush	1	2	3	.	.

Head of Household	WM 21-60 yrs.	WM under 21 & above 60	WF all ages	Blacks 12-50	Blacks under 12 & above 50
Lawrance Duncan	1	3	7	.	.
Edward Smyth	1	.	6	.	.
Jno. Wisdom	2	4	5	.	.
Benj. Grysom	1	5	3	.	.
Benj. Howard	3	3	6	6	2
Thos. Stapp	1	2	2	2	1
Richard Green	1	3	5	.	.
Isaac Cook	1	1	4	.	.
Richard Brown	1	.	.	2	2
Elisha Abner	1	3	5	.	.
Thos. Huskison	1	1	2	.	.
Benj. Duncan	1	4	3	.	.
Wm. Vest	1	.	2	.	.
Russel Jones	1	6	5	3	4
Mary Aldridge	.	2	2	.	.
Annanias Allen	1	2	4	.	.
Thomas Robins	1	3	5	4	1
	97	176	275	40	39

[Three names crossed out; figures illegible]
Jeremiah Farguson
Joshua Jones
Moses Hulme

Inhabitants in Capt. Trible's District.
Taken in by me. James Fletcher
Pg. 1; column 1

Head of Household	WM 21-60 yrs.	WM under 21 & above 60	WF all ages	Blacks 12-50	Blacks under 12 & above 50
Wm. Allen or Allin	1	1	1	.	.
John Henson or Hinson	1	1	3	.	.
Wm. Donethan	.	1	1	1	1
Wm. McGill	1	3	4	.	.
Richard Barbar Sr.	.	1	1	.	.
Benja. Hamrick	1	3	3	.	.
Charles Hamrick	1	5	2	.	.
Cornelias Gwyn	1	2	1	.	.
Peter Jones	1	3	2	.	.
John Campbell	1	1	6	.	.
Jno. Sloan	.	.	1	.	.
Jesse Hays	.	3	3	.	.
Nathl. Barber	1	1	2	.	.
L. Berry Laws	1	2	7	.	.
Isaac Walker	1	1	2	.	1
Isaac Elledge	1	2	2	.	.
Solomon Greer	1	.	2	.	1
Isham Boman	1	1	4	.	.
Isaac Norman	1	4	4	.	.
Jno. Gilreath	1	3	4	.	.
Isaac Lowe Jr.	1	.	1	.	.
Milley Laws	.	1	2	.	.
Joseph Laws	1	.	1	.	.

Head of Household	WM 21-60 yrs.	WM under 21 & above 60	WF all ages	Blacks 12-50	Blacks under 12 & above 50
Thomas Elledge	1	3	3	.	.
Richd. Barber	1	.	.	.	.
Francis Hardgrave	1	3	5	5	2
Rachel Mitchell	.	2	5	.	.
Wm. Trible	1	2	6	.	.

Pg. 1; column 2

Head of Household	WM 21-60 yrs.	WM under 21 & above 60	WF all ages	Blacks 12-50	Blacks under 12 & above 50
Shadrack Trible	1	.	.	.	.
Jacob Elledge	1	4	3	.	.
Saml. Wilson	1	3	1	.	.
Wm. Smith	1	4	8	.	.
John Patterson	1	.	.	.	.
Agnes Patterson	.	2	6	.	.
Alexr. Holton	1	4	4	.	.
James Freeman	.	1	2	.	.
Mary Lowe	.	3	2	.	.
Elizabeth Underwood	.	.	1	.	2
Thomas Norman	1	.	2	.	.
Isaac Lowe	1	4	6	.	.
Reubin Smither	1	.	3	.	.
Thomas Elledge Sr.	1	1	2	.	.
Ben Elledge	1	.	1	.	.
Gideon Gilbert	2	2	3	.	.
John Laws, Pig River	1	1	2	.	.
John Keller	1	.	7	.	.
John Stafford	1	5	3	.	.
John Winn	1	1	4	.	.
Joseph Elledge Jr.	1	.	.	.	.
Robt. Casterson (?)	1	2	2	.	.
Walter Walters	1	.	4	.	.

Pg. 2; column 1

Head of Household	WM 21-60 yrs.	WM under 21 & above 60	WF all ages	Blacks 12-50	Blacks under 12 & above 50
Spilsby Trible	1	10	4	1	.
Alexr. McMullin	1	2	3	.	.
Joshua Greer	1	4	7	1	.
Wm. Isbell	1	.	1	.	.
Nicholas Mitchell	1	5	3	.	.
Thomas Lowe	.	4	3	.	.
Jesse Greer	1	2	5	.	.
Joshua Morgan	.	4	9	.	.
Caleb Lowe	1	4	4	.	.
Elijah Trible	1	2	1	.	.
Joel Hampton	1	2	2	.	.
John Morgan .	1	.	.	.	.
William Cocoram	1	.	4	.	.
John Greer	1	4	5	.	.
Joiles Martin	1	3	3	.	.
J. (?) Moses Williams	1	4	3	.	.
George Owins	1	3	2	.	.
Josiar Dyer	1	.	2	.	.

Head of Household	WM 21–60 yrs.	WM under 21 & above 60	WF all ages	Blacks 12–50	Blacks under 12 & above 50
Elisha Dyer	1	5	5	.	.
Thomas Addams	1	1	1	.	.
Zachariah Martin	1	1	1	.	.
Isaiah Sharoon	1	.	2	.	.
Benj. Hubbard	1	1	2	.	.
Jesse Brown	1	5	2	.	.
Stephen Trible	1	1	3	.	.
Robert Hays	.	2	2	.	.
Patrick Hamrick	1	2	6	.	.
John Grey	1	2	5	.	.
Pg. 2; column 2					
John Wilson	1	1	1	.	.
Wm. Lowe	1	.	.	.	.
Jesse Smith	1	.	.	.	.
Wm. Pelley	1	1	2	.	.
John Rivers	1	.	2	.	.
Joshua Stephens	1	5	5	.	.
James Reeves	1	.	2	.	.
James Chaney	1	5	2	.	.
Benj. Branahm	1	1	3	.	.
Jno. Montgomery	1	3	3	.	.
John Majors	1	3	4	.	.
Jacob Hampton	.	7	5	.	.
Andrew Moore	1	4	4	.	.
Wm. Addams	1	3	2	.	.
Rachel Hampton	.	1	1	.	.
Reuben Johnson	1	.	.	.	.
Benj. Johnson	.	4	3	.	.
Charles Walker	1	2	3	.	.
Ann Greer	.	.	1	3	3
Aquilla Greer	1	4	4	2	4
Charles Gwyn	1	1	4	.	.
Edward Roberts	1	2	2	.	.
Ezekiel Joines	.	2	2	.	.
Hawkins Donithan	1	1	1	.	.
Gabriel Smithers	1	2	4	.	.
Shadrack Laws	1	3	3	.	.
Samuel Allen	1	3	3	.	.
Benj. Donithan	1	.	.	.	.
	23	53	66	5	7

A List of the number of Souls in Capt.
Johnson's Dist. July 7th, 1787.
Returned by Ams. Hammon.

Head of Household	WM 21–60 yrs.	WM under 21 & above 60	WF all ages	Blacks 12–50	Blacks under 12 & above 50
Pg. 1					
Samuel Worner	.	2	3	.	.
William Lee	1	2	2	.	.
Robert Hamon	1	2	4	1	.
Ambrose Hamon	.	1	1	2	3

Head of Household	WM 21–60 yrs.	WM under 21 & above 60	WF all ages	Blacks 12–50	Blacks under 12 & above 50
George Lewis	1	2	7	.	.
Randolph Holbrook	1	6	4	.	.
William Hargis	.	2	1	.	.
Joseph Pruitt	1	2	3	.	.
Thomas Welch	1	1	4	.	.
James Gouge	1	6	5	1	.
James Alexander	1	2	2	.	.
John Amburgy Sr.	1	1	3	.	.
William Harris	1	1	7	.	.
Jacob Lyon	1	.	2	.	.
Thomas Larrance Jr.	1	.	.	.	.
William Loyon	1	4	4	.	.
Stephen Philip	1	1	1	.	.
John Higgins	1	1	3	.	.
Samuel Stancell	1	3	3	.	.
Philip Johnson	1	.	.	.	.
Rachel Johnson	1	4	4	.	.
Lilliam Clark	1	1	1	.	.
David Parker	1	2	1	.	.
Joseph Hamon	.	.	3	.	.
Edward Twiner	1	1	2	.	.
Benjamin Hamon	1	1	1	.	.
John Gambill	1	2	6	.	.
	86	177	260	14	11
Pg. 2					
John Holbrook Sr.	.	3	4	.	.
Thomas Johnson	1	1	3	.	.
Elisha Hedden	1	3	2	.	.
John Hand	1	1	2	.	.
John Adams Sr.	.	1	1	.	.
Emmanuel Rose	1	1	4	1	.
William Rice	.	5	3	.	.
John Poe	1	2	2	.	.
William Poe	1	.	3	.	.
Samuel Johnson	1	1	2	1	1
James Bradberry	1	3	3	.	.
Randolph Allexander	1	4	4	.	.
Jacob Stamper	1	2	3	.	.
John Turner	1	1	1	.	.
William Canady	1	5	5	.	.
Thomas Turner	1	3	4	.	.
Thomas Morgan	1	3	4	.	.
William Morgan	1	1	.	.	.
John Holbrook Jr.	1	1	1	.	.
James Fenley	1	3	2	2	.
Zachariah Holbrook	1	1	.	.	.
John Borwn	1	.	.	.	.
William Johnson	1	3	1	.	.
Benjamin Adams	1	1	5	.	.

Head of Household	WM 21-60 yrs.	WM under 21 & above 60	WF all ages	Blacks 12-50	Blacks under 12 & above 50
William Spiser	1	2	1	.	.
Jonathan Stamper Sr.	1	2	2	.	.
Joel Stamper	1	2	3	.	1
James Webb	1	4	3	.	.
Stephen Caudell	1	1	2	.	.
Rodger Turner	1	2	3	.	.
Jonathan Stamper Jr.	1	5	2	.	.
Pg. 3					
Arter Critchfield	1	2	3	.	.
Thomas Billings Sr.	4	1	4	.	.
William Bradberry	1	1	2	.	.
John Amburgy Jr.	1	.	1	.	.
John Hamon	1	3	6	1	1
John Townzen	1	3	1	.	.
Silues (Silas) Adkins	1	1	1	.	.
Robert King	1	2	3	.	.
William Wyett	1	4	4	.	.
George Combs	1	1	1	.	.
George Whetly	1	1	4	.	.
Jacob Baugher	1	1	2	.	.
William Hodges	1	3	3	.	.
John Burrough	1	1	3	.	.
George Pain	1	2	1	.	.
James Caudill Sr.	.	3	1	.	.
John Orear	1	3	4	.	.
Mary Gambill	.	1	2	2	5
William Holbrook	1	2	2	.	.
Edey Holbrook	1	.	4	.	.
John Cornwell	1	1	6	.	.
Samuel Hinds	1	.	1	.	.
Joseph Hinds	1	3	1	.	.
John Wyett	1	1	2	.	.
Thomas Joines	1	.	5	.	.
Willis Allexander	.	1	.	.	.
James Larrence	1	.	.	.	.
Thomas Larrence Sr.	1	2	3	.	.
James Caudill Jr.	1	2	3	.	.
Thomas Caudill	1	.	.	.	.
Esom Fugit	1	1	1	.	.
William Hamon	1	1	3	.	.
James Gambill	1	1	1	.	.
Joshua Botts	1	2	2	.	.
Jacob Adams	1	2	5	.	.
Archelus Craft	1	.	3	.	.
John Adams Jr.	1	1	2	3	.
Spenser Adams	1	2	2	.	.
Thomas Grimsley	1	1	2	.	.
Elexander Lyon	1	1	2	.	.
Stephen Hallowway	1	4	3	.	.
William Cornelus	.	3	2	.	.

July 3, 1787. In obedience to the Worshipfull Court of Wilkes that I have taken in the numbers of the soles in Captn. Carrell's District. Wm. Terrell Lewis.

Head of Household	WM 21-60 yrs.	WM under 21 & above 60	WF all ages	Blacks 12-50	Blacks under 12 & above 50
Pg. 1; column 1					
Sarah Gwyn	2	2	4	7	3
Peter Goode	1	3	5	.	.
William Wawles(?)	1	1	3	.	.
Ebenezer Mehuring	1	3	2	.	.
Ann Stubblefield	.	.	2	.	.
Simeon Carter	1	2	5	.	.
Thomas Anthoney	.	2	5	.	.
Benjaman Martin	1	5	7	5	7
John Parkes Sr.	.	1	1	3	.
William Carrell	3	.	4	.	1
Thomas Thurman	1	4	3	7	4
Thomas Parkes Jr.	.	2	2	6	1
James Killbor	.	1	2	.	.
Michel Vanwinkle	1	4	4	.	.
John Parkes	1	2	5	.	.
Rubin Parkes	1	5	5	.	.
George Parkes	1	2	3	.	.
Isaac Garrison	.	3	3	.	.
William Carrell	1	1	8	.	.
George Wheatley	2	4	4	.	.
William Slone	1	2	2	.	.
Daniel Wright	1	.	1	.	.
Jacob Waules	1	1	2	.	.
Samuel Parkes	1	8	2	.	1
Thomas Parkes	1	1	5	.	.
George Stubblefield	1	2	4	.	.
James Davis	1	3	4	.	.
William Davis	1	2	2	.	.
Gabrill Loving	1	3	7	.	.
Thomas Stubblefield	1	6	6	.	.
John Price	1	2	2	.	.
Joseph Yunger	1	.	.	1	1
Richard Wats	1	1	5	.	.
Benjaman Rose	1	2	3	.	.
John Rose Sr.	.	2	1	.	.
Timothey Buttery	1	.	4	.	.
William Tolbey	1	2	3	.	.
Abigall Barrett	.	3	4	.	.
Pg. 1; column 2					
Aaron Parkes	1	2	2	.	.
Ambross Parkes	1	.	.	.	.
Joel Lewis	1	.	3	11	6
James Henson	1	.	2	.	.
John Munkes	1	1	1	.	.

Head of Household	WM 21-60 yrs.	WM under 21 & above 60	WF all ages	Blacks 12-50	Blacks under 12 & above 50
Ann Darnell	.	3	3	.	.
John Mash	1	3	4	.	.
Andrew Cornelious	1	1	1	.	.
Isaac Killborn	1	2	1	.	.
Gabrill Phillips	1	.	2	.	.
John Hewes (?)	1	2	3	.	.
Lewis Hewe	1	1	2	.	.
Martha Dotson	.	2	2	.	.
Andrew Cannadey	1	1	4	.	.
Jacob Goodings Lycans	1	2	3	.	.
Jasper Billings	1	.	2	.	.
Richard Allin	1	5	4	.	.
	49	107	177	40	23

Capt. Judd's District. Number of souls taken by me. June 10th, 1787. Rowland Judd.

Pg. 1

Head of Household	WM 21-60 yrs.	WM under 21 & above 60	WF all ages	Blacks 12-50	Blacks under 12 & above 50
Peter Baker	1	2	4	.	.
Nathaniel Judd	1	3	4	.	.
Rowland Judd	1	2	2	.	.
Robert Judd	1	.	1	.	.
Sarah Bery	.	1	2	.	.
Benjaman Pinnil	1	.	1	.	.
Daniel White	1	1	2	.	.
John Baker	1	1	2	.	.
Thomas Reed	1	2	1	.	.
Benjaman Church	1	1	1	.	.
Lewis Whooton	1	3	4	.	.
Robert Hankins	1	1	3	.	.
George Hoper	1	1	2	.	.
Reubin Robins	1	1	2	.	.
William Colvard	1	.	1	.	.
Owen Hall	1	3	4	.	.
Luke Jinins	1	1	2	.	.
Robert Hall	1	2	1	.	.
Jacob McGrady	1	1	3	.	.
Joseph Hoper	1	1	2	.	.
John Haukins	1	2	4	.	.
Ransom Alphin	1	2	3	.	.
Elijah Denny	1	.	1	.	.
Henry Woody	1	3	4	.	.
Francis Ervin	1	2	2	.	.
William Yates	1	3	5	.	.
William McQuery	1	1	1	.	.
William Cash	1	5	2	.	.
Thomas Hoper	.	2	2	.	.
James Hays	1	2	2	.	.
Walter Brown	1	3	6	.	.
Francis Brown	1	4	5	.	.

Head of Household	WM 21-60 yrs.	WM under 21 & above 60	WF all ages	Blacks 12-50	Blacks under 12 & above 50
Isaac Perlear	1	1	4	.	.
William Kilbe	1	2	5	1	1
Alexander Buckanin	1	6	4	.	.
Wm. Viar or Viah	1	5	3	.	.
Nathaniel Birdyne	1	4	6	.	.
William Tiry	1	4	4	.	.
James Shepard Jr.	1	1	1	.	.
Andrew Vannoy	1	4	4	2	3
William Smith	1	2	2	.	.
James Duglas	1	5	3	.	.
Henry Adams	1	2	2	.	.
John Jinins	1	1	2	.	.
John Shepard	2	3	4	.	.
John Hall Sr.	2	1	3	.	.
John Hall Jr.	1	1	1	.	.
John Colier	1	1	1	.	.
John Hoper	1	2	1	.	.
John Miller	1	2	3	.	.
William Owen	1	3	5	.	.
James Crain	1	1	4	.	.
William Crain	1	2	2	.	.
Philoman Crain	1	2	4	.	.
Michal Killbe	1	1	3	.	.
Henry Pumphry	1	2	1	.	.
Samuel Birdyne	1	4	3	.	.
John Owen	1	1	1	.	.
James Sartin	1	.	1	.	.
Michal McDougel	1	2	1	.	.
George Barker	3	1	3	.	.

Pg. 2

Head of Household	WM 21-60 yrs.	WM under 21 & above 60	WF all ages	Blacks 12-50	Blacks under 12 & above 50
Thomas Owens	1	.	10	.	.
Francis Vannoy	2	3	4	.	.
John Robins Jr.	1	2	5	5	1
Rowland Judd Sr.	1	2	1	.	.
Luci Sartin	.	2	3	.	.
Elisabeth Adams	.	1	2	.	.
James Shepard Sr.	1	1	3	2	.
Adam Killbe	1	1	4	1	.
Thomas Pinnil	1	1	4	.	.
John Tiry	.	5	4	.	.
Robert Shepard	1	2	7	.	.
George Gordon	1	2	4	7	8
Henry Miller	1	1	2	.	.
Johnathan Wall	1	2	4	.	5
Benjaman Glover	1	1	1	.	.
Jesse Hall	1	3	5	.	.
John Rhoads	1	2	3	.	.
Luis Sabastin	1	3	4	.	.
Benjaman Sabastin	1	1	1	.	.

Head of Household	WM 21-60 yrs.	WM under 21 & above 60	WF all ages	Blacks 12-50	Blacks under 12 & above 50
Josiah Sartin	1	2	2	.	.
Owen Williams	1	2	4	.	.
David Owen	1	2	2	.	.
Spencer White	1	1	2	.	.
Michal Wardin	1	.	?	.	.
George Owen	1				7?
	186	164	245	18	24

Inhabitants Numbered in Capt. Gordon's District.

Pg. 1

Head of Household	WM 21-60 yrs.	WM under 21 & above 60	WF all ages	Blacks 12-50	Blacks under 12 & above 50
Nat¹. Gordon	1	1	1	.	.
David Hickerson	1	3	3	.	.
Elisha Reynolds	1	.	1	.	.
Thos. Newberry	.	4	3	.	.
Wm. Curry	.	1	2	.	.
Cornelius Anderson	.	2	1	.	.
Bird Hagood	1	6	4	.	.
Patrick Buckner	1	.	3	.	.
John Standley	1	2	6	.	.
James Martin	2	.	3	.	.
Stephen Harris	1	4	5	1	.
Jas. Smoote	1	.	2	.	.
Geo. Johnson	1	7	4	.	.
Richard Gains	1	.	2	2	2
Edmd. Gains	.	1	.	2	.
Jams. Reynolds	1	2	4	.	.
Benj. Johnson	1	.	.	.	.
Leonard Keeling	1	5	2	.	.
Osborn Keling	.	2	2	.	.
Rachel Darnil	.	1	1	.	.
Mary Souther	.	1	1	.	.
Michael Souther	1	.	1	.	.
Jas. Young	1	.	8	.	.
Isaac Darnel	1	1	8	.	.
Jas. Wilson	.	2	3	.	.
Farlin(?) Hagood	1	3	1	.	.
Jno. Cunningham	1	4	2	2	.
Benj. Wilson	1	.	1	3	2
Hilliar Roussou	1	4	4	3	2
Jno. Major	1	4	7	.	.
Wm. Johnson	1	5	3	.	.

Pg. 2

Head of Household	WM 21-60 yrs.	WM under 21 & above 60	WF all ages	Blacks 12-50	Blacks under 12 & above 50
Timothy Chandlow	1	3	5	.	.
Jno. Landsdown	1	1	1	.	.
Alexr. Gilreath	1	2	2	.	.
Wm. Pratt	1	2	4	.	.
Wm. Curry	1	.	2	.	.
David Johnson	1	2	2	.	.

Head of Household	WM 21-60 yrs.	WM under 21 & above 60	WF all ages	Blacks 12-50	Blacks under 12 & above 50
Travis Alexander	1	1	1	.	.
Elijah Vickers	1	1	2	.	.
Joseph Holiman	1	6	4	.	.
Nathan Curry	1	2	2	.	.
John Curry	1	3	3	.	.
Francis Reynolds	1	4	7	3	3
Joseph Hickerson	1	.	.	.	.
John Burk	1	3	4	.	.
Daniel Holeman	1	4	4	.	.
James Cargile	1	4	2	.	.
Josiah Chandlow	1	1	1	.	.
Wm. Bates	1	.	2	.	.
Henry Carter	1	3	5	1	1
John Shoemate	1	.	1	.	.
Chas. Hickerson	.	2	2	.	.
John Chandlowe	1	3	6	1	1
John Profett	1	4	7	.	.
Mathias Bates	1	.	.	.	.
Edward Bullen	1	1	3	.	.
Daniel Vannoys	1	2	2	1	.
Jesse Alexander	1	4	2	.	.
Patrick McCoy	1	2	2	.	.
John Cargile	3	1	4	3	.
Stephen Newbery	1	.	1	.	.
	70	144	235	52	42

Pg. 3

Head of Household	WM 21-60 yrs.	WM under 21 & above 60	WF all ages	Blacks 12-50	Blacks under 12 & above 50
Wm. Cargile	1	1	2	.	.
Ann Parkes	.	3	4	2	1
Benja. Parkes	1	.	.	.	.
Edmund Denney	.	3	5	1	.
Auston Blackbour	1	1	6	2	.
Jacob Standley	1	3	2	.	.
Mourning Wilkey	.	1	4	.	.
Jeffery Johnson	.	3	1	2	4
Elisha Reynolds	1	1	1	.	.
Robert Chandler	.	2	2	2	2
Silas Tompkins	1	2	4	.	.
Joseph Porter	1	4	5	.	.
Elijah Cornwall	1	.	1	.	.
Joseph Herndon	1	1	4	8	7
John Eastridge	1	3	3	.	.
Charles Gordon Sr.	1	.	1	11	12
Chapman Gordon	1	.	1	1	1
Charles Gordon Jr.	1	.	.	.	.
John Johnson	1	2	5	.	.
Spencer Humphress	1	2	4	.	.
James Fletcher	1	3	2	1	1

Head of Household	WM 21-60 yrs.	WM under 21 & above 60	WF all ages	Blacks 12-50	Blacks under 12 & above 50
Pg. 4					
Benj. Herndon	1	3	5	10	10
Peter Salley	1	4	4	.	.
Lenord Sails	1	1	5	.	.
John Rose	1	1	6	.	.
John Howard	1	2	4	.	.
Wm. Willcockson	1	3	2	.	.
John Watson	1	3	7	.	.
Wm. Hendrin	1	4	.	.	.
Charles Taylor	1	2	5	.	.
Pg. 5					
Evin Davis	1	4	3	.	.
James Fox	.	6	2	.	.
Wm. Terrel Lewis	.	1	1	2	4
Abraham Slacks	1	1	4	.	.
James Denney	1	3	4	.	.
Walter Wellch	.	4	1	.	.
Aron Phelpes	1	5	4	.	.
Baswell Pinkston	1	3	6	.	.
John Baker	1	.	2	.	.
James McBride	1	2	8	.	.
Wm. Chambers	1	3	2	.	.
Abraham Cook	.	5	3	.	1
Wm. Mitchal	1	3	4	.	.
Wm. Raglin	1	1	2	.	.
Hance Lackins	.	1	4	.	.
John Grant	1	.	3	.	.
Bazel Baker	1	1	1	.	.
Wm. Dennes	1	2	4	.	.
Elias Brown	1	.	2	.	.
James Denney	1	2	1	.	.
John Richardson	1	2	3	.	.
Rebecca Brown	.	6	2	.	.
Daniel Brown	1	1	1	.	.
Wm. Robards	1	.	1	.	.
John Readen	1	.	3	.	.
Pg. 6					
Absalom Wiggons	.	2	2	.	.
Sarah Munson	.	3	4	.	.
Wm. Jackson	1	1	3	.	.
John Dunkin	1	3	5	.	.
Richard Woolbanks	.	5	2	.	.
[Next not clear; appears to be					
Obediah Baker]	1	4	3	.	.
Wm. Jones	1	.	1	.	.
Bazel Baker	1	1	2	.	.
Elizabeth Robards	.	2	2	.	.
Elisha Lunsford	1	1	1	.	.
John Lunsford	.	5	?	.	.
Valentine Watson	1	.	1	.	.
Isham Harvell	1	5	3	.	.
Slip Mathis	1	2	4	.	.
Wm. Lunsford	1	4	4	.	.
James Norman	1	7	2	.	1
Randolph Mabury	1	2	3	.	.
Isaac Reaves	.	5	5	.	.
James Mehaffey	1	.	3	.	.
Thomas Mehaffy	1	2	4	.	.
John McConnall	2	1	2	.	.
Wm. Nance	1	2	6	.	.
John Campbell	1	.	.	.	.
Thomas Cook	1	6	5	.	.
	119	140			
Pg. 7					
Rosanah Robards	1	3	2	.	.
Mary Wilson	.	4	5	.	.
Susanah Jackson	.	.	6	1	1
Benj. Crabtree	1	.	.	.	.
Mary Pate	.	2	4	1	.
Benj. Lewis	1	.	.	.	.
Wm. Lewis	.	3	3	.	.
Wm. Lewis Jr.	1	2	2	.	.
Daniel Rash	1	6	4	.	.
Elijah Oliver	1	4	6	.	.
Mordeca Samuel	1	2	1	.	.
James Taylor	1	1	2	.	.
James Garvis	1	.	1	.	.
David Bandge	.	2	1	.	.
Saml. Nickelston	.	6	5	.	.
Francis Sandris	1	2	3	.	.
Sarah Mullis	.	2	3	.	.
Jonathan Hathman	1	7	5	1	1
James Garrison	1	4	3	.	.
George Combes	1	2	2	.	.
John Combes	1	1	5	.	.
	171	203			
Pg. 8					
Wm. Sail Sr.	.	3	3	3	6
John Huland	.	1	1	.	.
Wm. Robards	1	.	2	.	.
Henry Mertain	1	2	1	.	.
Robart Sisk	1	3	4	.	.
Cornelias Sail	1	4	5	2	1
Howard Walker	1	3	3	.	.
Stephen Pow	1	.	3	.	.
Mary Jones	.	1	3	.	.
James Robards	1	.	.	.	.
Benj. Johnston	1	1	1	.	.

181

STATE CENSUS OF NORTH CAROLINA 1784-1787

Head of Household	WM 21-60 yrs.	WM under 21 & above 60	WF all ages	Blacks 12-50	Blacks under 12 & above 50
George Robards	1	.	.	.	.
John Sail	1	.	.	.	.
William Allen	1	2	4	.	.
Thos. Sail	1	.	.	.	.
William Brown Sr.	.	2	3	.	.
Wm. Brown Jr.	1	1	4	.	.
Saml. Brown	1	.	1	.	.
George Denney	1	1	1	.	.
Charles Brown	1	.	1	.	.
Benj. Brown	1	.	?	.	.
Joshua Mise	.	3	5	.	.
		198	248		
Pg. 9					
Thomas Bandge	1	6?	4	1	3
Thomas Green	1	.	3	1	1
John Sisk	1	7	1	.	.
Timothy Sisk	1	1	1	.	.

Head of Household	WM 21-60 yrs.	WM under 21 & above 60	WF all ages	Blacks 12-50	Blacks under 12 & above 50
Jonathan Norton	1	1	5	.	.
Thomas Sisk	1	2	6	.	.
Mary Hill	.	3	2	.	.
William Leach	1	2	1	.	.
Sarah Upchurch	1	2	6	.	.
Nathan Smith	1	5	1	.	.
Samuel Bicknall	1	5	5	.	.
Robbin Kell	1	2	5	.	.
Saml. Gray	1	.	6	.	.
Isaac Mertain	1	.	1	3	3
William Thurston	1	2	2	4	6
John Bagby	1	.	2	.	.
James Gray Sr.	3	.	3	.	.
John Bourland	1	4	2	.	.
George Parkes	1	.	.	1	.
Sarah Mertain	.	2	2	3	2
John Mertain	2	2	2	1	2
		244	308		

On Back: "A List of Inhabitants in Capt. Gordon's District, 1787.

Armstrong, Andrew 161; Clem^t. 34; Hugh 145, 146; Isaac 102; John 15, 36, 143; Martin 143; Wm. 145.
Arnett, And^W. 20; James 20.
Arnold, Benj. 141; David 70; Edward 40; Hendry 143(2); James 166; John 40; Joseph 157; Joshua 124; Richard 12; Samuel 152; Solomon 165; William 41, 130, 141.
Aron, Elizabeth 64.
Arrington, James 167; [---]m 134.
Arthur, John 76a.
Artis, Mary 112.
Arwin, Richard 22.
Asbell, James 11.
Ash/Ashe, Charles 68; John B. 64.
Ashbe, Winifred 125.
Ashbourn, Anderson 23; John 23.
Asher, William 147.
Ashford, William 102.
Ashley, William 52.
Ashman, Lewis 50.
Ashmore, Walter 153.
Askew/Askyou/Askey, Godfrey 11; James 12; Jesse 92; John 53; John Sr. 12; Nathan 119; Thos. 88; William 56.
Askins, Elizabeth 27.
Aswell, Pierce 22.
Atherton, Jepthah 110.
Atkins, Jesse 104; William 20.
Atkinson, Amos 77; Elisha 88; Jas. 57; Mileah 78.
Austin/Auston/Austern/Audtin, Bryant 101; David 172; John 37, 80; Nat. 147; William 21.
Avera/Averee/Avery/Avra/Avree, Alex^r 84; George 144; Jacob 84; Lewis 84; Mary 84; Robert 133; Thomas 77, 121; William 84, 155.
Averitt/Avritt/Avirt/Avryt, Alex^r 84; Arthur 122; Benj. 117; Daniel 80; James 90; Jinkin 117; Mary 117.
Avis, Abraham 11; Dellah 82; Joseph 11; Sawyer 11.
Aythardson, Mrs. 123.
A[---], Ephrim 99.
A[---], Josies 100.

B[---], Joseph 100.
B[---], Sampson 100.
Backus/Bakhus, John 97.
Badget(t); see Baggett.
Baescom, Nich^s. 100.
Bagby, Davis 60; John 182.
Baggett/Baget/Badget/Baggot, Abraham 114; Allen 93; Hardy 114; James 80, 138(2), 153; John 49, 164; Nathan 115;

Shadrack 138; Thomas 93(2).
Bagley, Henry 46; Jacob 43; Joshua 133; Robert 81; Thomas 133; William 60, 91, 166.
Bailes, Boeter 150; Daniel 150; Margrit 79; Sarah 150; Wm. 151.
Bailey/Baley/Baaley, Abraham 88; Ann 127; Arthur 83; Bethuel 72; Cloe 83; David 73, 83, 104, 127, 128; Dianah 73; Ed^W. 150, 175; Henry 83; James 73, 88, 165; Jean 127; Jeremiah 159; John 35, 46, 129, 150, 159; Joseph 131; Joshua 73; Micajah 81; Patrick 127; Richard 159; Robt. 124; Sarah 29, 127; Simon 73; Stephen 46; Thomas 73; Wm. 44, 81, 83, 175; Yancey 18.
Bair, John 148; Patrick 148.
Baird, Andrew 172; Zebulon 171; also see Beard.
Baize, James 154; Nathaniel 154; Richard 154.
Baker, Andrew 171; Ann 62; Arthor 104; Bazel 181(2); Dempsy 11, 79; Elias 12; Henry 147(2); James 9, 10, 34, 61, 65, 78, 173; John 12, 30, 39, 92, 103, 179, 181; Jurdan 62; Lawrence 39, 43; Morris 173; Moses 144; Obediah 145, 181; Peter 179; Richard 12; Samuel 39; Soloman 11(2), 72; Susanah 12; Thos. 15; Wm. 39.
Bala, Benjamin 115.
Baldwin, Edwd. 20; Henry 19; John 19; Rachel 141.
Balentine, Edward 95; Nehemiah 95.
Baley; see Bailey.
Ball, A. 120; Daniel 166(2); James 166; John 135; Nathan 86.
Ballard, Catherine 163; Dev. 167; Dudley 162; Elias 93(2); Elisha 93; Elizabeth 165; Hester 82; James 92, 122; Jesse 93; Jethro 41; John 96, 99, 119; Joseph 119; Kedar 40; Mournin 163; Morm 151; Owen 162; Sarah 163; Silas 92, 95; Thos. 146, 150; Walter C. 61, 62; Wm. 62; Wiatt 163; Wm 163.
Ballinger, John 78; Mary 79; Wm. 79.
Balthrop, Augt. 165; John 164; Wm. 164.
Bandge, David 181; Thomas 182.
Banks, Charles 76; James 125; John 92, 175; Jonathan 125; Joseph 124; Moses 76; Nathaniel 175; William 113, 175.
Bankston, James 101.
Banner/Banor, Benjn. 149; Ephraim 149; Henry 148; Joseph 149.
Baptist, Ann 126.
Barber, Aaron 131; Bly 80; Chas. 11; Elizabeth 10; M. 121; Moses 132; Nath^o. 176; Richard 117, 176(2); Ruebin 78;

Brazlton, Jacob 51.
Breedlove, John 44.
Breene, Owing 111; William 111.
Breet, Jesse 84.
Bressie, Francis 52.
Brewer, David 81; George 108; Hezeciah 167; James 95; Jesse 68; John 95; Lewis 63; Moses 57; Robert 91; Ross 164; Thomas 94.
Brewster, Lott 27.
Brian/Briant; see Bryan.
Brice, Abigal 35; John 35; John Acton 88.
Brickell, John 63.
Bridges/Bridgers/Bridgess, Benj. 82; Druery 159; John 159; Joseph 78, 111; Richard 159; Thos. 69; Willis 114; William 77, 110, 115(2).
Bridgewaters, William 22.
Briefs, Cornelous 117.
Briess, Henderson 117.
Bright/Brite, Mary 128; Willis 16; [---]liam 15; [---]mas 15.
Brigman/Bridgman, Asha 141; Thos 72.
Brigs, Charles 130; John 41; Moses 24; Richard 40; Robert 143; Solomon 40; Thomas 143.
Brinkley, Abraham 67; Elisha 38; James 50; John 136; Josiah 40; Peter 50; Rachel 41; Richard 55; William 67, 167.
Brinn, John 74; Nicholas 74; Rich 74.
Brinson, Adam 120; Benja. 34, 111; Ganse 120; Geo. 120; Isaac 119, 120; John 119; Math 120.
Brintle, William 162.
Bristow/Bristowe, Edward 41; Elizabeth 47; Geo. 49; James 40, 49; John 49, 150; Joseph 41; Richard 50.
Britt, Joel 9; John 80.
Brittain/Britton, Edmond 35; Capt. James 14; Jesse 111; John 35; Thomas 27.
Brittle, Jeremiah 114; Jesse 112; John 114; Rowland 112; Sarah 112; William 114.
Broach, Jones 19.
Brock, Benj. 31; Besent 31; Jesse 33; Joseph 88; Lewis 29; Robt. 33; Samuel 51; Uriah 107.
Brockett, Benjamin 85.
Brockman, Majr. 20.
Brocksons, Adkin 85.
Brodie, John 47.
Brogdon, James 95; William 91.
Brook(s), James 35; Joseph 34; Stephen 72; Thomas 72; Wm. 39, 147, 149.
Brooker, John 107.
Broom, Burrel 66; Epps 112; Haley 112; John 66; Lucy 66.

Brosher, Thomas 125.
Brothers, Andrew 123; Job 123; John 23, 123; Jonathan 123; Joseph 128; Malachi 124; Miles 123; Richard 123; Samuel 123; Thomas 123, 128; William 123.
Broun; see Brown.
Brown/Browne, Abigail 167; Abner 93; Abraham 27; Alexr. 95, 126; Andrew 135; Benj. 182; Charles 182; Daniel 77, 181; David 94; Edward 87; Elias 181; Ellinor 143; Ephraim 135; Francis 179; Gideon 153; Hardy 39; Howel 88; Jacob 35, 94, 120, 135, 153; James 20, 39, 86, 93, 174; Jehu 153; Jerremyah 167; Jesse 34, 39, 68, 81, 177; John 23, 34, 68, 128, 141, 152, 164, 174(2), 175, 177; Joseph 42, 149, 159; Leonard 23, 175; Milly 19; Patience 62; Patrick 153; Rannal 143; Rebecca 181; Richard 84, 89, 176; Samuel 42, 43, 182; Thomas 95, 108; Walter 179; William 23(2), 60, 81, 87, 115, 141, 149(2), 173, 182(2); [bour]se 81; Willis 39.
Browning, Edmund 22; Eliz. 22; Geo. 22; John 94; Nicholas 22; Samuel 22; Thos. 94; William 23.
Broxin, Adkin 85.
Bruce/Bruice, Alexander 23; Geo. 55; Robert 21; William 66.
Bruer, Mathew 81; William 127, 174.
Brummit, Nimrod 49.
Brune, Owing 111; William 111.
Bryan/Bryant/Bryon/Brian/Briant, Alason 114; Arthur 80; Assa 79; Auston 35; Blake 84; Clerky 114; Edw. 86, 87; Elias 93; James 114; Jason 114; Jean 114; Jemmima 62; John 30, 78, 79, 84, 86, 106, 111; John H. 86; Jonathan 120; Joseph 90; Kedar 36; Lewis 77, 86, 93; Lucia 62; Lucy 83; Mary 155; Nathan 87, 89; Needham 93; Nicholas 29; Rebecka 36; Robert 93, 145; Rowland 48; Sarah 77; Thos. 106; Walter 29; Wm. 10, 68, 79, 80(2), 83.
Bryer, Benjamin 9.
Bryom, Benjamin 106.
Bryson, James 146; John 146(2).
Buck, Bya. 144; John 57; Stephen 10; Buck's Co. 135.
Buchamon/Buckhamon/Buckamin/Buchum, Alexr. 179; William 159.
Buckner, Patrick 180.
Buffellow, Matthew 110.
Bufkin, Sarah 26.
Buford, Yarrington 105.
Buie, John 139; Robert 139.

Thos. 131.
Mois, Isaac 152.
Molley, Henry 63.
Molten/Molton, Abra. 34; Jacob 143; John
36; Patrick 145.
Monday, William 103, 123.
Mondin, Benjn. 128; John 128; Peter 128;
Symon 128; Thos. 128.
Monger/Munger, Baley 112; John 112;
Samuel 112; William 112.
Monk, Nottingham 10(2).
Monna, George 104a.
Montague, Henry 53; Lattiney 53; Young 53.
Montfort, Henry 164; Joseph 64; Richard
60; William 122.
Montgomery, John 177; Sarah 28; --- 15,
104a.
Moody, Benjamin 107; Gilliam 107; Surrel
107; --tlian 15.
Moon, Lucreacy 96.
Mooney, Charles 74; Lawrance 69.
Moore, Agness 9; Co. 135; Alex^r. 52, 154;
Andrew 146, 177; Athony 109, 110; Ben-
jamin 47; Charles 53, 54, 70; D. 120;
David 154; Duke 116; Epafroditus 11;
Geo. 97, 151; Geo. L. 47; Henry 73, 109;
Hodges 94; Jams 10; James 71, 114(2),
153, 154; Jesse 99, 126; John 9, 57, 62,
74, 75, 78, 107, 141, 151, 154, 160, 172;
Joseph 95(2); Joshua 132; Lewis 169;
Mark 167; Margaret 26; Major 56;
Matthew 89, 150; Maurice 95; Randol 83;
Richard 108; Rubin 66; Saml. 25; William
45, 53, 57, 96, 141, 154; Willia 26.
Moorland, Bartlit 59; Edward 60.
Moras, Thomas 98.
Moreman, Andrew 138; Benjamin 138; John
138.
Morgan/Morgain/Morgen, Arnold 112;
Benjn. 127, 159; Caleb 65; Geo. 28;
Hardy 80; Humphrey 106; J. 120; James
29, 128; Jean 146; Job 126; John 29, 45,
79, 107(2), 130, 148, 176; Joseph 29, 31;
Joshua 176; Lemuel 128; Mark 71;
Matthias 40; Michael 107; Peter 57;
Rubin 148; Sampson 111; Saml. 20; Seth
127; Timothy 112; Thos. 177; Valintine
148; William 20, 79, 88, 98, 177.
Morphus, Bashford 83.
Morran, Samuel 65; William 65(2).
Morrell, Benj. 113; Zachariah 113.
Morres, Tho. 120.
Morrice, Mary 165.
Morris, Aaron 124(2), 128; Adley 65;
Benj. 95, 124, 128; Charrity 41; Dunston
67; Elizabeth 147; Ephraem 41; Geo
67(2); Griffin 65; Hammen 148; Haton

98(2); Hezekiah 65; Holloway 65;
Jacob 95; James 33; Jesse 65; John 55,
91, 98, 100, 102, 105, 124, 130; Jonathan
128; Joseph 124; Lamuel 76; Joshua 9;
Lamuel 76, 135; Mary 128, 165; Mordica
124; Nathan 128; Peter 36; Philemon
87; Rebeccah 70, 94; Richdson 130;
Saml. 167; Silvy 119; Thos. 85, 148;
Traviss 148; Valentine 141; William
43, 67, 87, 76, 125, 148, 173; Zachariah
124.
Morrison, Ann 138; John 138.
Morrow, John 31.
Morse, Howel 45; Samuel 55.
Morton, J. 121(3); John 47, 110; Mesback
22; R. 121.
Moseley, James 166; Jesse 164; John 159,
164(2), 166; Samuel 159; West 134;
William 104.
Moses, Sarah 66.
Moss, Benj. 94; Christopher 59; David 161;
John 10, 49, 63; Mary 94; Reuben 56;
Richard 169; Robt. 101; Sampson 107;
Samuel 104a; Sarah 94; Wm. 20, 94;
Wilkim 169.
Mothrel, Samuel 22.
Motley, Robert 65.
Mott, Benjn. 105; Moses 154.
Mouns, Richard 32.
Mount, Luke 136.
Moye, John 88; Co. 135.
Muckleyea, Loclan 152.
Mullen/Mulins, Henry 171; Isaac 130;
Joseph 130; Thomas 9; Wm 154, 174;
Zador 130.
Mullis, Sarah 181.
Mulone, see Malone.
Mulrain, --- 124.
Mumford, Mills 30; Zadock 31.
Mun, Malcum 84.
Muncas, William 144.
Mundine, James 86; John 85; Kitterill 85.
Munger, see Monger.
Munkes, John 178.
Munley, William 113.
Munro/Munroe/Munrow, Hanna 121; James
34, 36; John 104, 140.
Munson, Sarah 181.
Murdock, David 37.
Murear, Dominique 28.
Murphy/Murphe, Al^d (?Archibald?) 18;
Elisabeth 163; Gabriel 22; James 152;
John 22, 24, 139; N. E. 18; Rich^d. 144;
Robert 104; Silas 153; Thos. 20; Timo-
thy 30; Wm 30.
Murray/Murrey/Murry, Adam 29; Daniel
72; Duncan 79; James 24; Jonathan 24;

Nowell, see Noel.
Nowland, see Noland, Nolin.
Nowlen, see Noland, Nolin.
Nuckolls, Ann 44; C. 169.
Null, William Capt. 15.
Nunary, Anderson 58.
Nunn, Elijah 19; John 150; Richard 150;
William 151.
N----, Abner 100.
N----, Joseph 100.

Oadham, Aaron 116; Jacob 116; James 116;
Josiah 116; Moses 116.
Oaks, William 151.
Oates, James 33.
Obanyan, Briaset 152.
Obryan, Baasit 143; Dennis 50; Patrick 51.
O'Cain, John 93; William 93.
Odom, Demsey 39; James 81; John 38, 81;
Joocam 75; Kedar 39; Mills 40; Moses
113; Richard 142; Sarah 39; Uriah 38;
William 38.
Ogborne/Ogburn, James 84, 116.
Ogden, Mary 118; Tabitha 119.
Ogilvie, Harris 47; Kimbrough 47; Smith 47;
William 51.
Okay/Okey/Oakey/Oakley, Joseph 47, 52;
Micajah 52; Thos. 50; Wm 50; --- 15.
Oldham/Oudham, Geo. 24; James 24; Jesse
24; John 24; Moses 24; Richard 24.
Olds, Thomas 157.
Olivant, Henry 94.
Olliver, Alexr. 157; Andrew 10, 157; Elijah
147, 181; Francis 33; John 53, 82(2), 85,
113, 156; Joseph 157; Mary 53; Peter 53;
also see Alifer.
Olos, Thomas 146.
O'Malley, Mathews 27, Mike 64.
Oneal, Ailsebeth 83; Amos 83; Benj. 83;
Edwd. 19; Isham 78, 83; John 72; Moses
83; Patrick 83; Richard 159; Samuel 83;
Sarah 27; Wm. 83(2); Zachariah 83.
Onley, Penelope 42.
Orange, William 71.
Onear, John 178.
Orme, William 89.
Orre, James 24.
Orrell, James 119; Thomas 119.
Osher, William 98.
Osmont, Francis 38.
Oterson, Caleb 136.
Otwell, William 19.
Outerbridge, Stephen 9; William 92.
Outland, Josiah 115; Thomas 115.
Outlaw, Edward 13; George 10, 41; Jacob 12,
41; James 31, 41; Jos. 131; Levis 41.
Overbey, David 77.

Overmon, Benjn. 128; Chas. 132; Jas. 124,
127; John 124; Joseph 124, 129; Nathan
125; Onias 124; Othniel 125; Oziass 125;
Samuel 124; Thomas 125, 127; Wm. 124.
Overstreet, Henry 63; Rebeckah 140; Silas
140.
Overton, Lam[ll]. 131; Samuel 125.
Owen/Owens/Owins, Adam 159; Barnit 171;
David 61, 180; Fredrick 53; Geo. 176, 180;
James 53; John 50(2), 53, 90, 150, 179;
Thomas 51, 53(3), 107, 159, 179; Wm. 164,
179; Zachariah 159(2).
Ownsbey, Molley 59.
Oxley, John 12.
Ozburn, James 115.
Ozier, William 103.

P----, Samuel 100.
Pace, Geo. 109; Hardy 106; Patience 58;
Thos. 69, 70; Wm 106, 109.
Packer, Mathew 59.
Packet, Holladay 86.
Padget/Padgett, James 29, 175; Joab 37;
Joanna 156; John 155, 157; Moses 147.
Page, Benj. 102; Jese 80; John 96; Nath[l].
20; Vincent 95; Wm. 20, 96.
Paget, see Padget.
Pain/Paine, Geo. 178; James 164.
Pairtree, Homes 73; Noah 73.
Palin, Joseph 123; Thos. 123(2).
Palmer, Abel 126; David 125; Demsey 126;
John 103; Joseph 125; Lam. 75; Malachi
123; Sarah 126; Thos. 124, 125; Wm. 50,
125; Willis 123.
Pardue, Blackmon 49; Joseph 166; Patram
165; William 165.
Parford, John 153.
Parham, Avery 48; Ephram 49; Isham 48;
John 48; Lewis 49; Rebekah 69; Thomas
48(2), 49(2).
Parierton, Joshua 161.
Park/Parke/Parks/Parkes, Aaran 178;
Ambross 178; Andrew 111; Ann 180;
Benj. 180; Benorie 133; Catharine 110
(2); Francis 116; Geo. 178, 182; Humphy
133; James 111(3); John 26, 113, 178(2);
Moses 161; Robert 21; Rubin 178; Sam-
uel 178; Solomon 23; Tabitha 111;
Thomas 178(2); William 110, 112.
Parker, Aaron 65, 106; Amos 35, 41, 52;
Ann 39; Charles 65; Daniel 31; David
110, 111, 177; Demsey 39; Elisha 39,
148; Eliza 31; Francis 38, 116; Gabriel
83; Hardy 29; Henderson 114; Holiday
86; Isaac 39; Jacob 93, 106; James 38, 40,
43, 62, 67; Jeptah 54; Jerusha 33; Job 26;
John 30, 34, 43, 93, 111; Jonathan 31, 35,